Protest and Resistance in the Tourist City

T0293480

Across the globe, from established tourist destinations such as Venice or Prague to less traditional destinations in both the global North and South, there is mounting evidence that points to an increasing politicization of the topic of urban tourism. In some cities, residents and other stakeholders take issue with the growth of tourism as such, as well as the negative impacts it has on their cities; while in others, particular forms and effects of tourism are contested or deplored. In numerous settings, contestations revolve less around tourism itself than around broader processes, policies and forces of urban change perceived to threaten the right to 'stay put', the quality of life or identity of existing urban populations.

This book for the first time looks at urban tourism as a source of contention and dispute and analyses what type of conflicts and contestations have emerged around urban tourism in 16 cities across Europe, North America, South America and Asia. It explores the various ways in which community groups, residents and other actors have responded to – and challenged – tourism development in an international and multi-disciplinary perspective. The title links the largely discrete yet interconnected disciplines of 'urban studies' and 'tourism studies' and draws on approaches and debates from urban sociology, urban policy and politics, urban geography, urban anthropology, cultural studies, urban design and planning, tourism studies and tourism management.

This groundbreaking volume offers new insight into the conflicts and struggles generated by urban tourism and will be of interest to students, researchers and academics from the fields of tourism, geography, planning, urban studies, development studies, anthropology, politics and sociology.

Claire Colomb is Reader (Associate Professor) in Planning and Urban Sociology at the Bartlett School of Planning, University College London (UK), and holds a first degree in Politics and Sociology (Institut d'Études Politiques de Paris, France) and a PhD in Planning (University College London). Her research interests cover urban and regional governance, planning and urban regeneration in European cities, urban social movements, European spatial planning and territorial cooperation, and comparative planning. She is the author of *Staging the New Berlin: Place Marketing and the Politics of Urban Reinvention* (Routledge 2011).

Johannes Novy is Lecturer (Assistant Professor) in Spatial Planning in the School of Planning and Geography at Cardiff University (UK). He studied urban planning and urban studies in Germany, Italy and the United States and holds a PhD in Urban Planning from Columbia University, New York. His research interests cover urban and planning theory, urban (development) politics, urban tourism, leisure and consumption. He co-edited *Searching for the Just City* (Routledge 2009).

Contemporary Geographies of Leisure, Tourism and Mobility

Series Editor: C. Michael Hall, Professor at the Department of Management, College of Business and Economics, University of Canterbury, Christchurch, New Zealand

The aim of this series is to explore and communicate the intersections and relationships between leisure, tourism and human mobility within the social sciences.

It will incorporate both traditional and new perspectives on leisure and tourism from contemporary geography, e.g. notions of identity, representation and culture, while also providing for perspectives from cognate areas such as anthropology, cultural studies, gastronomy and food studies, marketing, policy studies and political economy, regional and urban planning, and sociology, within the development of an integrated field of leisure and tourism studies.

Also, increasingly, tourism and leisure are regarded as steps in a continuum of human mobility. The inclusion of mobility in the series offers the prospect of examining the relationship between tourism and migration, the sojourner, educational travel, and second home and retirement travel phenomena.

For a full list of titles in this series, please visit www.routledge.com/series/SE0522
The series comprises two strands:

Contemporary Geographies of Leisure, Tourism and Mobility aims to address the needs of students and academics, and the titles will be published in hardback and paperback. Titles include:

9. **An Introduction to Visual Research Methods in Tourism**
   Edited by Tijana Rakic and Donna Chambers

10. **Tourism and Climate Change**
    Impacts, adaptation and mitigation
    C. Michael Hall, Stefan Gössling and Daniel Scott

11. **Tourism and Citizenship**
    Raoul V. Bianchi and Marcus L. Stephenson

Routledge Studies in Contemporary Geographies of Leisure, Tourism and Mobility is a forum for innovative new research intended for research students and academics, and the titles will be available in hardback only. Titles include:

59. **Political Ecology of Tourism**
    Community, power and the environment
    Edited by Mary Mostafanezhad, Eric J. Shelton, Roger Norum and Anna Thompson-Carr

60. **Managing and Interpreting D-Day's Sites of Memory**
    Guardians of remembrance
    Edited by Geoffrey Bird, Sean Claxton and Keir Reeves

Protest and Resistance in the Tourist City

Edited by Claire Colomb and
Johannes Novy

Routledge
Taylor & Francis Group

LONDON AND NEW YORK

First published 2017
by Routledge
2 Park Square, Milton Park, Abingdon, Oxon OX14 4RN

and by Routledge
711 Third Avenue, New York, NY 10017

First issued in paperback 2018

Routledge is an imprint of the Taylor & Francis Group, an informa business

British Library Cataloguing in Publication Data
A catalogue record for this book is available from the British Library

Library of Congress Cataloging in Publication Data
Names: Colomb, Claire, editor. | Novy, Johannes, editor.
Title: Protest and resistance in the tourist city / edited by Claire Colomb
and Johannes Novy.
Description: Abingdon, Oxon ; New York, NY : Routledge is an imprint
of the Taylor & Francis Group, an informa business, [2016] |
Series: Contemporary geographies of leisure, tourism and mobility |
Includes bibliographical references and index.
Identifiers: LCCN 2016003610 | ISBN 9781138856714 (hbk) |
ISBN 9781315719306 (ebk)
Subjects: LCSH: Tourism–Social aspects–Case studies. | Cities and
towns–Case studies. | Tourism and city planning–Case studies.
Classification: LCC G155.A1 P79 2016 | DDC 338.4/791–dc23
LC record available at https://lccn.loc.gov/2016003610

ISBN 13: 978-1-138-34224-8 (pbk)
ISBN 13: 978-1-138-85671-4 (hbk)

Typeset in Times New Roman
by Cenveo Publisher Services

Contents

Figures and tables

Figures

Table

Contributors

Albert Arias-Sans is a geographer and member of the research group 'Territorial Analysis and Tourism Studies' at the Universitat Rovira i Virgili, Tarragona (Spain). He is currently a PhD candidate working on his doctoral dissertation on urban tourism in Barcelona. He has been academic coordinator of the Urban Management Postgraduate Programme at the Open University of Catalonia (2006–12) and has worked as a consultant on urban planning and tourism issues.

Non Arkaraprasertkul has degrees in architecture and urban design from the Massachusetts Institute of Technology (USA), in Modern Chinese Studies from the University of Oxford (UK), and received a PhD in anthropology from Harvard University (USA). His transdisciplinary research interests lie at the crossroads of architecture and the social sciences.

Emily Bereskin is a postdoctoral fellow at the Center for Metropolitan Studies, Berlin Technical University (Germany) and is part of the international research programme 'The World in the City: Metropolitanism and Globalization from the Nineteenth Century to the Present'. Her research applies an interdisciplinary approach to the analysis of urban development and ethnic conflict, with a focus on issues of segregation, territory and identity.

Anne-Marie Broudehoux is Associate Professor at the School of Design of the University of Quebec at Montreal (Canada). She received her doctoral degree in architecture from the University of California at Berkeley (USA) in 2002. She is the author of *The Making and Selling of Post-Mao Beijing* (Routledge 2004) and has published extensively on processes related to urban image construction in the context of mega-event preparations. She is currently working on a new book on the socio-spatial impacts of the Rio de Janeiro 2016 Olympic Games.

Lucia Capanema Alvares has a degree in Architecture and Urban Planning from the Federal University of Minas Gerais (Brazil), a Master's in City and Regional Planning from Memphis State University (USA) and a PhD in Regional Planning from the University of Illinois at Urbana-Champaign (USA). She is currently a professor at the Federal Fluminense University (Brazil) and has professional experience in participatory planning and tourism. Her research interests include community planning, social movements and urban conflicts, planning theories, landscape and the environment.

Claire Colomb is Reader (Associate Professor) in Planning and Urban Sociology at the Bartlett School of Planning, University College London (UK), and holds a first degree in Politics and Sociology (Institut d'Études Politiques de Paris, France) and a PhD in Planning (University College London). Her research interests cover urban and regional governance, planning and urban regeneration in European cities, urban social movements, European spatial planning and territorial cooperation, and comparative planning. She is the author of *Staging the New Berlin: Place Marketing and the Politics of Urban Reinvention* (Routledge 2011).

Nina Fraeser MA has been a research and teaching associate in the team of the Chair in History and Theory of the City at the Hafen City University Hamburg (Germany) since 2015. Based on her interdisciplinary approaches to European urban studies, her research interests focus on the intersection of urban social movements, urban politics and the production of spaces of resistance.

Daniel Garrett is an author, photographer, political scientist and visual sociologist, currently finishing a PhD at the City University of Hong Kong. His first book, *Counter-Hegemonic Resistance in China's Hong Kong: Visualizing Protest in the City*, was published in 2014. His research interests include Chinese domestic and foreign affairs, cyber culture and warfare, globalization, international relations, media studies, moral panic, political sociology, security studies, soft power and visual sociology.

Maria Gravari-Barbas, an architect, geographer and planner educated in Greece and France, is Professor of Geography at the University of Paris 1 Panthéon Sorbonne (France), Director of the Institute for Research and Higher Studies on Tourism and Coordinator of the UNESCO Chair 'Tourism, Culture, Development' of the same university. She has published extensively on urban tourism, heritage and architecture and has coordinated several edited books in French and English on those themes.

Sébastien Jacquot is Assistant Professor in Geography at the University Paris 1 Panthéon Sorbonne (France) at the Institute for Research and Higher Studies on Tourism. His research interests cover heritage and social and urban transformations in UNESCO World Heritage Sites, (urban) tourism, big data, (political) informality and urban studies.

John Lauermann is Assistant Professor of Political Economy at the Rhode Island School of Design (USA). He is trained as a geographer and his research focuses on urban political economy, regional development governance and mega-event/mega-project planning. His recent research has evaluated the urban development politics of bidding to host sports mega-events, using a globally comparative sample of (successful and failed) Olympic bids.

Jacob Lederman is Assistant Professor of Sociology at the University of Michigan-Flint (USA). His doctoral work focused on urban restructuring amid economic crisis in Buenos Aires. His research interests cover post-industrial redevelopment models, contentious politics and the transnational flow of urban policies.

Jason D. Luger is a human geographer who recently completed his PhD at King's College London (UK) and the National University of Singapore. His doctoral research focused on comparative urbanism, urban space and urban policy, as well as grassroots activist movements in the non-Western world, specifically Singapore. Other research interests and prior experience include urban and regional planning, economic development and urban regeneration policies.

Karina Machado de Castro Simão has a Bachelor's degree in Architecture and Planning and a Master's degree in Sustainable Heritage from the Federal University of Minas Gerais (Brazil), where she is currently a researcher in the Landscape and Urban Conflicts Observatories. Her research interests cover urban design, building, planning, urban morphology and urban evolution analysis.

Altamiro S. Mol Bessa is Professor of Urban Planning at the Federal University of Minas Gerais (Brazil) and trained in Civil Engineering, Architecture, Urban Planning, Tourism and the Environment. His main topics of interest are urban and architectural revitalization, the construction of urban landscapes through structural and image changes, and cultural heritage.

Johannes Novy is Lecturer (Assistant Professor) in Spatial Planning in the School of Planning and Geography at Cardiff University (UK). He studied urban planning and urban studies in Germany, Italy and the United States and holds a PhD in Urban Planning from Columbia University, New York. His research interests cover urban and planning theory, urban (development) politics, urban tourism, leisure and consumption. He co-edited *Searching for the Just City* (Routledge 2009).

Florian Opillard is a PhD candidate at the École des Hautes Études en Sciences Sociales in Paris (France) and a visiting researcher at the University of California Berkeley (USA). His main fields of study concern the geography of gentrification in North and Latin America and the comparative geography of urban social movements in the United States, Chile and France.

Deike Peters is Assistant Professor of Environmental Planning and Practice at the Soka University of America (USA). She has Master's degrees in Urban Planning and International Affairs from Columbia University and a PhD from Rutgers' Bloustein School of Planning and Public Policy. Her research focuses on comparative urbanization, environmental sustainability and complex decision-making around urban infrastructure megaprojects.

Thiago Pinto Barbosa is a PhD candidate at the Free University Berlin (Germany), with a Bachelor's degree in Social Sciences from the Federal University of Minas Gerais (Brazil) and a Master's degree in International Relations (Berlin). He is the co-founder of the Popular Committee of the FIFA World Cup's Victims in Belo Horizonte (COPAC-BH). His research interests cover urban policy and mega-events in Brazil, environmental and land conflicts, social movements, South–South relations and cooperation, postcolonial theories and political ecology.

Michaela Pixová is an urban geographer and post-doctoral researcher at the Institute of Sociological Studies, Charles University, Prague (Czech Republic). Her research focuses on the role of citizen participation and forms of activism in the post-socialist restructuring of Czech cities, urban social movements, youth subcultures, social exclusion and brownfield regeneration. In her doctoral thesis she focused on the spatial aspects of alternative cultures in Prague. She is the vice-president of the citizens' organization PragueWatch.

Antonio Paolo Russo is Assistant Professor at the Faculty of Tourism and Geography, University Rovira i Virgili, Tarragona (Spain) and a member of the research group 'Territorial Analysis and Tourism Studies'. He has a PhD in Economics from the Erasmus University Rotterdam. His research interests range from tourism studies to cultural and urban economics, topics on which he has published extensively. He is an independent advisor on urban regional tourism and cultural economy and management.

Jan Sládek is a teaching and research assistant at the Institute of Sociological Studies, Charles University, Prague (Czech Republic), where he also obtained his PhD. He studied urban sociology in New Orleans, Lyon and Prague. His research focuses on urban social movements and the socio-economics of housing and social housing. He is a consultant in the field of social housing and urban planning.

Michele Vianello is Assistant Professor in Architecture and Planning at the International Balkan University, Skopje (Macedonia), having recently completed his PhD at the IUAV university in Venice (Italy). He has a background as an urban designer and planner. His research interests cover urban social movements and collective actions influencing planning policies. He has conducted research in Italy and Macedonia and worked for planning advocacy groups in Kenya.

Acknowledgements

The idea for this book arose out of a session organized by Dr Johannes Novy, Prof. Susan Fainstein and Dr Claire Colomb at the annual conference of the Research Committee 21 (RC21) on the Sociology of Urban and Regional Development of the International Sociological Association in Berlin in August 2013. The success of the session, which attracted many paper proposals, inspired the two editors to invite contributions from a wider range of scholars through a call for proposals launched in early 2014, with a view to prepare an edited volume on the subject of protest and resistance in the tourist city.

We would like to acknowledge the financial support received from the *Deutsche Forschungsgemeinschaft* (DFG – German Research Foundation) which, through a small grant, funded the organization of a thematic symposium on 'Protest and Resistance in the Tourist City' in Berlin in November 2014. The event comprised a public symposium and an internal workshop which allowed us to bring together most of the authors who contributed to the book and discuss the themes developed in this volume. Other institutions were instrumental in supporting the symposium. In particular, we wish to thank the Center for Metropolitan Studies (CMS) at the Technische Universität Berlin for hosting the event. Logistical support also came from the Brandenburg University of Technology Cottbus-Senftenberg (BTU), while the socio-cultural centre 'Regenbogenfabrik' in Berlin-Kreuzberg and the newspaper *die tageszeitung* (taz) acted as partners in the organization of two public cultural events on urban tourism in Berlin and Barcelona aimed at a more general audience. The help and contributions of several individuals also needs to be acknowledged: Eyke Vonderau, Katharina Knaus, and Bryn Veditz (all CMS), Gudrun Dahlick, Judith Jahn and Christian Kehrt (all BTU), Christine Ziegler (Regenbogenfabrik Berlin), Edith Kresta (taz), Martin Düspohl (Kreuzberg Museum), Julian Schwarze (Bündnis 90/Grüne Friedrichshain-Kreuzberg), Monika Hermann (District Mayor of Friedrichshain-Kreuzberg), Eduardo Chibás (documentary film-maker, Barcelona), Nana A. T. Rebhan (documentary film-maker, Berlin), Martin Selby (Coventry University) and Fabian Frenzel (University of Leicester) all deserve our gratitude for their contributions to the Berlin symposium which laid the ground for this book.

Much appreciation also goes to several valued colleagues and friends with whom we have discussed the themes addressed in this book informally on various occasions, and who have provided us with helpful insights and ideas, in particular: Prof. Susan Fainstein (New York), Sandra Huning (Berlin/Dortmund), Reme Gomez and Albert Arias-Sans (Barcelona).

We would like to thank Emma Travis (Commissioning Editor for the *Contemporary Geographies of Leisure, Tourism and Mobility* series) and Philippa Mullins (Editorial Assistant for Tourism) for their patience and encouragement in the development of this book.

Our thanks, too, to the various individuals who have allowed us to reproduce their photographs of protests and urban landscapes around the world for this book.

Last but not least we wish to thank the contributors of the book for the work they have put in their chapters, their cooperation and their good-natured responses to our many detailed requests for revisions.

1   Urban tourism and its discontents

An introduction

Johannes Novy and Claire Colomb

The word 'Berlin', a crossed-out heart, a capital 'U', and an unmistakable message: when the 'Berlin does not love you' stickers first appeared on buildings and street furniture across Germany's capital in the summer of 2011 (Figure 1.1), there was considerable uproar and media attention. Their emergence did not come out of the blue, however, but reflected a conflict that had been brewing for some time. Boosted by ever-growing visitor numbers and revenues, Berlin's business elites and politicians celebrated the city's booming tourism trade throughout the 1990s and early 2000s as a kind of saviour for the economically troubled city, and proactively designed various campaigns to lure even more visitors to Berlin. The reaction of many residents, especially in Berlin's central residential neighbourhoods, towards the rocketing presence – and prevalence – of tourism in their midst has been, meanwhile, decisively less enthusiastic. Against the backdrop of the city's profound socio-spatial restructuring after the fall of the Wall in 1989, some residents had already, in the late 1990s, voiced concerns about what they perceived as a *touristification* of Berlin's inner city. By the early 2010s concerns about the negative impacts of its success as a tourist destination had become so widespread that even national and international media began to pay attention to the issue (see, *inter alia*, Hollersen and Kurbjeweit 2011; Duvernoy 2012). Graffiti with slogans like 'No more rolling suitcases' and 'Tourists f*** off' became an almost ubiquitous sight in Berlin's districts; fierce debates at community meetings about the conversion of residential apartments into holiday rentals became more frequent. Anonymous posters citing Hans Magnus Enzensberger's famous words – 'The tourist destroys what he seeks by finding it' (Enzensberger 1996) – echoed a sentiment that a growing number of residents expressed quite openly: the city, they felt, was in danger of falling victim to its own success.

Meanwhile, on the other side of Europe, in August 2014 photographic evidence of an incident which took place in Barcelona made headlines in the local, national and international press: three young Italian male tourists wandered around naked in broad daylight in the streets and shops of La Barceloneta, Barcelona's waterfront neighbourhood, without being stopped by the police and oblivious to the outrage caused to passers-by and locals. Angry residents posted pictures on social media, which prompted a deluge of journalistic attention beyond the boundaries

Figure 1.1 'Berlin does not love you' sticker, 2012.

Source: Jonathan Adami.

of the Spanish state (i.e. Kassam 2014). Various residents' associations from the historic district of Ciutat Vella – Barcelona's Old City, which concentrates a significant part of tourist flows – had, for years, been campaigning against the negative impacts of the tourist economy on their neighbourhoods, such as the proliferation of short-term rental apartments, problems of noise and anti-social behaviour linked with 'drunken tourism', or the occupation and commodification of public space by cafe terraces. These associations got together and started quasi-daily demonstrations (Figure 1.2) outside the District and City halls to demand that politicians implement tighter control and regulation of the city's tourism economy and, more broadly, to plead for a change in the city's urban development model under the motto 'Barcelona is not for sale'. A well-known Barcelona housing activist, Ada Colau (2014), wrote an opinion piece in English in the *Guardian* to explain to an international audience why 'mass tourism can kill a city – just ask Barcelona's residents'. Eighteen months later she became Barcelona's new mayor, following local elections which saw a left-wing grass-roots movement which emerged out of citizens' activism and local urban social mobilization get into power, *Barcelona en Comú*. One of the central themes of the 'Barcelona in Common' campaign was tourism's negative impacts on the city's socio-economic fabric and the need to 'regulate the sector, return to the traditions of local urban planning, and put the rights of residents before those of big business' (Colau 2014: n.p.).

Figure 1.2 'Anti-tourism' demonstration by residents of La Barceloneta neighbourhood, Barcelona, 30 August 2014.

Source: Maurice Moeliker.

Currently the third and fifth most visited cities in Europe by bednight volumes (European Cities Marketing 2014), both Berlin and Barcelona have recorded particularly steep increases in tourist numbers since the early 1990s. It is perhaps no surprise that the impact of tourism on these cities' urban and social fabric have been increasingly contested. Yet manifestations of discontent, protest and resistance like the ones described above are not as exceptional as Berlin's and Barcelona's local media have tended to describe them. In Italy, individuals and groups are campaigning to help 'Save Florence' and the art-infused city's local heritage from the damage inflicted by mass tourism (Figure 1.3). In New Orleans, new hotel developments as well as a proliferation of unlicensed short-term rentals is provoking dissent by neighbourhood groups and affordable housing advocates who are concerned that the 'Big Easy' is 'in danger of losing its identity' (Moskowitz 2015) (Figure 1.4). New companies such as Airbnb have exploited the profits to be made from the so-called 'sharing economy' by offering online advertising and management platforms for individuals to rent their home, or part thereof, for short-term periods of time to tourists and visitors. This is having visible impacts on local housing markets, and similar protests have emerged in other cities (e.g. San Francisco – see Opillard in this volume). In Lisbon, local residents have formed a community group called 'People live here' (*Aqui mora gent*) in response to the city's growing 'party tourism' phenomenon. Meanwhile,

Figure 1.3 Concentration of tourists in Florence, July 2015.
Source: D. L. Ashliman.

in Hong Kong, there has been a strong backlash against the large numbers of mainland Chinese travellers (see Garrett in this volume), while cities in Central and Latin America and the Caribbean too are replete with examples of tourism-related struggles (see Betancur 2014).

Across the globe, from established tourist cities such as Venice or Prague to less traditional tourist destinations in both the global North and South, there is thus mounting evidence that points to an increasing politicization of what hitherto had essentially been a non- or minor issue in urban political struggles in most cities. This politicization manifests itself in different ways: in some contexts residents and other stakeholders take issue with the growth of tourism as such, as well as the impacts it has on their cities; in others, particular forms and effects of tourism are contested or deplored; and in numerous settings, as will be discussed in this volume, contestations revolve less around tourism itself than around broader processes, policies and forces of urban change perceived to threaten the right to 'stay put', the quality of life or the identity of existing urban populations.

It might nonetheless be misleading or premature to conclude that there is a global 'revolt against tourism', as Elisabeth Becker (2015) recently argued in the *New York Times*. Clearly, we are seeing a proliferation of *forms of contestation* – big and small – *surrounding* tourism. However, given their oftentimes different causes, characteristics and concerns – and taking into account that many of them

Figure 1.4 Contesting the impact of the proliferation of short-term tourist rentals, New
          Orleans, 2015: a billboard by artist Caroline Thomas.

Source: Caroline Thomas.

are not *against* tourism as such – one should avoid the pitfall of making them
appear more similar or uniform than they are in reality. This volume has been
motivated by the fact that the rise of urban tourism as a source of contention and
dispute has thus far received relatively little systematic attention and analysis.
Critical urban and tourism studies have certainly produced valuable empirical and
theoretical findings regarding what we have described as urban tourism's increasing 'politicization from below'. However, to our knowledge, so far no coordinated attempt has been made to provide a wide-ranging international overview (in
English) of the types of controversies, conflicts and protests that have emerged in
response to tourism's ascendancy within the contemporary urban fabric, as well
as its increasingly significant role in the economic and political agendas of urban

policy-makers. The present volume attempts to fill this gap. It contends that controversies, debates and protests surrounding urban tourism not only warrant investigation in their own right, but also offer a useful lens through which fresh light can be cast on the profound role tourism plays in contemporary cities, as well as on the current 'urban moment' more generally with its attendant conflicts and contradictions. In theoretical terms, the book seeks to connect the largely discrete yet interconnected disciplines of 'urban studies' and 'tourism studies'. More widely the book borrows from, and links up with, debates from the following disciplines: urban sociology, urban policy and politics, urban geography, urban anthropology, cultural studies, urban design and planning, tourism studies and tourism management.

This introductory chapter aims to establish the context within which the rise of urban tourism as a powerful force of urban change and as a source of contention is situated. Conceptualizing the rise of (urban) tourism as both indicative and constitutive of broader processes of economic and social change, it will first provide some critical reflections on the nature of tourism as a social phenomenon. The section that follows will discuss the formidable growth of urban tourism in recent decades, and the role it has acquired in urban development strategies and governance. The subsequent section will provide a short review of the transformation of urban conflicts and social movements in cities in general. Tourism is only one – albeit increasingly potent – force of rapid urban change and is closely intertwined with other forces, as further discussed below, which may themselves be the object of contestation. The subject matter of 'protest and resistance in the tourist city' is thus best understood as part of wider struggles around contemporary urban restructuring, the transformation of urban governance and the 'Right to the City', even if not all tensions surrounding urban tourism easily fit into such a framework of analysis. Embedded in a discussion of the book's objectives and underlying research questions, the final section will present a taxonomy of the conflicts, contestations and struggles surrounding tourism that can be observed in cities of the Global North and South and thereby introduce the chapters of the volume.

Coming to terms with (urban) tourism

The fundamental premise that underpins this volume is as simple as it is frequently overlooked, namely that tourism is fundamentally political. In fact, the process of defining, conceptualizing and measuring tourism is itself, from the onset, deeply political. The way tourism is accounted for and made sense of locally, for instance, has usually been shaped by the hotel industry and associated businesses. As the key local stakeholders in tourism development, they often purport what counts as tourism and what does not, and most statistics and data compiled on the local level reflect their interests and needs: the emphasis rests on visitors staying in hotels and similar establishments while day-trippers, people visiting friends and relatives, or those renting short-term (often unlicensed) holiday apartments were at least until recently either not accounted for or only insufficiently so. As a result, the conventional wisdom in the policy, scholarly and media spheres has tended in most contexts to equate 'tourists' with 'hotel guests' – a restrictive and increasingly flawed definition.

Yet what is actually meant by the term 'tourism'? And what does it mean to be a tourist? There is still much contention and debate over the meaning of those terms, and it is beyond the scope of this chapter to revisit the intense debates that have surrounded those issues. For the purposes of this volume, we adopted a deliberately broad understanding of tourism. A *tourist*, in line with the definition by the United Nations World Tourism Organization (UNWTO), is understood as someone who 'travels to and stays in places outside the usual environment for not more than one consecutive year for leisure, business and other purposes' (UNWTO 1995: 1). Tourism is conceptualised as 'the sum of phenomena and relationships arising from the interaction of tourists, business suppliers, host governments, and host communities' (McIntosh and Goeldner 1990, cited in Hall and Jenkins 1995: 7).

The pervasiveness of tourism for contemporary societies rests not only with the ever-growing numbers of people participating in it, but also with the wider impacts it has on the world we live in and the way we look at – and act in – it. While not going as far as Munt's assertion that we live in a world in which 'tourism is everything and everything is tourism' (cited in Gale 2008: 4), we nonetheless contend that it is hard to overestimate tourism's influence as a social force. In today's hyper-connected world, few places remain whose cultures, economies, social relations and spatial dynamics are not impacted by tourism. Moreover, the 'gaze' (Urry 1990) of ever more consumers, entrepreneurs and policy-makers is increasingly shaped by tourism.

Furthermore, rather than grouping tourists into a homogenous whole and conceiving tourism as a distinct and easily separable phenomenon, we stress that tourism is highly variegated and that its forms and practices intersect and overlap with other patterns of consumption, production, mobility and leisure. The boundaries between tourist and non-tourist practices in cities, for instance, have always been fluctuating, but have become increasingly blurred in recent decades as a result of increasing global mobility, a growing fluidity between travel, leisure and migration, a breakdown of the conventional binary divide between work and leisure, a disruption in the concepts of 'home' and 'away', as well as changes in the consumption patterns and preferences of middle- and upper-class city dwellers. Affluent city residents have been found to increasingly behave 'as if tourists' in their own cities, that is to engage in activities that are indistinguishable from those of visitors (Lloyd and Clark 2001: 357). Tourists visiting cities are increasingly likely to be frequent and experienced travellers who are familiar with the places they visit and/or seek to experience 'ordinary' or mundane spaces as locals would. Besides, growing numbers of 'temporary city users' (Costa and Martinotti 2003; Maitland and Newman 2009) that are neither readily identified as 'tourists' nor as 'locals', e.g. second-homers, frequent business travellers on short-term assignments, mobile 'creatives' or artists in temporary residence, or students going on exchanges, also make it increasingly difficult to establish a clear-cut distinction between tourism and everyday life. These 'temporary city users' have become more prevalent in a number of cities over the past decades and their practices have visible impacts on urban spaces and socio-economic relations in the city (Novy 2010).

As regards the supply side, sharp demarcations are also difficult to establish. Tourism relates to production activities that are dispersed across different branches of the economy; tourism resources (apart from accommodation) are in most urban contexts rarely solely produced for, or consumed by, tourists and efforts by local elites to transform urban environments into 'places to play' (Judd and Fainstein 1999) are rarely, if ever, exclusively driven by a desire to cater to the 'visitor class' (Eisinger 2000) alone. Rather, as will be discussed below, such efforts have to be seen in the context of a more general turn towards leisure and consumption in urban economic development. This underscores the need to address tourism not in isolation from, but in the context of wider social, political and economic processes. This has been recognized for some time: grounded in development and dependency theory, the first critical analyses of tourism as an activity predominantly organized by the capitalist system flourished in the 1970s (Jafari 2003; Weaver 2004). Since then, there has been a significant expansion of scholarship from both political-economic as well as cultural-interpretive perspectives that have highlighted the embeddedness of tourism within broader processes of economic and social change, such as globalization, industrial and regional restructuring, the turn towards entrepreneurial governance or the rise of 'postmodern' consumerism and the associated commodification of cultures and places.

That tourism is not only imbricated with but also central to many of the critical issues relevant to the understanding of contemporary societies was, meanwhile, for a long time not acknowledged by scholars outside the field of tourism studies. Instead, many scholars in sociology, geography and related disciplines did not view tourism as worthy of serious study. The sustained growth of tourism in recent decades has defeated such a view. According to the UNWTO (2015), tourism worldwide – as measured by international arrivals – has experienced a more than 40-fold increase, from approximately 25 million in 1950 to more than 1.1 billion in 2014. This trend is set to continue: international tourist arrivals worldwide are expected to reach 1.4 billion by 2020 and 1.8 billion by the year 2030. Urban tourism is thereby said to represent a particularly dynamic segment of tourism activity. Reliable statistics are hard to obtain, yet it is widely assumed that cities represent a key driver of overall tourism volume growth: a recent industry report suggested for instance that the volume of city trips increased by a staggering hard-to-believe 47 per cent from 2009 to 2013 alone (ITB 2013: 7).

Despite this – and the fact that urban environments worldwide have historically been among the most significant of all tourist destinations (Karski 1990) – urban tourism was for a long time not afforded much attention. Urban tourism suffered until well into the 1990s from what Ashworth (1989) famously called a 'double neglect . . . whereby . . . those interested in the study of tourism have tended to neglect the urban context in which much of it is set, while those interested in urban studies . . . have been equally neglectful of the importance of the tourist function of cities' (p. 33). This has changed in recent years, as urban tourism has been receiving an increased amount of scholarly attention. Works which address the chief concerns of this volume remain rather scarce, however, as most research thus far took a 'practical' and prescription-minded perspective and ignored the premise exposed earlier: that (urban) tourism is eminently political and consequently prone to controversy and social conflicts.

From marginal to integral: tourism's changing role in urban development politics and processes of urban change

That tourism transforms the spaces in which it develops, and that the changes it brings about are not always positive or desirable, has been recognized ever since the existence of tourism as a known phenomenon. Henri Stendhal, who coined the word 'tourist' to refer to an individual who travelled for pleasure, commented peevishly on the growth of tourism mobility that occurred during his lifetime. Writing about a visit to Florence in 1817, he complained that the city of his dreams was being occupied by too many visitors and remarked that Florence was 'nothing better than a vast museum full of foreign tourists' (cited in Culler 1981: 130). Conflicts between tourists and locals have also been documented since the 1800s, such as tensions in coastal towns in early Victorian Britain in response to the growth of (working-class) leisure mobility (see Morgan and Pritchard 1999; Churchill 2014) or the resentment that early forms of 'urban poverty tourism' (Steinbrink 2012) sparked in cities like London or New York. Such conflicts – while in no way trivial to those involved – were in the wider scheme of things of rather minor significance, however, and were afforded relatively little attention.

As a scholarly concern, urban tourism generally was, as noted earlier, for a long time deemed a peripheral topic, and policy-makers and planners – a few exceptions notwithstanding – typically also devoted only little attention to what was widely considered a 'marginal social activity' (Beauregard 1998: 220). Today the opposite is true, as a result of broad processes of economic, social and political change widely analysed in urban geography, sociology and politics. Cities – as a result of economic globalization and the rescaling and transformation of state activity – have been subjected to a series of unprecedented changes involving a profound restructuring of their economic bases, a transformation of their demographic composition and social class structure, as well as a significant remaking of the contexts for local governance. Cities' economies experienced a marked shift away from manufacturing towards service and knowledge-based industries. Urban politics became more and more a politics of economic development and entrepreneurialism as cities were forced into a global interurban competition for investment and economic growth. Consumption, culture and leisure moved centre stage in cities' political economy as productive sectors in their own right and as favoured means to achieve competitive advantage. And urban planners and policy-makers became increasingly preoccupied with place marketing and image-making policies so as to valorise cities as value-generating units (Harvey 1989, 1990).

Tourism emerged in this context as an attractive development option not only because of the increased recognition of its economic potential. Rather, it was seen as compatible with and conducive to other policies that came to characterize the 'new urban politics' from the late 1970s and early 1980s onwards (Hall and Hubbard 1998). Examples of the latter include traditional amenity-based development strategies to lure investment capital, residents and businesses; culture-based strategies (Bianchini and Parkinson 1993; Zukin 1995; Evans 2001; Miles 2007), or the more recent 'creative city' craze that has gripped mayors, planners and policy advisors in Europe, North America and elsewhere. Tourism moreover has been perceived by urban policy-makers and elites as an economic sector easy to promote, requiring little public investment besides promotional campaigns to stimulate the overall growth of the sector (Greenberg 2008; Colomb 2011) and measures supporting the 'tourist-friendly' reshaping of the city's spaces (e.g. through more policing of tourist hotspots). Against the backdrop of declining urban industrial bases and fiscal crises, it increasingly turned into a critical means to reposition cities in a rapidly changing economic environment and/or reaffirm their standing in an evolving metropolitan hierarchy (Fainstein *et al.* 2003: 2). Following the 2008 economic crisis, which affected global flows of foreign direct investment and visitors, many city leaders have often chosen to intensify, rather than roll back, place marketing and tourism promotion policies, even in a context of fiscal austerity and massive cuts in public spending.

Such arguments are more applicable to some contexts than others. Most of the foundational analyses of contemporary urban restructuring, including cities' shift towards leisure and consumption, are overwhelmingly rooted in the experience of European and North American cities. In many parts of the world, urban dynamics differ decisively from those whose experience dominates the (Anglophone) urban studies literature to this day (see Robinson 2006). Contrary to the suggestion by Fainstein *et al.* (2003: 8) that 'virtually every city sees a tourism possibility and has taken steps to encourage it', the elevation of tourism as a policy objective has not reached all places and contexts. But places that do not aspire to develop tourism get fewer and fewer – even the North Korean government has begun to market the country as a tourist destination – and many of the above-mentioned trends first observed in Western cities are also increasingly influencing the trajectories of cities in other contexts as well, in part due to the global emulation between city elites (see, *inter alia*, Broudehoux 2004; Yeoh 2005) and the globe-trotting travels of various forms of neoliberal urban policies (McCann and Ward 2011).

Neoliberalization refers to a combination of two processes: 'the (partial) destruction of extant institutional arrangements and political compromises through market-oriented reform initiatives; and the (tendentious) creation of a new infrastructure for market-oriented economic growth, commodification, and the rule of capital' (Brenner and Theodore 2002: 362). While neoliberalization strategies display important geographical variations (ibid.), many authors stress that place marketing and tourism promotion form a key component of the neoliberal policy experiments carried out in various cities and regions. Urban leaders have supported various initiatives to fuel the growth of the tourism sector in their cities in partnership with the private sector, mobilizing the cultural, social and physical capital present in their city in the process (see, *inter alia*, Hoffman *et al*. 2003; Spirou 2011). Frequently assisted or influenced by international institutions such as the World Bank and the Inter-American Development Bank, local and national governments in the Spanish and Portuguese-speaking Americas had begun, for instance, already in the late 1970s, to pursue the redevelopment of central locations, especially, heritage/historic centres, for tourism consumption, and in doing so transform them into 'wealth production machines' and prepare the ground for tourism gentrification (Betancour 2014: 4). Such efforts are prominently discussed by Latin American researchers and viewed as crucial expressions of a specific model of urban development that emerged as a result of the neoliberal reforms undertaken in the region (Janoschka *et al*. 2014).

In parallel, it is well documented that the restructuring processes of recent decades – in which activities previously deemed peripheral to the 'productive city', such as tourism and leisure, moved centre stage in cities' political economy – coincided with and contributed to an intensification of inequalities of various kinds. The contemporary city is not only one increasingly 'consumed by consumption' (Miles and Miles 2004: 172), but also one that is increasingly fragmented or divided. Urban inequality has grown considerably in most countries of the world and it has become increasingly clear that there is a flip side to the 'renaissance' or 'triumph' cities are said to have experienced in recent decades (see, *inter alia*, Porter and Shaw 2013). Escalating rents and housing prices make them increasingly unaffordable for low-income groups, while the most dynamic and desirable destinations among them are increasingly turning into exclusive playgrounds for the rich. That increasing social polarization and inequality, as well as gentrification and the destruction of low- and mixed-income communities, have become defining characteristics of the current urban moment is not accidental but in part the direct, often even deliberate, result of political actions such as the reduction of welfare spending, the dismantling of public housing and the shift towards market-oriented and property-led urban development strategies.

Urban tourism is intrinsically related to these trends in several ways. In terms of public policy, it has emerged as a popular priority in the boosterist agendas of local governments and growth coalitions, thus being granted public funding and investments which may have opportunity costs for other policy fields (e.g. welfare). Urban tourism has also frequently been found to perpetuate lopsided development patterns and contribute to existing or new patterns of urban inequality. Already in the 1970s there were significant debates about the uneven relations tourism entails and creates, but these debates were confined mainly to non-urban destinations – especially poorer, so-called 'Third World' countries. Dismissing 'the economics of tourism' and especially its central assumption that tourism represents a 'passport for development' that is unequivocally good for local communities, Turner and Ash were among the first to point out that the tourism industry involved substantial opportunity costs (see Pleumarom 2012). They described how tourism schemes overexploited cultural and natural resources, inflated prices beyond the reach of average levels of purchasing power, and disrupted and displaced traditional economies:

> The locals build the resorts and serve in them which, if fully controlled by foreigners, will contain few really worthwhile jobs. In the meantime, the fields return to weeds; the locals lose their ability to produce anything of direct practical use to themselves. While they've been building the resorts, they haven't been building the schools, the irrigation systems or the textile factories which would educate, feed or clothe them [. . .] For the sake of this industry, they can lose their land, their jobs and their way of life – for what?
>
> (Turner and Ash 1975, cited in Pleumarom 2012: 94)

Such intellectual critiques gave rise to the search for alternative development paths which were more conducive to local host communities' well-being (see Jafari 2003; Weaver 2004). However, their impact on discussions concerning tourism in cities remained for a long time rather limited. More extensively discussed in urban (tourism) research is another important line of criticism levelled against tourism: that tourism contributes to a commodification and destruction of cultures and places, and tends to set dynamics in motion that can lead to an erosion of precisely those attributes that constituted the original attraction for tourists to visit (Sorkin 1992; Zukin 1995; Harvey 2001).

These two lines of criticism have taken on particular relevance in the case of urban tourism, not just because of its quantitative growth, but also because of qualitative changes in the nature and geography of tourism flows. In many cities, urban tourism has spread geographically across urban space to new areas which lacked conventional tourist attractions – and were until recently not planned or marketed as tourist zones. New neighbourhoods have become increasingly desirable sites of tourism, leisure and consumption, e.g. the districts of Prenzlauer Berg, Friedrichshain, Kreuzberg and Neukölln in Berlin (Novy and Huning 2008) or London's East End (Brick Lane and Shoreditch (Maitland 2006). In some cities of the Global South, e.g. Brazilian and South African cities, tourists have been increasingly attracted to informal settlements, something referred to as 'slum' or 'favela tourism' (Frenzel *et al.* 2012; Broudehoux in this volume). Throughout the 1990s and the 2000s, such neighbourhoods became established destinations widely mentioned in tourist guidebooks, especially those catering for a young audience eager to 'go off the beaten track' (Maitland and Newman 2009).

The emergence of these neighbourhoods as 'new tourism areas' (Maitland 2006, 2007; Maitland and Newman 2004) is the outcome of the convergence of a number of trends (Novy and Huning 2008) which can be broadly classified into sociological, demand-related factors (i.e. the diversification of tourist audiences; the changing cultural practices of the new middle classes, e.g. in Europe in part due to the rapid development of low-cost airlines; the blurring of boundaries between tourism and other forms of mobility and practices of 'place consumption' (see Selby 2004)) and supply-side explanations (which include the role of local policies, place promotion and tourism marketing). In many cities, the local state and tourism marketing organizations have begun to promote such 'new tourism areas' for their vibrant sub- and counter-cultural and artistic scenes and 'authentic', 'off-beat' feel, for example in Berlin (Novy and Huning 2008; Colomb 2011, 2012), Amsterdam and Melbourne (Shaw 2005) or Paris (Vivant 2009). Ethnic diversity too has been mobilized in urban tourism strategies, e.g. in New York (Hoffman 2003), London (Shaw *et al.* 2004) or Berlin (Novy 2011a, 2011b). Occasionally described as 'touristification' (Bianchi 2003; Stock 2007), such processes of symbolic and physical appropriation and commodification have consequences for the spaces and people concerned, as discussed below. This multifaceted transformation of urban spaces under the influence of tourism flows, and the role of increasing tourist demand as a contributing and accelerating factor in broader urban transformation processes (e.g. gentrification), explain why urban tourism has become an increasingly contested topic, and why tourists have become an increasingly popular bogeyman in conflicts concerning urban restructuring processes.

Protests, resistance and (new) urban social movements in the tourist city: contestations in context

Many of the forms of protest and resistance surrounding urban tourism which are explored in this volume (further discussed in the next section) need to be put into the context of recent developments in the fields of urban activism and protest more generally – and the ways scholars have made sense of them. This section gives a brief overview of these developments, although it should be acknowledged that not everywhere can we observe structured or visible forms of collective mobilizations surrounding urban tourism. In some cities, as will be discussed in a number of chapters, we can discern micro-practices of resistance or individual adaptation to tourism flows and their impacts, which do not take the shape of fully-fledged social mobilizations for various reasons.

The role of the city as a space for the mobilisation and staging of protest has attracted increasing attention in recent years and a lot of developments, although disparate and disjointed, point to an upsurge of urban mobilisations and contestations. These mobilisations and contestations do not always revolve around territorially bounded urban issues. Instead, cities frequently – as was, for example, the case with Occupy New York, the Arab Springs or the Puerta del Sol protests in Madrid – serve as arenas within which broader political struggles that are not primarily urban-oriented are fought (Miller and Nicholls 2013: 452; Rodgers *et al.* 2014). Significantly, however, urban development processes and urban politics as such have also become increasingly contested in a variety of contexts and in a wide range of forms. This in itself is not new: the concept of urban social movements coined by Castells (1977) captured the emergence, in the 1960s and 1970s, of new social movements 'rooted in collectivities with a communal base' and/or with 'the local state as their target of action' (Fainstein and Fainstein 1985:

189). Castells' early categorization of urban social movements (1983) identified three types: those focusing on issues of collective consumption; those defending the cultural and social identity of a particular place; and those seeking to achieve control and management of local spaces, institutions or assets. The concept of urban social movements was subsequently broadened to refer to citizen action centred on urban issues, irrespective of its potential or actual effects (Pickvance 2003). Such social mobilizations have taken different forms and shapes in different national and local contexts, and have followed a path-dependent trajectory of transformation influenced by local opportunity structures and specific combinations of state-market-civil society relations.

Mayer's conceptualization of the evolution of urban social movements over time (2009), while simplifying a complex reality, points to some common trends of change across many parts of the Global North. In the 1990s, the strengthening of neoliberal municipal agendas which mobilized urban space as an arena for growth and market discipline led to a renewed politicization of urban struggles which challenged the effects of urban entrepreneurialism, increasing policing and surveillance and corporate urban development (e.g. anti-gentrification struggles under slogans such as 'Reclaim the Streets'). Recent scholarly contributions on urban social movements and contestations of contemporary forms of urban governance have highlighted the continuous transformation of the scope and agenda of movements since the 2000s in the face of the 'increasingly authoritarian, uneven and unjust nature of an ever more "neoliberalized" global political economy' (Purcell 2003: 564). In the context of the transformation of urban economic development agendas discussed in the previous section, and more recently of the 'austerity politics' following the 2008 economic crisis, several scholars have identified the emergence of new types of movements and coalitions which have begun to challenge, in particular, the consequences of the neoliberalization of policies in various fields (Koehler and Wissen 2003; Leitner *et al.* 2006; Mayer 2009, 2013).

Henri Lefebvre's concept of the 'right to the city' (1968) – a right both to use urban space and to participate in its social and political production – has in fact become a 'major formulation of progressive demands for social urban change around the world' (Marcuse 2009: 246). Activists in many parts of the world with various backgrounds and objectives have adopted it as a motto for broad urban social mobilizations protesting economic and environmental injustice, austerity politics, speculative gentrification and displacement, neighbourhood destruction, homelessness, etc. and demanding the creation of more just and democratic cities (Brenner *et al.* 2012). The US-based 'Right to the City' Alliance is one such example – a coalition of community-based groups, worker and labour rights' organizations, housing rights campaigners, environmental activists and migrant and minority groups united in their opposition against neoliberal economic and urban policies and social and environmental injustices of various kinds (Marcuse 2009; Mayer 2009).

Nicholls (2008) argues that the formation of such broad coalitions often results from a particular urban restructuring threat which acts as a 'structural push'.

Tourism and its impacts, in some localities, can be perceived as such a 'threat' by local actors, when it reaches a certain tipping point (e.g. as has been the case in Barcelona in recent years). It may crystalize the discontent which exists in a latent way with regard to various processes of urban and neighbourhood change which have negatively affected residents over the years, and are not caused by tourism per se. The city is a site of struggles over what type of urban development model should be prioritized, and tourism is often part and package of a broad economic model which has increasingly generated popular discontent. As the majority of chapters in this volume demonstrate, the conflicts surrounding tourism are rarely only about a crude tension between 'hosts' and 'guests', but instead reflect wider struggles over urban restructuring and socio-spatial transformations and who benefits and loses from them. A particularly good example of this is the complex links between 'touristification' and 'gentrification' processes, which are difficult to disentangle. The growth of tourism has been one factor among others which has fuelled changes in the residential markets of various cities. The increase in new hotels and hostels, as well as the sharp rise in the conversion of residential apartments into holiday rentals – a major topic of contention in various cities such as New York, Paris, Barcelona, Berlin or San Francisco (see Opillard in this volume) – has contributed to housing shortages and rent increases in neighbour-hoods which were already affected by gentrification processes.

Additionally, there is further evidence that in several cities marked by a visible 'cultural' or 'creative' turn in urban economic development – i.e. where the government has promoted a development agenda based on the marketing and promotion of creative industries, cultural consumption and urban tourism – a surge in activism and social mobilization around the consequences of such policy orientations has been witnessed (Novy and Colomb 2013). In various cities, protests led by coalitions of various actors, including cultural producers and 'creative milieux', have increasingly voiced their concerns about the ways in which culture and the arts are instrumentalized in post-industrial image econo-mies, how cities' existing social and cultural capital – old and new – is lost or commodified as a result of rampant gentrification, commercial development and/ or tourism, and how increasing rents displace low-income residents, cultural producers and alternative social and subcultural projects. In that context it is important to note that former urban social movements which became consoli-dated into more established community initiatives can themselves become the object of tourism practices or of the tourist gaze (see Fraeser in this volume), in particular in the case of alternative cultural spaces and initiatives such as (former) squats (see Pruijt 2003, 2004, Uitermark 2004 and Owen 2008 on the – contested – transformation of part of the Amsterdam squatting movement into providers of cultural services). Just like Mayer (2003) showed how the social capital present in some urban social movements has been instrumentalized by the state for economic competitiveness and social cohesion objectives, 'creative' and 'cultural' capital can be instrumentalized in the same way in marketing and economic development policies which seek to encourage urban tourism, consumption and the attraction of 'creative' workers and firms more generally (Colomb 2011).

Harvey, in *Spaces of Capital* (2001), stresses that contradictions – and thus conflict – emerge from this appropriation and commodification of a locale's cultural capital upon which consumption-driven urban economies and tourism are based. First, the exploitation of local marks of distinction with the potential to yield monopoly rents inevitably tends to lead to homogenization, which decreases uniqueness and 'erase(s) the monopoly advantage' which can be extracted from a place, item or event – something commonly discussed by critical cultural geographers in their investigation of tourism and place marketing strategies around the world (e.g. Kearns and Philo 1993). Second, drawing on uniqueness and local specificities to maintain a competitive edge and appropriate monopoly rents implies that capital has to 'support a form of differentiation and allow of divergent and to some degree uncontrollable local cultural developments that can be antagonistic to its own smooth functioning' (Harvey 2002: n.p.). These contradictions, according to Harvey, open 'new spaces for political thought and action within which alternatives can be both devised and pursued', but also could 'lead a segment of the community concerned with cultural matters to side with a politics opposed to multinational capitalism' (2001: 410) and favour alternatives based on different kinds of social and ecological relations (2002). This can help generate new coalitions or mobilizations bringing together the materially 'deprived' and the intellectually and politically 'discontented', as recent 'forms of (post-)Occupy collaborations that bring together austerity victims and other groups of urban "outcasts" with (frequently middle-class-based) radical activists' have shown in some places (Mayer 2013: 5).

Tourism related protests are, as several chapters in this volume show, frequently part of, or at least connected to, wider efforts to defend and reclaim the right to the city, challenge the predominance of exchange value over use value in the production of the built environment, and create 'cities for people, not for profit' (Brenner *et al.* 2012). At the same time, however, it is also important to recognize that not all tourism-related mobilizations readily slot into such a framework of analysis, and that not all of them can reasonably be regarded as 'progressive'. Tensions surrounding tourism involve different actors with different motives and agendas, and mobilizations clearly can be defensive, reactionary, exclusionary or even racist. To not recognize that NIMBYism ('Not In My Back Yard'), i.e. the defence of narrow interests around issues of individual property and consumption, is at play in some cases would be naive. It is equally important to acknowledge that tourism (and tourists) often provides a scapegoat for urban ills that they are barely responsible for. Moreover, (middle-class) individuals who are prolific travellers themselves, or came to settle in an urban area for the same reasons which draw visitors, often seem to complain loudest when tourism-related issues surface in their neighbourhoods. It is therefore not all that surprising that voices critiquing or resisting tourism are regularly accused of being hypocritical, self-serving and parochial. Such accusations, while sometimes true, are also regularly wrongly employed by representatives of the tourism industry, local media or policy-makers to discredit legitimate local mobilisations, stifle debate and draw attention away from the fact that tourism development has in many contexts emerged as an object of increasing contestations for understandable reasons. One consequence of these contestations has been that tourism in cities is increasingly recognized as what it is: increasingly consequential and inherently political (Burns and Novelli 2007; Hall 1994). Its political nature stems from the environment and circumstances in which it takes place, the decisions and underlying interests and power structures – sometimes proximate and sometimes remote – that shape it, as well as the profound, frequently socially and spatially uneven outcomes it involves.

Tourism's 'politicization from below'

The aim of this book is to analyse and better understand what type of conflicts and contestations around urban tourism have unfolded in contemporary cities across the world, and to explore the various ways in which community groups, residents and other organizations have responded to – and challenged – tourism development in cities in an international perspective. Our focus lies on the rise of urban tourism as a source of contention and the actors, causes and consequences of the multiple and variegated struggles around tourism that have emerged in recent years. The guiding questions which have structured the volume are as follows: Where and at what scale do conflicts and protests occur? What do they revolve around? Who are the actors and protagonists involved? What are their motives, demands and agenda, and how do they articulate them? Who are the target(s) of their demands or protests – the state, the tourism industry/the market, tourists? What impacts and consequences do manifestations of protest and resistance have? In particular, how do the local state and the tourism industry respond to them? What kinds of alternative approaches to tourism development (if any) are being proposed?

The present volume seeks in a modest way to shed light on these questions by bringing together a collection of theoretically rich and empirically detailed contributions by scholars from around the world. The aim is not to provide an exhaustive or representative overview, but to explore the diversity of struggles around urban tourism across different places and spaces, as well as the variety of disciplinary perspectives which can be used to make sense of these. This is reflected in the diverse backgrounds of the contributors to this volume – sociologists, anthropologists, geographers, political scientists, planners and architects. While the 16 chapters selected for the volume adopt a deliberately broad view of the subject, the majority of chapters align with our premise that tourism is increasingly the cause of unease and contestation and therefore experiences a 'politicization from below'. The contributions to the book cover more than 16 cities across Europe, North America, South America and Asia, which have been the recipients of increasing tourist flows. In those cities, residents have begun to note the effect of tourism on their daily life more clearly.

In some cases, this has led to the emergence of forms of collective mobilizations specifically set up around tourism-related issues, either at the city-wide scale (e.g. in Berlin, Chapter 3; in Hong Kong, Chapter 6; in Venice, Chapter 9;

or in Barcelona) or in particular neighbourhoods or sites (e.g. in Barcelona's Park Güell, Chapter 13). In other cases, existing forms of community activism (e.g. residents' or neighbourhood associations, housing rights collectives) or existing urban social movements have increasingly turned their attention towards tourism-related issues and incorporated them into their agenda as part of broader claims about: the defence of quality of life and public space management (e.g. in Paris, Chapter 3); neighbourhood restructuring, heritage protection and the 'right to stay put' in historic city centres (e.g. in Prague, Chapter 4 and in Valparaíso, Chapter 7); housing shortages, tenants' rights and rapid gentrification (e.g. San Francisco, Chapter 7); the desirability of new urban projects and questions of urban density (e.g. Santa Monica, Chapter 5); or the social impacts of mega-events (e.g. Belo Horizonte, Chapter 12 and more generally in many cities which were candidates for hosting the Olympic Games, Chapter 11). In other contexts, no structured or visible forms of collective mobilizations surrounding urban tourism might exist, but micro-practices of resistance (e.g. in the use of space by locals) against the impacts of touristification and forms of 'micro' or infra-politics' (see Chapter 2 for a discussion) can be uncovered (e.g. in Paris, Chapter 2 and in Singapore, Chapter 16).

All cities covered in the book are complex local societies divided by social, economic, class, ethnic and other lines. Local residents, individuals and groups are not homogeneous 'communities' who react to the prevalence of urban tourism in the same way. The potential benefits of urban tourism (and its costs) are consequently also the object of struggles between people, economic actors and social groups, who may enter into conflicts about: who can and should reap the positive benefits and profits generated by the tourist economy, based on unevenly distributed forms of cultural and economic capital (e.g. in Shanghai, Chapter 15 and Buenos Aires, Chapter 14); which kind of tourism they wish to see in the space they occupy (e.g. in the favelas of Rio de Janeiro, Chapter 10 or in a squatted building complex and alternative social-cultural centre in Hamburg, Chapter 17); the political, symbolic and economic use of tourism in societies marked by ethno-nationalist conflict (e.g. in Belfast, Chapter 8 and to an extent in Hong Kong, Chapter 6). In some contexts, thus, tourism has the capability to exacerbate or mitigate existing or latent urban conflicts (among social groups and between particular groups and the state) seemingly unrelated to tourism in the first place (see Chapter 8 on Belfast).

The main issues and themes of contention in most of the struggles surrounding urban tourism, at the risk of oversimplification, are about:

- the negative effects and externalities caused by tourism on people and places (which tend to become more intense and widely spread as tourism increases) (Table 1.1);
- equity impacts, i.e. the distribution of the costs and benefits of urban tourism among various groups and spaces – often very unevenly spread;
- the politics of urban tourism, including especially what is perceived as a skewed political agenda in favour of the 'visitor class' and the prioritization of development for exchange value over development for use value in the definition and conduct of public policies.

Table 1.1 The impacts of urban tourism on people and urban spaces: sources of conflicts

ECONOMIC	• Changing market demand for goods and services (from serving local needs to catering for the visitor economy, e.g. bars, souvenir shops) • Loss of small independent shops and growth of chain and franchised establishments • Increasing commercial rents and consumer prices → **(Commercial/retail gentrification (loss or displacement of resident-serving businesses)** • Increase and spatial expansion of tourism accommodation industry (hotels, hostels, bed & breakfast establishments, commercial vacation rental operators) • Increase in the number of second homes • Increase in the number of (short-term) rental housing units put on the market by individuals (owner-occupiers, tenants or landlords renting part or all of a housing unit, e.g. through online platforms) • Increasing property values and rents → **(Residential gentrification/displacement of low income residents and loss of housing units for long-term residents** • Conflicts between social and economic agents around who benefits from the visitor economy (e.g. conflicts about wages in the hotel industry, street vending or the 'tourist tax')
PHYSICAL	• Overcrowding and resulting problems (e.g. traffic congestion) • Deterioration of public spaces (e.g. through tacky souvenir stores, vandalism, etc.) • Privatisation and/or commodification of public space (e.g. proliferation of cafe terraces or enclosure of tourist sites) and community resources • Disruption of the aesthetic appearance of communities/ spread of 'sameness' • Environmental pressures (production of waste, litter, increasing water demand ...) • Land-use conflicts (e.g. the use of land for tourism-related activities vs. the use for housing, light manufacturing, etc.) • Over-development, 'land grabs', forced evictions and creative-destructive spatial dynamics • Physical manifestations of commercial and residential gentrification (see above)
SOCIAL AND SOCIO-CULTURAL	• Commercialisation, exploitation and distortion of culture (tangible/intangible), heritage and public space • 'Festivalisation' and 'eventification' • Invasive behaviour of tourists (voyeurism and intrusion)/ conflicts arising from different uses of and behaviour in public space (e.g. 'party tourism') • Problems of public order (crime, prostitution, 'uncivil' behaviour, etc.) • Repressive policies (e.g. anti-homeless laws)

(Continued)

Table 1.1 (Continued)

	• Heightened community divisions (e.g. between tourism beneficiaries and those bearing the burden, between alternative visions of what is heritage) • Loss of diversity/cultural homogenisation (e.g. loss of alternative spaces for artists or sub-cultural scenes) • Changing demographic make-up and tense relations within host communities between long-term residents and 'outsiders' (linked with gentrification dynamics)
PSYCHOLOGICAL	• Feelings of alienation, of physical and psychological displacement from familiar places (real or perceived) • Feeling of loss of control over community future • Loss of a sense of belonging or attachment to the community • Feelings of frustration and resentment among local people towards visitors

Source: Compiled by authors.

The book is structured as follows. Chapters 2 to 6 each offer an overview of the conflicts and social mobilizations surrounding tourism at the scale of an entire city, analysing in a detailed way the rise, and forms, of contention around aspects of urban tourism. In Paris (France), the quintessential tourist city, Gravari-Barbas and Jacquot (Chapter 2) argue that there are no coherent mobilizations against tourism as such, but that existing residents' associations and other actors have integrated claims about the impacts of the visitor economy in mainstream fights for quality of life, led by (middle-class) residents. They also show that resistance to tourism can take the shape of daily practices (e.g. of mobility in the city) of 'infra-' or 'micropolitics', as well as of bottom-up tourism approaches developed as alternatives to mainstream tourism.

Novy (Chapter 3) analyses the rise of discontent and protest surrounding the impact of growing tourist numbers in Berlin (Germany) in recent years. Embedded in a discussion of tourism's trajectory since the city's reunification and the key tenets of urban development and governance that shaped it, his analysis sheds light on the depoliticization and subsequent repoliticization of tourism as a policy field and posits that tourism-related mobilizations, while not uniform in their messages, are not so much 'anti-tourist' as they are critical of the city-state's approach to tourism development.

Pixová and Sládek (Chapter 4) analyse the forms of citizens' protest and resistance which have emerged in reaction to the touristification of Prague's historic core (Czech Republic), and show that they are integrated within broader, and relatively recent, forms of civic engagement and social mobilizations surrounding urban issues in post-socialist Prague. Activists tend to blame the city's problems on poor governance, management and public policy, not on tourism or tourists as such.

Peters (Chapter 5) analyses the recent conflicts surrounding urban development in Santa Monica (USA), one of California's premier tourist destinations, where newcomers (in particular skilled workers in the creative sectors) and temporary visitors clash with long-term residents in their visions for the city's future. Three different vignettes discuss how hotel workers struggle for living wage ordinances and fair treatment in the tourism service industry; how residents fight back against the perceived over-densification of their city; and how the sharp increase in short-term vacation rentals exacerbates the area's housing affordability crisis and is thus contested.

In Hong Kong, Garrett (Chapter 6) demonstrates that struggles surrounding urban tourism need to be understood against the backdrop of ideological and geopolitical concerns and disputes: the steep rise in mainland Chinese tourists and day trippers have had increasingly visible and contested impacts on Hong-kongers' daily lives and have led to the emergence of anti-Chinese tourism demonstrations. These are part of broader struggles surrounding the relationship between the People's Republic of China and the Hong Kong Special Adminis-trative Region, illustrated by the emergence of Hong Kong City State, localist and nativist sentiments.

Chapters 7 to 12 each address one particular sub-theme within the wider strug-gles surrounding tourism issues outlined above. Opillard (Chapter 7) provides a comparison of current tourism gentrification processes in San Francisco (USA) and Valparaíso (Chile), and of the discontents and forms of protest which they have generated in two very different contexts. San Francisco's corporate-led tour-istification and the emergence of new key actors in the tourism industry, such as Airbnb, has fuelled existing gentrification process and intensified the displacement of local residents. This has been contested by housing activist movements which have stepped up their mobilization around the regulation of the so-called 'sharing economy'. In Valparaíso, the designation of the historic core as a UNESCO World Heritage Site has led to new flows of investment and restructuring of the urban fabric which have triggered the gentrification of some neighbourhoods, contested by long-term residents.

Bereskin (Chapter 8) offers a slightly different take on the central theme of the book and studies the interaction of tourism development, protest and the long-standing ethnonationalist conflict in Belfast, Northern Ireland. Government tour-ism policies since the mid-1980s have exacerbated the economic, spatial and symbolic exclusion of the communities who have most suffered from the legacy of 'the Troubles', but sidelined communities have used tourism as a tool of protest by creating alternative tourism offers to challenge state narratives, culti-vate group recognition and secure economic benefits. Tourism has created a new field of interaction between the city's Catholic and Protestant communities, at times provoking cultural identity contests and competition between the two communities and at other times providing opportunities for intergroup contact and cooperation.

Vianello (Chapter 9) analyses the social mobilizations which have emerged to challenge cruise tourism in one of the world's cities most heavily threatened by tourism: Venice (Italy). The Committee *No Grandi Navi – Laguna Bene Comune* (No Big Ships – Lagoon as a Commons) has brought together various social actors (e.g. radical left-wing activists linked with social centres and middle-class environmental campaigners) to actively lobby public authorities for more stringent regulations of the cruise ship traffic in the lagoon, in a challenging political context which has prioritized the growth of cruise tourism (and related investments) at all costs.

Broudehoux (Chapter 10) discusses the emergence of a new form of urban tourism – slum tourism – in the squatter settlements of Rio de Janeiro (Brazil), and shows the multiple forms it has taken in the context of 'pacification' programmes for the *favelas*. She examines the relationship between visitors, residents and intermediary agents in these new forms of tourism, the conflicts and tensions generated, and the critiques and modes of resistance developed by the residents of these informal communities.

Lauermann (Chapter 11) discusses the urban politics of protesting sports 'mega-events' like the Olympics, which are used as catalysts for economic growth through a boost of the visitor economy. While mega-events can generate temporary gains in tourism economies and facilitate the pursuit of longer-term urban development goals, the mega-event planning process often bypasses normal processes of democratic deliberation and can introduce a 'democratic displacement' in the city. The chapter reviews the role of anti-bid social mobilizations (which contest Olympic projects at the early stages of planning) and their role in disrupting existing models of event-led urban development in the tourist city.

Capanema Alvares *et al.* (Chapter 12) further discuss the contested politics of mega-events as a tool of urban economic development and tourism policy, by looking at the socially contested and contentious impacts of the large-scale projects developed in a mid-sized Brazilian metropolitan area, Belo Horizonte, in preparation for the 2014 FIFA (Fédération Internationale de Football Association) World Cup and 2016 Summer Olympic Games hosted in Brazil. The huge public investments and stringent policy measures taken to prepare and sanitize urban spaces in Rio and other cities for those mega-events have come under mounting criticisms from a variety of actors. In June 2013, the country was shaken by the largest demonstrations in twenty years, triggered by a brutally repressed protest against the rise in public transport fares in São Paulo. Up to one million protesters took to the streets across the country to protest various issues, among which was the questionable amount of public expenditure spent on mega-event related projects to the detriment of social infrastructure, and the brutal evictions to make way for the construction works accompanying the preparation of those mega-events, as the case of Belo Horizonte illustrates.

Finally, Chapters 13 to 17, which are all characterized by the use of ethnographic approaches and in-depth, in situ observation, offer a series of case studies focusing on particular spaces or neighbourhoods which are used as lenses to address particular issues. Arias-Sans and Russo (Chapter 13) address the tensions between pressures for privatization and demands for commoning in over-used tourist spaces, discussing the contestations surrounding the plan to enclose part of the Park Güell, a major tourist attraction in Barcelona, Catalonia (Spain). Following the structure of a Greek tragedy, the chapter narrates the different stages of the conflict and unpacks the various arguments at stake between different social actors.

Lederman (Chapter 14) discusses how different categories and classes of local residents grapple with the opportunities presented by the growing visitor economy in San Telmo, a historic neighbourhood of Buenos Aires (Argentina), a country marked by an acute economic crisis in the early 2000s which left many impoverished. Drawing upon extensive observation of a street-based tourist market, he shows how vendors and artisans engage in complex strategies of symbolic ownership of the street by creating multiple linkages to local institutions and appealing to legitimized artistic identities and forms of cultural production. The chapter illustrates how tourism profoundly reflects and reshapes existing forms of social stratification between city residents, as benefits from the lucrative visitor economy are shaped by the hidden mechanisms of social and cultural power and capital.

Arkaraprasertkul (Chapter 15) also uses an ethnographic lens to investigate another type of conflict over the material benefits generated by the growing visitor economy – between the old and the new residents of an increasingly popular traditional *lilong* neighbourhood in Shanghai (China). Young creative entrepreneurs have settled in the city's downtown, rundown historic alleyways, building small-scale, often unlicensed businesses such as cafes and design stores which have contributed to the successful transformation of such neighbourhoods into tourist attractions. As a result, tensions have arisen between different categories of residents over the unequal distribution of the benefits from the growing tourism and leisure economy, which has led to a crackdown on such activities by public authorities. The chapter illustrates another form of protest and resistance – one against the implications of the new creative activities, and the visitors they attract, in a historic residential neighbourhood, rather than one of protest against tourism as such.

Luger (Chapter 16), in the case of Singapore, analyses how individual micro-practices of what he terms 'guerilla tourism', combined with an emerging social mobilization, have questioned the state-led tourism promotion agenda which has prioritized elite spaces such as the Botanic Gardens – Singapore's first UNESCO World Heritage Site – over less formal spaces which have important collective memory and environmental value for local residents. He shows how a loose network of grassroots groups have come together to reclaim and stop the destruction of Bukit Brown, the largest Chinese cemetery outside of China. Through the concept of 'guerilla tourism', conceptualized as an example of de Certeau's 'going off the pathway', the author shows how alternative (tourism) narratives are performed through the act of transgressing boundaries and walking, contesting and reshaping the hegemony of consumption-led urban development in the authoritarian tourist city.

Fraeser (Chapter 17) shows how forms of social protest and cultural resistance have themselves become, or been packaged as, 'tourist attractions'. Through the case of the Gängeviertel, a small building complex in the heart of Hamburg (Germany), she shows how a space of resistance can take advantage of its attractiveness for policy-makers and tourists alike, notwithstanding the co-optation and commercialization that this entails and the ambiguous consequences for the nature of the space. The primacy given by the Gängeviertel's activists to openness to visitors (more than radical autonomy) has turned the quarter into some kind of alternative tourist attraction, attracting both passive consumers and engaged visitors who wish to get involved in the social, cultural and political practices of the Gängeviertel collective and thus become part of its commoning process.

As this book is a first attempt to address the topic, it inevitably has weaknesses and limits. First, beyond the identification of a number of frequent issues and common themes in the present section, we have not developed a fully-fledged analytical framework for a systematic comparison between the cases, which are too disparate for that. Second, some themes which have acquired a lot of political resonance in recent years and are the object of high-profile debates in many locations, would have warranted more detailed analyses, in particular the proliferation of short-term tourism rental practices and the impacts they have on housing markets and neighbourhood change in various cities (hinted at in the case of Paris in Chapter 2, San Francisco in Chapter 7 and Santa Monica in Chapter 5) (Figure 1.5). Third, we have not discussed questions of methodology nor that of the researcher's positionality in relation to the topic under investigation. As researchers are also tourists (in their free time) or 'temporary city users' (when doing field work in urban

Figure 1.5 Banner and poster directed at tourists who rent (often unlicensed, illegal) short-term holiday apartments, Barcelona, 2010 and 2013.

Source: left, Evan Bench; right, Claire Colomb.

locations), they too contribute to the processes at play in tourist cities. In some cases, researchers are activists, engaging in collective mobilizations in their city to deal with some of the contentious issues evoked in this book, as individual citizens or as 'experts'. Fourth, the book barely addresses cases (of which there are plenty) where tourism activities and practices are relatively well integrated into urban space and appear accepted by local residents – or at least are not too contentious. There would be analytical value in studying why this may be the case, and whether this is related to questions of scale and the nature of tourism flows and practices, or of public policy and the regulation of tourism in urban space.

We are aware that the book, because of its focus on conflict, protest and resistance, might be perceived as presenting a one-sided and overly negative picture of tourism as a phenomenon and contemporary force of urban change. However, it should not be read as an attack on tourism as such. We are critical of tourism in its current form but do not suggest that tourism is by definition exploitative and destructive. Nor do we subscribe to portrayals of the practices and experiences of being a tourist or traveller (which we all engage in) as being inevitably 'tragic' or even 'vaguely pathetic' in their character (Harrison 2003: 25). Tourism can – and often does – create numerous benefits for both visitors and host communities. At the same time, however, we recognize that its practice and structures are rooted in unequal power relations and unsustainable development patterns which frequently inhibit any real ability for those being visited to assert control over tourism development, and cause largely negative consequences for the world we occupy (as residents) and travel through (as visitors). For this reason, the developments described and analysed in the present book should be addressed with both further research and action. This includes both a critical questioning and challenging of the way tourism operates and is dealt with in cities' political arenas, as well as intensified efforts to envision new forms of (state, community and market-led) regulations of the visitor economy and develop alternative forms of tourism. This is particular important as urban tourism flows are unlikely to weaken in the near future. The possibility of supply-side shocks resulting from terrorism, epidemics and natural catastrophes or sharply rising petrol and mobility prices notwithstanding, tourism will most likely not go away anytime soon, which is why more attention is needed to understand – and deal with – its impacts on cities.

References

Ashworth, G. J. (1989) 'Urban tourism: an imbalance in attention', in C. P. Cooper (ed.), *Progress in Tourism, Recreation and Hospitality Management*. London: Bellhaven Press.

Beauregard, R. (1998) 'Tourism and economic development policy in US urban areas', in D. Ioannides and K. G. Debbage (eds), *The Economic Geography of the Tourist Industry*. London and New York: Routledge.

Becker, E. (2015) 'The revolt against tourism', *New York Times*, 17 July. Online. Available at http://www.nytimes.com/2015/07/19/opinion/sunday/the-revolt-against-tourism.html.

Betancur, J. J. (2014) 'Gentrification in Latin America: overview and critical analysis', *Urban Studies Research*. Online. Available at http://www.hindawi.com/journals/usr/2014/986961/.

Bianchi, R. V. (2003) 'Place and power in tourism development: tracing the complex articulations of community and locality', *Pasos: Revista de turismo y patrimonio cultural*, 1(1): 13–32.

Bianchini, F. and Parkinson, M. (eds) (1993) *Cultural Policy and Urban Regeneration: The West European Experience*. Manchester: Manchester University Press,.

Brenner, N. and Theodore, N. (2002) 'Cities and the geographies of "actually existing neoliberalism"', *Antipode*, 34(3): 349–79.

Brenner, N., Marcuse, P., and Mayer, M. (eds) (2012) *Cities for People, not for Profit*. London and New York: Routledge.

Broudehoux, A.-M. (2004) *The Making and Selling of Post-Mao Beijing*. New York and London: Routledge.

Burns, P. M. and Novelli, M. (eds) (2007) *Tourism and Politics*. Philadelphia: Elsevier.

Castells, M. (1977) *The Urban Question*. London: Edward Arnold.

Castells, M. (1983) *The City and the Grassroots*. London: Edward Arnold.

Churchill, D. (2014) 'Living in a leisure town: residential reactions to the growth of popular tourism in Southend, 1870–1890', *Urban History*, 41(1): 42–61.

Colau, A. (2015) 'Mass tourism can kill a city – just ask Barcelona's residents', *Guardian*, 2 September. Online. Available at http://www.theguardian.com/commentisfree/2014/sep/02/mass-tourism-kill-city-barcelona.

Colomb, C. (2011) *Staging the New Berlin. Place Marketing and the Politics of Urban Reinvention Post-1989*. London: Routledge.

Colomb, C. (2012) 'Pushing the urban frontier: temporary uses of space, city marketing and the creative city discourse in 2000s Berlin', *Journal of Urban Affairs*, 34(2): 131–52.

Costa, N. and Martinotti, G. (2003) 'Sociological theories of tourism and regulation theory', in L. M. Hoffman, S. S. Fainstein and D. R. Judd (eds) *Cities and Visitors: Regulating People, Markets, and City Space*. Oxford and New York: Blackwell.

Culler, J. (1981) 'Semiotics of tourism', *American Journal of Semiotics*, 1(1–2): 127–40.

Duvernoy, S. (2012) 'Tourist-bashing turns ugly in Berlin', *Reuters*, 14 September. Online. Available at http://www.reuters.com/article/2012/09/13/us-germany-berlin-tourists-idUSBRE88C0ZT20120913.

Eisinger, P. (2000) 'The politics of bread and circuses: building the city for the visitor class', *Urban Affairs Review*, 35(3): 316–33.

Enzensberger, H. M. (1996) 'A theory of tourism', *New German Critique*, 68: 117–35.

European Cities Marketing (2014) *ECM Presents the Results of Tourism in Europe through Its Benchmarking Report 2014*, 24 July. Online. Available at http://www.europeancitiesmarketing.com/ecm-presents-results-tourism-europe-benchmarking-report-2014/.

Evans, G. (2001) *Cultural Planning: An Urban Renaissance?* London: Routledge.

Fainstein, S. S. and Fainstein, N. I. (1985) 'Economic restructuring and the rise of urban social movements', *Urban Affairs Review*, 21(2): 187–206.

Fainstein, S. S, Hoffman, L. M. and Judd, D. R. (2003) 'Introduction', in L. M. Hoffman, S. S. Fainstein and D. R. Judd (eds) *Cities and Visitors: Regulating People, Markets, and City Space*. Oxford and New York: Blackwell.

Frenzel, F., Koens, K. and Steinbrink, M. (eds) (2012) *Slum Tourism: Poverty, Power and Ethics*. London: Routledge.

Gale, T. (2008) 'The end of tourism, or endings in tourism?', in P. Burns and M. Novelli (eds) *Tourism and Mobilities: Local-Global Connections*. Wallingford: CABI.

Greenberg, M. (2008) *Branding New York: How a City in Crisis Was Sold to the World*. London and New York: Routledge.

Hall, C. M. (1994) *Tourism and Politics: Policy, Power, and Place*. Chichester: Wiley.

Hall, C. M. and Jenkins, J. (1995) *Tourism and Public Policy*. London: Routledge.

Hall, T. and Hubbard, P. (eds) (1998) *The Entrepreneurial City*. Wiley: Chichester.

Harrison, J. (2003) *Being a Tourist: Finding Meaning in Pleasure Travel*, Vancouver: UBC Press.

Harvey, D. (1989) 'From managerialism to entrepreneurialism: the transformation in urban governance in late capitalism', *Geografiska Annaler*, 71B: 3–17.

Harvey, D. (1990) *The Condition of Postmodernity*. Oxford: Blackwell.

Harvey, D. (2001) 'The art of rent: globalization and the commodification of culture', in D. Harvey, *Spaces of Capital*. London and New York: Routledge.

Harvey, D. (2002) 'The art of rent: globalization, monopoly and the commodification of culture', in L. Panitch and C. Leys (eds) *A World of Contradictions. Socialist Register 2002*. Pontypool: Merlin Press. Reproduced online. Available at http://www.16beavergroup.org/mtarchive/archives/001966.php.

Hoffman, L. (2003) 'The marketing of diversity in the inner city: tourism and regulation in Harlem', *International Journal of Urban and Regional Research*, 27(2): 286–99.

Hollersen, W. and Kurbjeweit, D. (2011) 'A victim of its own success. Berlin drowns in tourist hordes and rising rents', *Spiegel Online*, 16 September. Online. Available at http://www.spiegel.de/international/germany/a-victim-of-its-own-success-berlin-drowns-in-tourist-hordes-and-rising-rents-a-786392.html.

ITB (2013) *World Travel Trends Report 2013/2014*. Online. Available at http://www.itb-berlin.de/media/itb/itb_dl_all/itb_presse_all/WTTR_Report_2014_Web.pdf.

Jafari, J. (2003) 'Research and scholarship', *Journal of Tourism Studies*, 14(1): 6–16.

Janoschka, M., Sequera, J. and Salinas, L. (2014) 'Gentrification in Spain and Latin America – a critical dialogue', *International Journal of Urban and Regional Research*, 38(4): 1234–65.

Judd, D. R. and Fainstein, S. S. (eds) (1999) *The Tourist City*. New Haven, CT: Yale University Press.

Karski, A. (1990) 'Urban tourism: a key to urban regeneration?', *The Planner*, 76(13): 15–17.

Kassam, A. (2014) 'Naked Italians spark protests against antics of drunken tourists in Barcelona', *Guardian*, 21 August. Online. Available at http://www.theguardian.com/world/2014/aug/21/naked-italians-protests-drunken-tourists-barcelona

Kearns, G. and C. Philo (eds) (1993) *Selling Places. The City as Cultural Capital: Past and Future*. Oxford: Pergamon Press.

Koehler, B. and Wissen, M. (2003) 'Glocalizing protest: urban conflicts and global social movements', *International Journal of Urban and Regional Research*, 27(4): 942–51.

Lefebvre, H. (1968) *Le Droit à la Ville*. Paris: Anthropos.

Leitner, H., Peck, J. and Sheppard, E. S. (eds) (2006) *Contesting Neoliberalism*. New York: Guilford Press.

Lloyd, R. and Clark, T. N. (2001) 'The city as an entertainment machine', in K. F. Gotham (ed.) *Critical Perspectives on Urban Redevelopment*. Amsterdam: Elsevier Science.

McCann, E. and Ward, K. (eds) (2011) *Mobile Urbanism. Cities and Policymaking in the Global Age*. Minneapolis, MN: University of Minnesota Press.

Maitland, R. (2006) 'Cultural tourism and the development of new tourism areas in London', in G. Richards (ed.) *Cultural Tourism: Global and Local Perspectives*. New York: Haworth.

Maitland, R. (2007) 'Tourists, the creative class and distinctive areas in major cities: the roles of visitors and residents in developing new tourist areas', in G. Richards and J. Wilson (eds) *Tourism, Creativity and Development*. London and New York: Routledge.

Maitland, R. and Newman, P. (2004) 'Developing metropolitan tourism on the fringe of Central London', *International Journal of Tourism Research*, 6(5): 339–48.

Maitland, R. and Newman, P. (eds) (2009) *World Tourism Cities: Developing Tourism Off the Beaten Track*. London and New York: Routledge.

Marcuse, P. (2009) 'From critical urban theory to the right to the city', *City*, 13(2–3): 185–97.

Mayer, M. (2003) 'The onward sweep of social capital: causes and consequences for understanding cities, communities and urban movements', *International Journal of Urban and Regional Research*, 27(1): 110–32.

Mayer, M. (2009) 'The "Right to the City" in the context of shifting mottos of urban social movements', *City*, 13(2): 362–74.

Mayer, M. (2013) 'First world urban activism. Beyond austerity urbanism and creative city politics', *City*, 17(1): 5–19.

Miles, M. (2007) *Cities and Cultures*. London: Routledge.

Miles, S. and Miles, M. (2004) *Consuming Cities*. Basingstoke: Palgrave Macmillan.

Miller, B. and Nicholls, W. (2013) 'Social movements in urban society: the city as a space of politicization', *Urban Geography*, 34(4): 452–73.

Morgan, N. and Pritchard, A. (1999) *Power and Politics at the Seaside: The Development of Devon's Resorts in the Twentieth Century*. Exeter: University of Exeter Press.

Moskowitz, P. (2015) 'How New Orleans is in danger of losing its identity', *Vice Magazine*, 27 February. Online. Available at https://news.vice.com/article/how-new-orleans-is-in-danger-of-losing-its-identity.

Nicholls, W. (2008) 'The urban question revisited: the importance of cities for social movements', *International Journal of Urban and Regional Research*, 32(4): 841–59.

Novy, J. (2010) 'What's new about New Urban Tourism? And what do recent changes in travel imply for the "Tourist City" Berlin?', in J. Richter (ed.) *The Tourist City Berlin. Tourism and Architecture*. Berlin: Braun.

Novy, J. (2011a) 'Urban ethnic tourism in New York City's neighborhoods – then and now', in V. Aytar and J. Rath (eds) *Gateways to the Urban Economy: Ethnic Neighborhoods as Places of Leisure and Consumption*. London and New York: Routledge.

Novy, J. (2011b) 'Kreuzberg's multi- and intercultural realities. Are they assets?', in V. Aytar and J. Rath (eds) *Gateways to the Urban Economy: Ethnic Neighborhoods as Places of Leisure and Consumption*. London and New York: Routledge.

Novy, J. (2013) 'Städtetourismus, Stadtteiltourismus und der Mythos städtischer Steuerung. Das Beispiel Berlin', in K.-H. Wöhler (ed.) *Destination Governance*. Berlin: Erich Schmidt *Verlag*.

Novy, J. and Colomb, C. (2013) 'Struggling for the right to the (creative) city in Berlin and Hamburg. New urban social movements, new spaces of hope?', *International Journal of Urban and Regional Research*, 37(5): 1816–38.

Novy, J. and Huning, S. (2008) 'New tourism areas in the new Berlin', in R. Maitland and P. Newman (eds) *World Tourism Cities. Developing Tourism off the Beaten Track*. London and New York: Routledge.

Owens, L. (2008) 'From tourists to anti-tourists to tourist attractions: the transformation of the Amsterdam squatters' movement', *Social Movement Studies*, 7(1): 43–59.

Pickvance, C. (2003) 'From urban social movements to urban movements: a review and introduction to a symposium on urban movements', *International Journal of Urban and Regional Research*, 27(1): 102–9.

Pleumarom, A. (2012) 'The politics of tourism and poverty reduction, responsible tourism: concepts, theory and practice', in D. Leslie (ed.) *Responsible Tourism: Concepts, Theory and Practice*. Wallingford: CABI.

Porter, L. and Shaw, K. (eds) (2013) *Whose Urban Renaissance? An International Comparison of Urban Regeneration Strategies*. London: Routledge.

Pruijt, H. (2003) 'Is the institutionalization of urban movements inevitable? A comparison of the opportunities for sustained squatting in New York City and Amsterdam', *International Journal of Urban and Regional Research*, 27(1): 133–57.

Pruijt, H. (2004) 'Squatters in the creative city: rejoinder to Justus Uitermark', *International Journal of Urban and Regional Research*, 28(3): 699–705.

Purcell, M. (2003) 'Citizenship and the right to the global city: reimagining the capitalist world order', *International Journal of Urban and Regional Research*, 27(3): 564–90.

Robinson, J. (2010) *Ordinary Cities: Between Modernity and Development*. London: Routledge.

Rodgers, S., Barnett, C. and Cochrane, A. (2006) 'Where is urban politics?', *International Journal of Urban and Regional Research*, 38(5): 1551–60.

Selby, M. (2004) *Understanding Urban Tourism: Image, Culture and Experience*. London: I. B. Tauris.

Shaw, K. (2005) 'The place of alternative culture and the politics of its protection in Berlin, Amsterdam and Melbourne', *Planning Theory and Practice*, 6(2): 149–69.

Shaw, S., Bagwell, S. and Karmowska, J. (2004) 'Ethnoscapes as spectacle: reimaging multicultural districts as new destinations for leisure and tourism consumption', *Urban Studies*, 41(10): 1983–2000.

Sorkin, M. (ed.) (1992) *Variations on a Theme Park*. New York: Hill & Wang.

Spirou, C. (2011) *Urban Tourism and Urban Change: Cities in a Global Economy*. London and New York: Routledge.

Steinbrink, M. (2012) '"We did the slum!" Urban poverty tourism in historical perspective', *Tourism Geographies*, 14(2): 213–34.

Stock, M. (2007) 'European Cities: towards a recreational turn?, *Hagar. Studies in Culture, Polity and Identities*, 7(1): 115–34.

Uitermark, J. (2004) 'The co-optation of squatters in Amsterdam and the emergence of a movement meritocracy: a critical reply to Pruijt', *International Journal of Urban and Regional Research*, 28(3): 687–98.

UNWTO (1995) *Technical Manual: Collection of Tourism Expenditure Statistics*. Online. Available at http://pub.unwto.org/WebRoot/Store/Shops/Infoshop/Products/1034/1034-1.pdf.

UNWTO (2015) *UNWTO Tourism Highlights*. Online. Available at http://mkt.unwto.org/publication/unwto-tourism-highlights-2015-edition.

Urry, J. (1990) *The Tourist Gaze*. London: Sage.

Vivant, E. (2009) 'How underground culture is changing Paris', *Urban Research and Practice*, 2(1): 36–52.

Weaver, D. B. (2004) 'Tourism and the elusive paradigm of sustainable development', in A. Lew, C. M. Hall and A. M. Williams (eds) *Companion to Tourism*. Oxford: Blackwell.

Yeoh, B. S. (2005) 'The global cultural city? Spatial imagineering and politics in the (multi)cultural marketplaces of South-east Asia', *Urban Studies*, 42(5/6): 945–58.

Zukin, S. (1995) *The Cultures of Cities*. Oxford: Blackwell.

2 No conflict?

Discourses and management of tourism-related tensions in Paris

Maria Gravari-Barbas and
Sébastien Jacquot

Paris, a 'world tourism city' (Maitland and Newman 2009), was the first metropolitan tourist destination in Europe. Since the nineteenth century, tourism has intrinsically formed part of the urban development of the city. Some of its most famous places are the result of major tourism events, such as the International Exhibitions of 1889 and 1901. By contrast with other major European urban tourism destinations, such as Berlin or Barcelona, mass tourism development in Paris was not a recent phenomenon of the past two decades caused by relatively recent developments such as a notable mega-event (e.g. the Barcelona Olympic Games of 1992) or political development (e.g. German reunification). Paris is certainly facing several issues related to the management of major tourism flows: the hyper-concentration of tourists in particular sites and areas such as Le Marais, Montmartre or Notre Dame; tourism gentrification, commercial mono-activity and the commodification of a number of key tourist sites; rent increases, etc. Nevertheless, we do not seem to observe in Paris the large-scale public expressions of hostility vis-à-vis tourism which have manifested themselves in recent years in cities such as Barcelona or Berlin and have been widely reported in the European media. While the residents of Paris may complain about the visible impacts of the presence of tourists in the city (e.g. noise, street congestion or concentrations in specific night spots), this does not amount to what we could identify as an organized, large-scale opposition to tourism. This chapter aims to contribute to the understanding of this paradox – that there seems to be 'no tourism conflict' in Paris.

How can we explain this lack of (noticeable) contestation? Is it due to the fact that tourism is considered a consensual and banal social phenomenon in a metropolis such as Paris? To what extent is tourism a component of the way broader metropolitan issues are framed? What kind of resistance to tourism can we identify in Paris? This contribution is organized in four sections. We first give an overview of the Paris 'tourismscape'[1] (van der Duim 2007) as it was historically formed and as it has been evolving more recently. The second section sketches a theoretical approach to the idea of 'resistance' and introduces the notions of 'infrapolitics' or 'micropolitics', which we argue are more appropriate to grasp the non-institutionalized, non-formalized forms of resistance to tourism witnessed in Paris, which are subsequently described in that section. In the third section we outline the increasing demands for the public and private regulation of (some impacts of) tourism which have emerged in recent years. Finally, the fourth section analyses examples of alternative forms of tourism as possible expressions of resistance to mainstream and mass tourism.

Old and new Paris tourismscapes

Paris is a global tourist destination and the first tourist city in Europe, attracting 29.3 million tourists in Paris *intra muros* in 2013 (46.8 million in the broader Paris city-region) (OTCP 2014). The main tourist areas have been identified as the *Paris Central Tourist District* (Duhamel and Knafou 2007), comprising the Champs-Elysées, the Marais, Île Saint-Louis, the Latin Quarter and Montmartre. According to a study carried out by the Comité Régional du Tourisme (CRT) Paris-Île-de-France and IPSOS Marketing in 2009 (CRT 2010), even repeat visitors coming back to Paris for a second or third visit tend to visit the same places: the Louvre, Montmartre or the Eiffel Tower. The Louvre welcomed 9.2 million visitors in 2013 (70 per cent of which were foreigners) and the Musée d'Orsay 3.5 million.

The density of geotagged pictures posted on social networks (Flickr, Panoramio) – largely by tourists[2] – reveals the most photographed areas in Paris (Figure 2.1) and draws the contours of a polycentric tourism map. In the centre of Paris two main axes are clearly visible. The first follows the river Seine, from the Île Saint-Louis to the Eiffel Tower. Along the river we find, from East to West, most of the major tourist sights of Paris: Notre Dame, the Orsay museum,

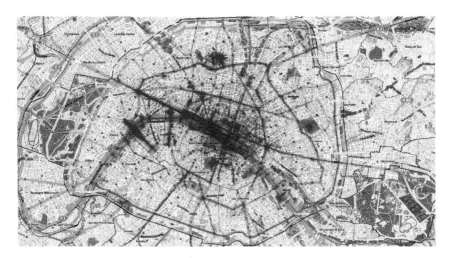

Figure 2.1 Tourism hotspots in Paris: 'heatmap' of the highest densities of pictures posted on Flickr, 2009–13.

the Quai Branly Museum or the Eiffel Tower. The second axis stretches from the Louvre and the Tuileries Gardens to the Champs Elysées, up to the Arc de Triomphe. The map also shows other areas of tourist concentration south of the river Seine (i.e. the Latin Quarter, the Sorbonne University and the Panthéon) and, on the northern bank, in the historical district of the Marais. In the north of the city, Montmartre also appears as a major tourist hotspot.

The tourist hotspots of Paris are the result of the accumulation of tourist guides' prescriptions and related tourist practices over a long period of time (Hancock 2003). The Baedeker guide in 1894 specifically recommended the Louvre, Notre Dame, the Sainte-Chapelle and the Concorde, among others (Cohen 2000). The itinerary proposed by that guide followed the axis starting in the Louvre and ending at the Place de l'Etoile, which, to this day, is still charac-terized by the highest degree of tourist activity. Successive urban interventions in Paris – some of them related to major international events in the nineteenth century such as the Universal and International Exhibitions of 1855, 1867, 1878, 1889 and 1900 – resulted in the production of a consolidated *tourismscape*, whose expansion steadily continued throughout the twentieth century through more international events hosted in Paris (e.g. the International exhibition of 1937) but also, from the 1960s onwards, through the active enhancement of the city's urban and architectural heritage. The Marais is a good example of the crea-tion of a major cultural and tourism district through the recovery of the splendid classical architecture of the area. Following the creation of a protected historic district (*Secteur Sauvegardé*) in 1963, the *Plan de Sauvegarde et de Mise en Valeur du Marais* guided the refurbishment of the *hôtels particuliers* (aristocratic townhouses) of the area and the transformation of the former economic activities (mainly small-scale craft and manufacturing) into cultural ones (APUR 2004). Heritage restoration contributed to the gentrification of the Marais district and encouraged the development of new activities related either to creative industries (fashion, design) or to the night economy. In addition, the relocation of gay bars and venues from Les Halles to the Marais resulted in the consolidation of the latter as a hotspot of Parisian nightlife.

The analysis of tourism concentrations in Paris therefore clearly highlights a small group of consolidated tourism areas in the city (Bauder *et al.* 2014). But it also allows us to identify new tourism development areas which, while remaining less visited compared to the hotspots mentioned before, have experienced a new tourism demand which we could describe as 'off the beaten tracks' (Maitland 2010, 2013). A new geography of tourism in Paris has indeed slowly emerged since the 1990s (Freytag 2008; Gravari-Barbas and Fagnoni 2013). This is in part related to the urban planning policies developed during the last decades of the twentieth century in the Eastern part of Paris, which aimed at rebalancing the historical disparity between the wealthy Western part of the city and the poorer neighbourhoods in the East. New large-scale redevelopment projects have been implemented in former industrial areas (Ingallina and Park 2009), such as La Villette (a major cultural complex and urban park built on the site of the city's old slaughterhouses) or Bercy (where former wine warehouses were redeveloped as an entertainment and shopping 'village'). New tourism patterns similar to those analysed by other scholars in London (Pappalepore *et al.* 2011) or Berlin (Füller and Michel 2014) can therefore also be observed in Paris. Even if they do not match numerically the concentrations witnessed in the established hotspots of Paris, tourism patterns are now clearly visible in specific areas such as Belleville, Bastille, the Canal Saint-Martin area, La Butte aux Cailles, etc. Tourism development in these districts has been encouraged by public and private initiatives, with the creation of associations dedicated to tourism development, using urban walks as an instrument to encourage visitors to discover new districts, as will be discussed in the final section of this chapter. A considerable number of local associations, start-ups and enterprises have been created over the past years in order to deal with new tourist demand, for instance *Ça se visite*, *Like a local*, *Parisiens d'un jour*, *Meeting the French*, *Balades Paris chanson*, *Paris le nez en l'air*, etc.

The development of a new geography of tourism in Paris towards these new districts has happened in parallel with processes of gentrification in the same areas (Clerval 2013). Researchers have highlighted the convergence between tourism development and the urban and social changes of some districts, specifically through gentrification processes (Gladstone and Préau 2008). In London, for instance, old and new gentrified areas are visited by tourists who are keen to discover 'everyday life' (Maitland 2008). We could therefore hypothesize that in Paris, the tourist can sometimes be a 'gentrifier', partly in relation to second-home ownership (Chevalier *et al.* 2013), as for example in Berlin Prenzlauer Berg (Dörfler 2010) or in New York (Gravari-Barbas 2014). While gentrification has been a widespread phenomenon in Paris for decades, beginning in the Marais after the creation of the protected historic district in 1962, it has extended more recently to districts such as Belleville in the north-east of Paris (Clerval 2013). These newly gentrified areas have also become sites of 'new tourism' development. But the development of a new geography of tourism in Paris, in parallel to gentrification processes, has not, thus far, raised massive or visible opposition. It appears generally accepted by the local population due, to an extent, to locally driven answers to international tourism demand.

Forms of resistance to the impacts of tourism in Paris

If compared to the situation witnessed in other European cities in recent years, e.g. Barcelona or Berlin, as mentioned in the introduction to this volume (see also Novy 2013), there does not seem to be visible manifestations of anti-tourist/anti-tourism opposition in Paris: no 'anti-tourists' graffiti in public spaces, no large-scale mobilizations on social networks,[3] no noticeable reactions in the local and regional newspapers to the issue of mass tourism flows. While we do not observe open conflicts and large-scale institutionalized or formalized mobilizations against tourism, we do, however, observe the development of what we have termed processes of 'infra' or 'micropolitics', through which Paris residents seek to avoid tourist nuisances.

When thinking about resistance (to unwanted social phenomena), it is actually useful to distinguish between several regimes of action, on the basis of their visibility, intentionality and relation to hegemonic powers. Whereas resistance is often analysed in terms of collective mobilizations, i.e. institutionalized and visible social movements, a number of analyses identify everyday and hidden practices as 'arts of resistance' (De Certeau 1990; Scott 1990). This notion of resistance has been developed in studies that build on Foucault and Gramsci, in order to understand the agency of the subaltern and dominated. These arts of resistance also imply a capacity to subvert hegemonic discourses and rely on 'hidden transcripts' (Scott 1990). They constitute 'infrapolitics',[4] a concept that refers mainly to the politics of the dominated (Bayart *et al.* 2008), which are not always intentionally 'political' (Bayat 2010). In that perspective, the lack of noticeable protests about a specific issue does not mean that no resistance exists.

In this chapter we assume that the above mentioned concepts are not only relevant to understanding the urban poor or visibly dominated citizens, but that the terms 'infra' or 'micropolitics' can be used to refer to hidden practices and non-visible actions in a more general context, e.g. to understand resistance in the tourist city. In this sense, resistance cannot be conflated with collective mobilisation, defined as an institutionalized and visible political movement directly challenging hegemonic discourses, e.g. in the urban context by claiming a right to the city and its amenities (Burawoy 1991) or fighting globalized dominant development models, including tourism-inspired ones (Stacy 1994). What then are the 'infrapolitics of tourism' and who are the subjects of resistance? Several studies have dealt with such forms of resistance in the metropolis (Burawoy 1991) but few have been conducted in tourism studies (Cheong and Miller 2000; Owens 2008). They are mainly concerned with forms of resistance by local communities, overwhelmingly in non-urban settings such as Goa (Zafer Dogan 1989; Routledge 2001; Saldanha 2010), through the use of the notion of 'identity resistance'. Resistance may challenge tourism development, or tourism strategies and the politics that define who is legitimate as a beneficiary from tourism, as in the case of the resistance of street vendors in Cusco (Steel 2012) (see also Lederman in this volume).

In this chapter we argue that rather than illustrating a case of explicit, formalized social resistance challenging hegemonic urban trends, Paris represents a particularly interesting case of 'infrapolitical' and 'micropolitical' resistance, which can also be observed in other tourist cities. As shown by Quinn in the case of Venice (2006), various microtactics involving negotiating time and space demonstrate the local residents' practical knowledge of tourist practices and their efforts to avoid crossing tourist hotspots. In Paris, the residents of the Montmartre district tend to avoid sites such as the Place du Tertre or the surroundings of the Montmartre Basilica.[5] A similar phenomenon is observed in the Notre Dame cathedral area: while tourists spend time sitting on the square, enjoying the setting and taking pictures, local residents strategically remain on the north side of the street alongside the *parvis* and the Jean-Paul II square (Mermet and Chapuis 2011; Chapuis *et al.* 2013).[6] Residents adapt their daily mobility practices to the rhythms of tourism flows: for instance, residents of Abbesses (Montmartre) or of the pedestrian streets of the Marais (such as rue des Francs-Bourgeois) avoid frequenting their neighbourhood on Saturday or Sunday. Moreover, as was implicitly said in 1992 in the second edition of the *Assises du tourisme parisien*, a public workshop reflecting on the role of tourism in the city of Paris, the 'legendary aggressiveness' of Parisians against tourists may also be interpreted as an exasperated reaction against the huge numbers of tourists or as microtactics of creating distance (Vial 1992).

Reactions to tourism may be more organized, such as those expressed against short-term apartment rentals, which can be interpreted as a form of micropolitics. As in other tourist metropolises, short-term vacation rentals have increased in Paris. The discourse promoted by defenders of Airbnb and similar services (see Introduction to this volume) insist on the opportunities that short-term rentals offer to local residents: the additional rental revenue is supposed to allow them to continue living in hyper-gentrified neighbourhoods. However, the proliferation of vacation rentals across the city has been the cause of numerous conflicts (around nocturnal noise, disturbance of the neighbourhood life, changes in local retail, etc.) that have led to both residents' complaints and new regulations. For instance, a number of commonhold or condominium associations (*copropriétés*) introduced new regulations that made it illegal for a building's tenants/owners to sublet their apartments for short-term vacation rentals and sued those who continued to do so. The City of Paris also introduced new measures aimed at controlling the proliferation of such rentals. In December 2014, the *Conseil de Paris* published a list of 257 addresses (containing over 8,000 apartments) that the city would have a 'right of first-refusal' (pre-emption right) to buy, in order to convert the housing units into subsidized (social) housing. According to O'Sullivan (2014: n.p.) 'the idea is to give [the city of] Paris the ability to act as a social mix monitor, stepping in to prevent social segregation in the public interest if they feel it is under threat.' In May 2015, the relevant municipal services controlled 1,868 apartments in 98 buildings mainly in the Marais district, in order to identify those that were not the main residence of their owners and had not received the authorization to be rented out on a short-term basis. While most of the controlled apartments were identified through a search of the Airbnb website, it is interesting to note that several others were brought to the attention of the authorities by local residents. According to the Deputy-Mayor in charge of housing, some residents complained about their building being transformed into an 'informal hotel' (*Le Figaro*, 22 May 2015).

A different example of mobilization is the reaction against the 'love locks' on the Pont des Arts and other Parisian bridges. This 'invented' tourism tradition, which started in 2008, consists of hanging locks with two lovers' names on the bridge railings, and throwing the keys into the river Seine. Apart from visual pollution, love locks are considered by many a degradation of the UNESCO-protected historical heritage of that part of Paris. In the case of the Pont des Arts, the weight of the locks has endangered some elements of the bridge itself (in June 2014, part of a railing collapsed). Perhaps ironically, the most visible mobilization against love locks was initiated by two American residents of Paris, who were previously visitors to the city and had settled there.[7] They created a website (www.nolovelocks.com) and an online petition that was signed by more than 10,000 people, and were invited to discuss the issue with the City Council staff under the mayor Anne Hidalgo elected in 2014. The mobilization led to the installation of new railings, to an awareness-raising campaign encouraging tourists to demonstrate their love in alternative ways less harmful to the city's heritage, and to the deployment of policemen preventing informal street vendors to sell locks to tourists.

Problems related to tourism are also managed on a more regular basis, through the activities of several residents' associations which aim at the improvement of quality of life in various Parisian districts that experience heavy tourism flows: *Les Amis du Champ de Mars* around the Eiffel Tower, *Vivre le Marais* in the Marais area, *ADDM 18 (Association de Défense de Montmartre et du 18ème)* in Montmartre and other associations in Belleville and la Butte aux Cailles, among others. Some associations date back to the 1970s (*ADDM 18*), the 1980s (*Vivre le Marais*) or the 1990s (*Les Amis du Champ de Mars*), and have a relatively large membership (around 1,800 for *Vivre le Marais*, 300 for ADDM[8] or *Les Amis du Champ de Mars*). These associations were not set up for the purpose of dealing with the impact of tourism as such, but with a variety of 'quality of life' issues, such as local heritage preservation, urban planning, green spaces and street cleaning. The impact of tourism has been an occasional issue of concern, but not the only one.

In the Southern part of the Marais ('SoMa'), a vibrant district considered the epicentre of gay life in Paris, the number of bars, night establishments and restaurants has increased considerably in recent years. The noise issue has become central to local debates, due to the increase in outdoor terraces, especially since the ban on indoor smoking. The main struggle of the *Vivre le Marais* association concerns the control of unauthorized terraces in public space. This topic has been one of the main reasons that recent new members joined the association. Each opening of a new club or bar has been followed by local opposition, in which residents put banners on their windows calling to 'stop the noise', and the association regularly calls for the police to enforce the rules of occupation of the public realm. As a result of their actions, some bars have been temporarily closed. It is, however, important to underline that tourism and tourists as such have not been at the core of these conflicts. Tourists are certainly part of the patrons of clubs and bars, but the initiatives taken by the association as well as non-organized residents have been directed against the managers and owners of the contested venues, not against tourists. More generally, tourism as such is not mentioned in the discourses of these associations, and the legitimacy of tourism development in the area is hardly, if ever, contested.

There is, however, a small number of conflictual issues explicitly related to tourism, such as the presence of tourist buses and informal street vendors and the congestion of key sites. Local mobilizations tried to ban the mass presence of tourist buses in the 1990s in the Marais and, more recently, around the Eiffel Tower and Montmartre. The main arguments are environmental (air pollution) or related to qualify of life. The first mobilization dates back to 1985: a petition which gathered 3,000 signatures against tourist buses in Montmartre, Rivoli and Madeleine, under the impetus of the association *Plateforme des comités parisiens d'habitants* (created in 1965 by various residents' associations) which denounced the nuisance posed by tourist buses. The Montmartre association has been the most active on that topic: tourist buses have been accused of adding to the deterioration of the buildings (due to the narrowness of the streets leading to the top of the Montmartre hill) and the environment (through air pollution and noise). In 1985, local authorities complied with the association's demand to ban tourist buses from the hill of Montmartre and forced them to park and drop off groups on the Barbès Rochechouart boulevard. In 1986 the protests broadened to address the transformation of restaurants and shops due to an increase in tourism. In the 1990s, local residents of Montmartre asked local authorities to expand the area covered by the tourist bus ban. Their activities involved ad hoc collective actions to block car traffic. More recently, residents' groups from the neighbourhoods in which the bus parking spaces are located have also called for more regulation of bus stands (*Collectif des Riverains des boulevards Clichy Rochechouart*).

The presence of informal street vendors has also become an issue from the 2000s onwards. In some areas, a considerable number of informal street vendors from Senegal or Pakistan sell tourist souvenirs or counterfeit goods. They are concentrated around the Trocadéro and the Champs de Mars or on the stairs leading to the Montmartre Basilica. Near the Louvre and Notre Dame, groups of female street vendors have developed various tactics to extort money from tourists.[9] This shows how the concentration of tourism can contribute to the emergence of 'nuisance' issues which affect not just residents, but also tourists themselves. The presence of various marginal activities and informal vendors, often from migrant origin, has become a topic of concern for local residents who have begun to alert public authorities, as did the association of residents *Les amis du Champ de Mars*.[10]

Tourism, in Paris, does not constitute a widely acknowledged and specifically identified 'public problem' for local residents' associations. But as discussed above, some of its impacts have been the focus of issue-specific mobilizations. It is telling, in that respect, that some associations make a point of distinguishing, in their public letters, their critique of specific tourism-related nuisances from the broader issue of the presence of tourists and tourism in the city, towards which a generally positive attitude prevails. Interviews carried out with members of Paris residents' associations[11] revealed that tourism is regarded as a 'normal' trend and phenomenon for Paris, an unavoidable fact that will keep on growing. Despite the overcrowding of some districts during the weekends, local associations do not demand the reconsideration of the regulations allowing the opening of shops on Sundays (which is only authorized in specific tourist zones such as the Champs-Elysées, Montmartre, the Rivoli street, etc.). It is noticeable that despite the aforementioned problems such as overcrowding, nightlife noise or short-term apartment rentals, not a single association has called for restrictions to seek to reduce the numbers of tourists themselves, even in the most touristic areas such as the Marais.

In their public discourse or during interviews, the members of residents' associations have developed two strategies in their argument. First, they do not distinguish between tourists and local users. They are aware that both locals and tourists patronize the trendy bars in Abbesses or Marais, and that the precise proportion of each group is hard to determine. In Montmartre, a member of the local association *ADDM 18* labelled the Parisians that go there on weekends as 'local tourists' (interview October 2014). Second, they focus on the responsibility of local stakeholders: the bar manager who extends his/her terrace, encroaching on public space and reducing the space available for walking; the nightclub owner who does not manage the noise generated by customers; the local politicians who appear unwilling to regulate these nuisances, etc. In some cases, it has even been in the name of tourism that some protests have been led. For instance, the argument developed by the association *Amis du Champ de Mars* in the upper-class districts surrounding the Eiffel Tower consists of saying that the general improvement in the quality of life in the area would also benefit tourism.

Tourism in Paris seems so unquestionable that even the '*f*** tourism*' graffiti written on the walls and *parvis* of the Montmartre Basilica in April 2014 were not interpreted by politicians as a protest against tourism, but as an anarchist attack against the sacred place of the Basilica.[12] Problems, tensions and conflicts related to tourism are visible in the quintessential 'tourist city' that is Paris. What is noticeable, however, is that the protests that have emerged in response to the above mentioned issues are hardly, if ever, directed at tourism primarily, let alone at tourists themselves. Their presence seems to be considered – and accepted – as an inherent part of urban life, integral to the kind of city which Paris is.

How can we explain the relative absence of organized, widespread protest or resistance against tourism in Paris compared to the situation observed in Barcelona or Berlin in recent years? In Berlin, protest has been partly linked to anti-gentrification movements (see Novy in this volume). In Paris, although gentrification has been spreading to the whole city and has resulted in large-scale urban transformation, there is no clearly visible, socially and politically articulated resistance to gentrification. In fact, protests in central and wealthy districts, such as the hyper-gentrified Marais, are rather concerned with fighting against the building of new social housing units. And in more peripheral and more recently gentrified neighbourhoods in the eastern part of Paris, such as Belleville, the Canal Saint Martin Area, or the Château-Rouge district, mobilizations against gentrification are either weak or non-existent (Clerval 2013). What therefore are the political demands of the residents' associations which criticize some of the side effects of touristification, if they are neither about tourism per se nor about broader processes of metropolitan transformation such as gentrification?

Increasing demands for the public and private regulation of tourism

As discussed above, there exists today various residents' associations in the districts in Paris. They cover different scales: for instance, *Vivre le Marais* covers the 3rd and 4th districts of Paris, but in these two districts other associations have also been created, some of them with a very localized focus, e.g. a few streets

(*Collectif Pierre au Lard*). The members of *Vivre le Marais* are mostly owner-occupiers and belong to the upper-middle class. When analysing the agenda and demands of these residents' associations, it is worth reflecting whether they are an expression of 'NIMBYism', i.e. homeowners acting defensively to preserve their own self-interests without considering those of others or of the city at large. These associations mainly campaign for quality of life in their neighbourhoods, dealing with topics such as street cleaning, the fight against noise and other nuisances, and in some cases, opposition against street vendors or against the building of new social housing units. Nevertheless, their campaigns are often underpinned by broader arguments that connect specific, personal opposition/protest with broader social issues, operating a 'generalization of the justification' (Boltanski and Thévenot 1991). Neighbourhood nuisances arising from the night-time economy are, for instance, discursively framed with reference to the problem of youth alcoholism and drug abuse. These associations legitimize their actions through various strategies: reference to the legal context (that local authorities are regularly accused of not enforcing), the use of moral arguments as well as general allusions to the 'public interest', e.g. by invoking heritage and environmental protection.

These strategies are accompanied by networking activities. In 2009, 30 associations created a federation, *Vivre Paris* (whose name reflects the leading role of the association *Vivre le Marais*), bringing together national NGOs (such as *Les droits du piéton* or *Association des Paralysés de France*) and 24 local associations, mainly formed by local residents (the term *riverains* is omnipresent in their names). Many of these associations share a preoccupation with nightlife regulations, as indicated in the names of some of them: *Droit au sommeil, halte aux nuisances* (Right to sleep, stop nuisances) in the 5th district; *Collectif pour une cour tranquille* (Group for a quiet yard) in the 10th district. The associations which constitute the *Vivre Paris* network represent 19 of Paris's 20 districts, but do not include residents' associations from the Parisian suburbs. Networking, however, extends beyond the city, as relations were established with other French associations dealing with similar topics (e.g. in Strasbourg, Toulouse, Nantes) and even in other European tourist cities (e.g. Lisbon, Berlin, Barcelona) to share knowledge and best practice, for instance about noise regulation. These networking activities are a key element of the legitimacy of Paris's residents' associations, in order to present the problems they encounter in their neighbourhoods as widely spread, generalized problems. Legitimization by generalization relies therefore on two concomitant approaches: spatial/geographical generalisation, and appeal to broader moral and intellectual arguments that go beyond the associations' immediate interests to encompass issues that appear of 'public interest'.

In terms of collective action, these associations use various complementary strategies. They first have to 'create a cause' by circulating petitions, writing public letters or blogs (for instance the blog *Vivre le Marais!*). They justify the legitimacy of their cause by conducting inquiries, taking pictures or describing the problem very precisely with reference to the spaces and stakeholders that are involved, as well as to the legal context. They construct a nuisance as a 'public problem' (Cefaï 1996). In terms of their spatial strategies, their members tend not to demonstrate in the streets or to occupy public space, but rather make signs of protests visible on the outer part of private homes and buildings, e.g. through posters and banners hanging from windows (Figure 2.2). Although these associations claim to be apolitical, their activities are characterised by intensive and continuous working relationships with local politicians, in the context of frequent interpersonal relations, another characteristic of micropolitics. They also publicly challenge political candidates before local elections to push the issues they care about, such as the problem of nightlife nuisances, to the centre of local political debates.

Figure 2.2 Protest banner against the proliferation of bars and night economy establishments in Le Marais: 'Quartier en danger: non à la mono-activité' ('Neighbourhood in danger, no to mono-activity'), 2015.

Source: Claire Colomb.

Nevertheless, they do not publicly support any political party and their members hold a diversity of political opinions.

Besides voicing their complaints through social media or the press, their most successful strategy consists of negotiating with local authorities to trigger public action or the regulation of contentious issues. The need to control short-term apartment rentals, or the issue of 'love locks', have generated a wide consensus among public actors and associations, as mentioned above. The calls for local regulation have been made in the framework of the existing relations between residents' associations and local authorities at both the municipal (city-wide) and district levels. For instance, the members of the association *DDMA 18* (Montmartre) have frequent contacts with district councillors about local issues, and its representatives are always present during the District Council sessions to defend the protection of local heritage and quality of life against small encroachments by tourist-oriented uses. *Vivre le Marais* has over the years established itself as an important local player: its representatives can easily obtain an appointment with municipal councillors and regularly meet with the police chief to discuss various problems in the district.

Residents' associations have even lobbied at the national level, through elected members of the French parliament, to promote further regulation of night-time activities or short-term apartment rentals. These associations are therefore not protesting or resisting from 'outside' the political system, but are regularly negotiating with public authorities. This confirms and reinforces their legitimacy. They do not fight for alternative models of urban development as such, and they do not question tourism development as a whole, taking it for granted. To them, the fight for a greater 'quality of life' is a question of balance between uses and users, and not about challenging, or creating alternatives to, the current status quo in terms of urban development and local decision-making.

This does not mean that there always is a convergence between these associations' agenda and local authorities. One of the main motives of the associations' discontent was the plan announced by the Paris City Council to develop and expand the city's nightlife so as to make it competitive with that of Berlin, Amsterdam or Barcelona. This conflict is rooted in an old debate about Paris and its supposed 'museification', which was recently reactivated in the context of the increasing competition among European capitals for urban attractiveness. Instead of the *capitale de la nuit* (nightlife capital), Paris was accused of being the *capital de l'ennui* (capital of boredom).[13] This accusation emerged from the trade union of bar and nightclub owners, who tried to legitimate their activities with two main arguments: the local economic benefits of nightlife in a period of economic crisis; and their critical contribution to the city's competitiveness as a place to live, visit and invest in the competition between cities. The municipality of Paris responded to their concern and launched a 'summit' of the main actors and stakeholders of the Paris nightlife (*Etats généraux de la nuit*), appointed a 'Night Mayor'[14] and developed other initiatives to support and nurture Paris's nightlife.

Several local residents associations, however, firmly opposed those initiatives, and created the already mentioned federation of associations *Vivre Paris* which gathered various local associations fighting against night activities and nuisances. These associations argued that the weakening of the local regulation of nightlife would worsen the situation. Following several meetings with local politicians, this federation managed to have an impact on the overall approach of the municipal government with regard to nightlife. The Barcelona example, and in particular the social mobilizations against the tourism-fuelled nightlife in the district of La Barceloneta, was used as a negative example to show that Barcelona had begun to pay the price for its tourist (over)-development and lax regulation of nightlife activities.

The control of vacation rentals, particularly Airbnb, was also developed through a process of collaboration between residents' associations and local authorities. For decades the municipality of Paris, faced with a chronic lack of tourist accommodation, had tried to encourage alternatives to hotels. In 1974, the Paris Tourist Office established a list of residents who were willing to host tourists, from which point bed and breakfast formulas were encouraged. These initiatives were not seen as antagonistic to residents' interests. However, the huge success, in recent years, of online rental platforms such as Airbnb, and the choice made by many landlords to turn flats into short-term holiday rentals, have had considerable impact on the housing market and have generated new problems and demands for regulations. The mushrooming of short-term rentals has been accused of accelerating real-estate speculation and housing shortages. Since 2014 the City Council of Paris (in particular its Councillor for Housing Ian Brossat), led by a left-wing government, has taken a tough stance towards the uncontrolled and rampant expansion of the number of vacation rentals. New legislation and regulations do not concern the temporary touristic use of a property, which remains legal, but its exclusive touristic use.[15] Nevertheless, public authorities do not have accurate data about apartments rented out through the Airbnb platform, and their control by legal means is still a challenging task. Given the fact that the municipal government reacted rather quickly on this issue, residents' associations played a watchdog role rather than one of outright protest on this issue. Nevertheless, the arguments put forward by these associations and by the socialist City Council are not the same: while the Council acts in the name of safeguarding flats for Parisians and the control of housing speculation, residents' associations complain about the noise and nuisances generated by tourist flats for their surroundings. The case of the Old City of Venice is regularly mentioned in the public debates, appearing as the counter-model to avoid at all costs.

To conclude, on the whole, one may argue that residents' associations in Paris do not accuse tourism as such of being a danger for the city. Rather, they blame specific categories of local stakeholders for exploiting tourist activities outside of established rules. Protest and resistance against tourism in Paris is not led by alternative or left-wing movements linking tourism and gentrification or tourism and capitalism. The issue of tourism's impacts appears to be part of more mainstream fights for 'quality of life', led by middle- or upper-middle-class residents who are often part of the gentrification process that has transformed the social base of most of Paris's districts. Nevertheless, a different kind of activity could be characterized per se as forms of resistance to (mainstream forms of) tourism: those that seek to introduce 'new tourism' or new social models that challenge the way tourism develops in the city.

Alternatives to mainstream tourism as an implicit form of resistance?

As regards the development of alternative forms of tourism in Paris, two initiatives deserve particular attention. The first is concerned with the relationship between tourists and residents and is part of a wider global trend – the development of the 'Greeters'.[16] Local associations such as *Parisiens d'un jour* (Parisians for a day), founded in 2007, have promoted tours conducted by local residents, mostly in the central districts of Paris. What is specific to Paris is the fact that this development has been widely encouraged by public authorities, in contrast to other cities where this process remains quite independent, or even controversial as in Buenos Aires.[17] According to the former vice-mayor of Paris in charge of tourism, the Paris Greeters can contribute to fight the reputation of Parisians being rude with tourists, through the voluntary exchanges which locals develop with visitors to introduce them to their neighbourhoods (Todd 2013). The former district mayor of the Marais, Dominique Bertinotti, actively tried to encourage more contacts between tourists and locals in order to pacify their relationship in one of the most heavily visited parts of the city. In fact, far from strictly belonging to two separate worlds, tourists and residents in the Marais share the same infrastructure and venues for leisure and consumption (Chapuis *et al.* 2013). However, it is interesting to note that the above-mentioned residents' associations campaigning for quality of life issues did not participate in these 'Greeters' initiatives. A clear gap appears between those associations' concerns and agenda and the district mayor's aim of fostering better relationships between the permanent and the transient (tourist) population of the Marais.

The second trend which has contributed to a shift in the relationship between tourism and urban development is the growth of tourism in more deprived areas of Paris, i.e. in the less wealthy, more multi-ethnic districts or even in the suburbs outside the *périphérique* (ring road). This trend started with the development of tourism related to the ethnic diversity of the metropolis (Rath 2007). The city of Saint-Denis, on the northern fringe of Paris, is a good example of the way in which tourism development in a 'peripheral' area can potentially challenge more conventional forms of tourism in central areas. In Saint-Denis, the systematic promotion of tourism dates back to the end of the 1990s, stimulated by the Soccer World Cup (whose main stadium was built in Saint-Denis). Saint-Denis has suffered from a bad image in the mass media due to social and economic problems (deindustrialization, unemployment, concentrations of deprivation and urban violence), which led the municipal government to implement new development strategies (Bertho 2008). At the beginning of the 2000s, the inter-communal organization Plaine Commune, an institutional structure that gathers various municipalities around Saint-Denis, developed various actions to promote its industrial, social and cosmopolitan heritage and promote tourism on the fringes of Paris (Jacquot *et al.* 2013).

For instance, an 'interpretation centre' was created in the garden city of Stains, a social housing settlement built between 1921 and 1933. This form of tourism may be regarded as 'tourism off the beaten track' (Maitland and Newman 2009) in a geographical sense, due to its location in the suburbs of Paris.

Additionally, this form of tourism development relies on different principles than more mainstream forms of urban tourism. First, tourism is not necessarily seen as a form of mobility that implies an overnight stay (according to the WTO definition), but as a way to discover a place through a short visit, including by Parisians or residents of the city-region who are seen as potential tourists. Second, tourism is used as a way to encourage a new gaze upon parts of the city-region which were formerly regarded as derelict or in decline (e.g. former industrial areas). Third, local residents are supposed to play a key role in this shift, not only as beneficiaries of tourism-led economic development, but as co-participants in the symbolic upgrade of their neighbourhoods. The tourism development plan (Plaine Commune 2012) advocates a 'participatory' model of tourism that relies on locals' contributions. Moreover, it is based on a conception of 'local heritage' which differs from the traditional approach to heritage in central Paris – one that is based on intangible social or industrial urban heritage rather than on monuments and museums.

Such initiatives have to be read within the context of a long-standing contrast between Paris and the suburbs in terms of tourism development, although Parisian suburbs have experienced a boom in hotel construction since the end of the 1990s due to the lack of available development sites in central Paris (Decelle and Jacquot 2013). While these hotels have started to bring considerable amounts of tourists to the suburbs, they have sometimes been accused of transforming the Paris periphery into a 'tourism dormitory'. Local tourism initiatives in the suburbs, such as that mentioned above, are by contrast based on the promotion of endogenous resources and heritage, and designed as alternatives to dominant tourism approaches. Recently, the political reorganization of the Paris metropolis and the creation of the Grand Paris city-regional authority (which took effect on 1 January 2016)[18] has encouraged a number of local political leaders, such as the president of the Plaine Commune inter-municipal association, P. Braouezec, to call for an alternative conception of metropolitan development in the Paris city-region – one based on polycentrism to counteract the hegemony of central Paris over its fringes. This would include alternative tourism and heritage policies in support of new forms of territorial development in the suburbs.

By contrast, the development of new forms of tourism in districts with high levels of migrants and ethnic minorities is not only happening in the suburbs but also in central Paris, in northern and eastern districts such as Belleville, Strasbourg-Saint-Denis, La Goutte d'Or, or 'le Petit Mali' (Little Mali). Such forms of 'ethnic' tourism have not been developed by public institutions, as in Plaine Commune, but promoted by local associations of various kinds, such as Belleville Insolite, an association created to support tourism in Belleville by promoting its multiculturalism (Corbillé 2009), Anardana, an association which organizes urban walks to discover Indian migratory cultures or Bastina, an association rooted in the responsible and sustainable tourism movement. These associations all share a willingness to put migrants or ethnic minorities at the centre of tourism practices as guides, interlocutors and main characters (Chapuis and Jacquot 2014), not as a mere object of spectacle (Shaw *et al.* 2004). Migrant-led tours can enable the development, through tourist-oriented discourses, of narratives which challenge dominant forms of urban development that threaten the existence of migrant communities. For instance, a North African tour in the district of Goutte d'Or openly evoked the eviction of migrants from that area in the context of large-scale urban renewal operations.[19] Alternative tourism initiatives are therefore not only alternative to mainstream tourism. They are also political in the sense that they contest, explicitly or implicitly, the dynamics of metropolitan transformation, in this instance in a number of multi-ethnic districts of central Paris as well as in Parisian suburbs. In that sense, it is not *resistance to tourism*, but a *resistance that uses tourism* and its codes, which contributes to challenge dominant urban dynamics and their consequences on urban spaces and residents.

Conclusion

In this chapter we have argued that the patterns of mobilization surrounding tourism-related issues in Paris are different from those recently witnessed in Berlin or Barcelona, as the city is not the theatre of forms of resistance to tourism per se. No visible manifestation of protest against touristification as such can be observed. Can we conclude that there is 'no conflict' in Paris, the archetypal (and one of the most visited) tourist city? As demonstrated in this chapter, various forms of mobilization from local residents are in fact *related* to the impacts of tourism, but are not led *against* tourism or tourists. Since the waves of urban renewal which began in the 1960s, residents' associations (with mostly middle-class members) have appeared in various districts and at various scales, initially fighting against urban renewal operations, and from the 1970s onwards, for the preservation of 'quality of life' in Paris. At the same time, Paris has been subject to processes of gentrification, first in the historic core (e.g. the Marais from the 1960s), later on from the 1980s in more peripheral districts (such as Belleville in the 19th district). Residential gentrification made tourism-related tensions more visible and complex: the first wave of short-term vacation rentals appeared in trendy, desirable, already gentrified areas and contributed to super-gentrification processes, mainly in the Marais (illustrating the link between residential gentrification and touristification, also discussed by Opillard in this volume). This in turn fuelled new tourism-related tensions, exemplified by the denunciation of short-term vacation rentals by local residents.

The mobilizations which deal with tourism-related issues analysed in this chapter have various goals: to banish tourist coaches, to tackle the nuisances of nightlife in which tourists play a role, to deter buskers from playing music at night, to control the illegal renting out of apartments to tourists, etc. Nevertheless, these mobilizations are not directed against tourists as such. Our analysis of the agenda of residents' associations in Paris has shown that their claims are focused towards local stakeholders: bar and nightclub owners and managers, migrants and street vendors, booksellers on the banks of the Seine that sell love locks to tourists and, of course, the municipal and district governments. Protests and mobilizations are part of broader local social conflicts about the kind of city which Parisians want, and address wider issues such as the regulation of street life and nightlife, the priorities for urban residential development (for local residents or for commercial activities such as vacation rentals), the types of uses that should be prioritized in urban space and their temporal regulation. One may argue, however, that the agenda of these largely middle- and upper-middle-class residents' associations remains relatively defensive and focused on 'quality of life' issues, without challenging and questioning the social changes that have been occurring in these districts at the same time (i.e. rapid gentrification). Their mobilization has not reached the point at which the legitimacy of tourism as an instrument of urban development in Paris would be questioned. Tourism-generated issues are pragmatically accepted in the name of economic development.

Finally, we have briefly outlined the emergence of a counter-model of tourism development based on new relationships between tourists and locals, through various initiatives for 'alternative urban tourism' in central Paris and on its outskirts. First, the development of so-called 'Greeters' initiatives seeks to reconfigure relations between hosts and guests, although they are disconnected from the mobilizations for 'quality of life' analysed above. Second, the development of alternative, resident-focused forms of tourism in areas that have not traditionally been regarded as touristic – such as deprived suburbs or multi-ethnic central districts now presented as valuable 'ethnoscapes' (Appadurai 1996) – can be interpreted as a form of 'soft' resistance to dominant patterns of metropolitan tourism in the Paris city-region (characterized by a huge gap between centre and suburbs). In some cases, they can also challenge the narrative of dominant forms of urban development, by giving symbolic value to these areas through the construction of a tourism discourse and the encouragement of a tourist gaze.

Notes

1 According to van der Duim (2007) a 'tourismscape' is a combination of discourses, materiality and practices in a functional whole.
2 Figure 2.1 maps the metadata associated with the pictures posted on Flickr between 2009 and 2013 (amounting, for Paris, to 1.8 million pictures), i.e. the geolocalization of the pictures taken and posted by users. This map is part of a broader interdisciplinary research project on big data and tourism (see Chareyron *et al.* 2014), which relies on the automatic collection and subsequent analysis and interpretation of big data extracted from tourist social networks (Tripadvisor, Flickr, etc.) to map tourism flows in the city.
3 A marginal *Front anti-touristes* community exists on Facebook. However, it has very few members and only expresses a diffuse anti-tourism feeling without any clear position/arguments about the tourism phenomenon in Paris.
4 Infrapolitics 'evokes mobilizations that do not respond to the criteria for widely recognized forms of political action'. They can be understood as 'what lies beneath the threshold of politics, or of the political itself'. They are 'mobilizations whose means do not quite make the mark as political, compared to conventional ones (. . .) or practices which are not quite political either in terms of form or content' (Marché 2012: 3–4).

5 Interviews with local residents.
6 This publication is the result of a collective study about tourist and resident practices in the Marais carried out by students on the Masters in Tourism from the University Paris 1 Panthéon Sorbonne, coordinated by professors A. Chapuis, A.-C. Mermet, M. Gravari-Barbas.
7 In the case of love locks, a local association, *l'Association pour la Défense du Site de Notre-Dame*, was in close contact with the two American citizens who started the campaign, but the media focused on the fact that two Americans were trying to save Parisian heritage. Media reporting was a crucial factor for the quick intervention of the City Council.
8 As declared by the interviewed members of these associations.
9 Pretending to discover a gold ring on the floor, collecting micro-gifts from tourists for hearing and speech-impaired people, etc.
10 We could also analyse the fact that street vending migrants remain in touristic areas as a form of resistance, despite hostility from inhabitants and local authorities (Notarangelo and Jacquot 2014).
11 *ADDM 18* and *Vivre le Marais* (2014).
12 The Basilica was built after the Commune de Paris riots by conservative, pro-establishment Catholics. It still symbolizes for many the repression of the revolutionary *Communards* by conservative powers (Harvey 2003).
13 According to the title of an article from *Le Monde* on 30 November 2009 named 'Paris, quand la nuit meurt en silence' ('Paris, when the night is dying silently'), following a petition launched by nightclub owners and nightlife stakeholders.
14 The first (voluntary) 'Night Mayor' of Paris took office in November 2013. He was 'elected' for an indefinite period by 2,200 Parisian revellers in a ballot organized in Parisian night establishments. He defends the interests of night owls and Parisian revellers in front of the public authorities.
15 According to national legislation (with new modifications added in 2013 and 2014 to regulate short-term rentals) and local regulations from the municipality of Paris, the shift to a permanent tourist use is considered a change of use from residential to commercial, which is only allowed subject to a binding condition: in the central and western districts of Paris, any landlord who allocates an apartment to permanent tourist use has to put on the market a normal residential surface which is twice bigger, and in the eastern districts, one which is of the same size. At the same time, inspections of existing apartments have been stepped up, and a fine of up to 25,000 euros can be charged for each illegal tourist apartment.
16 A 'greeter' is a person who volunteers to share tips about his/her city through a tour 'off the beaten tracks' (Holmes and Smith 2012). The concept was developed in 1992 in New York City by Lynn Brooks, who has devised a new form of tourism based around the encounter between visitors and local residents. Several greeters' associations have been established since in several cities around the world – federated since 2005 in the Global Greeter Network.
17 According to the president of *Cicerones*, the Buenos Aires Greeters, interviewed in 2013.
18 The Greater Paris Metropolis is a political project of city-regional governance in the form of an inter-communal grouping of at least 126 municipalities, which has been granted competence over strategic planning, housing and economic development. It is intended to tackle the territorial inequalities between the various municipalities in the greater Paris region.
19 Participant observation, April 2014.

References

[Unless otherwise stated, all URLs were last accessed 5 August 2015.]
Appadurai, A. (1996) *Modernity at Large: Cultural Dimensions of Globalization.* Minneapolis, MN: University of Minnesota Press.

APUR (Atelier Parisien d'Urbanisme) (2004) *PSMV du Marais. Difficultés de gestion et d'application. Améliorations et modernisations nécessaires.* Paris: APUR.

Bauder, M., Freytag, T. and Gérardot M. (2014) 'Analyser les mobilités touristiques à Paris en combinant enquête visiteurs et GPS', *EspacesTemps.net*, 17 February. Online. Available at http://www.espacestemps.net/articles/mobilites-touristiques-a-paris/.

Bayart, J.-F., Mbembe, A. and Toulabor, C. (2008) *Le politique par le bas en Afrique noire.* Paris: Khartala.

Bayat, A. (2010) *Life as Politics: How Ordinary People Change the Middle East.* Stanford, CA: Stanford University Press.

Bertho, A. (2008) 'La plaine Saint-Denis dans l'entre-deux', *Projet*, 2: 23–30.

Boltanski, L. and Thévenot, L. (1991) *De la justification: les économies de la grandeur.* Paris: Gallimard.

Burawoy, M. (1991) *Ethnography Unbound: Power and Resistance in the Modern Metropolis.* Berkeley, CA: University of California Press.

Cefaï, D. (1996) 'La construction des problèmes publics. Définitions de situations dans des arènes publiques', *Réseaux*, 14(75): 43–66.

Chapuis, A. and Jacquot, S. (2014) 'Mettre en tourisme les présences migratoires à Paris. Le touriste, le migrant et la fable cosmopolite', *Hommes et Migrations*, 1308: 75–86.

Chapuis, A., Gravari-Barbas, M., Jacquot, S. and Mermet A.-C. (2013) 'Dynamiques urbaines et mobilités de loisirs à Paris: pratiques, cohabitations et stratégies de production de l'espace urbain dans le quartier du Marais', in E. Berthold (ed.) *Les quartiers historiques, pressions, enjeux, actions.* Québec: Presses Université de Laval.

Chareyron, G., Cousin, S., Da Rugna, J., Gabay, D. and Jacquot, S. (2014) 'La métropole du data mining: ce que l'exploration du web nous apprend des pratiques et imaginaires métropolitains', *Les Cahiers de la Métropole*, special issue: 56–8. Online. Available at http://labs.esilv.fr/publications/public/2014/CCDGJ14/LaMetropoleduDataMining.pdf.

Cheong, S.-M. and Miller, M. (2000) 'Power and tourism: a Foucauldian observation', *Annals of Tourism Research*, 27(2): 371–90.

Chevalier, S., Lallement, E. and Corbillé, S. (2013) *Paris résidence secondaire, Enquête chez ces habitants d'un nouveau genre.* Paris: Belin.

Clerval, A. (2013) *Paris sans le peuple, la gentrification de la capitale.* Paris: La Découverte.

Cohen, E. (2000) 'La hiérarchie monumentale de Paris au XXe siècle. Les étoiles dans les guides de tourisme consacrés à Paris', in G. Chabaud, E. Cohen, N. Coquery and J. Penez (eds) *Les guides imprimés du XVIe au XXe siècle.* Paris: Belin.

Corbillé, S. (2009) 'Tourisme, diversité enchantée et rapports symboliques dans les quartiers gentrifiés du nord-est de Paris', *Genèses*, 76: 30–51.

CRT (Comité Régional du Tourisme Paris Ile-de-France) and IPSOS Marketing (2010) 'Les repeaters britanniques, allemands et espagnols', *Les Etudes* (Comité régional du tourisme Paris-Ile-de-France), April: 1–8.

De Certeau, M. (1990) *L'invention du quotidien, les arts de faire.* Paris: Gallimard.

Decelle, X. and Jacquot, S. (2013) 'Coalitions publiques-privées et stratégies d'investissement hôtelier dans la constitution de la métropole touristique francilienne, entre centralités et périphéries', in M. Gravari-Barbas and E. Fagnoni (eds) *Métropolisation et tourisme, comment le tourisme redessine.* Paris: Belin.

Dörfler, T. (2010) *Gentrification in Prenzlauer Berg? Milieuwandel eines Berliner Sozialraums seit 1989.* Berlin: Transcript Verlag.

Duhamel, P. and Knafou, R. (2007) 'Le tourisme dans la centralité parisienne', in T. Saint-Julien and R. Le Goix (eds) *La métropole parisienne. Centralités, inégalités, proximités.* Paris: Belin.

Freytag, T. (2008) 'Making a difference: tourist practices of repeat visitors in the city of Paris', *Social Geography Discussions*, 4: 1–25.

Füller, H. and Michel, B. (2014) '"Stop being a tourist!" New dynamics of urban tourism in Berlin-Kreuzberg', *International Journal of Urban and Regional Research*, 38(4): 1304–18.

Gladstone, D. and Préau, J. (2008) 'Gentrification in tourist cities: evidence from New Orleans before and after hurricane Katrina', *Housing Policy Debate*, 19(1): 137–75.

Gravari-Barbas, M. (2014) 'Patrimoine, culture, tourisme et transformation urbaine: le *Lower East Side Tenements Museum*, NY', in G. Djament-Tran and P. San Marco (eds) *La métropolisation de la culture et du patrimoine*. Paris: Le Manuscrit.

Gravari-Barbas, M. and Fagnoni, E. (2013) *Tourisme et métropolisation. Comment le tourisme redessine Paris*. Paris: Belin.

Hancock, C. (2003) *Paris et Londres au XIXe siècle. Représentations dans les guides et les récits de voyages*. Paris: Éditions du CNRS.

Harvey, D. (2003) *Paris, Capital of Modernity*. New York and London: Routledge.

Holmes, K. and Smith, K. (2012) *Managing Volunteers in Tourism, Attractions, Destinations, Events*. London: Routledge.

Ingallina, P. and Park, J. (2009) 'Tourists, urban projects and spaces of consumption in Paris and Ile-de-France', in R. Maitland and P. Newman (eds) *World Tourism Cities: Developing Tourism off the Beaten Track*. London and New York: Routledge.

Jacquot, S., Gravari-Barbas, M. and Fagnoni, E. (2013) 'Patrimonialisation et tourisme dans la région métropolitaine parisienne. Le patrimoine, clé de la métropolité touristique?', in M. Gravari-Barbas and E. Fagnoni (eds) *Métropolisation et tourisme, comment le tourisme redessine Paris*. Paris: Belin.

Le Figaro (2015) 'AirBnB: 2000 logements contrôlés à Paris', *Le Figaro*, 22 May.

Maitland, R. (2008) 'Conviviality and everyday life, the appeal of new areas of London for visitors', *International Journal of Tourist Research*, 10(1): 15–25.

Maitland, R. (2010) 'Everyday life as a creative experience in cities', *International Journal of Culture, Tourism and Hospitality Research*, 4(3): 176–85.

Maitland, R. (2013) 'Backstage behaviour in the global city: tourists and the search for the "real London"', *Procedia – Social and Behavioral Sciences*, 105: 12–19.

Maitland, R. and Newman, P. (2009) *World Tourism Cities: Developing Tourism off the Beaten Track*. London and New York: Routledge.

Marché, G. (2012) 'Why infrapolitics matters', *Revue Française d'Etudes Américaines*, 131: 3–18.

Mermet, A.-C. and Chapuis, A. (eds) (2011) *Pour un tourisme durable, participatif, alternatif, dans le 4e arrondissement*. Paris: Université Paris 1 Panthéon Sorbonne, IREST.

Notarangelo, C. and Jacquot, S. (2014) 'Discorsi sull'illegalità nel cuore turistico di Genova. Gli ambulanti senegalesi al Porto antico', in L. Faldini (ed.) *Dal Mediterraneo al Baltico. Dinamiche sociali in area urbana. Atti del Convegno, Genova, 23 ottobre 2014*. Novi Ligure: Edizioni Epoké.

Novy, J. (2013) '"Berlin does not love you" – Notes on Berlin's "tourism controversy" and its discontents', in M. Bernt, B. Grell and A. Holm (eds) *The Berlin Reader: A Companion on Urban Change and Activism*. Berlin: Transcript Verlag.

O'Sullivan, F. (2014) 'Paris wants to keep central neighborhoods from becoming "ghettos for the rich"', *The Atlantic – Citylab*, 19 December. Online. Available at http://www.citylab.com/housing/2014/12/paris-wants-to-keep-central-neighborhoods-from-becoming-ghettos-for-the-rich/383936/.

OTCP (Office du Tourisme et des Congrès de Paris) (2014) *Tourisme à Paris. Chiffres-clefs 2013*. Paris: OTCP.

Owens, L. (2008) 'From tourists to anti-tourists to tourist attractions: the transformation of Amsterdam squatters' movement', *Social Movement Studies*, 7(1): 43–59.

Pappalepore, I., Maitland, R. and Smith, A. (2011) 'Exploring urban creativity: visitor experiences of Spitalfields, London', *Tourism, Culture and Communication*, 10(3): 217–30.

Plaine Commune (2012) *Schéma touristique communautaire, 2012–2016*. Saint-Denis: Plaine Commune.

Quinn, B. (2006) 'Performing Venice. Venetian residents in focus', *Annals of Tourism Research*, 34(2): 458–76.

Rath, J. (ed.) (2007) *Tourism, Ethnic Diversity and the City*. London and New York: Routledge.

Routledge, P. (2001) 'Selling the rain, resisting the sale: resistant identities and the conflict over tourism in Goa', *Social and Cultural Geography*, 2(2): 221–40.

Saldanha, A. (2002) 'Identity, spatiality and post-colonial resistance: geographies of the tourism critique in Goa', *Current Issues in Tourism*, 5(2): 94–111.

Scott, J. C. (1990) *Domination and the Arts of Resistance. Hidden Transcripts*. New Haven, CT: Yale University Press.

Shaw, S., Bagwell, S. and Karmowska, J. (2004) 'Ethnoscapes as spectacle: reimaging multicultural districts as new destinations for leisure and tourism consumption', *Urban Studies*, 41(10): 1983–2000.

Stacy, W. (1994) 'Disneyfication of the metropolis: popular resistance in Seattle', *Journal of Urban Affairs*, 16(2): 89–107.

Steel, G. (2012) 'Whose paradise? Itinerant street vendor's individual and collective practices of political agency in the tourist street of Cusco, Perou', *International Journal of Urban and Regional Research*, 36(5): 1007–2021.

Todd, T. (2013) 'Les "Greeters" français veulent offrir aux touristes un visage accueillant', *France 24*, 10 September. Online. Available at http://www.france24.com/fr/20130910-volontaires-greeters-tourisme-accueil-touristes-france-paris.

van der Duim, R. (2007) 'Tourismscapes: an actor-network perspective', *Annals of Tourism Research*, 34(4): 961–76.

Vial, C. (1992) 'Les deuxièmes Assises du Tourisme Parisien: La "plus belle ville du monde" menacée par le succès', *Le Monde*, 3 April.

Zafer Dogan, H. (1989) 'Forms of adjustment: sociocultural impacts of tourism', *Annals of Tourism Research*, 16(2): 216–36.

3 The selling (out) of Berlin and the de- and re-politicization of urban tourism in Europe's 'Capital of Cool'

Johannes Novy

The past decades have witnessed a tremendous outpouring of scholarly books and articles dealing with urban tourism. Most of these contributions agree that tourism in cities has grown substantially and that this growth is paralleled by equally substantial changes in the way tourism is being perceived – and dealt with – in cities' political arenas. Whereas tourism in most cities was, until well into the 1970s, only of little interest to policy-makers and other local elites, tourism since then has evolved into a key policy concern in cities throughout the advanced capitalist world. Today, as Fainstein *et al.* (2003: 8) note, 'virtually every city sees a tourism possibility and has taken steps to encourage it.' Berlin has been no exception. Many scholars have argued that tourism ever since the fall of the Berlin Wall in 1989 has played an important role in the city's economic and urban development policies (Colomb 2011; Krajewski 2006; Novy and Huning 2009). Berlin's popularity as a destination, if anything, contributed to the impetus for tourism promotion. While the city suffered for the most part of the 1990s and early 2000s from a declining or stagnating urban economy, tourism belongs to the few economic sectors that have seen vertiginous and almost uninterrupted growth since 1989. Visitor numbers in paid accommodations alone have almost quadrupled since the early 1990s to a record-breaking 11.8 million annual visitors and more than 28 million overnight stays in 2014, making Berlin Europe's third most popular urban tourism destination after Paris and London. If the current growth rate is maintained, the latest official target of 30 million overnight stays set for 2020 will be reached several years ahead of schedule and city officials already dream of surpassing Paris which recorded 36.6 million overnight stays in 2014 (Matthies 2014). Accordingly, tourism's economic impact has also increased considerably – as of 2014 it was estimated to contribute an astonishing 10.6 per cent to the city's gross domestic product (Nicola 2014).[1]

Given such figures, it is not surprising that tourism – at least rhetorically – is held in high esteem in Berlin's political arena. Policy-makers regularly praise the sector as a main driver of the city's economy and pledge their commitment to boost its development further. There is no paucity of rhetoric that lends support to the widely held view that tourism is afforded 'high priority (. . .) by city leaders' (Fainstein *et al.* 2003: 2). Rhetoric is one thing, while policy enactment is another, however, and while developments in Berlin in many ways appear to be in tune with dominant interpretations about tourism's rise to prominence as a policy concern, there are also aspects that challenge such interpretations. Tourism promotion in the context of wider place marketing activities has become a defining feature of Berlin's increasingly entrepreneurial approach to urban and economic development, but there are at the same time clear limitations with respect to local authorities' engagement with tourism. These limitations have become increasingly more apparent as tourism, after years of being effectively depoliticized and treated in technocratic fashion, became increasingly controversially discussed and contested. The city's approach to tourism is characterized by a host of contradictions, lacunae and inconsistencies that have led both those critical of tourism as well as tourism advocates to call for change. Whereas the latter are mainly concerned about the adverse effects resulting from tourism's growth for inner-city neighbourhoods and their inhabitants, the former act out of a concern about the future prospects of Berlin as a destination. They know that tourism carries within itself the 'seeds of its own destruction', that is that tourism, if unchecked and not properly planned for, can harm and even potentially destroy the very attributes and resources a destination's success relies upon.

This chapter aims to elaborate on the situation in Berlin in greater depth and will discuss its implications for our scholarly understanding of urban tourism as a policy field as well as the (future) development of the destination Berlin. It is based on more than ten years of research and fieldwork, involving interviews, participant observation and archival research.[2] The chapter will start with a short discussion of key theoretical and empirical contributions concerning the relevance of urban tourism as a policy concern in present-day cities. Embedded in a discussion of tourism's trajectory since the city's reunification and the key tenets of urban development and governance that shaped it, the next sections focus on the development of tourism policy and politics and what I term the *de-* and *re-politicization* of urban tourism in post-1989 Berlin. They will first demonstrate that Berlin's tourism policy in practice is replete with lacunae and contradictions, and that beyond promotional activities, it remains in an underdeveloped and fragmented state. Subsequently, by focusing particularly on the recent controversies surrounding tourism's growth in Kreuzberg and other centrally located neighbourhoods, the (re-)politicization of tourism as well as the reactions it sparked will be discussed. Characterizing the reality of tourism as a policy field and area of public sector intervention as inherently complex, contradictory and inchoate, the chapter's final section will reflect upon the causes and consequences of local authorities' rather limited engagement with tourism to date and notable absence of tourism planning and management.

Urban tourism, 'new urban politics' and public policy

The heightened importance of urban tourism as well as the forces underlying its rise to prominence are well documented (see the introduction to this volume) and do not need to be rehearsed at great length. There is now a large body of literature that attests that urban tourism has evolved into an extremely important economic and social phenomenon as well as a critical force of urban change (see, *inter alia*, Law 2002; Hoffman *et al.* 2003; Selby 2004; Spirou 2011). Similarly, it is well established that the heightened relevance of urban tourism is illustrative of broader transformations with regard to the role and function of cities as well as equally fundamental changes in production, consumption and mobility patterns in North America, Western Europe and many other parts of the world. Simply put, two closely related real-world phenomena have been at play from the late 1970s onwards: an escalating growth of tourism in cities as well as a growing economic but also symbolic importance of tourism as a result of broader restructuring processes in which service-, knowledge- and consumption-based industries came to take on a critical role for cities' economic well-being and 'competitive edge'.

Referred to variously as post-industrial, postmodern or post-Fordist, these restructuring processes have been paralleled and accompanied by important governmental changes at a range of geographical scales, including, on the local level, by what has come to be known as a shift from managerial to entrepreneurial or, more recently, neoliberal local governance (Harvey 1989; Hall and Hubbard 1998; Brenner and Theodore 2002). This shift has been described as a move away from the traditional managerial functions of welfare and service provision towards a 'new urban politics' (Hall and Hubbard 1998) emphasizing growth and competitiveness. The task of urban governments thus increasingly became the creation of attractive conditions to lure new investments, residents and jobs in a context of intensifying inter-urban competition. Both policy-makers and scholars in this context quickly identified urban tourism as an important issue for future policy: on the one hand because of its potential as an economic sector in its own right; on the other because of its 'symbolic weight', as tourism increasingly came to be seen as a major mechanism to boost a city's image and bring new life to areas affected by deindustrialization and decline (Fainstein *et al.* 2003: 2; see also Selby 2004: 16). Framed within a broad array of what the literature refers to as 'place marketing' strategies (Philo and Kearns 1993: 3) and indicative of the so-called 'festivalization' of urban politics (Häußermann and Siebel 1993), increasing investments in tourist-oriented attractions, festivals and events as well as tourism marketing are perhaps the most palpable manifestations of the increasingly proactive stance towards tourism that from the 1970s came to characterize urban policy. This has led many authors to argue that urban tourism, as part of a more general shift in urban policy towards leisure and consumption, had 'rightly or wrongly' become 'a cornerstone of modern urban management' (van der Borg 1991: 2).

What is surprising, however, is that comprehensive analyses concerning tourism politics and policy-making in cities remain few and far between. Scholars have produced well-informed studies on specific aspects – e.g. the effectiveness or efficiency of tourism policy in regeneration attempts, the role of public–private partnerships or 'regimes' in tourism development, etc. – but comprehensive studies of the politics of tourism, including the local state's involvement in tourism as well as the institutional arrangements, decision-making processes, interests and conflicts that shape policy-making, continue to be rare. With regard to cities, Hall's (2006: 260) famous dictum about the state of tourism politics research thus still holds true: considering the profound effects associated with tourism, it is indeed remarkable 'how little attention is given to the way in which tourism is governed and directed.'

The few studies that have looked at these issues suggest that the extent of the changes brought about by urban entrepreneurialism should not be overstated. They argue that city governments have, to varying degrees, pursued tourism promotion strategies for a long time (e.g. the nineteenth century) and that the growing recognition of tourism as a key issue in today's 'selling' of cities has not automatically resulted in a greater recognition and institutionalization of tourism as a policy field. Discussing the state of tourism policy in English cities, Stevenson *et al.* (2008: 744), for instance, found that tourism policy is often accorded a low status in cities' political arenas, which 'arises from its discretionary nature, a lack of clarity about what it is and how it fits with other more established areas, and a lack of interest from the local electorate and local politicians'. Van der Borg *et al.* (1996: 316), looking at heritage destinations, came to similar conclusions and found that the 'principle of laissez faire (. . .) dominated the attitudes of policy-makers and entrepreneurs towards tourism development' and that 'explicit tourism management policy that goes beyond promotion alone' was few and far between. Such perspectives do not question the widely held view about tourism's growing relevance in urban and economic policy per se, but they question the conventional wisdom about tourism's supposed importance in contemporary urban policy. They illustrate that this importance does not necessarily, as occasionally assumed, translate into 'a rich(er) institutional structure to regulate local tourism' (Fainstein *et al.* 2003: 6) and that there appear to be limitations with regard to local authorities' engagement with tourism. These limitations, according to some scholars, have become not less but more conspicuous in recent decades as a result of what has been termed the 'hollowing out of the state' (Jessop 1994), that is the increasing delegation and/or privatization of functions previously within the remit of public authorities. According to these perspectives, the rise of what became known as the 'new urban politics', and the underlying neoliberal public-sector reforms, have profoundly transformed both the objectives of tourism policy and the mechanisms for achieving them.

Hall (1999, cited in Hall and Jenkins 2004: 528), for example, posits that the role of government in tourism has undergone a 'dramatic shift from a traditional public administration model which sought to implement government policy for a perceived public good, to a corporatist model which emphasizes efficiency, investment returns, the role of the market, and relations with stakeholders, usually defined as industry'. According to him as well as a number of other scholars (see Pastras and Bramwell 2013; Dredge and Jenkins 2011), the pendulum has swung toward both *more* and *less* government interference in the tourism field. Tourism agencies and boards have been outsourced to public-private or to completely private companies acting as 'municipal agents'; the state's role in coordinating and directing tourism activities has been reduced to that of a facilitator of tourism growth and the provision of a suitable environment for businesses to thrive; and not local officials but private sector actors often set cities' agendas as to how tourism is dealt with.

The reasons for this shift are rooted in the assumptions underlying the rise of neoliberal reforms: the idea that markets are generally self-regulating and should whenever possible be left to work on their own; the hegemonic belief that what is good for the economy is good for society; and the conviction that private sector actors know best what would make them prosper and consequently should be given a strong position in policy-making (see Dredge and Jenkins 2011). One notable consequence of the above-mentioned shift has been that tourism, not unlike other policy areas (see Wilson and Swyngedouw 2014), has effectively been *depoliticized* in two ways. On the one hand, a *discursive* normalization and naturalization of neoliberal practices and approaches could be observed, making tourism development – as well as measures to promote it – a largely uncontroversial matter of technicalities rather than of political interests, potential conflicts and power. On the other hand, tourism has been in many contexts *practically removed* from the public realm of the formal political sphere: privatization and corporatization as well as backroom deal-making and so-called 'public-private partnerships' took hold and not only excluded many groups and communities from relevant decision-making processes, but ultimately also called the primacy of political institutions as having formative power to shape social life into question.

Berlin, a city in which tourism had been highly politicized for much of the twentieth century (albeit under different circumstances and in a different sense than today),[3] until recently exemplified this situation particularly well. This has changed: recent years have witnessed a proliferation of protests and mobilizations around tourism and the city government's approach to it. As a result, many questions that had been depoliticized and taken for granted have effectively been *re-politicized*: the costs and benefits of tourism, their distribution, as well as the question of how the local state should approach tourism are now being publicly discussed.

Tourism in Berlin: political priority, political afterthought, or both?

As with any public policy in more general terms, tourism policy involves more than formal, identifiable decisions or directives by governments. It has been defined as 'whatever governments choose to do or not to do with respect to tourism' (Hall and Jenkins 2004: 527; see also Hall 1994; Jenkins 1993). It is also, with reference to the alleged shift from government to governance, considered to extend beyond the sphere of formal government structures to involve action, inaction, decisions and non-decisions by other, non-state actors active in the policy process. To this end, scholars have highlighted the role of 'policy networks' (Laslo 2003) or 'policy communities' (Dredge 2004) comprising those who have a stake in tourism, as well as of urban 'regimes' or 'coalitions' (Fainstein and Gladstone 2003), in shaping tourism policy and development. A case in point is Häußermann and Colomb's (2003) discussion of tourism development in Berlin in the 1990s and early 2000s. In it, they argued that a public-private 'tourism coalition' made of Berlin's government (Senate) and other (private) actors with a stake in tourism had been instrumental in making tourism a priority in the city's economic and urban development policy.[4] Their analysis, however, left a lot of questions unanswered concerning the actual character of tourism politics and policy-making. Place marketing and urban development efforts aimed at 're-invent(ing) Berlin as a post-industrial service metropolis' (ibid.: 201) and enhancing the city's image as an attractive place to live, work, play and invest in are extensively elaborated upon, but relatively little is said about the specific field of urban tourism policy, the city-state's and other actors' approach to it, and their relationships to one another. What role, then, did tourism play in Berlin's political arena after the city's reunification and, more specifically, how can the attitudes and actions of the local state towards tourism development be described? As will be discussed in the following sections, evidence offers a somewhat contradictory picture with respect to this question. Tourism throughout the past decades seems to have been both the object of substantial attention as well as, paradoxically, of continuous and at times callous disregard.

Reunited and redefined. Destination Berlin, 1989–2010

Berlin's rise to fame as one of Europe's most sought after tourist destination began with a significant event: the collapse of the Berlin Wall in November 1989 paved the way for Germany's reunification, which was formally concluded on 3 October 1990 and led to a massive surge of tourism. Streams of visitors from all over the globe flocked into the city to sense the festive atmosphere that engulfed Berlin as world history unfolded. Accordingly, Berlin registered record-breaking numbers of hotel guests and overnight stays: 7.2 million overnight stays were recorded in 1992 alone, the highest figures ever recorded by West Berlin's Office for Statistics. Revenues for hotels, restaurants, bars, souvenir stores and other businesses benefiting from tourism all jumped to record levels and in doing so conveyed a first powerful sense of tourism's economic potency (Nerger 1998: 814). In the immediate aftermath of the city's reunification, tourism was, meanwhile, of secondary importance in the local political arena. This is because major decisions about the city's future development had to be made, the reintegration of the two halves of the city had to be organized, and the German parliament's decision to move the government seat from Bonn back to Berlin compounded the daunting challenges officials found themselves confronted with. Politically, tourism first became a topic of discussion in 1992.

Three years after the fall of the Wall, amid dropping visitor numbers and falling revenues, policy-makers, tourism industry representatives as well as the Chamber of Commerce called for measures to stem the tide and put the tourism sector back on the growth track. The main issue under discussion was the perceived need to reorganize and strengthen the city's tourism marketing activities (see Colomb 2011). At the time, tourism marketing was managed by two public sector organizations – the *Fremdenverkehrsamt* and the *Informationszentrum*

Berlin – and the ruling Grand Coalition of Christian Democrats (CDU) and Social Democrats (SPD) as well as private sector representatives agreed that more 'effective' and 'up-to-date' tourism marketing was needed. As a consequence, the decision was made to replace the two organizations that had previously dealt with the tourism promotion of West Berlin with a new public-private partnership – the *Berlin Tourismus Marketing GmbH* (BTM). Set up in 1993 and later renamed *Visit Berlin*, the BTM was established to fulfil two main roles: that of a service agency for its partners in the tourism industry, and that of an active broker for the travel industry and for tourists and travellers to Berlin (Colomb 2011). With this step, Berlin's policy-makers created a key element of the organizational structure that would shape tourism-related activities for years to come. This organizational structure was completed in 1994 when *Partner für Berlin* ('Partners for Berlin, Company for Capital City Marketing') was established in order to provide support for the repositioning of Berlin as Germany's new capital city and, in the words of its originators, 'foster [. . .] Berlin's image as a leading, competitive, future-oriented and international metropolis' (Partner für Berlin 1998).[5]

Notably, representatives of the private sector play a pivotal role in both organizations – both as shareholders and on the companies' boards.[6] Tied to the general shift of the time towards greater private sector involvement, the local state hence transferred many responsibilities it had previously performed in the realm of tourism marketing to new arrangements that – while in many ways reliant on public funding and contracts – are private in character and not part of the governmental apparatus. Within the latter, tourism remained a concern within the city's economic development department. Apart from small-scale measures aimed at assisting the tourism industry, the department's engagement, however, was mainly limited to acting as an interface between the public sector, the newly established marketing organizations as well as the tourism industry. The city's urban development department, meanwhile, engaged in activities to facilitate tourism growth and promote the city as a destination, but rarely did so in explicit terms. Few of its activities were devoted primarily to visitors and it was the BTM and, to a lesser extent, *Partner für Berlin* that, from the mid-1990s onwards, came to take on the leading role as the city's quasi-public authorities for issues relating to tourism marketing and development. Debates over tourism (policy) became in the course of the 1990s increasingly dominated by their representatives and spokespersons from business groups such as the local branch of Germany's Hotel and Restaurant Association (DEHOGA), while representatives of the state – be they members of the Berlin parliament, civil servants or elected government officials – relegated themselves increasingly to the sidelines.

Prior to the overhaul of the city-state's tourism marketing, tourism had been the subject of heated parliamentary debates that not only revolved around the promotional activities advocated by the Grand Coalition but also involved more general discussions about the role and relevance that should be ascribed to tourism politically as well as the kind of tourism that should be promoted. Once the new organizational structure was in place, such discussions became increasingly rare. Little explicit tourism policy to discuss and contest, as well as the fact that there were other urgent issues on the political agenda are sometimes cited as reasons for this. In light of the massive economic and social problems that characterized Berlin at the time, it is not all that surprising that tourism took a back seat in favour of other controversial issues – especially since tourism, in stark contrast to the poor performance of Berlin's economy as a whole, experienced accelerating growth in the course of the mid and late 1990s. The problematic or outright negative side effects of that growth were, at first, not that evident or at least not of much concern. Ultimately, however, the absence of political debates on urban tourism can also be attributed to the way political practices and thinking became increasingly attuned to neoliberal rationality. The prioritization of growth as the central objective of tourism policy became almost universally accepted and with it the idea that the state's involvement in tourism should be limited to the attainment of this goal. It was ironically under a coalition of the centre-left SPD with the socialist party *Die Linke* (formerly PDS), which had come into power after the demise of the Grand Coalition in 2001, that this doctrine was formalized. In the city's first conceptual document on tourism (*Tourismuskonzept*) after reunification – revealingly prepared by a private consultancy firm in close cooperation with BTM – the roles of the state and of the private sector institutions were described as follows:

> The task of the state is to improve the general conditions for the activities of the private sector as a precondition for employment effects, influx of purchasing power and tax income. The task of the private sector is to initiate and develop self-supporting economic cycles with ideas and capital.
>
> (SenWI 2004: 5, cited in Colomb 2011: 235)

Capital, however, came also in significant part from the state as the 'red-red coalition', in spite of its more general austerity course, steadily increased funding dedicated to tourism promotion. Declaring tourism a 'top concern' of his administration (Sontheimer 2004a), Klaus Wowereit, the city's mayor elected in 2001, moreover implemented a number of other initiatives to boost the city's image as a destination and expand its tourism trade. This led Hanns Peter Nerger, BTM's long-serving CEO, to claim that his government was doing more for the advancement of tourism in Berlin than any of its predecessors (in Sontheimer 2004b). Berlin – at a time when the city's overall economy had hit rock bottom and the city-state teetered on the edge of bankruptcy – had entered the new millennium with record-breaking tourism growth rates. These developments – along with the fact that policy-makers had somewhat come to resign themselves to Berlin's lack of competitiveness as a business destination – heightened the relevance that was ascribed to tourism as an economic sector with relatively low entry costs and potentially high returns as a source of revenue, employment and image building. Furthermore, tourism fitted well with the more general approach to urban and economic development the city government adopted, including in particular its efforts to target 'creative' people and branches as a tool for urban development and innovation. Tourism hence became an increasingly integral part, albeit often not a very explicit one, of broader creative city-policies and other 'place selling' efforts and by hitting new highs year after year, it not only steadily grew in economic strength but also became increasingly apparent as a powerful force of urban change.

Growth pains and growing discontent. Destination Berlin, 2010–2014

By the end of the first decade of the new millennium, the city elites' love affair with tourism was stronger than ever before. Fuelled by constant new records in the number of visitors and overnight stays, the booming tourism trade was stylized, with the enthusiastic support of the media, as a kind of saviour for the economically troubled city (see Gitschier and Lukosek 2010). The international attention Berlin received as a destination – which earned the city the title of 'Europe's Capital of Cool' in *Time Magazine* – added to the excitement. At the same time, however, it also became evident that that not everyone shared the excitement about Berlin's success as a destination.

Against the backdrop of a more general discontent with the city's transformation since its reunification, critical voices began to disturb and challenge the hitherto almost exclusively boosterist narratives surrounding tourism. Residents and community groups became increasingly vocal and raised alarm about the impacts of tourism on their communities, in particular in the mixed-use but predominantly residential neighbourhoods surrounding the city's centre that developed in the nineteenth century expansion of the city – e.g. Kreuzberg (in the Western part, Figure 3.1), Friedrichshain and Prenzlauer Berg (in the Eastern part). These neighbourhoods had, as one newspaper described it, over the years increasingly been 'conquered' by tourism (Bartels 2010) and to many observers the city government was complicit in this process due to its preoccupation with growth-focused strategies aimed at selling the city to outsiders. To many critics the latter amounted to a 'sell-out' of the city and its inherent qualities. Along with tourism's perceived (albeit not unequivocally substantiated) role as a contributing factor in gentrification processes, nuisance issues such as noise pollution, as well as concerns about a commercialization and ultimately 'touristification' of communities, this contributed to the problematization and politicization of what hitherto had essentially been a non-issue in political debates and struggles. Graffiti with slogans like 'No more rolling suitcases' and 'Tourists F*** off' became a regular sight (Figure 3.2), community meetings addressing tourism's detrimental effects became a regular fixture, and tourists – blamed for their complicity in gentrification processes – emerged as the favourite scapegoats boys of radical left-wing groups, who claim to 'defend' Berlin's neighbourhoods and its cherished 'free spaces'.

Fiercely criticized for mistaking cause and effect, for scapegoating tourists and for its occasional xenophobic undertones (see Alas 2011), the growing discontent and protests against tourism in Berlin have been the subject of intense debates. Some protesters doubtlessly can be characterized as knee-jerk advocates of a 'Not in My Backyard' mindset and some manifestations of protest can be described as contemptuous or outright maliciousness. Perhaps the most palpable example of

Figure 3.1 Kreuzberg: impressions of a neighbourhood in flux.

Sources (from left to right): Ya Po Guille (CC BY-ND 2.0), Alper Çuğun (CC BY 2.0), Uli Herrmann (CC BY-SA 2.0), Ben Garrett (CC BY 2.0).

the latter is the much publicized 'Proposal for an anti-tourism campaign 2011' by the leftist magazine *Interim*. It declared tourists to be legitimate targets in the fight against gentrification and encouraged readers to steal phones and wallets from visitors and engage in all sorts of other hostile and intimidating activities so as so as to scare them away (see Hasselmann 2010).

Such views have attracted a disproportionate amount of media attention but can hardly be described as representative of the protests as a whole. As regards the composition of the actors behind the latter and the agendas they pursue, it is important to note that there is no readily identifiable core, let alone single coordinating body that directs them. Instead, different groups and individuals with different backgrounds, motives and methods problematize tourism independently of one another and many of them have far less in common with one another than many of the media's generalizing portrayals of Berlin's alleged 'tourist hate' (Huffington Post 2012) suggest. Among those expressing discontent are old residents fearful of gentrification, but also gentrifiers fearing for their quality of life and capital gains. Others are mainly concerned about tourism's cultural impacts such as the much-decried 'disneyfication' of Berlin's ambiguous historic heritage. A surprisingly large number happen to be beneficiaries of the tourism trade themselves. The owner of *Freies Neukölln*, a now defunct bar in the increasingly sought after neighbourhood of Neukölln, is one such example. The bar used to be popular with international 'party tourists' and its owner caused considerable uproar with a video entitled *Offending the Clientele* that criticized its patrons for their indifference to the former working-class and migrant neighbourhood's extant character and provocatively attacked them – supposedly to generate debate – for being responsible for the area's rampant gentrification.

One may argue that it would have been more constructive to point the finger not at visitors, but at those responsible for the city's development and the regulation of tourism activities. This is exactly what others have done, such as Andreas Becker, the director of the *Circus Hostel*, one of the city's most popular low-cost accommodations. He contended that the conflicts surrounding tourism, including in particular those arising from the excessive 'party tourism' that regularly concentrates in certain areas, can be attributed to the local state's unwillingness to engage in tourism management and planning. 'The city has failed', he argued, adding that the resulting damage to the city's image and the tourism sector's reputation would be disastrous for the tourism industry (cited in Lüber 2014). This is not the only instance where tourism industry members have publicly criticized the city's approach to tourism development – or lack thereof. Critiques have also been raised about the unregulated boom of hotels and hostels (whose number has more than quintupled since 1993) and the resulting crowding out of small, independently owned accommodation, as well as the proliferation of short-term vacation rentals in the city. Exact figures do not exist, but recent estimates suggest that there are up to 23,000 of the latter in the city (Aulich 2015). A major bone of contention for many residents and tenant organisations who argue that they drive up housing prices and lessen the supply of regular rental units, these rentals are also viewed critically by many in the tourism industry as they provide competition to hotels, inns and bed-and-breakfasts. Such examples reveal that the tourism industry is not monolithic but made up of different players with different opinions and interests, and that not all of them subscribe to the laissez-faire approach to tourism adopted by the local state in the 1990s.

Significantly, the same must also be said of the 'local state'. The district government of Friedrichshain-Kreuzberg emerged, for instance, over the years as one of the fiercest critics of the Senate's handling of tourism-related matters.[7] Centrally located and often described as one of Berlin's liveliest and vibrant districts, Friedrichshain-Kreuzberg experienced a particularly strong influx of tourists since the early 1990s. In addition – perhaps unsurprisingly given the district's history as a major centre of political activism and countercultural activity – it is also one of the areas in which tourism is most controversially discussed. Local officials have in this context frequently sided with local residents and community groups who campaigned against the proliferation of holiday accommodation or took issue with other tourism-induced changes impacting their neighbourhoods.

Figure 3.2 'No more *Rollkoffer* [rolling suitcases]'. Anti-tourism graffiti in Berlin's public space, 2011.

Source: Jörg Kantel, CC BY-NC-SA 2.0.

It was the local branch of the Green Party (which has led the district council since 2006) that organized a controversial community meeting under the title 'Help, the tourists are coming!' in 2011, which led the media to depict the district as the epicentre of the rise of 'tourist-haters' (Haas *et al.* 2011). The district council's own capacity to impact the dynamics of tourism within its boundaries is, however, relatively limited. It acted several times in a manner which stretched its powers to the limits to block the construction of new hotels and hostels (Myrrhe 2010; see also Linde 2010) or prevent shops and restaurants catering to visitors from displacing other businesses. Ultimately, however, the district government is not in a position to tackle the roots of the challenges it find itself confronted with. What district representatives certainly achieved was to give higher visibility to the issue: especially the 'Help, the tourists are coming!' event received a great deal of attention in the media and the district's officials have regularly engaged in city-wide discussions to advocate for policy changes. Their critique concerns both the Senate's action as well as its inaction. They argue that the Senate follows an exclusively growth-oriented approach to tourism, chide it for acting negligently – or failing to act altogether – concerning negative externalities surrounding tourism's growth, and pressure it to move towards a 'new model driven by 'sustainable' goals and principles'. Tourism, rather than being a priority for the Senate, has according to their opinion yet to receive the political attention it deserves, as the Senate has not as yet addressed tourism as a management and planning issue (Linde 2010).

This view is also shared by representatives of the tourist industry. Some of them confirm that the overhaul of tourism promotion in the 1990s has led to a fundamental misunderstanding concerning the respective roles and responsibilities of the public and private sector. It has contributed to a situation in which they are wrongly targeted and blamed for things they are not responsible for, not having the resources nor the competences to carry out proper tourism management and planning. As one employee of Visit Berlin stated during the above-mentioned community meeting, '(The organized tourist industry's) task is to attract visitors, but it is still mainly the responsibility of the local government to plan for and manage tourist impacts.' Some industry representatives have also understood that tourism development, if too successful, may result in externalities which might ultimately negatively impact tourism's resource base and the future prospects of Berlin as a destination. Burkhard Kieker, since 2009 CEO of Visit Berlin, has, for example, at times been relatively outspoken about problems associated with tourism's growth, albeit not so much because of a concern over the integrity of the city and its neighbourhoods or its inherent social costs. Rather, as Kieker once explained in an almost Marxist terminology to the left-leaning newspaper *Die Tageszeitung* (Rada 2010), he was concerned that too much 'capitalist exploitation pressure' might jeopardize some of the city's main competitive advantages as a destination, in particular Berlin's famous subculture of temporary music clubs and bars, as well as its more general creative and alternative 'flair'. Likewise, an understanding took hold in the late 2000s and early 2010s that failing to address nuisance problems and residents' concerns might ultimately fall back on Berlin as a destination. A draft version of the city's latest tourism conceptual document (SenWTF 2011) included extensive references to issues such as overcrowding or late-night disturbances leading to conflicts between visitors and residents, and to the need to address them. Many of these references did not make it into the final version of the document, however, reportedly scrapped by government officials who sought to keep the issue out of the election campaign that took place in the autumn of 2011.

On the other hand, the organized tourist industry has repeatedly sought to downplay the degree and extent to which tourism poses a problem by suggesting that many of the perceived issues and conflicts surrounding tourism are owed to the city's 'catch-up effect' after reunification. 'Paris and London have had hundreds of years to get used to their many visitors. We've only had 20 so far,' Kieker stated in an interview (Duvernoy 2012), suggesting that more time may be needed for its residents to 'adapt' to Berlin's new role as a major tourist destination and come to terms with processes that would, according to him, be considered 'normal' in other cities (see the analysis of Paris in this volume), e.g. gentrification (Richter and Anker 2014).

Tourism politics in Berlin: on policy lacunae, conflicts and contradictions

The interpretation of processes like gentrification as 'normal' obviously does not sit well with many residents and community groups. Simultaneously serving as cause, context and consequence of the city's rise to prominence as a visitor destination, gentrification has for many years been one of the most salient and contested trends affecting Berlin. Mobilizations against tourism clearly have to be seen against the background of wider struggles and conflicts surrounding the changing socio-spatial landscape of the city and its social and cultural implications, as well as the state's complicity in the ongoing gentrification of Berlin's inner city, soaring housing prices as well as growing socio-economic inequality (Holm 2011, 2014). Over the past years, these struggles increasingly impacted policy-making processes. New rent-control legislation has come into force in 2015 (Russell 2015), previously phased-out public housing programmes were restarted and the city-state, since 2011 governed again by a coalition of Social and Christian Democrats, has vowed to undertake a range of other measures to tackle what is now recognized as a fully-fledged housing crisis.

As regards tourism, policy changes have all in all been marginal, however. In 2013 the city government passed a law to regulate the Wild West of vacation rentals but whether it is effective or not remains under debate (Aulich 2015). Apart from this, the Senate sticks firmly to the position that conflicts surrounding tourism have been blown out of proportion and that there are no significant problems to be solved. Referring to a survey carried out in 2013 which apparently revealed that 87 per cent of Berlin's inhabitants would not feel disturbed by tourism's impacts, a Senate report to the Berlin Parliament on the matter concluded that 'the bottom line is that there are (only) few disturbances, mainly in relation to individual sites, that are perceived as negative by local residents' (SenWiTechForsch 2014: 2). What the report does not mention is that the number of residents who responded that tourism negatively impacts their lives is two to three time higher in areas particularly affected by tourism growth: in Kreuzberg, roughly 'a third of local residents complain about noisy party tourists' as the title of one article put it (Fahrun 2014). Leaving the question of the poll's merit aside,[8] it is noteworthy that one of the main policy recommendations proposed by the Senate as a result in the above-mentioned report was the need to raise inhabitants' awareness of the 'economic significance of tourism' by means of 'inward marketing'. Part of *Visit Berlin*'s marketing budget (about €300,000 annually) was consequently earmarked in 2014 for campaigns directed at local residents. Instead of only selling Berlin to tourists, *Visit Berlin* now also increasingly engages in selling tourism to Berliners. Among other things it set up a website (https://du-hier-in.berlin) to enable residents to provide feedback, comments or inputs concerning tourism in Berlin and has begun to organize 'citizen workshops' to develop ideas to improve tourism in Berlin. Significantly, however, the workshops were, at most, semi-public in nature. In addition, until the time of writing (June–October 2015) few concrete results have resulted from them – except perhaps to provide grist to the mill of those who deride such efforts as little more than legitimation exercises.

Representatives of the organized tourist industry, however, know that not all challenges they find themselves confronted with are simply matters of 'perception' and can be glossed over by improved public relations. Indeed, they have in recent years more than once also advocated for changes on the ground, e.g. as previously mentioned, in the struggle against vacation rentals, in debates surrounding the swelling number of pub crawl tours and beer bike operators, or in the controversies about the shallow commerce that surrounds sobering sites of memory like the Holocaust Memorial or the former Cold War border crossing at Checkpoint Charlie. Amid signs of frustration about the slow pace of progress on mitigating these and related issues, there is also a concern that a recent shift in economic policy towards a strengthening of Berlin's high-tech and knowledge-intensive industries will make it even more difficult to convince the Senate to seriously engage with tourism. As one informant put it in 2014:

> (Politicians) pride themselves with tourism's success, but especially in recent years this hasn't translated into much as far as resources are concerned. [. . .] We don't need to be convinced that a need for management and planning exists but to them (rather than being a political priority) tourism is more of a cash cow that regularly produces handsome profits but requires little attention.

In cases where the current well-being or future economic prospects of tourism are at stake, it thus seems that the organized tourist industry does not necessarily stand in the way of more planning and, if necessary, of more regulation to address existing problems associated with tourism and prevent future ones from occurring. However, what I referred to as a *re-politicization* of tourism has also expanded the debate beyond issues of management and governance. Tourism development is increasingly 'seen' and discussed as what it is: fundamentally political. This means that distributive concerns and issues of power are raised, and that the prioritization of economic considerations over environmental and social ones that characterizes tourism policy are called into question. Tourism is increasingly recognized as embedded in a broader political economy, and as encompassing much more than the discourse of tourism as an 'industry' (and its narrow conceptualizations of the tourism phenomenon) suggests (Higgins-Desbiolles 2006: 1192).

The recent struggles surrounding tourism have consequently exposed two lacunae in the way tourism has been approached in Berlin's political arena: first, tourism has almost exclusively been dealt with as an economic sector. Responsibilities for tourism are subsumed within the economic development department or, as discussed, outsourced to the tourism industry itself, and there was until recently very little understanding of tourism beyond its role as an economic sector. The cultural, environmental, social and political implications

Figure 3.3 'Berlin loves you'. Signs of 'touristification' close to Checkpoint Charlie in Berlin's city centre, 2013.

Source: Thiemo van Assendelft, Mooibeeld.nl.

of the scapes and flows caused by visitors and people 'on the move' were for a long time barely addressed. Efforts to approach tourism more holistically and develop policy frameworks that are more reflective and sensitive to the features unique to host communities, to include those who are visited into relevant decision-making processes and enable them to reap more of the benefits tourism may bring have been minimal. Second, (policy) debates, if any, revolved until recently almost exclusively around tourists staying in hotels and formal accommodation, while other forms of travel behaviour were rarely addressed, although they too play a significant role in the ongoing reconfiguration of city space and city life. Tourists visiting friends and relatives, daytrippers, as well as a vast number of other transient city users that, by definition, are tourists too even if they are not easily recognized as such (Novy 2010; see the introduction to this volume) were for a long time only of peripheral concern to policy-makers and local officials. This is in part due to the fact that the organized tourist industry is dominated by the hotel and convention sectors, which means that it is their knowledge and expertise that shaped the direction of the field. The discussed lacunae indicate that a discrepancy exists between the rhetoric surrounding tourism as a policy field and what is being implemented in practice. Policy-makers may still describe tourism as their priority, but the reality is more complex, contradictory and inchoate than that.

Conclusion

This chapter addressed the frequently asserted prioritization of tourism as a policy field in contemporary cities and argued that in the case of Berlin tourism is perhaps better characterized as, paradoxically, both a political priority *and* afterthought. Tourism promotion clearly has become a defining feature of Berlin's entrepreneurial development politics, regardless of the political party in power, and the quest for tourism growth has exerted a strong influence on current urban and economic development practice and thinking. In light of the enormous economic relevance of tourism for the city, the political attention and resources devoted to tourism should, at the same time, also not be overstated. The city-state's real engagement with tourism is replete with lacunae and contradictions, and the significance of tourism beyond its economic consequences was for a long time barely considered. Depoliticized and largely outsourced to the tourism industry, tourism as a policy field in its own right remained in an under-developed state: local authorities' *inaction* with regard to addressing tourism-related issues was arguably at least as important in contributing to the profound reconfiguration of city space and city life through tourism as their interventions. The described re-politicization of tourism has changed this picture somewhat. Protests and public discontent pushed the Senate into a debate about tourism's ambiguous and unevenly distributed impacts, and forced it to address at least some negative externalities associated with tourism's growth, such as the uncontrolled proliferation of vacation rentals.

The debate over tourism's impacts, however, will likely not go away anytime soon, especially given the projected growth of tourism in the coming years. And why should it? Tourism in Berlin emerged as a bone of contention for all sorts of reasons, and some of these reasons certainly may appear more 'reasonable' than others. This does not change the fact, however, that the present mode of development deserves to be debated and contested. It has been neither equitable nor sustainable – as the growing talk about a need to protect tourism from ruining itself confirms. If Berlin's recent history is any indication, it will require more pressure and more mobilizations 'from below' for this to change.

Notes

1 The latest official data from 2011 estimates tourism's contribution to the GDP at 7.9 per cent (Visit Berlin 2012: 24).
2 Interviews with numerous stakeholders were a valuable source of information, but so, too, were countless participant observation activities. Interviewees and informants are not named in this chapter to ensure anonymity.
3 For a discussion of the decisively political nature of tourism development/marketing in Berlin from the time of the Weimar Republic to Germany's reunification see Colomb (2011: ch. 3).
4 Whether or not tourism can be viewed as an 'industry' continues to be debated, but the term 'tourism industry' is used here for brevity's sake.
5 Later renamed *Berlin Partners*, *Partner für Berlin* developed and implemented several ambitious programmes and projects including, from 1996 until 2002, the *Das Neue*

Berlin (The New Berlin) campaign which has been described as instrumental in Berlin's reimagining and repositioning over the last two decades (see Colomb 2011).

6 In fact, *Partner für Berlin* was initially completely in the hands of the private sector and it was only when the company was merged with the state-owned Berlin Business Development Corporation that the local state acquired 45 per cent of the company's shares.

7 Berlin is a city-state in the German federal system and has a two-tier government system divided between the city-wide administration, made up of a parliament and a government and administration (the *Senat*), and of semi-autonomous districts, the *Bezirke.*

8 Unfortunately, neither the questionnaire nor the dataset were made available to the author for analysis.

References

[Unless otherwise stated, all URLs were last accessed 15 December 2015.]

Alas, J. (2011) 'Stop blaming "party tourists" for Berlin's problems', *Der Tagesspiegel*, 9 March. Online. Available at http://www.tagesspiegel.de/weltspiegel/in-english/racism-and-xenophobia-stop-blaming-party-tourists-for-berlins-problems/3930536.html.

Aulich, U. (2015) 'Berliner vermieten 17.500 illegale Ferienwohnungen', *Berliner Zeitung*, 6 August. Online. Available at http://www.berliner-zeitung.de/berlin/knapper-wohnraum-in-berlin-berliner-vermieten-17-500-illegale-ferienwohnungen,10809148,31403662.html.

Bartels, G. (2010) 'Berlin – die eroberte Stadt', *Der Tagesspiegel*, 15 August. Online. Available at http://www.tagesspiegel.de/berlin/berlin-die-eroberte-stadt/1903598.html.

Brenner, N. and Theodore, N. (2002) 'Cities and the geographies of "actually existing neoliberalism"', *Antipode*, 34(3): 356–86.

Colomb, C. (2011) *Staging the New Berlin. Place Marketing and the Politics of Urban Reinvention Post-1989*. London: Routledge.

Dredge, D. (2004) 'Policy networks and the local organisation of tourism', *Tourism Management*, 27(2): 269–80.

Dredge, D. and Jenkins, J. (2011) 'New spaces of tourism planning and policy', in D. Dredge and J. Jenkins (eds) *Stories of Practice: Tourism Policy and Planning*. Farnham: Ashgate.

Duvernoy, S. (2012) 'Tourist-bashing turns ugly in Berlin', *Reuters*, 17 September. Online. Available at www.reuters.com/article/2012/09/17/germany-berlin-tourists-idUSL5E8KB9AB20120917.

Fahrun, J. (2014) 'Lärm und Dreck: Jeder Dritte in Party-Kiezen fühlt sich gestört', *Berliner Morgenpost*, 8 September. Online. Available at www.morgenpost.de/printarchiv/titelseite/article131998676/Laerm-und-Dreck-Jeder-Dritte-in-Party-Kiezen-fuehlt-sich-gestoert.html.

Fainstein S. S. and Gladstone, D. L. (2003) 'Tourism in US global cities: a comparison of New York and Los Angeles', *Journal of Urban Affairs*, 23(1): 23–40.

Fainstein, S. S., Hoffman, L. M. and Judd, D. R. (2003) 'Introduction', in L. M. Hoffman, S. S. Fainstein and D. R. Judd (eds) *Cities and Visitors. Regulating People, Markets, and City Space*. Oxford: Wiley-Blackwell.

Gitschier, L. and Lukosek, S. (2010) 'In der Krise: Touristen retten Berlin', *Der Tagesspiegel*, 1 September. Online. Available at http://www.tagesspiegel.de/wirtschaft/in-der-krise-touristen-retten-berlin/1916216.html.

Haas, B., Drachsel, C. and Bauer, T. (2011) 'Kreuzberger werden zu Touristen-Hassern', *Berliner Morgenpost*, 11 May. Online. Available at http://www.morgenpost.de/berlin/article104978925/Kreuzberger-werden-zu-Touristen-Hassern.html.

Hall, C. M. (1994) *Tourism and Politics: Policy, Power and Place*. London: Belhaven Press.

Hall, C. M. (2006) 'Tourism, governance and the (mis-)location of power', in A. Church and T. Coles (eds) *Tourism, Power, and Space*. New York and London: Routledge.

Hall, C. M. and Jenkins, J. M. (2004) 'Tourism and public policy', in A. Lew, C. M. Hall and A. M. Williams (eds) *Companion to Tourism*. Oxford: Blackwell.

Hall, T. and Hubbard, P. (1998) *The Entrepreneurial City: Geographies of Politics, Regime and Representation*. Chichester: Wiley.

Harvey, D. (1989) 'From managerialism to entrepreneurialism: the transformation in urban governance in late capitalism', *Geografiska Annaler B*, 71(1): 3–17.

Hasselmann, J. (2010) 'Chaoten wollen Berlin-Touristen angreifen', *Der Tagesspiegel*, 19 December. Online. Available at http://www.tagesspiegel.de/berlin/linksextremismus-chaoten-wollen-berlin-touristen-angreifen/3637400.html.

Häußermann, H. and Colomb, C. (2003) 'The New Berlin. Marketing the city of dreams', in L. M. Hoffman, S. S. Fainstein and D. R. Judd (eds) *Cities and Visitors. Regulating People, Markets, and City Space*. Oxford: Wiley-Blackwell.

Häußermann, H. and Siebel, W. (eds) (1993) *Festivalisierung der Stadtpolitik*. Wiesbaden: VS Verlag für Sozialwissenschaften.

Higgins-Desbiolles, F. (2006) 'More than an "industry": the forgotten power of tourism as a social force', *Tourism Management*, 27(6): 1192–208.

Hoffman, L. M., Fainstein, S. S. and Judd, D. R. (eds) (2003) *Cities and Visitors. Regulating People, Markets, and City Space*. Oxford: Blackwell.

Holm, A. (2011) 'Gentrification in Berlin: Neue Investitionsstrategien und lokale Konflikte', in H. Herrmann, C. Keller, R. Neef and R. Ruhne (eds) *Die Besonderheit des Städtischen*. Wiesbaden: VS Verlag für Sozialwissenschaften.

Holm, A. (2014) 'Berlin's gentrification mainstream', in A. Holm, M. Berndt and B. Grell (eds) *The Berlin Reader: A Compendium on Urban Change and Activism*. Berlin: Transcript.

Huffington Post Canada (2012) 'Berlin tourist hate: gentrification fuels battle between locals and travellers', *Huffington Post Canada*, 12 May, Online. Available at http://www.huffingtonpost.ca/2012/12/05/berlin-tourist-hate_n_2240869.html.

Jenkins, J. M. (1993) 'Tourism policy in rural New South Wales: policy and research priorities', *Geojournal*, 29(3): 281–90.

Jessop, B. (1994) 'Post-Fordism and the state', in A. Amin (ed.) *Post-Fordism: A Reader*. Oxford: Blackwell.

Krajewski, C. (2006) 'Städtetourismus im "Neuen Berlin" zwischen Authentizität und Inszenierung', in P. Reuber and P. Schnell (eds) *Postmoderne Freizeitstile und Freizeiträume. Neue Angebote im Tourismus*. Berlin: Erich Schmidt Verlag.

Laslo, D. H. (2003) 'Policy communities and infrastructure of urban tourism', *American Behavioral Scientist*, 46(8): 1070–83.

Law, C. (2002) *Urban Tourism: The Visitor Economy and the Growth of Large Cities*. London: Continuum.

Linde, C. (2010) 'Der 13. Bezirk', *Mieterecho*, 341, July: 17.

Lüber, K. (2014) 'Who does the city belong to?', *Goethe*. Online. Available at http://www.goethe.de/en/kul/mol/20442881.html.

Matthies, B. (2014) 'Rekordzahlen in der Hauptstadt. Touristen lieben Berlin', *Der Tagesspiegel*, 19 February. Online. Available at http://www.tagesspiegel.de/berlin/rekordzahlen-in-der-hauptstadt-touristen-lieben-berlin/11392250.html.

Myrrhe, A. (2010) 'Trendbezirke lehnen weitere Billighotels ab', *Der Tagessspiegel*, 18 September. Online. Available at http://www.tagesspiegel.de/berlin/laermbelaestigung-trendbezirke-lehnen-weitere-billighotels-ab/1936408.html.

Nerger, H. P. (1998) 'Städtetourismus am Beispiel der Berlin Tourismus Marketing GmbH', in G. Haedrich, C. Kaspar, K. Klemm and E. Kreilkamp (eds) *Tourismus-Management. Tourismus-Marketing und Fremdenverkehrsplanung*. Berlin and New York: De Gruyter.

Nicola, B. (2014) 'Berlin beats Rome as tourist attraction as hordes descend', *Bloomberg Business*, 4 September. Online. Available at http://www.bloomberg.com/news/articles/2014-09-03/berlin-beats-rome-as-tourist-attraction-as-hordes-descend.

Novy, J. (2010) 'What's new about new urban tourism? And what do recent changes in travel imply for the "Tourist City" Berlin?', in J. Richter (ed.) *Tourist City Berlin*. Berlin: Braun.

Novy, J. and Huning, S. (2009) 'New tourism (areas) in the "New Berlin"', in R. Maitland and P. Newman (eds) *World Tourism Cities: Developing Tourism Off the Beaten Track*. London and New York: Routledge.

Partner für Berlin (1998) *The New Berlin*. Berlin: PfB.

Pastras, P. and Bramwell, B. (2013) 'A strategic-relational approach to tourism policy', *Annals of Tourism Research*, 43: 390–414.

Philo, C. and Kearns, G. (1993) 'Culture, history, capital: a critical introduction to the selling of places', in C. Philo and G. Kearns (eds) *Selling Places: The City as Cultural Capital, Past and Present*. Oxford and New York: Pergamon Press.

Rada, U. (2010) 'Reichtum macht bräsig und erstickt Kreativität', *Die Tageszeitung*, 7 August. Online. Available at http://www.taz.de/1/archiv/digitaz/artikel/?ressort=bl&dig=2010%2F08%2F07%2Fa0207&cHash=8e29e13a82.

Richter, C. and Anker, J. (2014) 'Tourismus-Chef Kieker – "Berlin ist nicht der Ballermann"', *Berliner Morgenpost*, 14 September. Online. Available at http://www.morgenpost.de/berlin/article132232382/Tourismus-Chef-Kieker-Berlin-ist-nicht-der-Ballermann.html.

Russell, R. (2015) 'Berlin becomes first German city to make rent cap a reality', *Guardian*, 1 June. Available at: http://www.theguardian.com/world/2015/jun/01/rent-cap-legislation-in-force-berlin-germany.

Selby, M. (2004) *Understanding Urban Tourism: Image, Culture and Experience*. London: I. B. Tauris.

SenWiTechForsch (Senatsverwaltung für Wirtschaft, Technologie und Forschung) (2014) *Bericht des Senats. Konzept zur Akzeptanzerhaltung des Tourismus*. Drucksache Nr. 17/1400 (II.B.87).

SenWTF (Senatsverwaltung für Wirtschaft, Technologie und Frauen) (2011) *Tourismuskonzept Berlin. Handlungsrahmen 2011+*. Online. Available at http://www.berlin.de/imperia/md/content/senwirtschaft/tourismuskonzept2011.pdf?start&ts=1301582288&file=tourismuskonzept2011.pdf.

Sontheimer, M. (2004a) 'Tourismus ist Chefsache', *Spiegel Online*, 5 July. Online. Available at http://www.spiegel.de/reise/staedte/interview-mit-klaus-wowereit-tourismus-ist-chefsache-a-307258.html.

Sontheimer, M. (2004b) 'Diese Stadt macht süchtig', *Spiegel Online*, 24 August. Online. Available at http://www.spiegel.de/reise/staedte/berliner-tourismus-diese-stadt-macht-suechtig-a-314549.html.

Spirou, C. (2011) *Urban Tourism and Urban Change: Cities in a Global Economy*. London and New York: Routledge.

Stevenson, N., Airey, D. and Miller, G. (2008) 'Tourism policy making: the policy-makers' perspectives', *Annals of Tourism Research*, 35(3): 732–50.

Van der Borg, J. (1991) *Tourism and Urban Development*. Amsterdam: Thesis Publishers.

Van der Borg, J., Costa, P. and Gotti, G. (1996) 'Tourism in European heritage cities', *Annals of Tourism Research*, 23(2): 306–21.

Visit Berlin (2012) *Wirtschaftsfaktor für Berlin: Tourismus- und Kongressindustrie*. Online. Available at http://press. visitberlin.de/sites/default/files/wirtschaftsfaktor_2012.pdf.

Wilson, J. and Swyngedouw, E. (eds) (2014) *The Post-Political and Its Discontents: Spaces of Depoliticization, Spectres of Radical Politics*. Edinburgh: Edinburgh University Press.

4 Touristification and awakening civil society in post-socialist Prague

Michaela Pixová and Jan Sládek

Soon after the fall of communism in 1989, the Czech capital started to rank among Europe's top tourist destinations, attracting visitors from all over the world with its beautiful architecture, historical atmosphere and dark yet appealing totalitarian legacies. The number of people visiting the city of 1.2 million has substantially grown, reaching a record of almost 6.1 million visitors and 14.8 million overnight stays in 2014 (CSO 2015a). Despite multiplying complaints about the 'touristification' of Prague's historic city centre, the authorities have welcomed the increase in tourist flows for its economic benefits. The implications of the touristification process are most tangible in certain parts of the Prague Monument Preserve (PMP), an 8.6 km² area in Prague's historic core (covering the districts of Prague 1 and part of Prague 2), whose valuable assets are being exploited and residents pushed out. Between 1900 and 2001, the number of permanent residents in the PMP decreased from 170,000 to 53,000 (Polívková 2001).

The existence of a 'tourist' and 'non-tourist' Prague is affecting the city's socio-spatial structure and human ecology (Hoffman and Musil 2009). Despite early warnings from academic commentators (Cooper and Morpeth 1998; Hoffman and Musil 1999; Simpson 1999), these detrimental effects were long ignored. Only recently have various citizen initiatives and Prague's planning institutions started to react to those negative effects. So far, however, little academic attention has been paid to how the city's residents respond to the impacts of mass tourism, particularly by means of protest and resistance. This chapter is based on research that aims to fill this gap. First, Prague's historic core and its development in a changing political-economic context will be introduced. Then the area's touristification, depopulation and the post-socialist laissez-faire approach to urban transformation will be discussed. Subsequently, bottom-up social mobilizations in post-socialist Prague will be introduced. The last section will provide insight into the focus, modes of action and claims of contemporary urban social mobilizations around urban issues related to the historic core of Prague.[1]

Prague's historic core in a changing political-economic context

Until the Second World War, Prague's urban development patterns mirrored other developed European cities (Musil 2001). Prague's core was the heart of the city's life, distinguished by a high concentration of historic buildings, heritage sites, as well as diverse functions linked with key administrative and economic activities and people's everyday life. The central district of Prague 1 was a zone of residence for a considerable population – in 1880, the 116,000 residents of Prague 1 formed one third of Prague's population. As the city grew, in 1921 the 112,000 residents of Prague 1 formed just over 15 per cent of Prague's population (Ouředníček and Temelová 2008). The proportion of residents living in Prague 1 decreased throughout the entire twentieth century, falling to around 50,000 (approximately 5 per cent of the entire city's population) in the 1980s (Ouředníček and Temelová 2008). However, in comparison with most Western European capitalist cities, the city centres of many socialist cities underwent a slower depopulation, retaining their cultural, political and social life (Sýkora 2009). Due to the flaws of the centrally planned economy, housing was scarce, and most of the limited capital investment was drained away to the construction of huge peripheral housing estates (Smith 1996). In Prague, the historic core suffered dilapidation, but the absence of major investments and large-scale redevelopment saved its historic fabric (Musil 2001). In 1971, the Czechoslovak government designated 8.6 square kilometres of the historic core as the PMP, where redevelopment and reconstruction was to be controlled by the historic preservation authorities (Horak 2007: 102–3). Even under socialism Prague attracted about half a million foreign tourists per year (Horak 2007).

In socialist Czechoslovakia, where most dwellings were under state or cooperative ownership, centrally located housing had no special economic value arising from its location. Housing was provided to people by means of the socialist system of housing allocation (Sýkora 2009), creating a new form of ideologically driven socio-spatial inequality: 'old people, low income households and Romani people were concentrated (or forced to stay) in decaying city centres', while newly built housing in peripheral estates was typically allocated to younger workers and families (Musil 2001: 292). Despite the low quality of housing in the historic core, the area remained a relatively populated, socially and functionally mixed area (Musil 2001).

After the Velvet Revolution of 1989, the country's democratization and national market reforms led to profound changes in Prague's physical and social structure. In the city centre, many buildings were privatized (Sládek 2013) and restituted to their pre-war owners (Lux and Mikeszová 2012). Some properties were transferred to municipal ownership. Many long-term residents lost housing security due to new, often unclear ownership relationships and rent deregulation. Fuelled by a non-existent social housing policy, many people faced a precarious housing situation (see Lux 2004). Prague was also hit by a huge influx of foreign investment and visitor flows. The historic core gained a prime position in the newly emerging urban economy, and its decaying buildings and streets were quickly restored and upgraded. In 1992, the UNESCO (United Nations Educational, Scientific, and Cultural Organization) agreed to put 866 hectares of Prague's historic centre on its World Heritage List. The pressure for commercial development and the ever-increasing number of international tourists were now the determining forces in the historic core, which has been said to have undergone a process of 'touristification' and turned into a 'tourism ghetto', according to some authors (Kadlecová and Fialová 2010; Dumbrovská and Fialová 2014), as described in the next section.

Touristification, depopulation and the laissez-faire approach

While the population of the Prague 1 district has kept decreasing (with 30,561 permanent residents in 2011 – four times less than a century before – i.e. only 2.4 per cent of Prague's population (CSO 2014)), the number of tourists in Prague has kept growing, reaching 6.1 million tourists in 2014 (more than double compared to 2000). Official statistics only include visitors staying in Prague's official accommodation facilities; the estimate of actual visitors is thus likely to be much higher. Although smaller in size and population, Prague has ranked among top European destinations for urban tourism such as London, Paris, Rome, Madrid or Berlin. One of the first studies on the impact of tourism in the historic core of Prague was conducted by Simpson (1999), who concluded:

> The relatively non-regulative approach to development, particularly where it is considered of economic benefit, has already brought about considerable land-use change in the area. Land use is being rapidly transformed (often from residential to commercial uses), the traditional resident population is being displaced and the overall atmosphere and congestion of the streets is being negatively influenced by the city's visitors. The research, therefore, illustrates a clear need to manage tourism-related activity within the historic core of Prague, if its quality of life for residents and the very character which attracted tourists in the first place are not to be eroded substantially.
>
> (p. 182)

Simpson pointed to the city officials' laissez-faire approach, which allowed commercial uses to rapidly squeeze out the core's residential function and displace the resident population, making space for unregulated and unmanaged booming tourism-related uses (Simpson 1999). Depopulation was further accelerated by an extreme rise in property prices instigated via privatization auctions, triggering a dramatic increase in the functions serving upmarket needs, such as hotels, restaurants and shops for tourists and high-income groups (Sýkora 1993, 1999).

The process of depopulation itself was also socially unequal. Some residents were able to buy their apartments and resell them at significantly higher market rates. The less lucky ones did not obtain ownership of their apartments due to house restitution regulations, or obstacles imposed by local authorities (increasingly aware of the value of centrally located dwellings under municipal ownership). Many residents were then gradually pushed out owing to rising rents or evictions. According to Cooper and Morpeth (1998), some of the new landlords used various dubious tactics to evict lower-income and elderly populations in order to replace them with higher-income tenants or more profitable functions. The private sector generated unprecedented pressure for commercial development, due to which not only residential functions, but also everyday services, such as shops used by permanent residents, were being gradually pushed out of the historic core (Sýkora 1999).

In her study, Simpson (1999) warned against the deterioration of the local atmosphere, the unique sense of place and identity of the historic core, and their replacement with globalized consumption practices and a standardized tourist experience. Insensitive and unregulated approaches towards tourism in Prague's historic core led to street congestion, 'internationalization, creeping homogeneity and a shift away from a "true" history towards a more sanitized and popularized identity', as well as 'a substantial erosion of the sense of place and identity of the historic core' (p. 182) (Figure 4.1). A decade later, a detailed study of the impact of tourism on the most exposed parts of Prague's historic core was undertaken by Kadlecová and Fialová (2010), who observed the attributes of a 'tourism ghetto', 'a compact part of urban area where common city functions have gradually been pushed away, or suppressed by the commercial function, namely by a one-track offer of tourist industry services' (Kadlecová and Fialová 2010: 3). Another recent study conducted by Dumbrovská and Fialová (2014) came to a similar conclusion as Simpson fifteen years ago:

> The Royal Path and the entire Old City and Lesser Town are losing their original values of residential area and transforming into a tourism ghetto. The development of tourism in Prague is not sustainable in the long term and if this negative development continuous without proper regulation, Prague will sooner or later be faced with the effect of a tourism trap.
>
> (p. 23)

Three studies conducted over fifteen years (Simpson 1999; Kadlecová and Fialová 2010; Dumbrovská and Fialová 2014) consequently illustrate the uninterrupted process of the touristification of Prague's historic core throughout the post-socialist history of the city. They all point out that, to date, efforts to put a halt to this unsustainable development have been non-existent or inefficient.

What has caused this situation? In their study of tourism-induced gentrification in Prague, Cooper and Morpeth mention that early post-socialist politicians were highly determined to support accelerated 'compatibility with neo-liberal accumulation regimes' (1998: 2253). In Prague, the desire to achieve the urban model of Western capitalist societies triggered an accelerated introduction of free-market principles and a laissez-faire approach to urban development. Horak's study of Prague's post-communist institutions and democratic development suggests that this approach allowed the creation of a widespread system of corruption in Prague's development, owing to which local politicians have tended to strongly support extensive private capital investments and avoid establishing any long-term planning strategies (Horak 2007). In addition, Cooper and Morpeth refer to the neglect of 'the broader social and environmental objectives of minimizing social exclusion and protecting the nation's cultural heritage' in the post-socialist Czech Republic (1998: 2253), which led to various inappropriate and ill-considered cases of handling historic property and sites (Bečková 2005; Biegel 2005; Horak 2007).

Figure 4.1 Prague's Old Town Square as a 'theme park'? Congestion, touristification and loss of functions for local residents, 2015.

Source: Author.

The emergence of bottom-up social mobilizations surrounding urban issues in post-communist Prague

In post-communist countries, civil society and its forms of mobilisation and action strategies often differ from those in established democracies (Jacobsson and Saxonberg 2013). Czech civil society has a long tradition and has played an important role in the nation's history; however, it was negatively affected by the repressive and restrictive socialist rule. Some forms of civil activism nonetheless existed even during that era (e.g. Vaněk 2002; Jehlička 2005), most notably in the form of the dissident movement, eventually enabling the fall of Communism (Flam 2001; Buden 2013). Nevertheless, the enthusiasm of the Velvet Revolution quickly disappeared and civil society in post-communist Czechoslovakia again became passive (Císař 2008). Thus far, the legacies of the former regime continue, such as the remaining strong role of the state, the public's belief in the state's paternalistic role, the absence of a strong middle class and the interrupted tradition of charitable donations and volunteering, among other factors (Vajdová 2005: 21). Additionally, surveys of social and political involvement show declining public trust in political institutions (except for local municipalities) and a decline in party membership (Kunštát 2014).

Contemporary Czech political activism is characterized by low individual participation. It is quite diversified, including cases of radical activism, self-organization and episodic mass mobilizations, and is dominated by post-materialist demands, mainly concerning the environment and human rights (Císař 2013). With the exception of radical activism, Czech political activism mostly relies on pressuring and lobbying public authorities, and less on collective public protest. The most active of the new social movements are represented mostly by small professionalized advocacy groups with a substantial transactional capacity, i.e. the ability to cooperate with other activist organizations in pursuing their interests, and with an agenda largely influenced by foreign donors (Císař *et al.*, 2011).

With the exception of *Klub Za starou Prahu* [*The Club for Old Prague*] (*KZSP*), a long-existing interest group which has defended Prague's heritage since 1900, forms of activism explicitly concerned with urban issues (including tourism, as will be discussed later) did not fully develop until 2010. In the 2010 municipal elections many voters expressed a clear 'no!' to twenty years of ODS (Civic Democratic Party) politics in Prague, which were characterised by the lack of inclusion of 'a broad range of interest communities in decision-making processes' (Cooper and Morpeth 1998: 2273) – which typically took place behind closed doors (Horak 2007) – and resistance against formulating 'any systematic policy for guiding decision-making' in relation to conservation and development in Prague's historic core (Horak 2007: 201). In 2010 many people therefore voted for a newly created right-wing party, TOP 09. ODS nonetheless created a coalition with the third most voted party (the Czech Social Democrats), side-lining TOP 09 and ostensibly attempting to ensure the continuation of the existing politics and entrenched processes, including constraints on bottom-up, grassroots activities.

Around 2010, members of the public started to increasingly organize in order to protect the city's urban and social fabric, as well as the interests of ordinary residents. With an increasing frequency, active citizens began to criticize urban governance patterns driven by a laissez-faire approach and corruption, and the concomitant touristification, commercialization and depopulation of the inner city. Such issues, initially criticized only by local residents affected by the impacts of touristification on their everyday life, gradually began to be addressed by other activists, and the historic core became a contested area for different groups. Contemporary demands to improve the situation in the historic core, as well as action strategies towards achieving them, are quite complex and diverse. In the following section dealing with the spread of civic engagement and the opening of the municipal government to public input after 2010, we will see that part of the public authorities eventually began to acknowledge the need to reform the ways in which the city's development is managed and have started to engage in a dialogue with activists and urban advocacy professionals.

Most forms of civil engagement analysed in our research are not directly aimed at tourism, but rather at the general deterioration of Prague's historic core (of which the tourism industry is a cause). Both older and younger forms of engagement were identified. Early forms predominantly consisted of individual (or small groups of) residents fighting against displacement, e.g. the defunct *Sdružení nájemníků Prahy* [*Prague 1 Tenants' Association*]; individuals and civic groups concerned with historic preservation (most notably the above mentioned *KZSP*);

and various associations focused on cultural and communal life in centrally located neighbourhoods (*Sdružení občanů a přátel Malé Strany a Hradčan – SOPMSH* [*Association of Citizens and Friends of the Lesser Town and Castle District*]; the somewhat younger *Komunitní centrum Kampa* [*Kampa Community Centre*] and *Sdružení občanů a přátel čtvrti Na Františku* [*Association of Citizens and Friends of the Na Františku Neighbourhood*]), which occasionally engage in protest activities.

Newer forms of engagement since 2010 have mostly consisted of initiatives, associations, NGOs and campaigns led by individual activists. They include Prague's well established, although still relatively young advocacy NGO, *Auto*Mat*, which concerns itself with cycling and public space. It has lobbied for a permanent closure of automobile traffic on Smetanovo nábřeží, a street along the banks of the Vltava River in the historic core. Other groups formed since 2010 include *Praguewatch*, an activist civic association engaged in watchdog activities in the field of urban planning; *Pražské Fórum*, a voluntary civic association pressing for a more transparent and open municipal government; *Buskerville*, a civic initiative founded for the purpose of supporting and promoting busking in Prague; *Piána na ulici* [*Pianos in the Street*], a project enlivening Prague's public space with pianos; *Pragulic*, a social enterprise employing homeless people as alternative tour guides; *Corrupt Tour*, a satiric project for tourists interested in Prague corruption; and *Pražská služba*, an artist group making art interventions to point out various issues in public space. To this list can be added the new association *Pro Jedničku* [*For Prague 1*] (later renamed *Pro1*), founded by discontented residents of Prague 1 in 2014, whose critique of the situation in the historic core resulted in their candidacy in municipal elections. *Pro1* is the only group which has explicitly targeted tourism-related problems such as 'alcohol tourism' – the so-called pub crawls – and Segway tours (Figure 4.1). Also indicative of an increase in bottom-up activism, and therefore included in our research, are the initiators of petitions aimed at saving the following venues and businesses threatened with eviction in the historic core: *U Černého Vola* pub, *La Casa Blů* bar, a traditional hardware shop on 28 Října Street, and a public library in the Castle District. In addition, we included the activities of Prague's squatters and anarchists, a relatively small group making radical claims in the fields of housing and social justice which, over the past few years, have concentrated some of their activities on the historic city centre.

Focus, modes of action and claims of the new urban social mobilizations in the historic centre of Prague

From housing insecurity to collective action: evolution and popular forms of activism in the historic core of post-1989 Prague

Amid the post-socialist euphoria of the 1990s, the first cases of civil activism were initiated by *KZSP* and local residents dealing with issues connected to the processes of housing privatization and restitution. Through this activity, local residents gained their first political experience and laid the foundations of local civic and political life in the historic core. Eventually, the early core of active citizens who challenged the situation in the historic core evolved into a heterogeneous group of people with different levels of political experience – ranging from activists to professional politicians – and with different domiciles – ranging from historic core dwellers to residents of other parts of Prague, and even to people residing outside the city. Some of them pursue their activities to defend personal interests (e.g. *Sdružení nájemníků* fighting against rent deregulation), while others seek to protect the quality of life in the historic core more broadly (e.g. petition initiatives to defend small businesses used by locals), engage in building local communities and cultural life (e.g. events organized by *SOPMSH*) or improve public space and the historic core's management and planning (e.g. activities of *Auto*Mat*).

As previously mentioned, Czechs generally prefer non-violent individual strategies, such as interpellations at city council assemblies, contact with politicians and institutions, publicity in the media or awareness-raising activities (e.g. one active resident, a member of *Pro1*, fought pub crawls and pedestrian-threatening Segway tourism by filming them and sending the videos to relevant institutions). Contested issues that concern larger collectives often involve petitioning. Petition initiatives have mostly been concerned with the use and management of public space and municipal property (e.g. a petition against the use of the Lesser Town Square as a car park; various petitions against expelling traditional and popular enterprises from municipal premises) or activities deemed insensitive to the area of historic preservation and negatively impacting its quality of life (e.g. noisy pub crawls).

Demonstrations are, on the other hand, less commonly used. In 2004 and 2005, there were a few small demonstrations against a new act facilitating further rent deregulation. Attendance was low, since many residents affected by the deregulation did not believe in their ability to affect change. According to a former member of *Sdružení nájemníků Prahy 1* and a lifelong Prague 1 resident who lost his dwelling due to privatization, tenants also tended to be afraid of their landlords. In addition, demonstrators lacked the support of the general public, which was affected by rent deregulation to a lesser extent, or not at all. The demonstrations were ineffective, and many people's housing situation worsened. Somewhat more successful were demonstrations against scandals surrounding heritage protection. Between 2011 and 2013, hundreds of mostly middle-class intellectuals and heritage lovers repeatedly demonstrated against the planned demolition of a house on the corner of Wenceslas Square and Opletalova Street and the intention to replace the undamaged 100-year-old building with a new shopping mall. The protest comprised various other strategies, such as petitions, letter-writing, interpellations and awareness-raising via the media. At the time of writing, the building was still standing, but its fate remained unclear.

The most substantial public mobilizations thus far seem to have been aimed at protecting spaces embodying the city's memory, not surprising in a city where most citizens are proud of the local history and where relatively few face severe material deprivation. Citizens have become increasingly engaged in protecting the way the city was built and used by previous generations, and have fought to preserve specific areas with a distinct *genius loci*, comprising not just heritage sites, but also famous and traditional businesses. These are the causes which have attracted a relatively higher participation in demonstrations against certain demolitions within the PMP, or behind the success of the petition aimed at saving the traditional pub *U Černého Vola* (signed by 4,600 people within the first two days of being launched).

The spread of civic engagement and the opening of the municipal government to public input after 2010

As explained above, an important turning point in relation to citizens' engagement in urban matters was the municipal election of October 2010. In November 2010, citizens' disillusion with Prague politics culminated in two demonstrations against the new city government. Prague then saw an unprecedented development of new citizen initiatives and civic associations concerned with various urban issues. Significantly, these events had important implications in terms of the attitude of the city government towards public input into policy-making. After the 2010 election, the political opposition decided to respond to the public critiques of Prague's management, planning and development. As a result of turbulent turnovers in the municipal government (i.e. several changes of coalition partners), the TOP 09 member Tomáš Hudeček became Prague's councillor for urban planning. In 2012, a platform called *Metropolitní ozvučná deska* [Metropolitan Sounding Board] (*MOZD*) was established to allow representatives of civil society, professionals, academics and politicians to discuss ways of improving the much criticized urban management of the city, including its historic core. In 2013, Hudeček won the post of mayor, and instituted a transformation of the *City Development Authority of Prague* [*Útvar rozvoje města – URM*] into the *Prague Institute of Planning and Development* [*Institut plánování a rozvoje hl. m. Prahy – IPR*], initiating the preparation of Prague's new land-use plan and new strategic plan, both of which would have implications for the historic core.

Several activists representing civil society organizations concerned with urban issues (most notably *Auto*Mat*, *KZSP*), including some of the newer ones (*Praguewatch* and *Pražské Fórum*), were invited to join MOZD to discuss the city's future and new planning documents. Public discussions were also dedicated to the situation in the historic core. A debate on 16 June 2014 was also joined by the Prague City Tourism office, and all MOZD participants agreed that the city centre's touristification process has many drawbacks. However, the prevailing solution proposed has been to advocate the provision of better quality services and the promotion of Prague to a more discerning tourist clientele, i.e. people with higher purchasing power. So far, these discussions have not led to any policy change. The dominant rhetoric of the municipal authorities and other professionals seems to remain focused on the financial gains from tourism, and does not tackle the decreasing liveability of the city centre. Despite the improved attitude of the city government towards public input, incentives for social mobilizations thus remain numerous. Our research identified three broad types and forms of mobilization concerning the historic core of Prague, which differ in terms of their members, methods of action and agenda. These three types, and tensions between them, are analysed in the following sections.

Advocacy and lobbying in Prague 1 district

The slow opening of Prague's city government towards public input is not reflected in all Prague districts. Our research revealed increasing citizens' partici-pation in the assemblies of the Prague 1 District Council, and many individual attempts to contact politicians in order to voice various claims and complaints. However, these are often ineffective. So far the district authorities of Prague 1 have not taken steps towards developing more inclusive forms of decision-making. The fragmentary nature and frequent ineffectiveness of Prague 1 residents' protest activities has resulted in the formation of a new civic association, *Pro1*, which was founded by a group of discontented residents of Prague 1 in 2013 and officially registered in 2014. The group was led at the time of writing by Kateřina Klasnová, a former party politician who became popular among local active residents for her willingness to listen to their complaints, unlike most other representatives of the local government. Members of *Pro1* have been active regarding various issues – against Segway tourism, disturbances caused by organized but unregulated 'alco-hol tourism', massive development projects (mainly new shopping malls and hotels), illegal buildings, the expansion of night economy establishments, non-transparent sales and leases of municipal property and other cases of wasteful expenditure by the local government. Klasnová argued, in an interview, that 'many people think they are alone with their problems' and that *Pro1* can help channel their claims. Individuals can use the group's social capital and knowledge to help solve their issues, and their individual efforts gain more relevance with the group's backing. During the municipal election in October 2014, *Pro1* representatives joined forces with the local Green Party to form the group *Zelená pro Jedničku* [*Green for One*], gaining two councillors on the Prague 1 District Council.

New creative strategies and the fight for public space

Since 2010, issues in the historic core have started to be increasingly addressed by means of 'creative' strategies, such as events, performances, festivals, theme tours, etc. They are mostly pursued by a younger generation, representing part of what could be called Prague's 'creative class', comprised of freelancers, artists and people working in NGOs, whose modus vivendi is to network, both online and offline. Their activities and initiatives, often inspired by foreign examples from other European cities, are driven by specific individuals and quickly change. A typical area of interest is public space: the desire to creatively change the spaces of people's everyday lives and to bring locals (back) into public spaces, especially the historic core, where public space has become dominated by tourists and tourism infrastructure.

Creative strategies in public spaces challenge or highlight contested and controversial issues, sometimes accompanying other forms of protest. An example of this was a human chain created around a block of buildings as a symbolic disagreement with the closure of the Latin bar *La Casa Blů* – one of the last original establishments in the city centre, popular with both locals and foreigners living in Prague, that has not yet fallen sacrifice to retail gentrification. The event was accompanied by petitioning. Both activities were organized by a regular patron with no previous activist experience. *Praguewatch* has organized several thematic tours aimed at critiquing various cases of bad urban development in Prague. In cooperation with *Pražské Fórum*, it organized a parade of activists dressed in medieval costumes and touring around sites epitomizing heritage destruction, reading out loud descriptions of misconduct by authorities, developers and private owners, and criticizing the work of Jan Kněžínek, the then director of the Prague City Hall Heritage Department.

Thematic tours have also been organized by the following groups. *Pragulic*, a social enterprise, employs homeless people as tour guides with the intention of improving the public perception of homelessness. By bringing their clients to sites that conventional visitors never visit or overlook, *Pragulic* provides an alternative to the standard tourist experience. The *Corrupt Tour* is organised by a small organization which seeks to disrupt the dominant glamorizing narratives about the historic core by showing sites that embody the city's clientelistic politics, and by introducing tourists to the city in a less superficial way. Despite its subversive character, the organizers see their enterprise as yet another form of touristic exploitation of the city, i.e. making profit from the city's touristic potential. A positive change in public space was achieved by the initiative *Buskerville*, a small group of musicians who managed to achieve institutional changes leading to the simplification of the system of permits needed by buskers to perform in public spaces – mainly in the historic core. Prior to that, it had been quite rare to encounter live performers in the streets of Prague. Finally, an example of a festival was a series of five street fairs called *Nábřeží žije!*, organized by *Auto*Mat* and other local actors. The fairs took place on Smetanovo nábřeží Street, along the banks of the Vltava River, which has spectacular views of Prague Castle and Charles Bridge. The idea of the fairs was to challenge the street's heavy automobile traffic by turning it temporarily into a space that can be experienced in a pleasant, cultural and sociable way. Obtaining a permit from the authorities to organize such a large-scale event was facilitated by *Auto*Mat*'s long-term professional advocacy in the planning processes of the City of Prague.

The right to the historic core – small-scale radical and resistance activities

More radical claims and forms of resistance occur through the activities of a group of Prague squatters and their supporters, numbering approximately 100. In the Czech Republic, squatting is highly repressed, and after the eviction of the last famous squat in Prague (*Milada*) in 2009, the group's agenda has mainly focused on finding a suitable space for a cultural and social squat. While being spatially unanchored, the hitherto rather self-focused group embarked on a broader critique of the housing market, especially speculative practices, increasing unaffordability and the development of the city's spaces according to their exchange value instead of their use value, serving mostly the interests of the elites and their consumption patterns. The group started to promote people's right to the city and attempted to bring attention to particular issues, including a few in Prague's historic core, where the criticized phenomena are the most tangible. It has organized several rallies, parades and happenings; since 2009, several underused buildings in the city centre have been symbolically occupied, most notably the public baths on Apolinářská Street and the sixteenth-century palace in the Pohořelec, Castle District.

The group has also engaged in helping several tenants affected by their landlords' speculative practices. In the first case, a new landlord attempted to compel remaining tenants to move out of his building in Prague 1 by providing emergency accommodation to people evicted from *Milada*. Squatters nonetheless helped the tenants fight off the owner's contested displacement practices (Pixová 2013). Three years later, a few squatters were asked to help the only remaining tenant in an abandoned residential building in Prague 2, who sought protection from being extorted by his landlords after he had won a lawsuit against their attempt to unlawfully evict him. Having his apartment repeatedly robbed and wrecked, the tenant invited squatters to occupy part of the house in order to gain their protection. In both cases, the landlords eventually managed to enforce their commercial interests by expelling the unwanted dwellers.

The group is still hoping to start a cultural and social squat. Until recently, their marginal position within society and their distrust of authorities inhibited them from turning to professional lobbying or advocacy at the institutional level, and limited their strategies to (mostly unsuccessful) negotiations with private owners of underused property, events and rallies, and raising awareness via the Internet and alternative media. Nonetheless, in 2014 and 2015, some of the squatters joined with other active citizens – mostly young people such as students, artists and activists involved in other mobilizations – and created the initiative *Klinika*, named after an abandoned state-owned clinic that the initiative has claimed for community purposes. The initiative had relatively far-reaching public support and at the time of writing (June 2015), it had been granted temporary permission to use the building by the government. The clinic is not located in the centre of Prague; nonetheless, successful negotiations with national, municipal and district governments are a precedent which can potentially facilitate similar negotiations for buildings in the historic core.

Lines of divisions between urban social mobilizations

If one considers the objectives and strategies displayed by the various citizens' groups mobilized about the city's historic core, a particular distinction emerges, which reflects Prague's divided nature due to tourism as depicted by Hoffman and Musil (2009). Our analysis of mobilizations related to the historic core has shown that residents of the historic core tend to defend their homes, the historic core's liveability, or worry about how district governments manage public resources, while the quality of public space, heritage protection, or the way the city at large is planned, regulated and managed, are issues advocated by activists regardless of their place of residence (i.e. including residents from the wider city who do not live in Prague 1). These broader aspirations are typically driven by the desire to develop Prague as a city that is inclusive, vibrant, diverse, liveable, pedestrian friendly, 'authentic' and with a sustainable tourism industry, but in some cases these aspirations go against the interests of the local residents of Prague 1.

One example was the attempt to permanently close automobile traffic on Smetanovo nábřeží Street, on the basis of an experiment in which the street was used for a fair, called *Nábřeží žije!* (*Living Waterfront*), over five autumn Saturdays in 2013. Preceded by a year-long debate, the event was supported by municipal authorities (especially IPR) as a response to the campaign of several NGOs, particularly *Auto*Mat*, which were advocating a more comprehensive and inclusive management of particular parts of the city centre. Smetanovo nábřeží Street was denounced as an example of a particularly attractive space ruined by the dominance of automobile traffic, and municipal authorities were criticized for their neglectful approach towards local residents and their alleged interests. However, closing traffic on this particular street clearly had not been discussed with local residents – active citizens from the historic core were actually opposed to it, complaining about traffic getting diverted to other neighbourhoods. Members of *SOPMSH* especially complained about the Lesser Town, on the other side of the river, being hit the hardest during the five Saturdays when *Nábřeží žije!* took place.

An inverse example of such antagonism stems from activists' different understanding of the notions of quality of life and public space. While the *Pro1* association has lobbied against the loud and repetitive noise of busking activities, the *Buskerville* initiative has invested a lot of energy into facilitating live performances in the streets. Live performances are attractive for tourists and residents who live outside of the historic core, but locals find them disturbing. *Buskerville* nonetheless argues that the authorities have replaced the repression of busking with ill-advised regulations; busking is supported only in a limited number of areas, and buskers therefore fight for those areas, sometimes even by overpowering each other's music. Non-existing regulations for the length, volume or type of performance further deepen the conflicts. *Pro1* members have also been complaining about night disturbances, disorder and untidy streets caused by tourists participating in pub crawls. These are further perpetuated by a lack of policing, the continuous expansion of the night-time economy in the area around Dlouhá Street and by concentrations of taxis. These complaints are often dismissed by citizens from other parts of Prague, who argue that life in the city centre cannot be expected to be calm. Since many Prague citizens avoid the city centre, few of them are aware of the current situation, nor of the fact that pub crawls might gather up to two hundred drunken foreign visitors who cannot be managed by the usual two-person police patrols. The authorities have dealt with the problem by publishing a map demarcating areas where night noise ordinances apply and installing signboards alerting people to these ordinances.

Controversy also surrounded the case of the group *Pražská služba* painting over the famous Lennon Wall mural in the Lesser Town in white and writing in black 'WALL IS OVER'. Since the 1980s, the wall had been covered by graffiti connected to John Lennon, becoming a symbol of global ideals and young people's resistance against communism. *Pražská služba* reacted to the fact that the wall, which the communist regime had kept repainting, had now become a tourist attraction empty of political meaning. The intervention raised both outrage and support.

Conclusion

The citizens of Prague are well aware of the effects of Prague's touristification. They are nonetheless not against tourism and tourists. From their perspective, tourism itself is not the true cause of problems and conflicts in the historic core. The adverse impacts of tourism, such as commercialization, depopulation and decreasing liveability, are rather seen as the consequence of mismanaged development, mainly blamed on the laissez-faire approach and corruption of the municipal government. To date, explicit opposition against tourism, although small in scale, has been triggered only by the phenomenon of 'alcohol tourism' and Segway tours. Other mobilizations have been mostly driven by opposition to various cases of further deterioration of the historic core, i.e. the demolition of historic buildings, the evictions of traditional venues and businesses or new developments in the PMP. Actors involved in these contestations are both residents of the historic core, as well as activists and organizations concerned more broadly with various urban issues in Prague, frequently concerning heritage conservation and the quality of public space. Most contestations are non-violent, mainly based on communication and lobbying of the authorities or creative strategies. Pressure is typically expressed by petitioning, while demonstrations are usually held only if other strategies fail to bring about change.

With the exception of Prague's squatters, who challenge capitalist urban restructuring by employing direct action in claiming their right to use abandoned buildings, other Czech activists are not making radical claims and are rather 'reformists'. Their demands are based on the belief that most problems, including those connected with tourism, can be solved by good governance and a more efficient performance of the authorities. From their perspective, this would lead to the harmonious development of the entire city, allowing the historic core to function as a sustainable mixed-use area that satisfies both the needs of tourism and local residents. The municipal government has been under mounting pressure to take good care of public spaces and the city's heritage and memory, and replace its laissez-faire approach with more regulation and strategic planning.

In comparison with the initial absence of citizen activism in the 1990s, our research has shown a renaissance of bottom-up activities in local political life on various urban issues. The picture of existing mobilizations in Prague is, however, rather scattered, characterized predominantly by isolated events, endeavours and struggles pursued by groups and individuals that scarcely communicate with each other. Due to the prevailing reformist approach and paternalistic attitude of the Czech public and Czech state, many active citizens have attempted to enter the formal realm of municipal politics. Since 2010, many new political groups and parties (mostly labelled 'independent') have emerged, and in 2014 the number of people running for municipal elections was the highest since 1989 (234,000 in 2014 compared to 160,000 in 1994) (CSO 2015b). Some of their candidates, including quite a few activists from the movements described in this chapter, were successful. However, tourism and the influx of tourists into the city has not, to date, been a central topic in Prague's formal political arena, and tangible policy changes in this area do not look likely. The city government might ban Segway tours or regulate pub crawls. There might be more attractive things to do in the city centre for locals or fewer demolitions of historic buildings. But for the moment, the historic core's touristification process will most likely remain untamed, at least while urban tourism flows are in full bloom.

Note

1 The research is based on long-term observation of developments in Prague's historic core over the period 2009–15, and on 21 in-depth interviews conducted between April 2014 and July 2015 with active citizens and representatives of initiatives related to various local issues. Respondents varied in age and political experience; eleven respondents resided in the historic core, ten outside. Unstructured interviews were also performed with representatives of relevant institutions (i.e. the Prague Institute of Planning and Development, the municipal council and Prague City Tourism – the institution responsible for the city's tourism marketing). This research was supported by Grant no. 14-24977P from the Grant Agency of the Czech Republic as part of the project 'Contested Czech Cities: Citizen Participation in Post-Socialist Urban Restructuring'.

References

[Unless otherwise stated, all URLs were last accessed 4 July 2015.]

Bečková, K. (2005) 'City Hall is not a good guardian of national heritage protection interests', *Bulletin of the Association for Old Prague*, 35(3): 9–12.

Biegel, R. (2005) 'System of national heritage protection and its problems in Prague', *Bulletin of the Association for Old Prague*, 35(3): 5–8.

Buden, B. (2013) *Konec postkomunismu: Od společnosti bez naděje k naději bez společnosti*. Prague: Rybka Publishers.

Císař, O. (2008) *Politický aktivismus v České republice. Sociální hnutí a občanská společnost v době transformace a evropeizace*. Brno: Centrum pro studium demokracie a kultury.

Císař, O. (2013) 'A typology of extra-parliamentary political activism in post-communist settings: the case of the Czech Republic', in K. Jacobsson and S. Saxonberg (eds) *Beyond NGO-ization. The Development of Social Movements in Central and Eastern Europe*. Aldershot: Ashgate.

Císař, O., Navrátil, J. and Vráblíková, K. (2011) 'Staří, noví, radikální: politický aktivismus v České republice očima teorie sociálních hnutí', *Czech Sociological Review*, 47(1): 137–67.

Cooper, C. and Morpeth, N. (1998) 'The impact of tourism on residential experience in Central-eastern Europe: the development of a new legitimation crisis in the Czech Republic', *Urban Studies*, 35(12): 2253–75.

CSO (Czech Statistical Office) (2014) *Sčítání lidu, domů a bytů 2011.* Online. Available at https://www.czso.cz/csu/sldb.

CSO (Czech Statistical Office) (2015a) *Cestovní ruch v Hl. m. Praze v roce 2014.* Online. Available at https://www.czso.cz/csu/xa/cestovni-ruch-v-hl-m-praze-v-roce-2014.

CSO (Czech Statistical Office) (2015b) *Volby.cz.* Online. Available at http://volby.cz/.

Dumbrovská, V. and Fialová, D. (2014) 'Tourist intensity in capital cities in Central Europe: comparative analysis of tourism in Prague, Vienna and Budapest', *Czech Journal of Tourism*, 3(1): 5–26.

Flam, H. (2001) *Pink, Purple, Green. Women's, Religious, Environmental, and Gay/ Lesbian Movements in Central Europe Today.* New York: Columbia University Press.

Hoffman, L. M. and Musil, J. (1999) 'Culture meets commerce: tourism in postcommunist Prague', in D. Judd and S. Fainstein (eds) *The Tourist City.* New Haven, CT: Yale University Press.

Hoffman, L. M. and Musil, J. (2009) *Prague, Tourism and the Post-industrial City.* Chicago: Great Cities Institute, University of Illinois at Chicago.

Horak, M. (2007) *Governing the Post-Communist City: Institutions and Democratic Development in Prague.* Toronto: University of Toronto Press.

Jacobsson, K. and Saxonberg, S. (eds) (2013) *Beyond NGO-ization. The Development of Social Movements in Central and Eastern Europe.* Aldershot: Ashgate.

Jehlička, P. (2005) 'The Czech environmental movement's knowledge interests in the 1990s: compatibility of Western influences with pre-1989 perspectives', *Environmental Politics*, 14(1): 64–82.

Kadlecová, V. and Fialová, D. (2010) *Královská cesta v Praze – vizitka Česka.* Paper presented at the conference *Aktuální problémy cestovního ruchu*, Jihlava, 3–4 March. Online. Available at http://geography.cz/wp-content/uploads/2009/11/pozvanka.pdf.

Kunštát, D. (2014) *Důvěra ústavním institucím v březnu 2014. Zpráva z výzkumu CVVM.* Online. Available at http://cvvm.soc.cas.cz/media/com_form2content/documents/c1/a7202/f3/pi140324.pdf.

Lux, M. (2004) 'Housing the poor in the Czech Republic: Prague, Brno and Ostrava', in J. Fearn (ed.) *Too Poor to Move, Too Poor to Stay.* Budapest: Local Government and Public Service Reform Initiative.

Lux, M. and Mikeszová, M. (2012) 'Property restitution and private rental housing in transition: the case of the Czech Republic', *Housing Studies*, 27(1): 77–96.

Musil, J. (2001) 'Vývoj a plánování měst ve střední Evropě v období komunistických režimů', *Sociologický časopis*, 37(3): 275–96.

Ouředníček, M. and Temelová, J. (2008) *Socioekonomická analýza území MČ P1. Druhá etapa plnění úkolu 1.1. – 30.4.2008.* Online. Available at http://www.praha1.cz/cps/media/Socioekonomicka_analyza_uzemi_MC_Praha_1_-_Etapa_II.pdf.

Pixová, M. (2013) 'Spaces for alternative culture in Prague in a time of political-economic changes of the city', *Geografie – Sborník ČGS*, 118(2): 221–42.

Polívková, H. (2001) 'Aktualizace studie Pražské památkové rezervace', *Věstník Klubu Za starou Prahu*, no. 1–2. Online. Available at http://stary-web.zastarouprahu.cz/ruzne/ppr1.htm.

Simpson, F. (1999) 'Tourist impact in the historic centre of Prague: resident and visitor perceptions of the historic built environment', *Geographical Journal*, 165(2): 173–83.

Sládek, J. (2013) 'The privatisation of state housing stock in the Czech Republic – a path dependent process?', *Sociológia*, 45(3): 267–89.

Smith, D. M. (1996) 'The socialist city', in G. Andrusz, M. Harloe and I. Szelenyi (eds) *Cities After Socialism*. Oxford: Blackwell.

Sýkora, L. (1993) 'City in transition: the role of rent gaps in Prague's revitalization', *Tijdschrift voor Economische en Sociale Geografie*, 84(4): 281–93.

Sýkora, L. (1999) 'Proměny vnitřní prostorové struktury postkomunistické Prahy', *Acta Facultatis Studiorum Humanitatis et Naturae Universitatis Prešoviensis – Folia Geographica*, 32(3): 98–103.

Sýkora, L. (2009) 'Post-socialist cities', in R. Kitchin and N. Thrift (eds) *International Encyclopaedia of Human Geography*, Vol. 8. Oxford: Elsevier, pp. 387–95.

Vajdová, T. (2005) *Česká občanská společnost 2004: po patnácti letech rozvoje. Zpráva z projektu CIVICUS Civil Society Index pro Českou republiku*. Online. Available at: http://docplayer.cz/348478-Ceska-obcanska-spolecnost-2004-po-patnacti-letech-rozvoje-zprava-z-projektu-civicus-civil-society-index-pro-ceskou-republiku-1.html.

Vaněk, M. (2002) *Ostrůvky svobody – kulturní a občanské aktivity mladé generace v 80. letech v Československu*. Praha: Votobia.

5 Density wars in Silicon Beach

The struggle to mix new spaces for toil, stay and play in Santa Monica, California

Deike Peters

The ocean-side community of Santa Monica is one of California's premier tourist destinations. It covers just under 22 square kilometres and is home to about 90,000 residents. Santa Monica is encircled on all sides by Los Angeles (LA), a city of 3.5 million people that in turn lies at the heart of the LA metropolitan region, which – at 18 million people spread out across 12,500 square kilometres – is one of the largest urban agglomerations in the world. Market analysts contend that Santa Monica has now gone 'from beach town to boom town' (White 2013), with a slew of dense, mixed-use development projects slated for completion in the near future that many see as a tipping point in the city's development. Creative industries (film, fashion, new media and tech companies) along with tourism activity dominate the economic landscape. Urban tourism has now been clearly recognized as a driving force in the urban politics and governance of US cities (Judd 2002; Eisinger 2000), and Santa Monica is no exception. Newcomers and temporary visitors clash with long-term residents in their visions for the city's future, and the new, developer-friendly climate in Santa Monica is seen in stark contrast to 'the People's Republic of Santa Monica's' earlier tradition of lower-density, slow growth, progressive urban development policies that were focused on the supply of public benefits. Yet these public benefits – well-maintained parks, affordable housing, good public transit and parking – were precisely the key elements that distinguished Santa Monica from its larger neighbour Los Angeles and made the city a more attractive place to live, work, visit and play in the first place.[1]

In the case of Santa Monica, the somewhat familiar story of a well-governed, progressive, attractive place becoming victim of its own success contains some interesting twists, and these will be the focus of this chapter. Following a short historical review linking developments in Santa Monica to longer-term and larger processes of urban revitalization, the chapter will unpack the complex scales of protest and resistance in tourism-related developments. Three different vignettes will discuss (a) the unionization efforts of Santa Monica's hotel workers; (b) residents' reservations and resistance against additional densification in general and three key visitor-oriented development sites in the Civic Center, Bergamot and Downtown areas in particular; and finally (c) new debates surrounding the recent heavy 'airbnbfication' of housing in Santa Monica and in

Figure 5.1 Aerial view of Santa Monica, 2015.

Source: Google Earth, map data by Google, labels added by author.

adjacent Venice Beach. The vignettes will reveal new fault lines among protagonists, not just between recent and long-term residents but also along ethnic, generational and class lines. There is an important flip-side to the cliché of the elderly, white anti-development resident: a majority of Santa Monicans between the ages of 18 and 24 strongly supports new hotel development, and over 70 per cent of Hispanics are in support of proposals for new hotels in downtown (Godbe Research 2014: 60–1). At the same time, young and minority residents are typically those most affected by the housing affordability crisis in the city, while the recent influx of young, mostly white and often well-to-do tech workers moving down from Northern California's Silicon Valley additionally complicates the picture in Santa Monica.

Santa Monica, California: from beach city to 'Silicon Beach' boom town

From beach city to 'Silicon Beach'

Santa Monica is one of America's quintessential 'tourist cities'. As California became the United States' 31st state in 1850, the Mexican ranchos of Santa Monica changed hands and declined. Tourism soon became an inseparable ingredient in the city's prosperity. As gold seekers arrived in Southern California, Santa Monica quickly developed into the region's first recreational resort, with vacationers sometimes prospecting for gold along the beaches (Garbee *et al.* 2007: 20). Soon after the arrival of the Southern Pacific Railroad in the 1890s, Santa Monica lost out to San Pedro as the location for Los Angeles' major seaport, enabling the town to maintain its quaint seaside charm. Tobacco millionaire and land developer Abbot Kinney developed the Ocean Park neighbourhood and its adjacent 'Venice of America', providing significant new residential areas alongside Santa Monica's first of many major amusement parks. A whole string of wooden piers were built, key among them the Santa Monica Pier, the only one remaining today. Railroad and development magnate Henry Huntington invited the Hawaiian-Irish surfer George Freeth to the coast in 1907 to promote his Pacific Electric Railroad lines, paying him to demonstrate his skills at several venues along the beach. Freeth's surfing and swimming lessons drew significant crowds and are credited with increasing ridership along Pacific Electric's beach routes. The city's population doubled to exceed 30,000 by the 1920s, and resort tourism became increasingly important in the city's economic mix. The Miramar Hotel and the Club Casa del Mar opened their doors and the area surrounding Marion Davis' Ocean House mansion became known as the Gold Coast. Santa Monica Bay became a key location for film production and film-star living.

Donald Douglas Sr built his first Aircraft Plant along with the airfield at Clover Park in Santa Monica in 1921, employing over 40,000 people by the early 1940s, many of them women. Douglas remained the area's largest employer throughout the 1950s (Garbee *et al.* 2007: 27). From the late nineteenth century until the 1950s, a large number of amusement piers lined the Santa Monica shoreline, yet all but one were eventually brought down by storms, fire or bankruptcy. The opening of the Santa Monica freeway in 1966 promised to improve accessibility and bring additional economic development but it was routed through and thus tragically decimated Santa Monica's long-established African-American enclave in the Pico District. Throughout the 1960s and 1970s, the city's economic base changed significantly. The Douglas plant closed in 1968. Some health and sports-related businesses opened but the economy slowed overall. Many residents liked the slower pace of life in the city. By the late 1970s, Santa Monicans for Renters' Rights (SMRR) was founded and soon emerged as a major local political force, gaining a council majority by the early 1980s and being instrumental in passing a rent control ordinance, partially as a response to early gentrification along Main Street and other parts of Ocean Park.

A new indoor mall, Santa Monica Place, was built in 1980, directly competing with the adjacent outdoor mall that opened in 1965 on Third Street. The eventual revitalization and transformation of the outdoor mall into the highly successful Santa Monica Third Street Promenade further cemented Santa Monica's reputation as a desirable place for play and stay. The city re-zoned multiplexes out of other areas, forcing them to relocate along the mall, bringing in millions of dollars of investment. Interestingly, Third Street's successful reinvention was not led by local business leaders but by then-mayor Denny Zane, one of the early SMRR leadership figures and someone Santa Monica residents inherently trusted (Pojani 2008: 147).

Since the late 1980s, economic and tourism development have been on a steady upward trend, much of it owing to the high quality of life progressive politicians were able to create and maintain in Santa Monica by consistently investing in public infrastructure, services, education and public amenities. The 1990s saw the opening of several new high-end hotels in the city, most notably Shutters On The Beach between the pier and Pico Boulevard, the Loews and Casa del Mar. The coastal stretch running from Santa Monica to Venice and Marina del Rey is now considered Southern California's second most popular tourist destination, behind Disneyland but ahead of Hollywood and Downtown Los Angeles (Wallace *et al.* 2014). In the new millennium, hotel development became increasingly complemented with the relocation of major tech firms to the area.

Although Santa Monica is generally considered a model city for urban sustainability planning in the US (Farr 2012: 78; Riposa 2004), it still struggles to keep its famous beaches clean and water healthy (NRDC 2014: 2). Santa Monica also houses a large homeless population, is increasingly gridlocked by traffic and faces issues of displacement and a crisis of affordability.

Play, toil and stay: Santa Monica as a place to visit, work and live in

Santa Monica's 92,185 residents have a median income of $62,816 (City Data n.d.). Two-thirds are renters, 63 per cent are White and 13 per cent Hispanic. Compare this to LA's 3.9 million residents: their median income is $46,491, 52 per cent are renters (still the highest among major US cities) and the racial mix is 49 per cent Hispanic, 28 per cent White, 10 per cent Asian and 8.5 per cent Black (Civic Publications 2015). Median rents in Santa Monica climbed to $3,595 by mid-2015, compared to $2,300 in the LA metro area (according to www.zillow.com). Santa Monica has over 9,000 businesses, including branch offices for entertainment industry giants like MTV Networks, Universal Music Group and Lionsgate Universal and technology giants such as Google, Apple, Microsoft and, soon, Intel. In recent years, many tech start-ups from the Bay Area's Silicon Valley have relocated or opened new offices in Santa Monica, Venice and nearby Playa Vista, earning the area the name Silicon Beach.

The city's official tourism board, the Santa Monica Convention and Visitor's Bureau (SMCVB), recorded record numbers for 2014: 7.9 million visitors generated $1.72 billion in revenue. Visitors' average length of stay was just 1.44 days (but overnight visitors stayed an average of five days). With a transient occupancy tax rate of 14 per cent, these overnight stays added $45.5 million to the city's General Fund (up 7.6 per cent from 42.3 million in 2012). Overnight visitors accounted for 67 per cent of visitor spending in 2014, down from 77 per cent the previous year. International visitors accounted for 55.5 per cent of visitors in 2014 and mostly came from Australia/New Zealand, England, Canada, Mexico and various EU countries (SMCVB 2015). Two-thirds of visitors mainly visit Santa Monica for pleasure/vacation, but one key business event is the American Film Market, held every November in the Loews Hotel. The AFM brings 8,000 people from 70 countries to Santa Monica for a week to sell, finance or buy films. Beach hotels are converted into movie marketplaces and the whole city is abuzz with movie screenings, conferences and parties.

Tourism as an integral part of urban development in Santa Monica: conflicts and key stakeholders

Santa Monica is a city with a lively history of political activism. Resident groups are sometimes divided between renters and homeowners and between business owners and employees, but overall, a loud and strong political force exists in this city advocating for 'slow(er) growth', i.e. a kind of economic growth that shuns massive development projects and resists city plans for additional office development even when it comes packaged as part of mixed-use projects that also propose residential and hotel units. Santa Monica may only have about 90,000 residents, but with work commuters, beachgoers and tourists, the city's daytime population can swell to anywhere from 250,000 to 450,000 people, with weekend congestion at times surpassing weekday rush hour traffic. Not surprisingly, many residents are thus increasingly wary of any developments further exacerbating this trend.

Urban politics in Santa Monica has also long been defined by a stark contrast between its upper class, increasingly super-rich, celebrity-studded and over-whelmingly white North of Montana area, where the median sales price for residential homes lay above $3 million in 2014 and median household incomes are above $115,000, and the Pico area to the south, where individual homes sell for a quarter of the price and median household incomes are around $57,000.

Santa Monica has been governed by a city charter reliant upon a mayor–council system since 1906, but corruption and inefficiency in the 1930s brought about the adoption of a new city charter in 1946, which is still active today. It is still based on a council system, with seven city council members reviewing, setting and passing key local laws and decisions. Political forces in the city remain divided between (the nominal majority of) renters and (politically well organized) home-owners as well as business owners and developers, including hotels. For the last three decades, the political action committee (PAC) Santa Monicans for Renters Rights (SMRR) has dominated Santa Monica local politics. All council members, school board officials and planning commissioners elected in the 2013 mid-term elections had been endorsed by SMRR.[2] SMRR is by no means a monolithic organization, however, covering a spectrum ranging from fierce anti-development individuals to moderate players more amenable to responsible development. In 2014, SMRR for the first time endorsed a slate of all anti-development candidates. Renters also cover an increasingly wide demographic spectrum, representing many different ethnicities, income brackets and political viewpoints.

Hotel workers are politically organized through Unite Here! Local 11, the local hospitality workers union that traditionally turned out to support SMRR-endorsed candidates, often joining forces and bringing in lots of volunteers for door-to-door campaigns. The fight for hotel workers' unionization and living wage campaigns was primarily led by an organization called Santa Monicans Allied for Responsible Tourism (SMART). But few hospitality workers can afford to live in Santa Monica, which weakens their voice. On the pro-development, pro-business side, the key local PAC is Santa Monicans United for a Responsible Future

(SMURF). They often stand diametrically opposed to the city's leading anti-development group Santa Monica Coalition for a Livable City (SMCLC). In 2014 a new anti-development group called Residocracy rose to the fore over resistance against a large mixed-use project in the Bergamot area, a fight described in more detail in vignette II. Many other specific-purpose PACs supporting or fighting a multitude of causes exist, most recently relating to the closure of Santa Monica's small aircraft airport.

Protest and resistance in the tourist city: three vignettes

The three vignettes below illustrate some of the central fault lines that exist in urban economic and tourism development in Santa Monica today.

Vignette I: Hotel workers campaigning for a living wage – protesting and resisting tourism-related exploitation

Despite the city's heavy reliance on tourism, workers and residents have resisted 'selling out' to tourism's private interests. The movement that received the most attention is the living wage campaign led in the early 2000s by Santa Monicans Allied for Responsible Tourism (SMART). While eventually evolving into a much broader community movement, SMART formed in 1996 to fight an effort by the Fairmont Miramar Hotel, a historic beachfront luxury hotel in downtown Santa Monica, to decertify its union. Originally built in 1924, the Fairmont then remained the city's last unionized hotel. The coalition included the Hotel Employees and Restaurant Employees Union (HERE), community activists, clergymen as well as the Los Angeles Alliance for a New Economy (LAANE), a local research and advocacy organization (Erskine and Marblestone 2006: 250). After its success in the union fight, the coalition moved on to a tackle a new element of workers' rights: a living wage.[3] Benefitting from city investment and a policy that froze hotel development in the 1980s, many of Santa Monica's hotels still paid some of the lowest wages in the state – an average of $14,250 a year with no health benefits (Flad 2002; Gottlieb *et al.* 2006). In 1997, supported by LAANE, the Los Angeles City Council passed a living wage, and Pasadena passed its own ordinance during the same time period. Inspired by LAANE's success in LA, SMART decided to bring the living wage to Santa Monica, specifically to the exploited hotel workers of the city's tourism industry. Mobilizing a broad-based coalition of community activists, hotel workers, college students, law students and community members new to activism, SMART popularized the idea of introducing a living wage in Santa Monica and by 2000 had drafted a living wage ordinance (LWO) to recommend to the Santa Monica City Council. The proposed ordinance was designed to target the businesses in the city's coastal zone, which benefitted the most from the tourism industry and had the greatest proportion of low-wage workers (Erskine and Marblestone 2006: 251). The living wage itself was set at $10.69/hour plus health benefits (or an additional $2.50/hour if not provided).

Before the city could approve or reject the proposal, a business coalition of opponents pre-empted SMART's LWO by getting its own 'living wage' proposal placed on the November 2000 ballot as Proposition KK. The coalition misleadingly called itself Santa Monicans for a Living Wage, and proposed a much weaker LWO that featured a wage of $8.52/hour and applied only to city employees and businesses receiving $25,000 in city contracts, thus covering only about 62 people in total. Thanks to intensive campaigning and canvassing by SMART Proposition KK did not pass (Erskine and Marblestone 2006: 252). After the election, the City Council began working again with SMART and the business community to draft an LWO for the city. Some of the council members were concerned about the legality of indirectly targeting a specific industry and as a result, the actual ordinance adopted by the City Council was less ambitious than the original proposal, dropping the required wage to $10.50/hour and applying only to businesses grossing more than $5 million in a year (City of Santa Monica 2001).

The LWO nonetheless met business opposition yet again, this time with a coalition called Fighting Against Irresponsible Regulation (FAIR). FAIR lead a referendum campaign to put the recently approved LWO on the ballot for repeal. Despite SMART's efforts to discourage people from signing petitions, FAIR got the required 10 per cent of voters to sign, and Measure JJ to repeal the LWO appeared on the ballot. In another act of questionable politics, three weeks before the election, FAIR used the Political Reform Act to create three committees called 'Quality Schools Coalition', 'Pro-Choice Voters Committee' and 'Democratic Voters Ballot Guide' and sent out pamphlets to make it appear as if these groups were against the Santa Monica LWO. Predictably, on voting day, Santa Monica's LWO was rejected and subsequently repealed. SMART later organized a public hearing on the election to expose FAIR's deceptive tactics, but while FAIR was found guilty, the repeal held (Erskine and Marblestone 2006: 253–5).

Despite the LWO's failure at the polls, Santa Monica and HERE did not give up on the living wage. In 2005 the city of Santa Monica officially adopted an LWO into its city code, setting a moving living wage requirement for city employees and the employees of city contractors that reached $15.37 in 2014, as per the Santa Monica Municipal Code, Chapter 4.65. Additionally, several hotels came to individual agreements with the union and others instated higher wages as part of their development agreement (DA) process with the city (Islas 2013a, 2013b). The political climate in the rest of LA County has also been changing quickly. In 2012 Long Beach passed a minimum wage of $13/hour. Los Angeles, meanwhile, passed a minimum wage of $15.37 for all hotel workers in 2014 (Lowery 2012; Walton 2014) and then made national headlines in 2015 with a commitment to push its general minimum wage to $15/hour by 2020 (Lazo 2015).

Vignette II: Residents waging density wars: protesting and resisting dense mixed-use projects

Homeowners and renters in Santa Monica are often united in their concerns over overdevelopment in Santa Monica, but alliances can be brittle. This second vignette is best begun by a quick look at Santa Monica's Land Use and Circulation Element (LUCE), a hefty 540-page major planning document approved in 2010 after a series of lengthy and heated public debates that started in 2004 (City of Santa Monica 2010). Visionary in many ways, Santa Monica's LUCE won several major local and national planning awards. Among other things, the plan calls for the development of a new Specific Plan for Downtown, the city's main commercial and visitor destination, and dedicates significant attention to two other major areas where battles over development have been fierce: the Civic Center Area, for which a Specific Plan is already in its implementation phase, and the so-called Bergamot Area, a clustering of creative sector venues where residents successfully mixed plans for a major mixed-use redevelopment project in 2014.

In fact, by regular North American urban development standards, the LUCE is incredibly restrictive, specifying that almost all of the city's remaining undeveloped land area should be conserved and that land use changes in the city should be directed to commercial and industrial areas that comprise only 4 per cent of the land area, mainly concentrated around the Civic Center and Bergamot areas. Both areas lie mostly within walking distance of a new light rail line that is set to open in 2016, allowing residents, workers and visitors direct transit access to many key LA locations, including Downtown LA. The intention to locate future development near this important new transit line was a huge impetus for the development of the LUCE, and for rethinking development in Santa Monica more generally.

In the Civic Center area, two adjoining redevelopment projects have just been completed. The area is cut off from the dense, vibrant Downtown commercial area by the I-10 Freeway and features overly wide streets and an overabundance of parking lot space. The landscape 'starchitecture' firm, James Corner Field Operations, best known for designing the Highline in NYC, moulded six acres of surface lots into the award-winning Tongva Park, completed in the fall of 2013. With its different themed hills, meadows, curved walkways alongside drought-tolerant gardens and striking vista points overlooking the ocean, the park became an instant hit with many residents and visitors. Immediately adjacent to Tongva Park, the Village at Santa Monica mixes 160 affordable rental units with 158 luxury residences developed by Related Companies and partners. A central feature is the 'walk street' through the site that connects pedestrians from Main Street to Ocean Avenue and is dotted with retail, restaurants and landscaped plazas. Public reactions to the project cover the entire spectrum from praise to outrage. The LEED-Silver-certified affordable Belmar apartments, which included work/live studios with roll-up fronts as well as 1–3 bedroom apartments, were targeted at artists, actors and other creative class workers rather than low-income hotel or other service sector workers, who were priced out of Santa Monica long ago. Lottery applications were provided via the Actors Fund (2013). Rents were as low as $439/month for studios and $650/month for three bedrooms, compared to Santa Monica's average rental price of $2,600/month (Logan 2014). The two luxury condo complexes, the Waverly and the Seychelles, meanwhile, offer 1–3 bedroom residences priced between $1 and $4 million dollars.

Amenities offered at these locations are largely congruent with those of a high-end luxury hotel.

For the Bergamot area, the City developed an entirely new plan. In June 2013, a draft document of over 200 pages was released after extensive community feedback (City of Santa Monica 2013). Like the LUCE, the Bergamot Area plan was a solid planning effort that sought to address the essential struggles of densification in Santa Monica via a long-term vision that hoped to transform this rather drab light-industrial and commercial area into a transit-accessible, bike- and walk-friendly district for creative-class workers and, increasingly, outside visitors. Planners envisioned the future of the area as one where visitors would arrive by light rail or bicycle to enjoy the art galleries, improved amenities and dining options as well as a new boutique hotel. However, while planning efforts for a revamped Bergamot Arts Center appear to be moving forward, the corresponding plans for the adjoining Bergamot Transit Village were toppled by community resistance.

On 4 February 2014 Santa Monica's City Council approved the Bergamot Transit Village (BTV), a massive 765,000 square foot (about 70,000 square metres) mixed-use development project on the site of an old Papermate factory sitting adjacent to the future Exposition light rail transit stop at 26th Street and Olympic Avenue. BTV included 375,000 square feet of creative office space, 29,300 square feet of retail and 330,000 square feet of housing (471 apartments and 27 live/work units for artists). As a commercial developer, owner Hines underemphasized the residential potential of the site while at the same time drawing the immediate ire of locals worried about additional traffic impacts in an area with already nightmarish congestion.

In January 2014, Residocracy, a new 'slow-growth' group emerged, quickly vying to become a major political force. Residocracy founder Armen Melkonians led the campaign for a veto referendum petition, which was also supported by SMRR, SMCLC and many other community groups including all seven surrounding neighbourhood associations. They were mainly concerned that BTV would bring up to 7,000 new daily car trips to the area.[4] Their petition gathered 13,500 signatures, far more than the 6,091 required, thus forcing the City Council to act. Rather than put the veto referendum on the 4 November 2014 election ballot, the council voted to rescind the development plan. Residocracy's activism ultimately resulted in the developer Hines walking away from the entire project and selling the Papermate factory site to another developer, Clarion, which wants to reactivate existing entitlements and simply redevelop the site for office use as of right. Clarion will thus not need to provide any of the community-oriented benefits or innovative street redesigns associated with the larger mixed-use residential/retail/office project, although their bland project will still generate similar amounts of additional car trips. As Barragan (2015) aptly summarized, 'BVT opponents were worried about traffic and they're going to get it anyway.' Clearly, slow-growth proponents once again held the upper hand in Santa Monica by successfully stopping a large mixed-use project, but the pyrrhic nature of this victory is hard to miss. The proponents of 'slow growth' are primarily older, white residents, many of whom are homeowners. This stands in sharp contrast to the 96 per cent of the

city's Hispanics and 75 per cent of Asian Americans who had been fully supportive of the Bergamot plan (Godbe Research 2014; Smith 2014).

Another important recent battleground for contested development takes us back
to the Fairmont Miramar Hotel. Located on Ocean Avenue just one block away
from the Third Street Promenade, the Miramar was designated as a 'prominent site'
for community development in the city's General Plan, according to the 2010
LUCE amendment (Epstein 2013). In 2011 the hotel proposed a LUCE-friendly
plan to develop the site into a mixed-use location with larger hotel rooms, underground parking, expanded food, beverage and retail space, condominiums, a one-
acre public park space and an off-site affordable housing project (Santa Monica
Daily Press 2011). The project sparked immediate controversy and fierce opposition by the adjacent Huntley Hotel. As the two largest hotels in Santa Monica, they
are clear economic rivals. The Huntley lies just to the east of Miramar on the other
side of Second Street, and Miramar's building plans put the Huntley's ocean views
in jeopardy. Given its size, the Miramar proposal is subject to the city's so-called
'float-up process', in which proposed projects are to be presented at public hearings
with the community and the Planning Commission before complete plans are
made. Public interest was tremendous: early hearings were standing room only.

While many were in support of the revitalization project, many other locals
were concerned about bringing in such dense development, especially when it
had the potential to block the ocean views of those who lived and worked nearby.
The Huntley, eager to fuel this fire, formed Santa Monicans Against the Miramar
Expansion (SMATME) and began distributing anti-development flyers and other
informational materials, warning of increased traffic, loss of street-level light and
calling the project 'Miramarmageddon' (Santa Monica Daily Press 2012). From
here the mudslinging continued, reaching almost comical proportions. Miramar
responded to the Huntley's campaigning with a PR strategy of its own, launching
a website called HuntleyFacts.com, which accused the Huntley of being against
organized labour (the Huntley is a non-unionized hotel) and affordable housing,
committing tax evasion and of making questionable campaign contributions to
try to block the Miramar expansion (Huntley n.d.). In response to public
comments Miramar changed its plan in 2013 to a layout that will maintain the
current footprint of the hotel (thus reducing ocean view obstruction), but also
features a 21-storey tower (Archibald 2013). This appeased many community
members, but some, including the Huntley, still continued to protest vehemently.
The fight has gone on in PR campaigns, opinion pieces, community polls and
threats of legal action. At the time of writing (mid-2015) Miramar was still planning to go through with their project but will have to continue to contest with
strong and adamant opposition from anti-development advocates.

Vignette III: Rethinking the new 'sharing economy' – protesting and resisting the 'Airbnbification' of Santa Monica

While many residents are opposed to new and expanded hotel operations, many
are equally dismayed at the recent expansion of 'hotel alternatives' in their city.

Similar to other popular urban tourist destinations around the world (see Opillard on San Francisco in this volume), Santa Monica has seen a spectacular rise in so-called 'sharing economy' offerings via sites such as Airbnb. The overall situation is still somewhat messy, murky and in flux, with less clearly defined front lines of protest and resistance than in the other two vignettes. Airbnb turns residents into hosts and thus into competitors for the hotel industry. By extension, it potentially pits increasingly squeezed renters in the least affordable market in the nation against struggling hotel workers. But while Airbnb may have started out in 2007 as (mostly) a 'sharing economy' concept promoting simple peer-to-peer rentals, it is now at a very different stage of its operations. At around $13 billion, Airbnb has a higher market value than hotel giants Hyatt or Wyndham (at $8.4 and $9.3 billion, respectively) (Bradshaw 2014, also cited in Saman 2015: 5). The highly successful 'culting' of its brand (Atkin 2004) is based upon establishing a sense of community among its customers who are to buy into Airbnb's 'San Francisco air mattress' founding myth. In a blatant act of self-boosterism and rhetoric of 'community building', the company released an 'analysis' immodestly entitled *Airbnb's Positive Impact in Los Angeles*, claiming that host incomes and visitors' spending generated an overall economic impact of $312 million while supporting 2,600 jobs (Airbnb 2015a, 2015b). This is how Airbnb characterizes its local 'community':

> Airbnb hosts in the City of Los Angeles have been welcoming guests into their homes since late 2008. Over the past six years, Los Angeles residents have formed a vibrant Airbnb community, sharing unique experiences with travellers from around the world. [. . .] Between May 2013 and April 2014, 4,490 Los Angeles hosts welcomed guests into their homes. [. . .] 38 per cent of hosts are low to middle income, [earning] below $65,900/year. Almost half of Airbnb hosts work in the arts, entertainment and recreation occupations.
>
> (Airbnb 2015a)

The spin in the corresponding press release is even more extreme, basically recasting Airbnb not as a multi-billion dollar business empire but as a charitable, environmentally beneficial endeavour that 'can help locals out' in multiple ways:

> 'Home sharing helps Angelenos stay in their homes, pursue creative careers, and share the city they love with visitors from around the world,' said Airbnb Regional Head of Public Policy David Owen. 'Nearly three quarters of all Airbnb hosts use the money they earn to stay in their homes and about 30 per cent of hosts say hosting helped them to start a new business.' [. . .] 'Many hosts are aspiring stars in the entertainment industry, and the additional income from Airbnb is what allows them to keep their LA dreams alive.' By helping residents share their homes, Airbnb also promotes the efficient use of existing resources and a more environmentally sustainable way of traveling. The study found that home sharing results in a significant reduction in

energy, water use and waste generation, compared to hotel stays, and also encourages sustainability awareness among both residents and visitors.

(Ibid.)

A closer look at Santa Monica's and Los Angeles' Airbnb market reveals this rhetoric that touts win-win 'creative class peer sharing' as a preferable, personalized alternative to hotel booking as a partial truth at best (for additional insights, also see http://www.insideairbnb.com). The listed units are a far cry from the proverbial 'actor's couch' lower-income tourists were supposed to crash on: nearly 90 per cent of the rental offers were for whole units, often listed by leasing companies with multiple units. By early 2015, as many as 8,400 hosts and more than 11,400 units were listed for rent in Los Angeles (which for the purposes of the report included all of Santa Monica) via the rental site, clearly indicating its growing influence on the Los Angles tourism sector. And Santa Monica and the adjacent beach community of Venice Beach together were responsible for a whopping 40 per cent of total Airbnb revenue in Los Angeles (Saman 2015: 29). Yet contrary to Airbnb's own claims, a report by the Los Angeles Alliance for a New Economy (Saman 2015) detailed how this impact is likely to be negative rather than positive, especially in the longer term:

> By incentivizing the large-scale conversion of residential units into tourist accommodations, Airbnb forces neighbourhoods and cities to bear the costs of its business model. Residents must adapt to a tighter housing market. Increased tourist traffic alters neighbourhood character while introducing new safety risks. Cities lose out on revenue that could have been invested in improving the basic quality of life for its residents. Jobs are lost and wages are lowered in the hospitality industry. [. . .] Airbnb has created a nexus between tourism and housing that hurts renters. The 7,316 units taken off the rental market by Airbnb is equivalent to seven years' of affordable housing construction in Los Angeles. In Venice, as many as 12.5 per cent of all housing units have become Airbnb units, all without public approval. There are 360 Airbnb units per square mile in Venice and long-time residents who never intended to live next to hotels now find themselves dealing with noise and safety concerns that negatively impact their quality of life.
>
> (Saman 2015: 2–3)

The report distinguished between three main categories of hosts, namely 'on-site hosts' who actually 'share' a room or other portion of their home, hosts who rent out a single unit and hosts who are actually leasing companies or landlords taking advantage of the lucrative short-term rental market. And while on-site hosts actually make up a majority of all listings (52 per cent), they only generate 11 per cent of all Airbnb revenue, while the multiple listers, who only make up 6 per cent of all agents, generate more than a third of all revenue. Generating considerable buzz and press in local Los Angeles real estate and urban development blog sites such as Curbed LA (Kudler 2013, 2015a, 2015b), the report prompted Airbnb to delete listings and cancel bookings for some of its biggest hosts, mostly in and around Santa Monica. A month after the report was released, the Santa Monica City Council voted unanimously to curtail allowable Airbnb operations to on-site hosting and to require hosts to obtain a business licence from the city and pay a 14 per cent hotel tax. This new legislation is tough for many Santa Monicans who relied on the additional rental income collected whenever they were away. Los Angeles mayor Eric Garcetti, meanwhile, simply wants to use taxes collected from Airbnb to bankroll a new affordable housing trust fund (http://www.lamayor.org/sotc).

The 'Airbnbification' of Santa Monica and surrounding Los Angeles is yet another indicator of changing practices of place consumption (as discussed in the Introduction to this volume). Indicative of the rise in so-called 'post-tourists', many visitors like to 'live like locals'. Sometimes, new practices purposely circumvent established regulations, taxes and protections in the hospitality industry. At the same time, we have witnessed impressive recent labour victories in the hotel worker arena. Clearly, more research is necessary in order to better unpack and unbundle the implications which the actions of new opportunists in the so-called 'sharing economy', such as Airbnb and others, have on urban tourist economies in highly valuable, high-profile and high-stakes markets such as Santa Monica's.

Concluding remarks: what does Santa Monica teach us about (new?) urban tourism?

When discussing patterns of protest and resistance in the arena of urban tourism in Santa Monica, a complex picture emerges that involves different interest groups – residents, employees and business leaders in the city. As the city densifies and its economy further develops and diversifies, the call for the equitable sharing of tourism profits from hotel worker unions intertwines with the struggle to equitably share increasingly scarce public spaces, infrastructures and amenities between new and old residents and a much larger daytime population that also includes hundreds of thousands of additional visitors and employees. The vignettes above detailed how hotel workers struggle for fair wages and fair treatment in the tourism service industry, how residents fight back against the perceived over-densification of their city and how hosts and commercial landlords now all welcome visitors to Santa Monica via new short-term sharing sites. Is Santa Monica a typical or an atypical example for protest and resistance in urban tourism and does it offer broader insights into the state of tourism in post-industrial cities across the Northern Hemisphere?

As is the case in other urban tourism hotspots around the world, Santa Monica's dual reliance on both a vibrant tourism sector and a strong creative class economy effectively blurs the boundaries between visitors and a new class of residents it seeks to attract. One might say that although, early on, Santa Monica at least partially fitted the characteristics of a typical 'tourist city' that continuously (re-)built infrastructures to attract tourists (Judd and Fainstein

1999), these spaces never became exclusionary, insulated tourist 'bubbles' (Fainstein 2007). In fact, Santa Monica's most important tourist amenities – the beaches, the Pier, the Third Street Promenade and, more recently, Tongva Park – are all public spaces and they can be equally enjoyed by locals and visitors who are drawn to Santa Monica as a general 'creative urban area'. Santa Monica is somewhat atypical in that it is already so thoroughly gentrified that there are really no 'alternative tourist spaces' left to discover. The city has reached a breaking point in terms of its affordability for lower- and middle-income residents, many of whom are regularly spending half or more of their income on rent.

But the case of Santa Monica also illustrates the nascent attempts to regulate the manifestations of the so-called new 'sharing economy', such as Airbnb. Moreover, old-fashioned progressive labour victories are not all a thing of the past. We also see that residents in the 'new tourist city' of Santa Monica are not always as monolithically divided between homeowners and renters as might be expected, but that differences are more apparent along race, class and generational lines. Many of Santa Monica's new tech sector-oriented residents crave rather than fear the construction of large new mixed-use developments that the older residents are so wary of. And younger and non-white residents are not just much more supportive of Santa Monica's efforts to ease its housing crunch and traffic congestion via transit-oriented mixed-use developments around the new Expo light rail line, they are also more likely to take advantage of its revamped bus system, its newly expanded network of bike lanes and its brand new bike sharing system. For the time being, however, a lot of what many planners and urban designers would consider 'progressive planning and policy-making' seems still to get trampled by the anti-density activism of particular groups of residents who continue to resist and resent both the advent and expansion of Silicon Beach and the advancement of beachgoers into their wealthy single-family home neighbourhoods.

Notes

1 The author would like to explicitly acknowledge the highly valuable input that her research assistant Renae Zelmar provided for this chapter. Specifically, she is responsible for the content that covers hotel worker unionization and LWO activism as well as the debate over the redevelopment of the Miramar Hotel.
2 Although candidates typically also receive formal endorsements from the Santa Monica Democratic Club, traditional Democratic or Republican party affiliations are insignificant in this socially progressive environment. In state and national elections, Santa Monicans always lean heavily Democrat, with 75 per cent of votes going to President Obama in 2012 and 74 per cent going to State Governor Jerry Brown in 2014.
3 Commonly defined, a living wage, as opposed to a minimum wage, is a wage that allows a worker to provide for most of the basic needs of his/her family without falling below the poverty line or requiring the assistance of government or poverty programmes (also see Erskine and Marblestone 2006: 249).
4 SMCLC also filed a lawsuit against the project, attacking the whopping 8,500-page Environmental Impact Report for not having sufficiently studied alternatives to the massive project. For additional details on the referendum, see http://ballotpedia.org/City_of_Santa_Monica_Bergamot_Transit_Village_%22Hines_Project%22_Veto_Referendum_%28November_2014%29.

References

[Unless otherwise stated, all URLs were last accessed 15 August 2015.]

Actors Fund (2013) *Application Cover Sheet Belmar Apartments*. Online. Available at http://www.actorsfund.org/others/pdfs/LA/BelmarFinalApplication.pdf.

Airbnb (2015a) *Overall Economic Impact* [of Airbnb in Los Angeles]. Online. Available at http://blog.airbnb.com/economic-impacts-los-angeles/.

Airbnb (2015b) *New Study: Airbnb Community Generates $312 Million in Economic Impact in LA*. Online. Available at https://www.airbnb.com/press/news/new-study-airbnb-community-generates-312-million-in-economic-impact-in-la.

Archibald, A. (2013) 'New vision for Fairmont Miramar', *Santa Monica Daily Press*, 21 February. Online. Available at http://smdp.com/new-vWoSon-for-fairmont-miramar/118563.

Atkin, D. (2004) *The Culting of Brands: When Customers Become True Believers*. New York: Portfolio.

Barragan, B. (2015) 'New owner of SaMo's old Bergamot Transit Village site wants it all to be office space', *CurbedLA*. Online. Available at http://la.curbed.com/archives/2015/03/new_owner_bergamot_transit_village_office_space.php#more.

Bradshaw, T. (2014) 'AirBnB valued $13B', *Financial Times*, 24 October. Online. Available at http://www.ft.com/cms/s/0/99312b96-5b05-11e4-8625-00144feab7de.html#axzz3Xj9LKyvd.

City Data (n.d.) *City Data Income Santa Monica*. Online. Available at http://www.city-data.com/income/income-Santa-Monica-California.html.

City of Santa Monica (2001) *City Council Minutes, 24 July*. Santa Monica, CA: City of Santa Monica.

City of Santa Monica (2010) *Land Use and Circulation Element (Final Adopted)*. Santa Monica, CA: City of Santa Monica. Online. Available at http://www.smgov.net/uploaded Files/Departments/PCD/Plans/General-Plan/Land-Use-and-Circulation-Element.pdf.

City of Santa Monica (2013) *Bergamot Area Draft Plan*. Santa Monica, CA: City of Santa Monica. Online. Available at http://www.smgov.net/uploadedFiles/Departments/PCD/Plans/Bergamot-Area-Plan/Bergamot-Area-Plan-Draft-June-2013.pdf.

Civic Publications (2015) *The 2015–2016 Guide to LA County Cities. Community Profiles*. Online. Available at http://www.civicpubs.org/portfolio.html.

Eisinger, P. (2000) 'The politics of bread and circuses building the city for the visitor class', *Urban Affairs Review*, 35(3): 316–33.

Epstein, A. (2013) 'Letter to our fellow Santa Monicans', *The Miramar Hotel*. Online. Available at http://www.miramarplan.com/letter-to-our-fellow-santa-monicans/.

Erskine, K. M. and Marblestone, J. (2006) 'The movement takes the lead: the role of lawyers in the struggle for a living wage in Santa Monica, California', in A. Sarat and S. A. Scheingold (eds) *Cause Lawyers and Social Movements*. Palo Alto, CA: Stanford University Press.

Fainstein, S. (2007) 'Tourism and the commodification of urban culture', *Urban Reinventors*, 2: 1–20.

Farr, D. (2008) *Sustainable Urbanism: Urban Design with Nature*. Hoboken, NJ: Wiley.

Flad, E. (2002) 'A "winnable issue"', *The Witness*, 85. Online. Available at http://www.thewitness.org/archive/may2002/fladwinnable.html.

Garbee, J., Gottesman, N., Helper, S. and Schwartz, M. (2007) *Hometown Santa Monica: The Bay Cities Book*. New York: Prospect Park Books.

Godbe Research (2014) *City of Santa Monica 2014 Development Survey*. Online. Available at http://www.smgov.net/WorkArea/DownloadAsset.aspx?id=46504.

Gottlieb, R., Freer, R., Vallanaintos, M. and Dreier P. (2006) *The Next Los Angeles: The Struggle for a Livable City*. Berkeley, CA: University of California Press.

Huntley (n.d.) *Get the Facts: Huntley*. Online. Available at http://huntleyfacts.com/.

Islas, J. (2013a) 'Living wage persists in Santa Monica a decade after losing at the polls', *Santa Monica Lookout*. Online. Available at http://www.surfsantamonica.com/ssm_site/the_lookout/news/News-2013/November2013/11_18_2013_Living_Wage_Persists_in_Santa_Monica_A_Decade_After_Losing_at_the_Polls.html.

Islas, J. (2013b) 'Union marches on city hall for higher wages in new Santa Monica hotels', *Santa Monica Lookout*. Online. Available at http://www.surfsantamonica.com/ssm_site/the_lookout/news/News-2013/September-2013/09_03_2013_Union_Marches_on_City_Hall_for_Higher_Wages_at_New_Santa_Monica_Hotels.html.

Judd, D. R. (ed.) (2002) *The Infrastructure of Play: Building the Tourist City*. Armonk, NY: ME Sharpe.

Judd, D. R. and Fainstein, S. (eds) (1999) *The Tourist City*. New Haven, CT: Yale University Press.

Kudler, A. G. (2013) 'Airbnb-affiliated lobbying group defeats Venice's attempt to regulate vacation rentals in Los Angeles', *CurbedLA*. Online. Available at http://la.curbed.com/archives/2013/11/airbnbaffiliated_lobbying_group_defeats_venices_attempt_to_regulate_vacation_rentals_in_los_angeles.php.

Kudler, A. G. (2015a) 'Can Airbnb survive in LA without big professional landlords?', *CurbedLA*. Online. Available at http://la.curbed.com/archives/2015/04/can_airbnb_survive_in_la_without_big_professional_landlords.php.

Kudler, A. G. (2015b) 'Meet LA's most prolific AirBnB host, with 78 units for rent', *CurbedLA*. Online. Available at http://la.curbed.com/archives/2015/03/airbnb_los_angeles_most_prolific_host_ghc.php.

Lazo, A. (2015) 'Los Angeles boosts minimum wage', *Wall Street Journal*, 10 June. Online. Available at http://www.wsj.com/articles/los-angeles-prepares-to-boost-minimum-wage-1433955616.

Logan, T. (2014) 'Rents in Southern California will climb faster in next two years, study says', *Los Angeles Times*, 7 October. Online. Available at http://www.latimes.com/business/realestate/la-fi-rents-in-southern-california-will-climb-20141006-story.html.

Lowery, W. (2012) 'Southern California – this just in', *Los Angeles Times*, 7 November. Online. Available at http://latimesblogs.latimes.com/lanow/2012/11/hotel-worker-minimum-wage-measure-passes-in-long-beach-.html.

NRDC (2014) *The Impacts of Beach Pollution. Testing the Waters*. Online. Available at http://www.nrdc.org/water/oceans/ttw/2014/ttw2014_Impacts_of_Beach_Pollution.pdf.

Pojani, D. (2008) 'Santa Monica's Third Street Promenade: the failure and resurgence of a downtown pedestrian mall', *Urban Design International*, 13: 141–55.

Riposa, G. (2004) 'Reinventing paradise: Santa Monica's sustainable city program', *Public Administration Quarterly*, 28: 222–51.

Saman, R. (2015) *Airbnb, Rising Rent, and the Housing Crisis in Los Angeles*. Los Angeles: Los Angeles Alliance for a New Economy.

Santa Monica Daily Press (2011) 'Developer submits plans for iconic hotel', *Santa Monica Daily Press*, 3 May. Online. Available at http://smdp.com/developer-submits-plans-for-iconic-hotel/78587.

Santa Monica Daily Press (2012) 'Hotel renovation fuels development debate', *Santa Monica Daily Press*, 13 February. Online. Available at http://smdp.com/hotel-renovation-fuels-development-debate/80220.

SMCVB (Santa Monica Convention and Visitors Bureau) (2015) *Santa Monica 2014 Tourism Economic and Fiscal Impacts and Visitor Profile*. Online. Available at http://live-smcvb.pantheon.io/wp-content/uploads/2015/04/2-Page-Econ-Imp-Summary-2014.pdf.

Smith, S. (2014) 'White Santa Monicans hate new development', *NextCity*. Online. Available at https://nextcity.org/daily/entry/white-santa-monicans-hate-new-development-latinos-love-it.

Wallace, E., Pollock, K, Horth, B., Carthy, S. and Elyas, N. (2014) *Los Angeles Tourism: A Domestic and International Analysis*. Los Angeles: LA Chamber of Commerce.

Walton, A. (2014) 'LA hotel employees join Santa Monica with highest minimum wage in the nation', *KPCC*. Online. Available at http://www.scpr.org/news/2014/09/24/46938/la-hotel-employees-join-santa-monica-with-highest/.

White, J. (2013) *HVS Hotel Market Insight: Santa Monica, CA*. Mineola, NY: HVS Global Hospitality Services.

6 Contesting China's tourism wave

Identity politics, protest and the rise of the Hongkonger city state movement

Daniel Garrett

For China, the world's largest outbound tourism source, politics and tourism have become unavoidably connected phenomena (Weaver 2010; Hall 1994; O'Brien 2011) – geopolitical, nationalistic and secessionist – as recent trends in the relationship between the People's Republic of China (PRC) and the Hong Kong Special Administrative Region (HKSAR) aptly illustrate. Buckling under the pressure of relentless mainland Chinese inbound tourism, the social and political costs of breakneck Chinese tourism to Hong Kong – ultimately proving inimical to the socialist nation building project – have precipitously accrued in recent years and provoked the emergence of nativist and secessionist sentiments seeking to defend and preserve the Hong Kong identity and way of life. This phenomenon has grown so much that expanding 'contentious performances' (Tilly 2008) staking bold claims against excessive Chinese tourist incursions and booming mainland tourism's deleterious impact on Hongkongers' daily lives *and* quality of life have become prominent symbols and signifiers of Hong Kong–China tensions, hegemonic crisis and 'moral panic' (Cohen 1972). Though unrepresentative of Hong Kong's broader protest culture in demographics, numbers, repertoires and temperament, anti-China tourism demonstrations, marches and rallies targeting mainland visitors to Hong Kong have become convenient and timely political scapegoats for hegemonic forces in Beijing and Tamar[1] to deploy in their broader 'life-or-death' struggle against insurgent democratic Hongkonger subalterns and rising transgressive young radicals. This has especially been the case since the emergence of the Occupy Central with Love and Peace and Umbrella Revolution (Occupy/Umbrella hereafter) movements in 2013 and 2014 respectively, and the pro-democracy forces' rejection of an undemocratic Chinese-dictatorial political reform package in 2015.

In the subsequent hegemonic panics over the backlash against mainland tourism, sensational headlines and dubious official claims of armed insurrection, economic catastrophe, reputational harm, rising separatism and social upheavals have almost become the norm. Most recently, following a handful of controversial anti-parallel trader[2] (APT) protests in Hong Kong's New Territories in February and March 2015, where scores of protesters were arrested and some accused of attacking mainland shoppers and tourists, many Chinese and HKSAR agents of social control and the regime's 'moral crusaders' and 'entrepreneurs'[3] strategically sought to construct, demonise, label and frame anti-mainlander tourism protests and perspectives as criminal, deviant, fascist, irrational, radical, racist, separatist, violent and xenophobic. The latter charge is especially ironic given the strident revanchist 'One Country' rhetoric and anti-Hongkonger enmity espoused by many regime and pro-establishment supporters in criticizing the APT protests and protesters.

More revealing, however, have been parallel political moves by hegemonic elements to conflate, distort and exaggerate these exceptional anti-mainlander voices and actions as defining elements of Hong Kong's wider pro-democracy movement and protest culture and emblematic of a Hongkonger independence movement – which they are not (yet). Likewise, hegemonic claims of severe economic impact and reputational harm to Hong Kong from these provocative yet numerically negligible anti-mainlander tourism protest episodes are dubious, and omit or minimize potentially exculpatory factors impacting tourism inflows and spending. These include such developments as China's corruption crackdown targeting purchases of luxury goods, Chinese government control of tourist inflows (especially the number of tour groups travelling to Hong Kong[4]), changing tourism patterns towards other regional destinations, seasonal ebbs and flows of tourism, and a national economy slowing months prior to APT protests in 2015 – or Occupy/Umbrella in 2014 (Resonance Insights 2014; Information Services Department 2014; Zhou 2014b).

Rather than protesters deterring visiting mainland tourists, instead it has been the Chinese tourism swell, other forms of mainland migration and relentless cultural, economic and political integration that have incited protesters and other Hongkongers' resistance to mainland tourism. As the record shows, long before tens of thousands of Hongkongers took to the streets of Admiralty, Causeway Bay and Mong Kok in late September 2014 as part of the Umbrella Revolution, the HKSAR had already been occupied by tens of millions of trolley-pulling mainland Chinese tourists. By the time Hong Kong SAR security forces lobbed 87 canisters of tear gas at peacefully demonstrating protesters, more than a quarter of a billion Chinese tourists[5] (Tourism Commission 2015; Commerce and Economic Development Bureau 2013) – what Siu *et al.* (2013) refer to as part of the 'Chinese Tourists' Wave' of inbound tourism (China Tourism Wave (CTW) hereafter) – had already visited the city over the past decade, inevitably creating, broadening and hardening locals' resistance to unremitting mainland tourism inflows. This spurred a litany of quotidian grievances unrelated to demands for genuine universal suffrage, but more connected to protecting the Hongkonger identity, sense of place and way of life. In short, the CTW and its consequences have contributed to the emergence of a broad and amorphous Defend Hong Kong movement of variegated actors, interests and ends. Put simply, unrestrained Chinese parallel trading and tourism have helped incite the emergence of a 'Hongkonger City State' movement.

After describing and situating the Chinese tourism swell to the HKSAR, this chapter introduces the genesis of APT protests and contextualizes the emergence of related City State, localist and nativist sentiments and resistance to mainland traders and tourists. Hesitant and halting regime measures to manage adverse tourism impacts and overbearing hegemonic responses to anti-tourism insurgencies in Asia's 'World City' are briefly reviewed before concluding this brief exploration.[6]

The 'China Tourism Wave'

Chinese tourism to Hong Kong has dramatically increased in recent years. So much so that online Hong Kong CTW discontents frequently derisively portray large crowds of Chinese tourists in Hong Kong as herds of 'Walkers' from the popular *Walking Dead* cable television series. Elsewhere dissidents (political and anti-CTW) have depicted tourists as mindless red hoards attacking and devouring the city, residents and resources. Some have also used the derogatory symbol and term 'Locust'[7] to describe the experience and effect of the mammoth mainland visitor wave on the city. Allusions to cultural assimilation, destruction and even the obliteration of Hong Kong via homogenizing colossal tourism swells are similarly alluded to by more fervent subalterns, who compare unwanted mainland cultural and linguistic encroachments connected to the CTW to the forced sinicization of Tibetan and Xinjiang regions. For instance, they frequently cite examples of mainland simplified characters and Putonghua use by local retailers and the government as squeezing out traditional Chinese characters and Cantonese, the main writing style and language/dialect used in the city.

In the 1990s, the debate over the future development of Hong Kong's tourism industry was largely rooted in conflicting predictions and perceptions of the forthcoming change of sovereignty on 1 July 1997 (Mok and Dewald 1999). As framed then by Hobson and Ko (1994: 8), pessimists darkly saw the looming handover as 'the end of the uniqueness of Hong Kong' and demise of its international tourism appeal while optimists giddily saw only vast 'opportunities as a regional tourism destination'. Following the Handover, China curtailed mainland travel to Hong Kong 'to demonstrate China's determination of keeping Hong Kong as a SAR and to alleviate Hong Kong people's fear that droves of people from China will enter Hong Kong after the handover' (Mok and Dewald 1999: 36). In 1997, the year the British colony of Hong Kong became a SAR of the PRC, the number of Chinese visitors to the city totalled only 2.2 million as overall tourist arrivals declined. However, this policy of caution and restraint by the Chinese government changed in 2003 following the Asian financial crisis, the outbreak of Severe Acute Respiratory Syndrome (SARS) and the 1 July 2003 democracy crisis[8] that affected political stability in the HKSAR.

By 2014, the number of mainlanders arriving in HK exceeded 47 million – a more than twenty-fold increase from 1997 and nearly seven times Hong Kong's population. Between 2003 – when Chinese authorities first liberalized travel to the SAR and Hong Kong's first major political crisis erupted over opposition to Chinese national security legislation and demands for democracy – and 2014 – when Occupy/Umbrella manifested – the number of mainland Chinese arrivals to Hong Kong had exploded, exceeding a quarter of a billion arrivals. Arrivals from

China have constituted more than half of all visitors since the 2003 liberalization of mainland tourism to Hong Kong under the Individual Visit Scheme (IVS) and subsequent iterations.[9]

Between 2010 and 2014, more than 173 million Chinese tourists visited the city (Tourism Commission 2015; Commerce and Economic Development Bureau 2013) – in other words, nearly 25 times the entire population of Hong Kong crowding into 25 per cent of Hong Kong's total land mass.[10] Mainland arrivals accounted for 75 per cent or more of all visitors since 2013 and represented at least two-thirds of all arrivals since 2010, when an additional liberalization of tourism to the HKSAR occurred. The share of Gross Domestic Product (GDP) occupied by the tourism sector steadily increased from 3.2 per cent in 2006 to 5 per cent in 2015 (Information Services Department 2015c). Reportedly, more than a quarter of a million Hongkongers are directly employed in the tourism sector, a pillar industry of the HKSAR economy (Information Services Department 2014).

Yet, the majority of these employment 'opportunities' are low-paid, low-skilled jobs in one of Asia's most expensive cities with more than a million in poverty and the highest degree of income inequality among advanced economies (HKSAR Census and Statistics Department 2011; Chen 2014; Ngo 2013; Yun and Hu 2013). Moreover, as members of a HKSAR government (HKSARG) think tank observed: 'There was little trickling down of the economic benefits gained from Mainland visitors. Big shopping malls and high-end shops gained the most from the surge of Mainland visitors' (Secretariat to the Commission on Strategic Development 2014b: 3). According to a 2010 discussion paper by the same think tank, 'the Mainland tourist market has become the most important area of growth for Hong Kong's tourism industry' (Secretariat to the Commission on Strategic Development 2010: 10). However, the Chinese tourism tsunami to Hong Kong has induced rising resistance and instability as strongly indicated in accumulating official, popular and scholarly discourses.

In the wake of the CTW, some Hongkongers claim they feel like strangers in their own home as tourists pour in and the HKSARG is increasingly perceived as pursuing almost exclusively Chinese, not local, interests. Some complain Hongkongers are now second-class citizens who are being re-colonized and that the city is being occupied by mainland immigrants and tourists. Hong Kong, others claim, is being transformed into a giant shopping mall or Disneyland for rich mainlander tourists. Relatedly, CTW-connected retail and residential gentrification have become major issues as neighbourhoods lose local character and heritage, becoming strip malls of infant formula, luxury goods and pharmaceutical outlets catering to parallel traders and mainland tourists.

Tellingly, the situating of major Umbrella Revolution occupation encampments in key shopping districts predominantly patronized by mainlanders incidentally illustrated the breadth of CTW commercial gentrification; for instance, along the borders of the Mong Kok occupation camp, there were at least 40 luxury goods stores (primarily) catering to mainland tourists (Grundy 2014). Similarly, earlier prominent displays of anti-CTW sentiment/protests (the so-called 'D&G' and 'Anti-Locust' performances) were situated in the iconic luxury shopping enclave of Canton Road heavily frequented by rich mainlanders (Garrett 2013; Garrett 2014b). Yet, it has been across the SAR that commodity and property prices have skyrocketed and shortages increased as mainlanders invest in property and buy goods they do not trust back 'home'.

Hongkongers also lament what they see as the weakening of the international character of Hong Kong and its 'East meets West' uniqueness as hundreds of millions of Chinese visitors transform the city into 'just another Chinese city'. Concomitantly, they claim rising corruption and the declining rule of law in Hong Kong are related to the 'mainlandization' of the HKSARG and Region[11] induced by massive mainland tourism, migration and accelerating integration.

The genesis of the anti-mainlander protests

APT and anti-CTW protests are symptomatic of significant underlying problems in China–Hong Kong relations under the 'One Country, Two Systems' (OCTS) framework that prohibits the introduction of the mainland's socialist system, provides for the SAR's liberal freedoms and protects Hong Kong's way of life for fifty years. The handful of controversial and confrontational APT and anti-CTW protests over successive weekends in February and March 2015 were arguably the most sensational anti-mainland visitor spectacles in terms of regime rhetoric, police violence and arrests, but they did not spontaneously erupt. Three years of increasingly transgressive (and aggressive) APT and anti-CTW protests preceded them. Albeit 2015 was the most disruptive in terms of tactics, 2014 was the most innovative, evocative and creative of the contentious performances with some episodes provoked by 'confrontations between Hongkongers and mainlanders' and others reacting to 'criticizing and patronizing comments by Chinese leaders and SAR officials' (Garrett 2015: 20). For instance, months before Occupy and Umbrella, 'Anti-Locust' (see Figure 6.1 and 6.2), 'Patriotic Parody' (see Figure 6.3), 'Luggage and Pride' and 'Toddler-gate'[12] anti-mainland tourist and APT spectacles targeting visitors' misbehaviours and conflicting cultural norms transpired (Garrett 2015: 78–96; Garrett 2014a, 2014b). By mid-2014, Chinese and HKSAR governments were already considering how to reduce the number of Chinese visitors as a result of those episodes and rising CTW resistance (Information Services Department 2014).

The year before, in 2013, tens of thousands of Hongkongers had petitioned the President of the United States of America online under the heading of 'Baby Hunger Outbreak in Hong Kong, International Aid Requested' over shortages of infant formula in the city caused by parallel traders illicitly transporting milk powder to the mainland. Transgressive YouTube videos mocking Chinese visitor behaviours and decrying their destruction and pollution of the Hong Kong Way of Life appeared. Anti-Chinese colonialism protest banners and 'F*** Chinese Dictators' T-shirts were brandished and deployed at the largest annual protest ritual in Hong Kong. In early 2012, contentious protest performances over mainland mothers (involved in a phenomenon dubbed 'birth tourism') and drivers, publication of the infamous 'Locust Ad',[13] Hong Kong retailers' discriminatory

Figure 6.1 Placard from the February 2014 'Anti-Locust' protest on Canton Road. It depicts a pro-Hongkonger identity composition inspired by the Japanese anime, manga and now film, 'Attack on Titan'. Hongkonger nativists envisioned themselves defending Hong Kong from a communist onslaught of mindless, voracious humanoid hordes (elsewhere represented as giant locusts) threatening the city and devouring its limited resources (and residents). The Lion and Dragon emblem and colonial flag are provocative identity markers for localists and nativists struggling against mainlandization and sinicization by the Chinese 'Other'.

Source: Author.

practices against locals in favour of Chinese tourists and calls for the 'liberation' of Hong Kong's New Towns from Chinese parallel trader occupations and tourism swarms first erupted (Garrett 2013) as the CTW broke and crashed untenably onto Hong Kong society.

Notably, in that same year (2012), the perceived cultural, economic and social downsides of oppressive tourism flows and the strident 'China-first' attitude of the HKSAR regime and pro-establishment camps' exploitation of ordinary Hongkongers so as to receive ever greater numbers of Chinese tourists, also became potent issues in the political sphere as radical pro-democracy politicians – in that year's Legislative Council elections – incorporated APT and CTW grievances in their election platforms and campaigns. At the same time, many members of the patriotic camp began to feel that Hong Kong had taken its most anticommunist stance since the 1967 riots and that an independence virus, isolationist thinking and 'mainland-phobia' were starting to spread throughout Hong Kong (Chan 2012a, 2012b; Economic Journal Insight 2014; Yang 2012).

Figure 6.2 'Anti-Locust' sticker declaring the popular Causeway Bay entertainment and shopping area a 'Hongkonger citizen'-only area off-limits to mainlander tourists, June 2014. In addition to the overt symbolic and verbal references to the derogatory Locust icon/label, the visual implicitly invokes Hongkongers' anger towards mainland birth tourism in the SAR with the pictorial inclusion of a 'baby locust'. Localist nation-building sentiments are also asserted in the subaltern construction of a 'HK citizen' category implicitly rejecting mainland and local regime categorizations of Hongkongers as Chinese citizens and just residents of Hong Kong.

Source: Author.

Pointedly, with the exception of 2015, all of these APT/anti-CTW developments and episodes firmly preceded the Occupy/Umbrella watersheds by months and years and were focused on the CTW's threat to Hong Kong and Hongkongers, not on democracy issues. Indeed, Chinese tourists were ubiquitous *and* welcomed unproblematically in Occupy/Umbrella occupation sites taking photographs (especially selfies with Umbrella Revolution-themed Chinese President Xi Jinping cutouts), collecting souvenirs, camping out in tents (enjoying the 'Occupy' experience), leaving messages of encouragement and support on 'Lennon's Wall' and other non-confrontational, quasi-supportive activities. Yet, as will be detailed later, the Occupy/Umbrella 'Hongkonger sentiments' have been held up by hegemonic proponents as iconic of the Taiwanization of Hong Kong politics.[14]

Figure 6.3 An APT/anti-CTW demonstrator wearing a pig mask and Cultural Revolution-
era Red Guard cap holds up a copy of Chairman Mao's *Little Red Book* during
the 'Patriotic Parody' protest in Mong Kok in March 2014. The protest responded
to senior mainland Chinese and HKSAR officials' criticism of APT/anti-CTW
protesters as 'unpatriotic'. The demonstrator was waving the book and yelling in
Chinese and English that he was a 'Chinese pig'. Protesters told Chinese shoppers
to be 'patriotic' and buy Chinese, not Hong Kong, goods and to go back to the
mainland. Mong Kok is a popular shopping and entertainment district in Hong
Kong heavily patronized by locals, foreigners and visiting mainland tourists.

Source: Author.

The emergence of APT protests is just one facet of a broader Hong Kong
resistance towards social and political problems generated by the CTW and
underlying relentless economic and physical integration with Socialist China
such as tourism gentrification, competition for scarce opportunities and resources,
commodity shortages and property inflation, cultural erosion, infiltration of
'mainland values,' overcrowding, degradation of Hong Kong's living environment and quality of life, etc. These anxieties and/or grievances are often held in
conjunction with other concerns over premature assimilation and integration of

Hong Kong into the PRC in contravention of promises made by China to Hongkongers under the OCTS framework and codified in the HKSAR Basic Law (BL). Significantly, the costs of the CTW have not been evenly distributed or experienced in Hong Kong society and disproportionately impact ordinary, low- and middle-income groups and youth, the first and last categories constituting primary demographics in APT protests. Though APT sentiments do not constitute the totality of anti-CTW or anti-mainland sentiment in Hong Kong, APT/anti-CTW protests and protesters have become symbols and public icons of underlying social and political problems seized upon by both hegemonic and subaltern forces contesting for control over Hong Kong.

Since at least 2012, APT/anti-CTW protests have been adopted by a growing number of incipient entities variously characterized by academics, government, media and the protesters themselves as 'nativist' or 'localist' – yet not everyone participating in an APT episode necessarily identifies with either (ambiguous) category. Affiliation and membership in these insurgent collectives is ad hoc, informal and fluid. That said, in the last few years, these groups and APT/anti-CTW sentiments have gained higher visibility and greater following in society. Yet, the APT protesters remain fringe political actors/voices who, through astute deployment of 'image events' (Delicath and DeLuca 2003) and postmodern action repertoires, have captured disproportionate public and regime attention with sensational symbolic displays and transgressive modes of resistance. In tandem, Cold War-era hegemonic anxieties ('peaceful evolution'), post-1989 regime insecurities ('colour revolutions' and 'Arab Springs') and colonial-era traumas (political and social ostracisation from mainstream Hong Kong society) held by the minority ruling forces in Beijing and Tamar (the site of the Central Government Office of the Hong Kong Government) have contributed to exaggerated threat claims and disproportionate security responses which, in turn, have elevated APT/anti-CTW protests and protesters' prominence, social capital and media visibility. Though marginalized in Hong Kong's political sphere, these dissidents have been effective in forcing the Chinese and HKSAR regimes to respond to Hongkongers' concerns where more 'polite politics' (Ho 2000) have failed.

Accordingly, APT protests/anti-CTW sentiments – as part of the securitization (Wæver 1995)[15] of the CTW industry and OCTS – have been portrayed as national security threats to China's social harmony and cohesion, accused of advocating separatist ideologies and seeking independence. At their most rudimentary level, they are seen by the Chinese regime as endangering the relationship between the HKSAR and the Central Authorities/Mainland and tarnishing the image of Hong Kong as a tourist destination (and OCTS as a viable political construct). Under duress from all corners, regime actors have conflated exceptional APT/anti-CTW protesters and movements with the mainstream pro-democracy movement and so-called radical protest actions like Occupy/Umbrella whom they similarly frame as national security threats, menaces which are likewise depicted as being under the control of external and foreign powers (Taiwan, the United States and the United Kingdom (UK)). Yet APT/anti-CTW protests and protesters are not the vanguard of a Western-inspired colour revolution; they are simply the latest folk devils and enemy images in the Chinese Communist Party's political struggle at home and abroad.

Making sense of the protests in their broader context

This section briefly elucidates geopolitical, nationalistic and separatist politics surrounding APT/anti-CTW actors, movements and sentiments, and corresponding incitements of subaltern Hongkonger City State sentiments/movements and reacting hegemonic independence panics. It describes how APT/anti-CTW protests and sentiments have become a volatile condensation symbol of Hongkonger–Mainlander conflict. Put differently, the CTW and resistance to it have become symbols of larger political struggles between Beijing and its 'unruly' subjects in the HKSAR. First, a sketch of the complicated and conflicted relationship Hong Kong enjoys with its sovereign is offered, before the rise of Hongkonger City State, localist and nativist entities frequently cited in anti-mainland tourism actions is discussed. The salience of a constructed 'Hongkonger, Not Chinese' ethnicity enumerated by some Hongkongers is raised.

Trouble in the 'shoppers' paradise'[16]

Hong Kong and China have a complicated, conflicted and problematic relationship. Once part of imperial China, the territory was begrudgingly handed over to Socialist China in 1997 after 156 years as a British colony. The return and transition from colony to SAR was controversial and fiercely contested, albeit perceived as inevitable. Some Hongkongers welcomed it, many did not, and others with no choice simply accepted it. Those that could – elites and middle class – left the colony or secured foreign passports as a back-up plan 'just in case' the Bamboo Curtain eventually descended.

Prior to the Handover the UK began the gradual introduction of limited representative governance. The substance and pace of these reforms were exceptionally contentious with China. Beijing saw many measures and the cultivation of democracy figures as intended to hijack governance of the SAR after the Retrocession (Qian 2005). Following China's military crackdown on student demonstrators in 1989, the British accelerated and enhanced efforts to democratize the colony. China vigorously objected and introduced obligatory national security legislation for Hong Kong into the BL to prevent the city from becoming a base of subversion.

Subsequent to the HKSARG's efforts to impose national security legislation on Hongkongers in 2003, the largest ever protest in post-Handover history (500,000 people) occurred, eventually forcing the regime's withdrawal of the legislation. Like 1989, this watershed irreversibly transformed China–Hong Kong relations and Hong Kong itself into 'a quintessentially political city over the issues of democracy, elections and universal suffrage' (Garrett 2009: n.p.). It also marked China's abandoning of its 'hands-off' policy over Hong Kong and the beginning of aggressive integration and sustained united front policies (Lo

2008; Loh 2010) – including people-to-people exchanges – a project inevitably facilitated by the liberalization of mainland tourism to Hong Kong in 2003/4.

Chinese tourism and the rise of the Hongkonger City State movement – 'localists' and 'nativists'

After 2003 a transformation of Hong Kong's political and protest culture also occurred. A new generation of Hongkongers embodying postmodern sensibilities and manifesting the aesthetics and identity politics of the new social movements emerged in response to perceived mainland and establishment threats to Hong Kong's cultural heritage, local identity and way of life (Garrett and Ho 2014; Cheung 2006; So 2011). Unlike prior generations, the siren lure of (false) prosperity and stability under capitalism and unremitting economic development were insufficient for securing the acquiescence of younger generations that were increasingly marginalized and pushed out of the Hong Kong Dream in the wake of hegemonic pursuit of ever greater numbers of mainland tourists and deeper mainland integration. Economic cooptation, the mainstay of the Chinese Communist Party's unification projects in Hong Kong and Taiwan (Yeun 2014), was no longer a 'magic weapon' for the Party.

Then, beginning in 2010, coinciding with a second colossal swell of mainland tourists (the first being 2003/4), Hong Kong's protest culture and relationship with Chinese authorities entered yet another new, albeit more combative, phase (Garrett 2015), one that ultimately led to the Occupy/Umbrella movements in 2014/15, the so-called 'era of disobedience' (Lam *et al.* 2014; Zhou 2014a) and the emergence of 'radical politics' (Cheng 2014) in Hong Kong. The advent of nativist/localist sentiments and groups at the core of the APT/anti-CTW protests in early 2015 have their genesis in this period. Allegedly, the most important ideological development was a 2011 award-winning book, *On the Hong Kong City State* – a text broadly credited by anti- and pro-regime forces as having inspired the so-called City State movement/sentiment (Hung 2014; Lam 2015).

The author, Chin Wan-kan, claimed Hong Kong's civil and moderate yet failed mainstream democracy movement, and China's persistent encroachments into Hong Kong's high degree of autonomy, germinated an impetus for a more action-oriented movement. More rousing, however, were the negative consequences of the CTW and Socialist Chinese nation-building projects like the HKSAR's failed 2012 Moral and National Education (MNE) scheme which had escalated tensions between Hongkongers and Mainlanders (Cheng 2014: 219–20). This, in turn, incited the rise of the Hongkonger City State, localist and nativist sentiments/ movements (ibid.).

Less sympathetically, Lo (2014: n.p.) avers that:

> The rise of nativism, or a strong local Hong Kong identity, has taken the form of young Hongkongers labeling mainlanders as 'undesirable' elements who deprive the people of Hong Kong of various services, including hospital beds for local pregnant women as mainland counterparts occupied many of

these beds, and embracing milk powder formula which remain the target of mainland tourists who lost confidence in the safety of mainland milk powder for their babies.

The politicization of the problems surrounding the CTW and mainland integration, Lo holds, had led 'some Hong Kong youth, fiercely identifying themselves as Hong Kong people', to view

> the influx of mainland tourists and even mainland students and talents, with animosity, as a threat to their rights, job opportunities and entitlements to local resources. The most extremist among them even argued that Hong Kong should be seen as a 'nation' with the right to self-determination.
>
> (Lo 2015: n.p.)

According to him, HKSAR politics have become 'Taiwanized' as populist and radical sentiments were rising out of control, energized by the secessionist ideology of 'Hongkongism' (Lo 2015).

Conversely, Cheng (2014) observed that the emergence of groups espousing radical politics and action since 2010 simply provided Hongkongers with a political platform and vehicle to voice politically incorrect 'grievances and emotions' regarding the negative outcomes of massive Chinese inflows, parallel trading and breakneck integration with the mainland (p. 220). He points to a diversity of nativist/localist groups like Chin Wan-kan's City State Movement, the Hong Kong Autonomy Movement, Hong Kong Nativism Power and others that fulfilled this need. For example, in September 2012, an iconic APT performance frequently cited by hegemonic critics, the 'Liberation of Sheung Shui'[17] Mass Transit Rail (MTR) station near mainland China, took place. Two symbolic acts by APT actors during the protest – waving a colonial-era British flag and a handwritten cardboard placard demanding 'Chinese Out!' – became controversially assertive icons frequently associated with the APT/anti-CTW movement and criticised by Chinese and HKSAR hegemonic forces.

One prolific Hong Kong-based pro-establishment commentator in the *China Daily*, Thomas Chan, for instance, claimed that use of the colonial flag was a 'strong political message that the action was one that pitched the colonial legacy of Hong Kong against the present state of the "One Country, Two Systems" with Hong Kong under Chinese sovereignty' (Chan 2012c: n.p.). Chan further opined the cardboard message 'revealed outright hostility towards mainlanders and amounted to a public denial that Hong Kong residents are Chinese' (ibid.) He averred that the appearance of colonial flags at an anti-MNE protest the same year against the HKSAR's mainland-tinted patriotic education scheme for students inherently linked the political movements, thereby revealing their anti-communist, anti-central government and anti-Chinese orientation and independence inclinations.

Soon after the 'Liberation of Sheung Shui' APT episode, another highly symbolic performance occurred on China's National Day in front of its Liaison Office in Hong Kong. During that event, the colonial flag was again displayed and demonstrators shouted at Chinese officials inside to leave, stating that the protesters were Hongkongers, not Chinese. Both the Sheung Shui and Liaison Office actions provoked condemnations by senior Chinese officials, such as former deputy director of the State Council's Hong Kong and Macao Affairs Office (HKMAO) Chen Zuoer and former director Lu Ping. Chen Zuoer remarked that 'the rise of a pro-independence force in Hong Kong is spreading like a virus' and Lu Ping scolded: 'Those who do not recognize they are Chinese should look at what is written on their passports or they should renounce their Chinese nationality' (Cheung and Lau 2012: n.p.).

'Hongkonger, not Chinese'

Contrary to the mainstream pro-democracy movement with whom the APT/anti-CTW sentiments and nativist/localists have been steadily conflated by regime figures, a key differentiating tenet shared among nativist and localist groups in Hong Kong distinguishing them from mainstream democrats is a focus on *local*, not *national* issues. This breaks with the traditional pro-democracy camp's position that perceives Hong Kong and Hongkongers as Chinese, and relatedly must fight for a democratic China as well as a democratic SAR. Instead, the City State, localists and nativists seek to protect Hong Kong from China, and to leave 'China' to the 'Chinese' – a position the Chinese Communist Party and its HKSAR patriots find abhorrent, albeit ironically, as the Chinese authorities repeatedly tell Hongkongers to keep out of mainland politics. At various levels, this has become a subaltern 'Hongkonger, not Chinese' versus hegemonic 'Chinese, not Hongkonger' identity conflict.

Another position held by many nativists/localists that the Party finds problematic is one that posits China as a (re-)colonizer of Hong Kong (and, by extension, its tourists are coming to the SAR to exploit Hongkongers' 'resources'.) Rather than relying on and becoming dependent on China (for tourism or in general), they advocate Hongkongers to be self-reliant and practise self-determination to realize the promised High Degree of Autonomy from the Central Government. Hence, an 'us versus them' rhetoric is frequently manifested in contentious performances not only during APT/anti-CTW protests, but also when they participate on the fringes of mainstream political rituals like the annual 1 July democracy march. Here they are not accosting parallel traders or tourists directly. Rather, they are staking subaltern identity claims, boundaries and markers and repudiating the hegemonic 'occupier'. This frequently involves displaying transgressive visuals of putative mainland visitor behaviours.[18]

For example, perhaps the most infamous protest performance occurred in 2013 when a loose-knit group of twenty to thirty Hong Kong nativists and supporters averring CTW grievances marched in the 1 July procession waving colonial and Lion and Dragon flags while brandishing a huge banner demanding: 'Chinese Colonists Get Out!' (Garrett 2015: 240). In addition, a crowdsourced subaltern Hong Kong video mashup entitled *Attack on China* (inspired by the highly popular Japanese anime and manga series *Attack on Titan*) conceptualizing APT protesters as 'defenders' of the 'Hongkonger City State' was released online (and quickly banned by China) days before the march was said to have embodied the spirit of Hongkongers 'Defending Our Hong Kong Land' (Garrett 2014c).

The Defend Hong Kong sentiment is also increasingly exhibited in a diversity of embodied displays adorning protesters and the urban infrastructure – functioning as boundary and identity markers – such as T-shirts and stickers declaring Hongkongers an endangered species, defining who 'Hongkongers' are, asserting 'Our Home, Our Say', exhorting 'Hong Kong is not part of China', pronouncing 'Hongkonger, not Chinese!', inciting '"Nation Building for [the] Hong Kong City State' and warning 'We Dare to Fight!'

Responses by the Hong Kong and Chinese governments

(Limited) measures by the HKSAR government

HKSARG responses to APT/anti-CTW and broader anti-mainland sentiment have been begrudging, incremental and limited – as well as furiously contested by pro-establishment vested interests in the accommodation, food and beverage, retail, transportation and tourism sectors. The HKSARG substantively began addressing problems first in 2012 following multiple high-profile APT/anti-mainland shopper displays and spreading Hongkonger–Mainlander conflicts garnering international attention. Hammered by the public for inaction, HKSARG public relations campaigns now repeatedly stress that they have 'got it', that they are 'very concerned' over the impact of PT/CTW on Hongkongers' daily lives and that they are taking action.[19] At the same time, HKSAR strategic communication strategy also emphasizes the intractability of the problem and the need to balance national and local interests and protect Hong Kong's tourism brand as Asia's World City. Because of the complex bureaucratic nature of the HKSARG response and the competing discourses and representations by Hong Kong SAR, local Chinese (Shenzhen and Guangdong Province authorities) and Central Government actors, a full accounting and assessment of the HKSARG response to the APT/anti-CTW crisis is beyond the scope of this chapter. Instead, the four most decisive measures to date are elucidated briefly. The efficacy and sufficiency of these measures are not discussed, but they are widely contested in Hong Kong and mainland media and official discourses.

The two most tangible responses have been the banning of mainland pregnant women from obtaining maternity spaces in Hong Kong and the institution of export controls over infant formula. Announced in 2012 and implemented in 2013, the controversial 'zero quota' policy for expectant mainland mothers aggressively tackled Chinese birth, benefits[20] and medical tourism that had become pervasive in Hong Kong. Prior to implementation, as many as 30,000 mainland mothers were reserving maternity wards annually. As with other discussions over reducing Chinese visitors, the 'zero quota' policy provoked panic declarations of hospitals closing and severe damage to Hong Kong's economy, image and medical tourism potential (Moy and Lau 2013) – none of which have occurred. Second, the government instituted export restrictions in 2013 on baby formula for infants and children under three years of age, allowing no more than two cans (1.8 kilograms) of powdered formula per person to be taken out of Hong Kong within a 24-hour window. By April 2015, the HKSARG claimed that joint operations with Shenzhen authorities had netted more than 1,300 cases of unlicensed exporting of over 11,400 kilograms of milk powder (Information Services Department 2015d).

Third, Hong Kong's public transportation rail provider twice limited the size and weight of luggage carried on its trains and established weigh station check-points along key routes patronized by parallel traders. Lastly, the HKSARG nego-tiated with the Chinese Central Government to first preclude and then adjust the existing multiple-entry Individual Visit Endorsement (IVE) scheme for Shenzhen residents in 2012 and 2015 respectively. In 2015, in comparison to 2014 mainland visitors numbers, a 30 per cent reduction of IVE visitors was to be achieved by limiting new IVE holders to one visit per week instead of allowing multiple daily entries; this reportedly would lead to an estimated 10 per cent reduction in overall mainland visitors (4.6 million) (Information Services Department 2015a) though its impact would not be felt immediately as existing permit holders were unaf-fected by the rollback.

'Enough, already!' – safeguarding cordial relations between the HKSAR and the Mainland

Though insignificant in numbers, resources and supporters and lacking any mature ideology or organization, the identity politics of the APT/anti-CTW and other anti-mainlander and anti-integration activists have succeeded in exposing the fragility of Beijing's hegemony over Hong Kong. The Central Authorities' concern over not just the increasing enmity between the mainland and Hong Kong but also the nature (bold, demanding, disrespectful, dismissive, flagrant) and visibility (on the mainland and abroad) of the growing Hongkonger resistance front appears to have reached, or is reaching, a tipping point.

In March 2015 a State Council established a semi-official think tank, the Chinese Association of Hong Kong and Macao Studies (the Association hereafter), staffed by former senior officials of the HKMAO, HKSARG and leading establish-ment academics, experts and opinion leaders, which warned that 'hostile rhetoric' on both sides (Hong Kong and China) would damage the relationship (Chan and Tsang 2015). Moreover, it asserted that the SAR's economic development was inseparable from the mainland and that nativist/localist sentiments and actions were counterproductive to the region's development (Gao 2015).

Stronger warnings were made by top Chinese and HKSAR officials, legal scholars and other moral entrepreneurs and securitizing agents in the same month. The most consequential and threatening remarks were those by China's number three leader, Zhang Dejiang, the chairman of the National People's Congress (NPC), who declared that calls for independence and separatism in Hong Kong surrounding the APT/anti-CTW/anti-mainlander protests/movements/sentiments had approached China's 'red line' and were 'intolerable' (RTHK 2015a; Cheung and Cheung 2015; China Daily 2015a). Zhang reportedly asserted the activists were attempting to 'alienate people on both sides of the border from each other' and told HKSAR patriots to stop them (Economic Journal Insight 2015). Of related significance was that no fewer than 15 English-language op-eds or editorials (e.g. in the *China Daily*, *Global Times* and *South China Morning Post*) were published that month castigating and warning against Hong Kong independence along Zhang's directions – typically with allusions or references to APT protests or anti-mainland sentiments in Hong Kong (China Daily 2015b; Ma 2015; Wong 2015; Wu 2015). Several media exhibited expressions of moral panic and 'enemy image-making', indicated through processes of dehumanization, distortion, exaggeration and fabrications: minor scuffles became riots; APT protester folk devils became 'enemies of the state', 'fascists', 'gangsters', 'rapists' and 'hate groups'. HKSAR Chief Executive C. Y. Leung also accused radical pro-democracy lawmakers of instigating the APT/anti-CTW protests, blamed protesters for diminished tourism numbers and warned that the impact of the protests 'could not be underestimated' (RTHK 2015b; RTHK 2015c). Subsequently, mainstream Hong Kong media have uncritically reproduced tenuous regime-asserted linkages between APT/anti-CTW/localism and diminishing tourism (Lam 2015).

Five months later, the HKSARG conveniently 'discovered' an alleged separatist bomb plot concocted by a never heard of militant localist group (the National Independent Party), accused of conspiring to disrupt a political reform vote in June 2015. Though no firm evidence was supplied at the time of writing (November 2015) and the governments' claims were widely viewed as dubious, the regime's 'moral entrepreneurs' and media mouthpieces wasted no effort in linking APT protesters, localists, nativists and radical pro-democracy elements to the putative terror cell, just as they had sensationally exaggerated and distorted many details of APT protests earlier in 2015. Given that Hong Kong's protest culture – even its more rambunctious, transgressive and uncivil APT/anti-CTW subset – is almost universally non-violent, these arguably can be seen as quite fantastical moral panic overtures to discredit Hongkongers espousing resistance to the CTW and relentless integration with Socialist China.

Conclusion

This chapter has briefly analysed the politicization of the CTW in Hong Kong and associated Hongkonger resistance movements, loosely situating them within the broader geopolitical context and nationalistic and separatist politics. It discussed the phenomena of APT/anti-CTW protests and sentiments juxtaposed against the crushing weight of the tourism tsunami. Begrudging and constrained HKSAR regime responses to manage tourism inflows, but not to assuage cultural, economic, social and political costs or to reduce tourist numbers, were identified. The complicated history and tedious contemporary relationship between Hong Kong and China were sketched, setting the ground for the rise of the Hongkonger City State, localist and nativist sentiments, groups and movements. Relatedly, the emergence of a constructed ethnicity – 'Hongkonger, not Chinese' – in response to excessive tourism inflows and relentless integration was broached as part of larger Hongkonger versus Mainlander identity politics. Hegemonic moral panic and securitizing responses demonizing, delegitimizing and attempting to subdue subaltern Hongkonger folk devils confronting China's tourism onslaught and putatively threatening the HKSAR–Mainland relationship were raised.

In short, this chapter primarily illuminated how, in the wake of more than a quarter of a billion Chinese tourist to Hong Kong since 2003, APT/anti-CTW protests and anti-mainland sentiments regarding tourism and integration have become volatile symbols of the intensification of the Hongkonger–Mainlander conflict. Significantly, Hong Kong's anti-Chinese tourism drama is not an exceptional case: in Taiwan the growing influx of Chinese tourists has become salient in electoral and protest politics involving identity and security debates, as well as affecting cross-Strait relations with many critical voices accusing China of using tourism 'as a tool of foreign policy and a tactic of territorial projects' (Rowen 2016: 8, 2014). In light of China's emergence as the world's largest tourism source and its government's increasing awareness of tourism's potential to add clout to its soft power and to otherwise influence international relations, it is not beyond the realms of possibility that similar conflicts might emerge elsewhere. These conflicts illustrate that tourism is not only a profoundly political phenomenon but can also have potentially far-reaching geopolitical – and even security – implications.

Notes

1 'Tamar' is the location of the HKSAR government complex.
2 Parallel traders (PTs) are mainland visitors buying lower priced goods in bulk and illicitly transporting them into China undeclared for resale; they operate independently or as part of organized buying rings or criminal syndicates and utilize Hong Kong's public transportation infrastructure. The HKSARG categorizes all 'visitors' as tourists; it claims PTs are not easily distinguishable from other visitors.
3 That is rule advocates and creators of public threats, who identify and lobby for some issue/thing/person to be seen as a social problem and who strongly advocate for social control responses (Becker 1963).
4 Travel between Hong Kong and the Mainland is controlled by China; Mainlanders visit as part of tour groups or under a special individual scheme limited to certain cities.
5 The total number was in excess of 270 million based on HKSAR statistics. Total mainland visitor arrivals between 2003 and 2009 accounted for some 97 million visitors. Between 2010 and 2014, another 173 million visitors arrived under expanded Mainland tourism schemes.
6 Competing subaltern anti-Mainland tourism protests, representations and sentiments, and demonizing enemy image-creating hegemonic discourses are taken as objects of interpretative analysis. Analysis is informed by the author's qualitative work visualizing HKSAR protest culture (Garrett 2013, 2015; Garrett and Ho 2014) and investigating political struggles between insurgent Hong Kong and domineering China (Garrett 2014b, 2014c). A broad corpus of official texts, hegemonic opinion journalism and subaltern paraphernalia collected via participant observation during APT/anti-CTW demonstrations, rallies, marches and mobilizations between 2011 and 2015 are drawn upon. This chapter does not assert to be an authoritative or exhaustive account of the identity and securitization politics related to the inflows of Mainland Chinese tourism to the HKSAR.

7 The label alludes to swarming insects descending on an area and devouring everything. It largely came to prominence in 2012 as Mainland tourists/traders allegedly stripped stores bare of goods; Mainland Chinese have also used the phrase to refer to urban migrants. HKSAR usage has provoked debate over whether it should be outlawed under racial discrimination laws.

8 On 1 July 2003 half a million Hongkongers marched against the imposition of new Chinese-mandated national security legislation. Concurrent demands were made for the introduction of universal suffrage. It was the largest march in post-Handover history and represented the first major political crisis in China–HKSAR relations.

9 The IVS programme initially covered four cities in Guangdong Province. It was subsequently expanded multiple times and presently includes 49 mainland cities. In addition to Beijing and Shanghai, all cities within Guangdong Province and major cities in the Pearl River Delta Region adjacent to the HKSAR are included. Since 2009, various residents of the Shenzhen Special Economic Zone next to Hong Kong have been allowed one-year multiple-entry permits. Since 2013 IVS visitors constitute the majority of mainland arrivals (Secretariat to the Commission on Strategic Development 2014a: Annex 2).

10 The HKSAR is a small, highly urbanized, dense enclave of 7.24 million people. Its bounded area constitutes 1,100 square kilometres of which only a quarter is urbanized thereby making it 'one of the most densely populated places in the world' with 6,690 persons per square kilometre (Information Services Department 2015b).

11 Region, as used in this chapter generally, refers to the territory of post-Handover Hong Kong (as opposed to the colony of pre-Handover Hong Kong). The HKSAR government and Chinese officials tend often to use Region or SAR whereas many Hongkongers use Hong Kong, especially those in opposition to CTW trends. There are also cultural and political nuances in how and when each term may be used, as well as historical factors. For instance, in many of the anti-CTW visuals and literature a clear distinction is made between the HKSAR/Region and Hong Kong: the former being a Chinese communist political entity – an alien other – and the latter referring to a cultural (and now also a political) identity.

12 These were high-profile performances occurring along the tourist and shopping areas of Tsim Sha Tsui, various New Towns and in Mong Kok. The 'Anti-Locust' protest in February on Canton Road – the premier luxury shopping district – and near the iconic Star Ferry kicked off the series which targeted high-end mainland shoppers, e.g. the 'patriotic parody' protest depicted in Figure 6.1 (March 2014). 'Luggage and Pride' events mocking Mainland tourists by walking slowly and loudly through shopping malls in large groups dragging luggage behind them and squatting in public areas transpired over the following months. 'Toddler Gate' responded to public defecation and urination by a mainland child in Mong Kok (and instances elsewhere such as children urinating in restaurants) with a roving photography exhibition of Mainlanders relieving themselves across Hong Kong was displayed with many other images of similar transgressions shared online.

13 In February 2012, local netizens crowdfunded a newspaper advertisement depicting a giant locust crouching over the city atop an icon of the Hongkonger identity, the 'Lion Rock'. Accompanying the illustration was the claim and appeal that 'Hong Kongers have had enough!' which asked: 'Would you like to see Hong Kong spend HK$1,000,000 every 18 minutes on the children of non-Hong Kongers?' (Garrett and Ho 2014: 352).

14 These proponents are academics, commentators and other opinion leaders enunciating a strong pro-establishment position advocating for and defending the HKSAR and Chinese regimes. Briefly, 'Taiwanization' in the HKSAR context refers to identity politics demarcating and privileging local cultural and political identities as distinctive from socialist mainland China. Local values and interests are privileged over national (Chinese) ones. Parallels also exist in anti-communist sentiment, desires to keep China

at a distance, concerns over influxes of Mainlanders and Mainland culture. Informal cooperation between some Hong Kong and Taiwan activists and politicians (especially the Sunflower Movement and Occupy/Umbrella actors) have goaded hegemonic accusations of independence conspiracies.

15 Securitization (Wæver 1995) refers to the designation by certain political actors of an issue, object or social problem as a 'security matter', thereby removing it from public debate, as security issues are claimed to be the sovereign purview of the state. Invocation of 'national security' primes the public to accept regime use of exceptional measures to respond to the 'threat'.

16 See Lin (2012) for a brief account of Hong Kong as a 'shopper's paradise'.

17 'Liberate' or 'liberation' are common catchphrases used in conjunction in APT actions in the New Territories such as 'Liberate Yuen Long' or 'Liberate Sha Tin'. It insinuates PTs have 'invaded' and 'occupied' Hong Kong's new town urban spaces; this is visually suggested in PTs' 'camping out' in large queues surrounding MTR stations and other sites.

18 A review of APT/anti-CTW off and online discourses since 2010 discloses an array of negative attitudes and behaviours commonly attributed to some mainland visitors by some Hongkongers. Claims are frequently 'substantiated' with visual 'evidence' of transgressive acts shared online as individual images or montages in mashups, e.g. via YouTube. Attitudes and behaviours frequently depicted include: arrogance, committing petty crimes like pickpocketing, corruption, defecating and urinating in public (lifts, restaurants, streets, train stations and passenger cars), lawlessness, lacking humanity, littering, rule-breaking, speaking loudly, acting rude, spitting, squatting in public, lack of culture and violent attitude. Separately, Loi and Pearce (2015) have noted at least 40 'troublesome behaviours' connected to Mainland Chinese tourists as perceived by Hongkongers.

19 A much publicized HKSARG study (Commerce and Economic Development Bureau 2013) claimed to have examined the SAR's ability to absorb additional tourists. It concluded that tens of millions more tourists could be accommodated. However, the report only assessed infrastructural capacity – not the socio-political or livelihood impacts of existing or expanded tourism inflows. Livelihood was mentioned, but not in terms of perceived adverse cultural, economic, social and political implications – simply in terms of potential revenue and the need to increase policing resources. Moreover, it explicitly dismissed parallel trading as salient to its 'assessment' of tourism capacity: 'given that combating parallel trade activities and Hong Kong's capacity to receive tourists are two separate issues and should not be discussed together, this report has not included parallel trading in our assessment or discussion' (p. 35).

20 Migration to Hong Kong is controlled by China. Children born in the SAR gain the right of abode and associated rights and benefits affiliated with HKSAR permanent residency.

References

[Unless otherwise stated, all URLs were last accessed 1 July 2015.]

Becker, H. S. (1963) *Outsiders: Studies in the Sociology of Deviance*. New York: Free Press.

Chan, S. and Tsang, E. (2015) 'Hong Kong protest sees arrests, but triads stay away', *South China Morning Post*, 1 March.

Chan, T. (2012a) 'A dangerous political trend', *China Daily*, 10 October.

Chan, T. (2012b) 'Rita Fan rejects talk of campaign against "one country, two systems"', *South China Morning Post*, 27 October.

Chan, T. (2012c) 'Social movements getting more politically motivated', *China Daily*, 4 October.

Chen, L. (2014) 'Beyond the Umbrella movement: Hong Kong's struggle with inequality in 8 charts', *Forbes*, 8 October.

Cheng, J. Y. S. (2014) 'The emergence of radical politics in Hong Kong: causes and impact', *China Review*, 14: 199–232.

Cheung, A. B. L. (2006) 'The rise of identity politics', *South China Morning Post*, 28 December.

Cheung, G. and Cheung, T. (2015) 'NPC boss Zhang Dejiang blasts supporters of Hong Kong independence', *South China Morning Post*, 6 March.

Cheung, G. and Lau, S. (2012) 'Love China or leave it, says Lu Ping', *South China Morning Post*, 1 November.

China Daily (2015a) 'Zhang warns against calls for HK independence', *China Daily*, 6 March.

China Daily (2015b) 'Hong Kong protesters attacking tourists are worse than gangsters', *China Daily*, 11 March.

Cohen, S. (1972) *Folk Devils and Moral Panics: The Creation of the Mods and Rockers*. London: MacGibbon & Kee.

Commerce and Economic Development Bureau (2013) *Assessment Report on Hong Kong's Capacity to Receive Tourists*. Hong Kong: HKSARG.

Delicath, J. W. and DeLuca, K. M. (2003) 'Image events, the public sphere, and argumentative practice: the case of radical environmental groups', *Argumentation*, 17(3): 315–33.

Economic Journal Insight (2014) 'Current social weather likened to events leading to 1967 riots', *Economic Journal Insight*, 18 August.

Economic Journal Insight (2015) 'Anti-parallel-trading activists stirring up enmity: NPC chief', *Economic Journal Insight*, 5 March.

Gao, F. (2015) '"Localism" voice endangers future of HK, *China Daily*, 30 March.

Garrett, D. (2009) *'One Country, Two Systems' in the 21st Century: A New Policy?* Paper presented at the International Symposium 'China's Rise and Its Impact on Asia: Democratization, Development and Culture', 20–22 March, Louisville, Kentucky.

Garrett, D. (2013) 'Visualizing protest culture in China's Hong Kong: recent tensions over integration', *Visual Communication*, 12(1): 55–70.

Garrett, D. (2014a) *Cyber Insurgency in China's Competitive Authoritarian Showpiece: The Hong Kong Special Administrative Region, Parallels with the Russian Federation*. Paper presented at the American Political Science Association (APSA) Annual Meeting, 'Politics after the Digital Revolution', 28–31 August, Washington, DC.

Garrett, D. (2014b) 'Framing the radicals: panic on Canton Road', Blog, *China Policy Institute*, 26 February. Online. Available at https://blogs.nottingham.ac.uk/chinapolicyinstitute/2014/02/26/framing-the-radicals-panic-on-canton-road-i/.

Garrett, D. (2014c) 'Superheroes in Hong Kong's political resistance: images, icons, and opposition', *PS: Political Science and Politics*, 47(1): 112–19.

Garrett, D. (2015) *Counter-hegemonic Resistance in China's Hong Kong: Visualizing Protest in the City*. Singapore: Springer.

Garrett, D. and Ho, W. C. (2014) 'Hong Kong at the brink: emerging forms of political participation in the new social movement', in J. Y. S. Cheng (ed.) *New Trends of Political Participation in Hong Kong*. Hong Kong: City University of Hong Kong Press.

Grundy, T. (2014) 'Mong Kok's 1/4 mile Occupy camp sits amidst 40 luxury stores', Blog, *Hong Wrong*, 16 November. Online. Available at http://hongwrong.com/luxury-store-gentrification/.

Hall, C. M. (1994) *Tourism and Politics: Policy, Power, and Place*. Chichester and New York: Wiley.

HKSARG Census and Statistics Department (2011) *Hong Kong 2011 Population Census – Thematic Report: Household Income Distribution in Hong Kong*. Online. Available at http://www.statistics.gov.hk/pub/B11200572012XXXXB0100.pdf.

Ho, K.-L. (2000) *Polite Politics: A Sociological Analysis of an Urban Protest in Hong Kong*. Aldershot: Ashgate.

Hobson, J. S. P. and Ko, G. (1994) 'Tourism and politics: the implications of the change of sovereignty on the future development of Hong Kong's tourism industry', *Journal of Travel Research*, 32(4): 2–8.

Hung, H.-F. (2014) 'Three views of local consciousness in Hong Kong', *Asia Pacific Journal*, 12(44): n.p.

Information Services Department (2014) *LCQ2: Control on the Number of Visitors to Hong Kong*. Hong Kong: HKSARG.

Information Services Department (2015a) 'HKSAR Government welcomes new measure to optimize "multiple-entry"', *Individual Visit Endorsements*. Hong Kong: HKSARG.

Information Services Department (2015b) *Hong Kong: The Facts (Population)*. Hong Kong: HKSARG.

Information Services Department (2015c) *LCQ1: Decline in Number of Visitors to Hong Kong*. Hong Kong: HKSARG.

Information Services Department (2015d) *Parallel Trading Meeting Held*. Hong Kong: HKSARG.

Lam, J. (2015) 'Is the rise of localism a threat to Hong Kong's cosmopolitan values?', *South China Morning Post*, 2 June.

Lam, J., Kao, E. and Zhao, S. (2014) 'Hong Kong's "era of disobedience" has begun, says Occupy leader as protesters join forces', *South China Morning Post*, 1 September.

Lin, J. (2012) '40 years of retail change but Hong Kong remains a shopper's paradise', *South China Morning Post*, 5 September.

Lo, S. (2015) 'HK needs to educate its youth', *China Daily*, 9 January.

Lo, S. H. (2008) *The dynamics of Beijing–Hong Kong relations: A Model for Taiwan?* Hong Kong: Hong Kong University Press.

Lo, S. H. (2014) *Integration and Adaptation: Contrasting Hong Kong with Macao*. China Policy Institute. Online. Available at https://blogs.nottingham.ac.uk/chinapolicyinstitute/2014/01/29/integration-and-adaptation-contrasting-hong-kong-with-macao/.

Loh, C. (2010) *Underground Front: The Chinese Communist Party in Hong Kong*. Hong Kong: Hong Kong University Press.

Loi, K. L. and Pearce, P. L. (2015) 'Exploring perceived tensions arising from tourist behaviors in a Chinese context', *Journal of Travel and Tourism Marketing*, 32(1–2): 65–79.

Ma, C. (2015) 'Hong Kong protests damage rule of law', *Global Times*, 18 March.

Mok, C. and Dewald, B. (1999) 'Tourism in Hong Kong: after the handover', *Asia Pacific Journal of Tourism Research*, 3(2): 32–40.

Moy, P. and Lau, S. (2013) 'Zero quote on mainland mums in hospitals "bad for economy"', *South China Morning Post*, 26 May.

Ngo, J. (2013) '1.3 million Hongkongers live in poverty, government says, but offers no solution', *South China Morning Post*, 28 September.

O'Brien, A. (2011) *The Politics of Tourism Development: Booms and Busts in Ireland*. Basingstoke: Palgrave Macmillan.

Qian, Q. (2005) *Ten Episodes in China's Diplomacy*. New York: HarperCollins.

Resonance Insights (2014) 'Chinese tourist shopping slowing with luxury sales falling 40% in Hong Kong', *Resonance*, 9 September.

Rowen, I. (2014) 'Tourism as a territorial strategy: the case of China and Taiwan', *Annals of Tourism Research*, 46: 62–74.

Rowen, I. (forthcoming, 2016) 'The geopolitics of tourism: mobilities, territory and protests in China, Taiwan and Hong Kong', *Annals of the Association of American Geographers*.

RTHK (2015a) 'Beijing in stern warning over independence call', *RTHK*, 6 March.

RTHK (2015b) 'CY Leung accused of being insincere', *RTHK*, 26 March.

RTHK (2015c) 'Pan-democrats behind protests: CE', *RTHK*, 22 March.

Secretariat to the Commission on Strategic Development (2010) *Hong Kong's Role in the Development of the Mainland* (translation). Hong Kong: HKSARG.

Secretariat to the Commission on Strategic Development (2014a) *Hong Kong's Relationship with the Central Authorities/the Mainland* (translation). Hong Kong: HKSARG.

Secretariat to the Commission on Strategic Development (2014b) *Summary of Views Expressed at the Fifth Meeting of the Commission on Strategic Development held on 26 May 2014*. Hong Kong: HKSARG.

Siu, G., Lee, L. Y. S. and Leung, D. (2013) 'Residents' perceptions toward the "Chinese Tourists' Wave" in Hong Kong: an exploratory study', *Asia Pacific Journal of Tourism Research*, 18(5): 446–63.

So, A. Y. (2011) 'The development of post-modernist social movements in the Hong Kong Special Administrative Region', in J. Broadbent and V. Brockman (eds) *East Asian Social Movements: Power, Protest, and Change in a Dynamic Region*. New York: Springer.

Tilly, C. (2008) *Contentious Performances*. Cambridge: Cambridge University Press.

Tourism Commission (2015) *Tourism Performance in 2014*. Online. Available at http://www.tourism.gov.hk/english/statistics/statistics_perform.html.

Wæver, O. (1995) 'Securitization and desecuritization', in R. Lipschutz (ed.) *On Security*. New York: Columbia University Press.

Weaver, D. B. (2010) 'Geopolitical dimensions of sustainable tourism', *Tourism Recreation Research*, 35(1): 47–53.

Wong, R. (2015) 'Shades of Ku Klux Klan in stir against parallel traders', *South China Morning Post*, 17 March.

Wu, A. (2015) 'Abusing people in the name of ending parallel trading only adds to the problem', *South China Morning Post*, 15 March.

Yang, S. (2012) 'Hong Kong needs rational expression', *China Daily*, 27 September.

Yeun, S. (2014) 'Under the shadow of China: Beijing's policy towards Hong Kong and Taiwan in comparative perspective', *China Perspectives*, 2: 69–76.

Yun, M. and Hu, F. (2013) 'Hong Kong's first poverty line puts one-fifth of people in need', *Bloomberg News*, 29 September.

Zhou, B. (2014a) 'Brand new chapter begins in Hong Kong SAR politics', *China Daily*, 3 September.

Zhou, B. (2014b) 'HK has to decide what it really wants', *China Daily*, 11 June.

7 From San Francisco's 'Tech Boom 2.0' to Valparaíso's UNESCO World Heritage Site

Resistance to tourism gentrification from a comparative political perspective

Florian Opillard

On 22 November 2014, two housing activism collectives, the Anti Eviction Mapping Project and Eviction Free San Francisco, called for a protest against 'the Airbnb takeover of San Francisco', USA (Anti-Eviction Mapping Project 2014), right in front of Fort Mason Center, which was hosting an 'Open Airbnb Host Conference'. Both organizations were denouncing Airbnb's role in the rapid gentrification and shortage of affordable housing in the city. After gathering in front of the entrance, the activists held signs that read 'Airbnb, don't evict me!' or 'I lost my apartment to a tourist. It's unfAirbnb'. Claiming that the so-called 'sharing economy'[1] is in fact a selfish economy, they raised the issue of Airbnb triggering the removal of units from the rental stock available to local residents, therefore aggravating the housing crisis responsible for the eviction of thousands of San Franciscans.

On 23 October 2014, a group of activists gathered in front of the *centro juvenil* (youth centre) in Barón, one of the 42 hills of Valparaíso, Chile, to organize a *pasacalles* (march) aimed at *ponerse de pie por su dignidad y patrimonio* (standing up for one's dignity and heritage). After setting up a banner, the crowd headed down the hill towards the ocean and stopped in front of the San Francisco church, a symbol of the city's slowly decaying historical heritage. The crowd then walked towards the recently destroyed Hospital Ferroviario, one of the city's working-class icons soon to be replaced by a luxury condominium with 'the best view of Valparaíso'. After several speakers defended the *verdadero patrimonio* (real heritage), the protesters ended the march chanting *¡Barón no se vende, el barrio se defende!* (Barón is not for sale, the *barrio* defends itself).

The comparison of the struggles unravelling in San Francisco and Valparaíso that these two incidents exemplify allows a cross-contextual analysis of what activism and resistance reveal in terms of processes of dispossession triggered by tourism capital flows. On the one hand, in the case of Valparaíso, the coordinated politics of tourism, in particular through the designation of some of the city's historic districts as a UNESCO World Heritage Site, appear to have dramatically fuelled the gentrification of some of the city's neighbourhoods (Jacquot 2005), such as Barón. On the other hand, San Francisco is currently experiencing what has been referred to as a 'hyper-gentrification process' (Brahinsky 2014) – in part caused by the so-called 'Tech Boom 2.0' (Opillard forthcoming). In this process, the existing housing crisis has been aggravated by the success of online short-term rental platforms such as Airbnb, through which landlords can profit from the growth of the 'sharing economy' and remove their properties from the regular rental market in order to rent them to visitors and tourists.

The concept of 'tourism gentrification' can be applied to both cases to encompass processes of economic, socio-demographic, cultural and material changes in urban space. Nonetheless, tourism gentrification per se has yet to be clearly defined (Gotham 2010), and it seems that the use of this concept tends to overlap between studies of tourism-induced city-centre rehabilitation (Salin 2002) or heritage reclamation (Jacquot 2006) on the one hand, and studies on gentrification on the other (Lees *et al.* 2010). Following Gotham (2010), in this chapter I argue that the concept of tourism gentrification is an effective tool to analyse the local effects of changes in policy decisions and of the intervention of new actors (Swyngedouw 1997; Brenner 2001) in cities currently experiencing the effects of a surge in tourism flows and capital. I also stress the fact that ethnographic observations of the resistance to distinct processes of tourism gentrification can help shed light on the intricate co-construction of urban development agendas and the surge of tourism flows.[2] The chapter first sketches the theoretical framework that makes the concept of tourism gentrification relevant for the understanding of global and local processes of power restructuring in contemporary (tourist) cities. These processes are then approached through the comparison of the politics of tourism, and of the resistance to their impacts, in the city of Valparaíso (Chile) and the City and County of San Francisco (United States).

Tourism gentrification: politics of scale, global and local shifts

In order to understand tourism gentrification processes, it is essential to elaborate upon their specificity with regard to paradigmatic processes of gentrification on the one hand, and to the increasingly complex nature of tourism developments and practices in the urban sphere on the other.

Waves of gentrification and urban change

Research on gentrification has attracted a lot of attention in past decades. The debates over the triggering of gentrification processes in various contexts have created a dynamic research field in which scholars have mostly argued over both demand-side and production-side explanations. On the one hand, demand-side explanations suggest that 'markets and (the) state respond to consumer demand for gentrification', making it essential to analyse the 'switch from suburban to urban aspirations' (Brown-Saracino 2010: 27) of what David Ley calls the 'new middle class' (Ley 1996). The emergence of a new consumer potential embodied in 'white collar workers associated with a post-industrial, service oriented economy' (Brown-Saracino 2010: 65) thus shapes gentrification processes while the market seizes the opportunity which these consumers' aspirations represent. On the other hand, the 'generalization' of gentrification patterns in multiple contexts has made it possible to talk about 'global urban strategies' (Smith 2002) and their specific enactment in various settings (Bridge *et al.* 2011; Lees 2012). Neil Smith's explanation of the gentrification processes through the rent gap, i.e. 'the disparity between the potential ground rent level and the actual ground rent capitalized under the present land use' (Smith 1996: 65), revealed the mechanisms by which gentrification can be a 'form of *collective social action* at the neighbourhood level' (ibid.), whether it is initiated by the state or by financial institutions. His depiction of the Lower East Side's battles in the 1990s specifically focused on the real estate market's mechanisms that contributed to the emergence of 'new frontiers' within the city (Smith 1996). In his later works, Neil Smith identified three waves of gentrification, which account for both the expansion and intensification of the process and the re-articulation of market and state relations (Hackworth and Smith 2001).

In light of the ongoing 'financialisation of urban production' (Le Goix and Halbert, 2012; Aalbers 2015), the global spread of gentrification, as well as the accelerating 'super gentrification' (Lees 2000) of world cities like New York, London or, indeed San Francisco, Smith's definition of these three waves is today more relevant than ever. An aspect that Smith only raised implicitly was the role tourist flows and the tourism-related investments and interests play in the production, extension and intensification of gentrification processes. This issue was later picked up and elaborated upon by Gotham (2010) who introduced the concept of 'tourism gentrification' to discuss how tourism – and in particular tourism-oriented promotion strategies – encourage and provoke gentrification. Focusing on the case of New Orleans' Vieux Carré (French Quarter), he highlighted especially 'the role of state policy [. . .] and the actions of large corporate entertainment firms' in the socio-spatial transformation of the neighbourhood, but at the same time claimed that tourism gentrification 'presents a challenge to traditional explanations of gentrification that assume demand-side or production-side factors drive the process' (p.149).

Tourism gentrification: power struggles, material and discursive impacts

The challenges researchers face when trying to identify the intricacy between tourism and processes of gentrification are numerous. One of them, which will not be thoroughly discussed here, is the disentanglement of tourism-related factors from other forces leading to neighbourhood change in particular cities. Another is the tackling of both demand-side and production-side models, a dichotomy that often confines the analysis of gentrification to both a predefined set of mechanisms – tourism practices versus tourism policy – and a strict causal link – individual practices influencing market-led developments, state policy filtering down to the local. Following the work of Gotham (2010), I argue that the concept of tourism gentrification is both a heuristic tool to overcome this dichotomy and an operational concept to seize the imbrication of global and local processes. On the one hand, the ever-increasing mobility and evolving consumption preferences of the middle class are said to have resulted in significant changes with regard to cities' tourism and leisure landscapes. On the other hand, numerous studies have identified tourism economic interests as an important factor contributing to policies resulting in gentrification, while the emergence – and the territorial impacts – of new actors such as Airbnb further complicates the interplay among forces shaping gentrification processes.

In this context, I argue here that tourism gentrification does not only refer to 'the transformation of middle-class neighbourhoods into a relatively affluent and exclusive enclave marked by a proliferation of corporate entertainment and tourism venues' (Gotham 2010: 148). Rather, I want to expand its scope to include the consequences of the power shifts provoked by tourism gentrification, insisting on the discursive processes accelerating or counteracting the transformation of gentrifying spaces. A constant struggle against erasure and for the persistence of collective memory lies at the heart of gentrification processes (Lee and Yeoh 2005), since both the commodification of collective memory (Kearns and Philo 1993) and the 'mutual forgetting of what came before the constructions of new buildings, restaurants, and businesses [are] critical to the creation of sites based on gentrified consumption' (Raquel Mirabal 2009: 17). The concept of tourism gentrification provides the opportunity to identify the ways in which changing touristic 'landscapes of power' (Zukin 1993) reconfigure both the way space is remembered and the way people identify with it.

The following section aims to illustrate the complexity of the processes of tourism gentrification, by firstly drawing attention to the declaration of parts of Valparaíso as a UNESCO World Heritage Site and the impact this has had on discursive and material processes of neighbourhood change. The city's designation process exemplifies the growing influence of new actors in local governance and urban development following the UNESCO nomination. The transformation of the city that has arisen as a result has been contested. Subsequently, I will explore how recent developments in the so-called 'sharing economy' have fuelled processes of gentrification in San Francisco, leading to political struggles over the legalization of a private corporation's practices, Airbnb. This illustrates the blurred lines between demand-side and supply-side analysis in tourism gentrification research.

Tourism policy and tourism gentrification in two neoliberal contexts

Tourism gentrification plays out differently in different places depending on a variety of factors – global, national and local, as well as agential and structural. In this section two case studies[3] – the city of Valparaíso, Chile and the City and County of San Francisco, United States – are explored to depict two very distinct types of urban tourism policies. On many levels, San Francisco and Valparaíso have more in common than one might expect. Both are coastal cities built upon dozens of steep hillsides; both cities' histories are intrinsically tied to their ports, and both cities were transformed into boomtowns and magnets for European immigrants during the Gold Rush. These and other similarities – both are, for example, well known for their unique and varied architectural heritage dating from the nineteenth and early twentieth centuries as well as a long history of countercultural and bohemian movements – should not obscure the gulf that otherwise separates them. One of the most prosperous cities in one of the most prosperous countries of the world, San Francisco is today experiencing a rapid growth in population, with an estimated 852,469 inhabitants growing by 5.9 per cent between 2011 and 2015 and an increase of visitors by 6.5 per cent between 2013 and 2014 to 18 million visitors. Its economic prosperity, thanks to the proximity of the Silicon Valley, makes it one of the most wealthy cities in the United States, with a median income reaching 75,604$ in 2013 (United States Census Bureau 2015). The demographic and economic situation of Valparaíso stands in sharp contrast. With an estimated population of 269,446 inhabitants in 2012, which decreased by 2 per cent between 2002 and 2012, Valparaíso, Chile's third-largest city and in the past sometimes referred to as the country's 'little San Francisco', is meanwhile facing a difficult economic situation: the average household income in 2009 was just above $12,000 a year, with high levels of inequality (Biblioteca del Congreso Nacional de Chile 2012). In parallel, the number of tourists who stayed in hotels in the Valparaíso region (*Quinta Región*) between 2010 and 2013 increased by 48 per cent from 537,371 to 799,246 (Instituto Nacional de Estadísticas 2013). Both cities' economies rely on their tourism industries in very distinct ways. While the Chilean central government and Valparaíso's local government count on tourism as a key sector to trigger the city's economic recovery, the ongoing tourism boom in San Francisco partly stems from the existing dynamism of the city's economy.

Heritage reclamation ('recuperación patrimonial') in the wake of the UNESCO designation: discourses and power struggles over the making of local heritage in Valparaíso, Chile

Valparaíso is remarkable for many different reasons: its cove shape and colourful houses sprinkling the city's 42 *cerros* (hills), the nineteenth-century architecture that European migrants (Germans, French, British, Italians) brought along with them, the artistic and bohemian lifestyle that still attracts many tourists. These amenities started to be thought of as touristic assets by local decision-makers in the 1990s with the city government's decision to submit a bid to become a UNESCO World Heritage Site. The process that led to the bid, as described by Jacquot (2005), lasted for ten years and was characterized by intense discussions, disputes and power struggles over what was unique to Valparaíso's local heritage (*patrimonio*) and consequently worthy of being included in the city's bid to be added to the UNESCO World Heritage list. In the first nomination dossier that the city government submitted to ICOMOS, the non-profit organization in charge of the evaluation of World Heritage Site candidacies, the discourse defining the *patrimonio* underlined the

> universal and noticeable values of the amphitheatre city, composed of the superposition of the geographical features of the bay, of specific architecture and urbanism, shaped by the natural landscape and anthropic intervention through the city's historic development, which ties together, combines and makes its own the natural and built elements.
>
> (Jacquot 2005: 395)

While the city government was elaborating the bid, the Chilean central government prepared a plan to support the development of the city. In 2000, the Ministry of Housing and Urban Planning developed a 'plan to revitalize the historic centre' (Jacquot 2007: 283), and in 2002 an exceptional initiative by the President Ricardo Lagos launched the *Plan Valparaíso*, which aimed at 'opening the seashore, promoting and facilitating investments and transforming Valparaíso into a heritage and cultural city' (ibid.).

The first UNESCO bid failed to convince ICOMOS and was turned down in 2000, according to Guerrero Valdebenito (2012) because of a lack of experience of local actors and insufficient preparation. The second attempt, this time designed by the city government, the regional administration, the Council of National Monuments and the national Ministry of Public Works, included a systematic listing of the buildings with heritage value. The perimeter concerned the areas closest to the harbour – the Barrio Puerto – along with two hills with a noticeable architectural landscape – the Cerro Alegre and Cerro Concepción, highlighting the 'exceptional testimony of a phase of the nineteenth century globalization' (Jacquot 2007).

Following the granting of the UNESCO designation in 2003, the material consequences of the implementation of the heritage preservation perimeter in terms of tourism gentrification processes have been quickly felt, albeit in different ways in different parts of the city. The hospitality industry, headed by the semi-public Corporation for the Promotion of Production (*Corporación de Fomento de la Producción*), rapidly increased the infrastructure to host national and international tourists in the two hills of the designated perimeter. In these two neighbourhoods, the city government additionally subsidized the painting of facades and street pavements by contracting a fifty million dollar loan from the Interamerican Bank for Development. Although there is no official data at the neighbourhood level on second-home ownership, evidence suggests that the designation of the UNESCO perimeter triggered the purchase of many properties by *santiaguinos* (inhabitants of Santiago de Chile, the capital city) and Europeans seeking to invest in real estate with the promise of high rates of return. In his works, Jacquot suggests that 'the *Santiaguinos* . . . are important agents of this gentrification, buying houses or apartments in Valparaíso, often as a second home' (2007: 322). The multiplication of hotels, *hospedajes* and restaurants following the UNESCO designation[4] is another indicator of the neighbourhood's transition, as revealed in an interview conducted in October 2014 with a French restaurant owner who had run his business in the Cerro Alegre since 1998. He described the rapid installation of restaurants alongside his own, the subsequent increase in rents and sale prices, and the pressure on small existing businesses, many of which were forced to move as a result.

The contrast between the hills mentioned above and the Barrio Puerto, Valparaíso's 'port neighbourhood' and one of the oldest, most traditional parts of the city, is striking. Also a part of the UNESCO preservation area, Barrio Puerto used to be a centre of commerce and social life and experienced a particularly drastic process of decline as a result of the demise of Valparaíso's maritime and port industry after the opening of the Panama Canal. The declining fortunes of the port led to high concentrations of socially marginalized groups (Retamales Quintero 2010), a lack of public and private investment as well as a dilapidation of the area's building stock. The replacement of the Barrio Puerto's historical narrative – i.e. the port as the vehicle of a long-standing social mix (Chandía 2013) – with the idea of heritage as a commodity (Aravena Nuñez and Sobarzo 2009) is symbolized by the increasing number of folkloric souvenir stores and walking tours depicting the local 'bohemianism'.

Today, the neighbourhood is at the centre of a second phase of touristic development, materialized by the imminent construction of a seaside resort called *Mall Barón*. This twelve-hectare project, facilitated by the privatization of Chile's harbour administration in 1997 (the *Empresa Portuaria de Chile*, renamed *Empresa Portuaria de Valparaíso* – EPV), follows the model of cities like 'Boston, New York and Baltimore [where] great investments were made in old abandoned port precincts which were transformed into public spaces of great value for their populations and in touristic sites' (MallPlaza 2012). In this area, real-estate developers have exerted intense pressures to bypass existing historic preservation ordinances as well as zoning and height restrictions (Jacquot 2007). While the first phase of heritage restoration which accompanied the UNESCO designation rested on the promotion of a nostalgic vision of the city's nineteenth-century apogee (Aravena Nuñez 2006; Aravena Nuñez and Sobarzo 2009; Gervais-Lambony 2012; Jacquot 2007), this latest phase is characterized by an emphasis on international festivals and conferences as a means to generate development and foster the 'revival' of the declining *ciudad puerto*. The yearly festival *Puerto de Ideas*, which seeks to promote the works of local and international top scientists (financed by the Coca Cola Foundation), has been located in the derelict Severín building, one of the most emblematic properties of the city that has laid in ruins for decades, from which tons of trash and waste were removed for the occasion. In his inauguration speech in 2014, the city mayor insisted on making this festival an opportunity to capture the attention of investors willing to help and 'recuperate' the *Barrio Puerto*, quoting the example of the imminent construction of a neuroscience research centre in the same building. The festival illustrates the local government's more recent ambition, alongside tourism development, to deploy – and exploit – cultural resources in order to transform Valparaíso from a trading, industrial city into a city of 'knowledge' and 'creativity', in line with the ideas of Landry (2000) and Florida (2002).

Tourism policy as apparent laissez-faire: the corporate-led touristification of San Francisco

With millions coming to see the Golden Gate Bridge, Alcatraz, the city's steep hills and the surrounding areas from Muir Woods to the Napa, Sonoma and Silicon Valleys, San Francisco is one of the United States' major domestic and international tourist destinations. The city is the third most popular urban destination in the country among international tourists behind New York City and Los Angeles, with 18 million visitors in 2014 generating a record-breaking $10.7 billion in visitor spending (San Francisco Travel Association 2015). Perhaps unsurprisingly then, tourism has also for a long time been recognized as a crucial driver of urban change. McDougall and Mitnick (1998), for instance, already claimed in the 1990s that San Francisco was subjected to a 'Disneyland-style thematization' as a result of the influx and influence of tourists: 'whole neighbourhoods have been destroyed, recreated, and redecorated as tourist destinations by urban planners who use the same strategies as film production designers to transform the city into a collection of picturesque facades' (p. 153). While San Francisco is often described as one of the few large US-American cities in which activists have had a real and sustained impact on urban and neighbourhood development (Hartmann 2002; Beitel 2013; Tracy 2013), tourism as a policy area has been dominated for decades by the interests of the tourism industry. Described by Chester Hartman as one of the 'principal driving forces behind the transformation of the city' (p. 20), the San Francisco Convention and Visitors Bureau (CVB), in particular, played an instrumental role in numerous initiatives to stimulate tourism development. It has now been renamed 'San Francisco Travel', a private, not-for-profit membership organization, 'aggressively marketing and selling San Francisco to attract visitors' (San Francisco Travel Association 2015). Exemplifying the 'thin line between the public and the private sector' (Hartmann 2002: 21) that tends to characterize tourism marketing organizations and headed by a Board of Directors made up of 45 business leaders from various companies, its vision is to 'ensure that San Francisco is the most compelling destination in the world'.

In the context of a very well structured and wealthy industry promoting the development of tourist attractions and convention centres, the recent emergence of corporations surfing the wave of the so-called 'sharing economy' tends to complexify the analysis. Online platforms like Airbnb and VRBO that allow owners and tenants to rent parts of or their entire apartments for short periods of time are both indicative of, and integral to, a profound reconfiguration of tourism practices and markets. Airbnb was started in 2008 in San Francisco and is today a company worth 25.5 billion dollars (Carson 2015), with approximately 500,000 listings and 350,000 hosts in about 34,000 cities around the world. At the time of writing it was estimated that the number of Airbnb listings in San Francisco was between 5,249 and 6,113 (Budget and Legislative Analyst's Office 2015), 34.7 per cent of them from hosts that have multiple listings (Cox 2015). Within the total number of listings, 59.2 per cent are entire homes with an average price of $261 per night. The geography of Airbnb listings in San Francisco reveals a

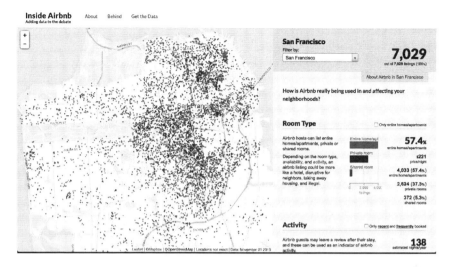

Figure 7.1 Screenshot of *Inside Airbnb* focusing on San Francisco as of 10 November 2015.

Source: http://insideairbnb.com, initially created by Murray Cox.

higher number of offers in the Downtown area, Haight and Ashbury, the Mission, the Castro and Bernal Heights, as shown in Figure 7.1.

Airbnb is currently the object of a major controversy over the role that short-term rentals play in San Francisco's housing crisis. The consequences of online rental platforms on local housing markets were described in a study delivered in May 2015 to David Campos, supervisor of the Mission District, showing for example that 'in the Mission, 29 per cent of [vacant rental housing units], or 199, were listed on the website. Another estimate states the Mission percentage could be as high as 40 per cent and as high as 43 per cent in the Haight' (Sabatini 2015). Although it has proven difficult to clearly link tenants' evictions and the surge in Airbnb listings (Said 2014a), some cases demonstrate that homeowners prefer to take their properties out of the rental market and rent them through the online platform, which allows them to significantly increase their rental income (Budget and Legislative Analyst's Office 2015). Loopholes in state legislation – mostly the Ellis Act[5] – allow landlords to exit the 'normal' rental market by evicting tenants from their properties without any justification, which facilitates the conversion of properties into permanent short-term rentals (Hill 2015).

The impact that online rental platforms have on the housing market has consequently been widely discussed in the local political arena, and companies like Airbnb are regularly accused of adding fuel to the housing crisis, which had already been deepened by the effects of the so-called 'Tech-boom 2.0' (Opillard forthcoming; Beitel 2013) that is affecting the Bay Area. Other than the effects that Airbnb listings have on the housing market, critiques have pointed out that Airbnb did not pay the city hotel tax from 2008 to 2014, thus owing the city 25 million dollars in hotel tax (Said 2014b), and that most of its 7,029 listings (Cox 2015) were not complying with local legislation which imposes a ceiling of 30 days on residential rentals.

Resisting tourism gentrification

Both the contexts and paths of tourism gentrification vary greatly in the two cities under investigation. On the one hand, Valparaíso's gentrification process stems from the prioritization of 'heritage' by both the central and local government as part of, and in parallel to, the UNESCO designation of a local protection perimeter, which has incentivized external investments from both individuals and international corporations. On the other hand, San Francisco's tourism gentrification can be ascribed, not least, to the long-standing influence of private tourism corporations in the local economy, as well as, more recently, the emergence of new players in the 'sharing economy' like Airbnb. Nonetheless, common elements emerge from this analysis: both cases of gentrification provoke the displacement of existing communities and their dispossession from their homes. Along with these processes, the narratives that contribute to building collective appropriation by long-term inhabitants tend to shift, and the power struggles that can be witnessed are those of communities fighting against the dispossession of their collective identity and memory of space. The last section of this chapter will focus on some of the communities' responses to processes of tourism gentrification, specifically stressing the contextual elements that seem to facilitate or restrict the possibilities for the building of grassroots mobilization, political power and control over the making of space.

San Francisco's community activism against
loss and displacement

In San Francisco, over the past years the housing rights and tenants' movement has again grown in importance. While it is not specifically directed towards tourism gentrification, it seeks to fight the consequences of gentrification at large, tourism gentrification being one of the many processes that provoke displacement and dispossession (Beitel 2013).

Groups and repertoires of contention in the housing movement

On 7 February 2014, after a series of local meetings in several districts of San Francisco called Neighbourhood Tenants Conventions, the Tenderloin Community School hosted the Citywide Tenants Convention. The convention was the first major event of the Anti-Displacement Coalition (SFADC) which had been established in 2013 by various community groups to 'address the wave of evictions and landlord harassment forcing thousands from their homes and neighbourhoods'

(Anti-Displacement Coalition 2014). The convention agreed on a joint resolution regarding San Francisco's deepening housing and affordability crisis that was later submitted to the Board of Supervisors, the legislative body within the government of the city and county of San Francisco. The convention also served as a starting point for the organization of two ballot initiatives: an anti-speculation tax (Proposition G) that was put up for vote to the citizens of San Francisco in November 2014 and failed to be accepted; and a ballot measure put up for vote in November 2015 asking voters to decide on tougher regulations on vacation rentals in private homes (Proposition F).

In the Anti-Displacement Coalition, two collectives have stood out: the Anti-Eviction Mapping Project (AMP) and Eviction Free San Francisco (EFSF). As a direct action group, EFSF exemplifies anti-capitalist community activism. The fight over cases of evictions mostly revolves around three modes of action: protesting in public spaces, rallying and publicly denouncing 'greedy' landlords and speculators. The AMP's modes of action correspond to the pattern of artistic and 'tech activism' specific to the Bay Area (Lallement 2015). Using technology as a tool to implement and empower community activism, the group makes maps, links housing developments and evictions to real-estate speculators and collects oral histories of displacement, using both their own collected data and the available data on evictions and housing ownership.

Both collectives are based in the Mission district, where the fight against displacement is historically strong. The Tenants Union acts as one of the main resources of many gravitating groups: it offers a workspace, material and technical support (mainly to EFSF and the AMP) in the Mission district, legal resources and volunteer-based tenants' counselling. The Housing Rights Committee, another 'housing clinic', provides space for meetings, banner making and legal support to tenants, backing the Tenants Union in its missions. Other organizations like Our Mission No Eviction and Causa Justa:Just Cause work more specifically to support Black and Latino residents, while the Chinatown Community Development Corporation actively supports the Chinese community.

The first and most visible project that the AMP group implemented was the Ellis Act Evictions Maps, which identified areas that have been struck the most by the displacement of tenants (Figure 7.2). The AMP's maps have had a great echo in the tenants' movement and have inspired the making of other maps more directly related to the fights around tourism gentrification (see Figure 7.1), as discussed below. They specifically shed light on the importance of the creation and use of data as a tool for social movements to produce alternative narratives on neighbourhood change and gentrification (Raquel Mirabal 2009).

The making of tourism as a public issue: the Airbnb
fight within the structure of political opportunities

The battle over Airbnb's right to offer short-term rentals has gained significant coverage in 2015. Up to February 2015, renting a space for less than 30 days was illegal in San Francisco, making a lot of Airbnb's rentals illegal. Yet the Board

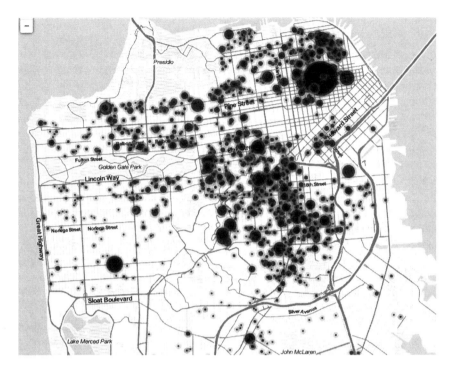

Figure 7.2 San Francisco Ellis Act evictions map by the Anti-Eviction Mapping Project, April 2014.

Source: http://www.antievictionmappingproject.net/ellis.html

of Supervisor's decision on 7 October 2014 to legalise most of the company's listings through David Chiu's (supervisor of District 3) legislation made it possible to rent out spaces within the limit of 90 days, as long as owners live in the rented space for the rest of the year and with the condition that they register with the City (Jones 2014). Some supervisors closer to the tenants' movement in the city, like David Campos (supervisor of District 9), opposed the measure in the Planning Commission, arguing that since it did not include any obligation for Airbnb to share their listings with the City, it deprived the municipal government of its capacity to enforce the 'Airbnb law'. Campos clearly stated the influence that the company is having in the preparation of local legislation concerning short-term rentals:

> I believe that home sharing and short-term rentals have a place in San Francisco but what doesn't have a place in San Francisco is the idea that a corporation can write a law, then ignore the very law that it wrote, and then refuse to provide the very basic information that is needed to enforce that law.
>
> (Raile 2014)

The fight in the Board of Supervisors over new legislation revealed the political tactics of Airbnb, whose 'board members Reid Hoffman, the co-founder of LinkedIn, and Silicon Valley super-angel Ron Conway basically bought the good graces of the president of the San Francisco Board of Supervisors through $674,000 in contributions to a supportive political action committee' (Schaal 2014). Intense campaigns took place in November 2015 over the vote on Proposition F and the election of the District 3 Supervisor. These revealed the omnipresence of Airbnb as a source of contention. While the organizations mentioned above were fighting to push for a pro-tenant candidate in District 3 – a district particularly affected by illegal Airbnb apartment conversions (Hill 2015) – the battle over Proposition F to toughen regulations on vacation rentals in private homes was subject to intense lobbying from Airbnb. The company invested 8 million dollars in the campaign against Proposition F, making it the most expensive campaign in the city's history. After the proposition was defeated in the ballot, Airbnb revealed its political strategy to invest in over '"100 clubs", a network of home-sharing "guilds" across the US', launching what the company calls an 'Airbnb host movement' to support the forthcoming conflicts with local governments (Lehane 2015) while comparing its political influence to that of the National Rifle Association (Alba 2015).

This local political fight underlined the importance of both the use and production of data to frame the political debate around the company's effects on the housing market: while Airbnb has refused to disclose its listings' data to public

Figure 7.3 Protest against Airbnb in North Beach, San Francisco, 2 October 2015.

Source: Peter Menchini.

officials, a policy analysis report by the Budget and Legislative Analyst's Office of the Board of Supervisor (Budget and Legislative Analyst's Office 2015) was transmitted to supervisor David Campos which underlines the effects of Airbnb on the housing market. For housing activists, the production of alternative data is also crucial. On a local level, both the AMP and EFSF groups have launched research projects on what they call 'Airbnb evictions' which turn apartments into short-term rentals. On a national level, the Inside Airbnb project developed by Murray Cox (Figure 7.1), 'an independent digital storyteller, community activist and technologist' (Cox 2015), offers alternative counts of the number of Airbnb listings, rate of occupancy and rate of multiple listings, contrasting with the data used by the Board of Supervisors' analyst. Like the AMP-produced maps, the map and graphics created by Murray Cox show how 'tech activism' provides tools to turn the effects of Airbnb into a public issue (Cefaï 1996).

Valparaíso's activism: community resistance against private developments

By contrast with San Francisco's well-structured and institutionalized tenants movement, participant observation in several organizations in Valparaíso revealed both the fragility and heterogeneity of collective movements. The following section will briefly explore the mobilizations surrounding tourism gentrification in Valparaíso and analyse the elements that contribute to the building of community political power over the making of space.

Tourism gentrification and the 'heritage governmentality'

In December 2013, the academic Pablo Aravena Nuñez and the lawyer Pablo Andueza delivered, along with more than fifty citizen organizations, a report to the UNESCO inspectors entitled *Valparaíso Reclamado* (Aravena Nuñez and Andueza 2013). It analysed local policy-making with regard to the World Heritage Site and stressed the influence of private corporations on decision making over urban planning issues: 'It is therefore worrying to see how the heritage management of the city – given up to the private sector without proper regulation – sometimes seems to be going straight "against" Valparaíso' (ibid.: 10–11). The dispossession described here corroborates the idea of a transfer of power to the private sector: 'Who administers our World Heritage Site? Everything indicates that only in appearances is it the entity designed by the nomination in 2003, which is to say the city government. In fact, EPV decides upon what to do on the seashore' (ibid.). The report reviews the recent history of the city's transformation. It insists on the several political shifts leading to the deep transformation of planning regulations and policies since Valparaíso's inscription on the UNESCO's World Heritage list. In this context, the Mall Barón appears to be only the 'tip of the iceberg': the extension of various industrial sites (Terminal 2 and Sitio 3) along with the touristic development for cruises (*terminal de cruceros*) show, according to the report, coordinated plans for intensive development of the seashore. These plans contradict many of the principles and recommendations put forward by UNESCO concerning the safeguarding of heritage sites as well as the zoning laws that had been put in place for the heritage area and its surroundings (ibid.: 21, 22, 23).

At the same time, this latest development phase is not at odds with but actually the direct consequence of the touristification of the city. I argue here, following Sobarzo (2008), that the spread of a heritage-based discourse in Valparaíso from the late 1990s onwards corresponds to the implementation of a 'heritage governmentality'. The concept is adapted from Foucault's definition of governmentality (Foucault 2004), which refers to the specific techniques of government and control of the modern state. Sobarzo insists on the neoliberal character of heritage governmentality, arguing that, in the case of Valparaíso, the weakening of state regulations and the concentration of power in the hands of lobbies

> is a distinctive trait of the explosion of the real estate market, and in particular in relation to the concept of 'heritage reclamation', which meant the disappearance of livelihoods relying on urban systems in the process of extinction (*barrios*, small stores, plazas and parks etc.).
>
> (2008: 5)

The city's heritage reclamation efforts appear to be crucial factors in the change in what Sobarzo (ibid.) calls the city's 'economic regime' since the early 2000s. Instead of developing and improving the living conditions of existing residents, the current hegemonic 'touristic logics' is characterized by several processes:

> 1. Fear by the tourist of the dreadful city [. . .]: dogs and trash in the streets, urban chaos, crime. 2. Generation of new peripheral zones due to the displacement of native populations. 3. Hygienisation of the access to the centres of capital: population shift in the heritage zones, renovation of the harbour zone, converted in touristic service centre. 4. Creation of a symptom which displaces the preoccupation for the origin of inequality towards its modes of expression: depoliticised 'chosisme' expressed through heritage. 5. Huge amounts of money transferred to the private sector straight from the State [. . .]. 6. Higher living costs inside the heritage perimeter [. . .]. 7. Decline of the small retail in the harbour zone and replacement by chains [. . .] and 8. Proletarianisation of the touristic jobs.
>
> (Ibid.: 8)

Drawing on the social and economic history of Chile's neoliberal turn since the military coup in 1973, Sobarzo sees the touristification of the city as the latest form of a neoliberal government intervention to expand the market's imprint (Paley 2001; Brenner and Theodore 2002; Sobarzo 2008; Aravena Nuñez and Sobarzo 2009).

Groups and repertoires of contention in the Coordinación
de Defensa de Valparaíso

In this context, the most visible battle in terms of resistance to tourism development is most certainly the ten-year fight against the construction of a resort and
commercial touristic complex on the city's seashore, the above-mentioned Mall
Barón, down the *Cerro Barón*. As Jacquot argues, the fight to preserve the seashore
from high-rise developments was in the 2000s frontally led by both *No al Mall
Barón* and the organization *Ciudadanos por Valparaíso*, two organizations which
produced a discourse over the preservation of an 'unaltered' authentic architecture
(Jacquot 2006). The fight to give the seashore back to the people is at present led
by the organization *No al Mall Barón*, which has been slowing down the construction process by challenging the project in many different ways, in particular by
resorting recurrently to a particular discourse invoking heritage, insisting on the
dissonance that a mall on the seashore would create with the nearby UNESCO
heritage site. In this case, *No al Mall Barón* utilizes the UNESCO narrative of a
preserved World Heritage City to counteract the increasing interest of private
developers in both the shoreline and the hill neighbourhoods.

The two groups mentioned above exemplified the fights led between 2005 and
2012 by mostly middle-class organizers with a strong capacity to project their
claims and discourse in the local, national and international media. In the early
2010s, a different kind of mobilization started to take shape, coordinating the
efforts of local groups in a citywide coalition called the *Coordinadora de Defensa
de Valparaíso* (CDV). On 12 April 2014, the most important fire that the city had
experienced in years killed 15 people, displaced more than 12,500 residents and
burnt 3,000 houses to the ground. This catastrophe itself tells a lot about the way
in which collective movements were then forced to both change the focus and
narrative of their actions. Before the fire, the *Coordinación de Defensa de
Valparaíso* was just beginning to take shape, fighting against the changes in the
plan regulador[6] that would allow massive urban development projects in the hilly
neighbourhoods of the city, where constructions are not solidified and often
illegal. With the fire, several distinct groups met in order to fulfil the role of the
overwhelmed municipal services by bringing food to affected residents and
helping victims of the fire. After a great deal of organizing, the CDV started
publishing press releases which insisted on the fact that 'the fire sheds light on
the insecurity and tough life that lots of inhabitants of the city heights are living,
abandoned by the state apparatus and in the midst of the municipal administration's
inefficacy' (CDV 2014). Adding to this debate, on 4 December 2014, the
Contraloría, the highest jurisdiction in Chile, identified the municipal government
as being mainly responsible for the fatal consequences of the fire as it failed to
ensure that sufficient fire protection measures were in place. This decision helped
to generate additional attention and support for the contentions and activities of
the CDV which, as it gained more visibility, decided to create a second field of
action, in the form of a network of neighbourhood organizations named *Cabildos*
(Councils).

The term *Cabildo* is used as a reference to the colonial times, during which the taking up of political power by local elites through the *Cabildos abiertos* (open councils) led to the process of Chilean independence. In Valparaíso, a number of community leaders from several hills decided to form the *Cabildo communal*, whose mission is 'to supplant the municipal management and criticise the plans to redevelop entire areas by displacing poverty', as one leader expressed it in an interview in December 2014. On a micro-local level, during the few months of my observation, from October to December 2014, four *Cabildos* were active, gathering each week from 15 to 30 people. Each *Cabildo* pursues its own specific issues, e.g. the issue of garbage accumulation and lack of drinking water in the Cerro Cordillera, or the development of a mall on the seashore and aggressive real-estate practices in the Cerro Barón. Each *Cabildo* is conceived as a tool for the coordination of several pre-existing organizations in its neighbourhood, among which are radical housing cooperatives (*Red Habitat Valparaíso*), autonomous community centres (*Centro Santa Ana*) and youth community centres (*Centro Juvenil Barón*).

In various cases within the small-scale fights led by the *Cabildos*, the notion of heritage has been re-appropriated and its meaning transformed. Heritage is then defined as the very neighbourhood infrastructure and facilities that allow citizens to have access to public services and fulfil their basic needs. The UNESCO preservation perimeter actually puts this specific heritage at risk, the *Cabildos* argue, by commodifying architectural icons and leaving aside social infrastructure. The *Cabildos* describe the transformation of the city's public services (swimming pools, libraries, hospitals, schools) and small-scale neighbourhood commercial facilities into private retail infrastructure as a sign of the city government's economic disinvestment. More specifically, the tourism industry along with real-estate developers are singled out as taking advantage of the recent process of 'heritage recuperation', making Valparaíso a touristic destination rather than a decent place to live for its inhabitants.

The fights surrounding the former Hospital Ferroviario, a vivid symbol of the last amenities used by railroad workers in the Cerro Barón, are a particularly relevant example of these struggles. Activists embarked on a multifaceted campaign to protect the hospital from demolition and redevelopment into a new condominium complex, ranging from the creation of banners (Figure 7.4), the fight through the municipal board and lawsuits for harassment of the elderly. Eventually, the Cerro Barón activist networks were not successful in protecting the building but the struggle initiated the production of a heritage claim called 'Heritage for whom?' (*¿Patrimonio para quién?*), making the former hospital a symbol for the struggle over community possessions.

In this context, the structuring of a coordinated political discourse by local mobilizations confronting municipal decisions reveals the intricacy of the combined impacts of tourism development and of the economic disengagement of the city government. On two different scales, both the CDV and local *Cabildos*, in their struggle, highlight the fact that tourism development has been the trigger that started the interest of the private sector in the city. Tourism gentrification in

Figure 7.4 March in the Cerro Barón in Valparaíso, 26 October 2014.

Source: Gabriel Ducros.

parts of the UNESCO perimeter and the growing interest of real-estate corporations for the shoreline therefore appear as two distinct but closely related processes.

Conclusion

International comparisons pose conceptual as well as practical challenges. They run the risk of correlating factors that rely on 'complex geographical contingencies' (Lees 2012: 161). Yet, within international comparisons lies the key to understanding how global dynamics and phenomena such as increasing tourism and mobility flows play out in specific contexts. The study presented here is aimed at a cross-contextual analysis of processes of dispossession triggered by tourism capital flows as well as of the community responses they sparked. In both cases, it was argued that the concept of 'tourism gentrification' can be applied, and that government policy and business interests have played a key role in facilitating the transformation the two cities have experienced. The cases of Valparaíso and San Francisco, in other words, lend support to Gotham's claim that tourism gentrification, rather than simply a reflection of market laws of supply and demand, is first and foremost indicative of an interplay of global and local forces as well as new institutional arrangements between actors in the public and private sector.

Significantly, however, these arrangements and interplays take on different forms in different contexts: Valparaíso's socio-spatial change needs to be examined in the context of the actions of 'traditional city boosters' like the ones Gotham identified in New Orleans, as well as the city's inscription in the UNESCO's World Heritage List. The case of San Francisco meanwhile is indicative of the emergence of a new player whose business model relies heavily on the 'disruption' of the traditional hotel industry and the housing market (Said 2012), but which also complexifies conventional production-side models of gentrification and the demand and supply distinctions they tend to rely upon. In addition, Airbnb brings about new challenges for those resisting processes of tourism gentrification. By exploiting the value-laden idea of 'sharing', creating the illusion of offering a business model that is owned by no one and open to all and, more recently, casting itself as a 'saviour of the middle class' (Said 2015) for residents feeling the squeeze of higher rents, Airbnb camouflages and 'sugarcoats' both the processes of dispossession its business contributes to and the profits it accumulates from these processes. 'Sugarcoating' – a term used by Slater (2006) to criticize depoliticizing, demand-side narratives of gentrification – is meanwhile also an issue locals grapple with in Valparaíso, where the virtue of historic preservation or reclamation of a certain kind of heritage has become an essential means for elites to (re-)assert their – moral and material – authority over urban space. Perhaps best thought of as the 'performative in the political' (Butler and Athanasiou 2013), such morally charged narratives, which underlie practices and policies, play a role which should not be underestimated in place and space making (Raquel Mirabal 2009). Future research on – and protests against – (tourism) gentrification are well advised to critically engage with them (Slater 2006).

Notes

1 The 'sharing economy' is a term which refers to an economic system relying on the sharing of services or goods between users, 'peer-to-peer' being one form of it. The term is being increasingly associated with start-ups such as Airbnb or Uber, using technology such as websites and mobile applications to put the users in contact.
2 This chapter borrows from the author's PhD research in the making, entitled 'Comparing the Territorial Dimensions of Anti-gentrification Activism. San Francisco, United States and Valparaíso, Chile', at the *École des Hautes Études en Sciences Sociales* (School for Advanced Studies in Social Sciences), 2013–16, Paris, France. Translations of Spanish and French sources into English in this chapter are the author's own.
3 Both case studies are grounded in three-month participant observation visits: in San Francisco, from February to May 2014, and in Valparaíso, from October to December 2014.
4 Companies such as Airbnb have not yet conquered the short-term rental market.
5 The Ellis Act is a California state law designed in 1986 allowing landlords to evict all their tenants in a building at once without justification. It is designed to prohibit 'local governments from forcing rental property owners to continue offering their housing for rent' (Tenants Together 2014).
6 Legal document that defines land uses in the city of Valparaíso.

References

[Unless otherwise stated, all URLs were last accessed 1 December 2015.]

Aalbers, M. (2015) 'Corporate financialization', in N. Castree *et al.*, *The International Encyclopedia of Geography: People, the Earth, Environment, and Technology.* Oxford: Wiley.

Alba, D. (2015) 'After victory, Airbnb compares its influence to the NRA's', *Wired*, 4 November. Online. Available at http://www.wired.com/2015/11/after-victory-airbnb-compares-its-influence-to-the-nras/.

Anti-Displacement Coalition (2014) *Keeping San Francisco Affordable for All of Us.* Online. Available at http://antidisplacementcoalitionsf.com/main/.

Anti-Eviction Mapping Project (2014) *Protest Airbnb's Takeover of San Francisco*, 22 November. Online. Available at https://www.facebook.com/events/448446991969287/.

Aravena Nuñez, P. (2006) *Trabajo, memoria y experiencia. Fuentes para la historia de la modernización del puerto de Valparaíso*, Valparaíso: Consejo Nacional de la Cultura y las Artes, Universidad Arcis, Centro de Estudios Interculturales y del Patrimonio.

Aravena Nuñez, P. and Andueza P. (2013) *Valparaíso reclamado. Demandas ciudadanas de la ciudad-puerto.* Valparaíso: Perseo Ediciones.

Aravena Nuñez, P. and Sobarzo M. (2009) *Valparaíso: patrimonio, mercado y gobierno.* Concepción: Escaparate Ediciones.

Beitel, K. (2013) *Local Protest, Global Movements: Capital, Community, and State in San Francisco.* Philadelphia: Temple University Press.

Biblioteca del Congreso Nacional de Chile (2012) *Reportes Estadísticos y Comunales 2012.* Online. Available at http://reportescomunales.bcn.cl/2012/index.php/Valpara%C3%ADso#Ingreso_promedio_de_los_hogares_CASEN_2003-2009.

Brahinsky, R. (2014) 'The death of the city? Reports of San Francisco's demise have been greatly exaggerated', *Boom: A Journal of California*, 4(2): 43–54.

Brenner, N. (2001) 'The limits to scale? Methodological reflections on scalar structuration', *Progress in Human Geography*, 25(4): 591–614.

Brenner, N. and Theodore, N. (2002) 'Cities and the geographies of "actually existing neoliberalism"', *Antipode*, 34(3): 349–79.

Bridge, G., Butler, T. and Lees, L. (eds) (2011) *Mixed Communities: Gentrification by Stealth?* Bristol: Policy Press.

Brown-Saracino, J. (2010) 'How, where and when gentrification occur?', in J. Brown-Saracino (ed.), *The Gentrification Debates: A Reader.* New York: Routledge.

Budget and Legislative Analyst's Office (2015) *Analysis of the Impact of Short-term Rentals on Housing*, 13 May. Online. Available at http://www.sfbos.org/Modules/ShowDocument.aspx?documentid=52601.

Butler, J. and Athanasiou, A. (2013) *Dispossession: The Performative in the Political.* Cambridge: Polity Press.

Carson, B. (2015) 'Airbnb is worth $25 billion after raising a massive $1.5 billion round', *Business Insider*, 26 June. Online. Available at http://www.businessinsider.com/airbnb-15-billion-round-values-the-company-at-255-billion-2015-6.

CDV Coordinadora de Defensa de Valparaíso, Laguna Verde y Placilla-Curauma (2014) *Cronica de una tragedia anunciada*, 22 April. Online. Available at https://www.facebook.com/permalink.php?story_fbid=278380592331625&id=274475759388775&fref=nf.

Cefaï, D. (1996) 'La construction des problèmes publics. Définitions de situations dans des arènes publiques', *Réseaux*, 14(75): 43–66.

Chandía, M. (2013) *La Cuadra, pasión, vino y se fue . . . Cultura popular, habitar y memoria histórica en el Barrio Puerto de Valparaíso*. Valparaíso: RIL Editores.

Cox, M. (2015) *Inside Airbnb* [website]. Online. Available at http://insideAirbnb.com/san-francisco/.

Florida, R. (2002) *The Rise of the Creative Class*. New York: Basic Books.

Foucault, M. (2004) *Sécurité, territoire, population: Cours au Collège de France (1977–1978)*. Paris: Broché.

Gervais-Lambony, P. (2012) 'Nostalgies citadines en Afrique Sud', *EspacesTemps.net*. Online. Available at http://www.espacestemps.net/articles/nostalgies-citadines-en-afrique-sud/.

Gotham, K. (2010) 'Tourism gentrification: the case of New Orleans' Vieux Carré (French Quarter)', in J. Brown-Saracino (ed.), *The Gentrification Debates: A Reader*. New York: Routledge.

Guerrero Valdebenito, R. M. (2012) 'Patrimonio cultural mundial, territorio y construcción de ciudadanía. Construcción y apropiación social del patrimonio cultural de la ciudad de Valparaíso-Chile', *Scripta Nova*, 16(388). Online. Available at http://www.ub.edu/geocrit/sn/sn-388.htm.

Hackworth, J. and Smith, N. (2001) 'The changing state of gentrification', *Tijdschrift voor Economische en Sociale Geografie*, 92(4): 464–77.

Hartman, C. (2002) *City for Sale: The Transformation of San Francisco*. Oakland, CA: University of California Press.

Hill, S. (2015) 'The unsavory side of Airbnb', *The American Prospect, Longform*, Fall 2015 Issue. Online. Available at http://prospect.org/article/evictions-and-conversions-dark-side-airbnb.

Instituto Nacional de Estadísticas (2013) *Turismo, Informe Anual, 2013*. Online. Available at http://www.ine.cl/canales/menu/publicaciones/calendario_de_publicaciones/pdf/turismo_2013.pdf.

Jacquot, S. (2005) 'Valparaíso, valeurs patrimoniales et jeu des acteurs', in M. Gravari-Barbas (ed.), *Habiter le patrimoine. Enjeux, approches, vécu*. Rennes: Presses Universitaires de Rennes.

Jacquot, S. (2006) 'La redistribution spatiale du pouvoir autour du patrimoine à Valparaíso (Chili)', in J. Lombard, E. Mesclier and S. Velut (eds), *La mondialisation côté sud. Acteurs et territoires*. Paris: IRD Éditions, Éditions rue d'Ulm.

Jacquot, S. (2007) 'Enjeux publics et privés du réinvestissement des espaces publics centraux: une étude comparée de Gênes, Valparaíso et Liverpool'. PhD dissertation, Angers, Université d'Angers.

Jones, T. S. (2014) 'Chiu introduces legislation to regulate Airbnb and short-term housing rentals', *SF Bay Guardian Online*, 15 April. Online. Available at http://www.sfbg.com/politics/2014/04/15/chiu-introduces-legislation-Airbnb-and-short-term-housing-rentals.

Kearns, G. and Philo, C. (eds) (1993) *Selling Places. The City as Cultural Capital: Past and Future*. Oxford: Pergamon Press.

Lallement, M. (2015) *L'âge de faire: hacking, travail, anarchie*. Paris: Seuil.

Landry, C. (2000) *The Creative City. A Toolkit for Urban Innovators*. New York: Routledge.

Le Goix, R. and Halbert, L. (eds) (2012) 'La ville financiarisée', *Urbanisme*, no. 384.

Lee, Y.-S. and Yeoh, B. (eds) (2005) *Globalisation and the Politics of Forgetting*. London: Routledge.

Lees, L. (2000) 'Super-gentrification: the case of Brooklyn Heights, New York City', *Urban Studies*, 40(12): 2487–509.

Lees, L. (2012) 'The geography of gentrification: thinking through comparative urbanism', *Progress in Human Geography*, 36(2): 155–71.

Lees, L., Slater, T. and Wyly, E. (eds) (2010) *The Gentrification Reader*. New York: Routledge.

Lehane, C. (2015) *Organizing in 100 Cities: The Airbnb Host Movement*. Online. Available at http://publicpolicy.airbnb.com/organizing-100-cities-airbnb-host-movement/.

Ley, D. (1996) *The New Middle-Class and the Remaking of the Central City*. Oxford: Oxford University Press.

McDougall, M. and Mitnick, H. (1998) 'Location: San Francisco', in J. Brook, C. Carlsson and N. J. Peter (eds), *Reclaiming San Francisco: History, Politics, Culture*. San Francisco: Citylights Books.

MallPlaza (2012) *La experiencia de otras ciudades puerto*. Online. Available at http://www.proyectopuertobaron.cl/portada-interior/la-experiencia-de-otras-ciudades-puerto.

Opillard, F. (forthcoming) 'Resisting the politics of displacement in the San Francisco Bay Area. Anti-gentrification activism in the Tech Boom 2.0', *European Journal of American Studies*.

Paley, J. (2001) *Marketing Democracy. Power and Social Movements in Post-Dictatorship Chile*. Oakland, CA: University of California Press.

Raile, D. (2014) 'Stickering it to the man: Airbnb packs SF City Hall for public meeting on home sharing law', *Pando*, 25 April. Online. Available at https://pando.com/2015/04/25/stickering-it-to-the-man-airbnb-packs-sf-city-hall-for-public-meeting-on-home-sharing-law/.

Raquel Mirabal, N. (2009) 'Geographies of displacement: Latina/os, oral history, and the politics of gentrification in San Francisco's Mission District', *Public Historian*, 31(2): 7–31.

Retamales Quintero, F. (2010) 'Vagabundos, mendigos, torrantes: Configuraciones sociales del habitar en la calle en el Barrio Puerto de Valparaíso'. Degree thesis in Anthropology, Santiago de Chile, Universidad Academia.

Sabatini, J. (2015) 'Airbnb rentals cut deep into SF housing stock, report says', *The Examiner*, 15 May. Online. Available at http://archives.sfexaminer.com/sanfrancisco/sf-report-says-units-rented-for-short-term-reduce-long-term-housing/Content?oid=2929888.

Said, C. (2012) 'Short-term rentals disrupting SF housing market', *SFGATE*, 10 June. Online. Available at http://www.sfgate.com/realestate/article/Short-term-rentals-disrupting-SF-housing-market-3622832.php.

Said, C. (2014a) 'SF cracks down on Airbnb rentals', *SFGATE*, 7 April. Online. Available at http://www.sfgate.com/bayarea/article/S-F-cracks-down-on-Airbnb-rentals-5381237.php#photo-6130507.

Said, C. (2014b) 'Airbnb to collect hotel taxes for San Francisco rentals', *SFGATE*, 1 April. Online. Available at http://www.sfgate.com/news/article/Airbnb-to-collect-hotel-taxes-for-San-Francisco-5365352.php.

Said, C. (2015) 'Airbnb, Uber cast themselves as saviors of the middle class', *San Francisco Chronicle*, 10 November. Online. Available at http://www.sfchronicle.com/business/article/Airbnb-Uber-We-are-the-saviors-of-the-middle-6620729.php.

Salin, E. (2002) 'Les centres historiques du Caire et de Mexico: représentations de l'espace, mutations urbaines et protection du patrimoine'. PhD dissertation, Paris, Université de Nanterre – Paris X.

San Francisco Travel Association (2015) *About*. Online. Available at: http://www.sanfrancisco.travel/about-san-francisco-travel-association.

Schaal, D. (2014) 'How Airbnb bought a San Francisco short-term rental law, lawsuit alleges', *Skift*, 4 November. Online. Available at http://skift.com/2014/11/05/how-airbnb-bought-a-san-francisco-short-term-rental-law-lawsuit-alleges/.

Slater, T. (2006) 'The eviction of critical perspectives from gentrification research', *International Journal of Urban and Regional Research*, 30(4): 737–57.

Smith, N. (1996) *The New Urban Frontier: Gentrification and the Revanchist City*. New York: Routledge.

Smith, N. (2002) 'New globalism, new urbanism: gentrification as a global urban strategy', *Antipode*, 34(3): 427–50.

Sobarzo, M. (2008) 'Gubernamentalidad patrimonial', *Revista Diseño Urbano y Paisaje*, 5(13): 1–12.

Swyngedouw, E. (1997) 'Neither global nor local: "glocalization" and the politics of scale', in K. Cox (ed.), *Spaces of Globalization*. New York: Guilford Press.

Tenants Together (2014) *The Speculator Loophole: Ellis Act Evictions in San Francisco*. Online. Available at http://www.slideshare.net/tenantstogether/ellis-act-report.

Tracy, J. (2013) *Dispatches Against Displacement. Field Notes from San Francisco's Housing Wars*. Oakland, CA: AK Press.

United States Census Bureau (2015) *State and County Quick Facts: San Francisco County*. Online. Available at http://quickfacts.census.gov/qfd/states/06/06075.html.

Zukin, S. (1993) *Landscapes of Power: From Detroit to Disney World*. Oakland, CA: University of California Press.

8   Tourism provision as protest in 'post-conflict' Belfast

Emily Bereskin

Just as growth in the tourism sector has been hailed as a solution to urban restructuring challenges such as post-industrial and post-socialist transformations in cities of the global North, so too has it been prescribed as a remedy for cities debilitated by violent conflict. Planners and policy-makers consider investment in tourism to be a fast, reliable means of regenerating damaged cityscapes and repairing war-torn economies. Tourism forms a fundamental component of reconstruction plans in Beirut, Sarajevo, Kigali, Nicosia, Cape Town and many other 'post-conflict' cities worldwide. In 2011 and 2013, the annual conferences of an international organization dedicated to promoting knowledge transfer among conflict-affected cities, the Forum for Cities in Transition, even featured 'Cultural Tourism as an Economic Driver' and 'Tourism Potential of a Divided City' as central panel discussions.

Tourism policies shape much more than visitor numbers. As discussed in the introduction to this volume, urban tourism alters social and spatial patterns of the city: delineating new neighbourhoods, changing centre/periphery relations, and generating (or exacerbating) socio-spatial polarization. Moreover, through its discursive and representational re-imaging practices, tourism transforms conceptions and understandings of place (Selwyn 1996; Urry 1990). In the conflict or 'post-conflict'[1] city, such changes map onto the divisions and hardships caused by the hostilities. This chapter examines Belfast, Northern Ireland as a case study in order to analyse how the politics of tourism development intersect with the politics of ethnic conflict in deeply divided cities with histories of violent conflict.

This chapter first analyses tourism development in Belfast from the beginning of the peace process in the mid-1980s, and examines its main socio-political ramifications. It then shows how communities excluded from the benefits of tourism-led regeneration and revenue have developed an alternative tourism offer to protest against their omission from the 'New Belfast' vision created and marketed by city leaders. Belfast's tourism debate differs from many cities in that faith in tourism's curative properties remains widespread, even among those it most negatively impacts. Local tourism protests do not challenge the prioritization of tourism as a development strategy or its deleterious effects. Instead, protests dispute *who* gets to shape the city's tourism offer and who shall benefit from any related economic and political gains. Alternative tourism provision has become a means of securing economic benefits for deprived communities and demanding recognition for cultural traditions and narratives stamped out or elided in official discourses. This alternative tourism industry, however, has itself created tensions, spurring competition between the city's Protestant and Catholic communities and exacerbating cultural identity contests.[2] Rather than constituting a separate, technocratic sphere of urban enterprise, tourism in Belfast has become, I will argue, a new terrain and mechanism for ethnonationalist struggles.

Tourism policy development in Belfast

The legacy of conflict

Belfast is the epicentre of an enduring ethnonationalist conflict, whose roots stretch back to the arrival of Protestant settlers in the predominantly Catholic Ireland in the 1600s. The modern conflict is rooted in the Irish Home Rule movement and the 1921 partitioning of the island into the Republic of Ireland and Northern Ireland, the latter of which remained in the United Kingdom. Following decades of institutionalized discrimination against the Catholic community within Northern Ireland, disputes about whether the region should remain in the UK or join Ireland took the form of an armed struggle commonly referred to as 'the Troubles' (1969–98). The conflict was officially settled in 1998 by the Belfast Agreement, a political accord which created power-sharing mechanisms based on consociational principles and instituted equality measures across a range of policy areas.

Although violence has dramatically decreased since the height of the Troubles, conflict is by no means a thing of the past. Mixing in upper- and middle-class communities is increasing, but Catholic and Protestant communities still lead predominantly separate lives, living in segregated neighbourhoods, attending separate schools and marrying within their own ethnic group (McKeown 2013; Nolan 2014). Individual and collective identities based on ethnicity remain highly salient, and group identities are still constructed in terms of opposition and antagonism (Cairns 2010). Particularly in working-class communities, a 'conflict ethos' (Bar-Tal 2000) continues to pervade social identity, communal relations and group goals. Outgroup members are viewed with mistrust and communities still prefer to live separated by physical security barriers, the so-called 'peace walls' (Jarman 2008). Violence and rioting, in particular in areas at the interface between Catholic and Protestant communities, remain a common occurrence, particularly in the summer parading months.

Over the course of this dispute, points of contention between the two communities have fluctuated in response to political events, broader structural shifts and changing societal attitudes (Ruane and Todd 1996). The once fundamental questions of governance structure and constitutional status have waned, and the conflict today has been reframed around issues of equality, balanced socio-economic opportunities, cultural parity of esteem and transitional justice. The flag protests, which saw over three months of violent and non-violent demonstrations in response to the removal of the Union Jack from Belfast City hall in December

2012 and early 2013, indicates the continued importance of cultural identity recognition and symbols in the region. This issue, coupled with problems of entrenched socio-economic deprivation, plays directly into tourism debates and protests.

'Confidently moving on': official tourism development in 'post-conflict' Belfast

Prior to the outbreak of the Troubles, Northern Ireland was a popular holiday destination, cherished for its impressive natural landscape and attractive seaside resorts (Boyd 2013). Unsurprisingly, tourism declined drastically during the conflict, with numbers falling in direct correlation to periods of violence receiving substantial media attention (Wilson 1993). Even long after the major episodes of violence had ceased, negative perceptions continued to deter tourists (Boyd 2013).

Policy-makers began strategizing Belfast's comeback long before the conflict was settled. Heartened by the prospects of stability portended by the 1985 Anglo-Irish Agreement, the Belfast Development Office, the Belfast City Council and the Department of the Environment partnered with private interests to construct a 'New Belfast' that would appeal to tourists and investors (Nagle 2010; Needham 1998; Neill 1993). However, as McCabe (2013) argues, Northern Ireland had no real hope for significant amounts of foreign direct investment (FDI) and tourism remained the region's best chance for economic recovery. Early regeneration efforts focused on the blighted city centre, which had been debilitated by the IRA's bombing campaign as well as the British government's securitization measures. The revitalization of Belfast's central district was designed as a 'heart transplant' that would expand outward to revive the wider city (Neill 1993). The council introduced grants to refurbish facades and set up floodlights to showcase 'architectural masterpieces' and 'hide wrinkles' (Needham 1998: 176). A new shopping centre was built on the city's high street, whose unshuttered glass facade intentionally symbolized optimism in the peace process (ibid.: 171). Waterfront Hall (begun 1993), the similarly vitreous convention centre erected along the Laganside waterfront, was the city's first serious bid for tourists: fully aware of the obstacle posed by Belfast's negative reputation, the City Council initially targeted markets of 'compulsory tourists', those who would be required to come to the city for events such as conventions and other business matters. These developments marked the beginnings of a transformation of the city centre and the waterfront into spatial showcases to spur the confidence of potential investors (Figure 8.1). These polished areas likewise shielded guests from the unpleasant realities found in the outlying residential estates, where the environment was still marked with paramilitary murals, watchtowers, barricades and other material manifestations of hostilities. City marketing reinforced the divide, with Belfast's working-class districts literally cut off of the city's tourism map.

The push for tourists continued throughout the peace process in the 1990s, and today tourism development has become entrenched as a first order of business in plans, policy papers and strategic documents across a swath of government departments. Development of the local industry is led by the Northern Ireland Tourism

Board (NITB), the Belfast City Council (BCC) and the Belfast Visitor and Convention Bureau (BVCB), a destination marketing organization founded immediately after the Belfast Agreement. However, provisions for tourism development are also found in the strategic plans for a number of government departments, e.g. the Planning Service of Northern Ireland (Pl.SNI), the Department of Enterprise, Trade and Investment (DETI), the Department of Culture, Arts and Leisure (DCAL), the Department of Regional Development (DRD) and the Department for Social Development (DSD). Collectively, these departments have directed a two-and-a-half decade makeover of the city centre into a lively commercial district with multiple shopping malls, active high streets and a thriving arts and cultural quarter. The city's largest undertaking has been the regeneration of Queen's Island into the 'Titanic Quarter', a 185-acre multi-use district branded after the famous liner constructed onsite. Anchoring the district is Titanic Belfast, 'the world's largest Titanic-themed visitor attraction', earmarked by the NITB as one of their five signature projects which they hope will attract 150,000 out-of-state visitors a year.

Since the 1980s, Belfast's physical refashioning has been accompanied by a persuasive re-imaging campaign aimed at combating deleterious perceptions of the city. While acknowledging curiosity in the conflict, both the NITB and the BCC avoid mentioning the Troubles in their marketing materials for fear that it will deter more visitors than it might attract. Instead, the NITB has focused on a normalizing presentation, highlighting benign attractions such as scenery, outdoor activities and shopping (Wilson 1993). The city's first attempt to engage with local history was 'Titanic Belfast', a city-wide branding strategy that sought to distract from the city's conflict history by presenting a 'selected and authorized past' (Short 2006: 121). Glossing over the institutionalized anti-Catholic sectarianism of

Figure 8.1 The recent upgrading of Belfast's Waterfront Hall, June 2015.

Source: Claire Colomb.

these industrial sectors, state agencies use Belfast's legacy as a manufacturing and shipbuilding powerhouse to present an industrious, resilient and prosperous city (see also Neill et al. 2013). In addition, visitor guides from the past five years have tested out a number of new images: Music City, Literary Belfast, City of Quarters and City of Festivals, all of which showcase the Renaissance ethos of the Northern Ireland tourism identity 'confidently moving on' (NITB 2010), while of the Belfast brand 'a unique history and a future full of promise have come to create a city bursting with energy and optimism' (BCC and NITB 2011: 3).

Since 1998, Belfast's tourism numbers and profits have grown steadily. From 1999 to 2012, the number of annual visitors to the capital grew by over 500 per cent, from 1.5 million to 7.6 million – peaking at 9.3 million in 2009 (BCC 2000; BCC 2012). Annual tourism spending has increased from £114 million to £416 million (ibid.); including both direct and indirect expenditure, the total contribution to the city's economy was £524 million in 2012 (BCC 2012). However, although these numbers represent significant growth, Belfast's tourism numbers remain much lower than similarly sized European cities and tourism flows are considerably smaller and less international than other cities in this volume. Seventy per cent of visitors came only for a day trip and only roughly 10 per cent travelled from outside Northern Ireland or the Republic of Ireland (ibid.).[3] Indisputable, however, is how radically international perceptions of the city have changed. Belfast has received numerous accolades in industry press, and consistently appears on top-ten destination lists, all of which are quick to highlight the

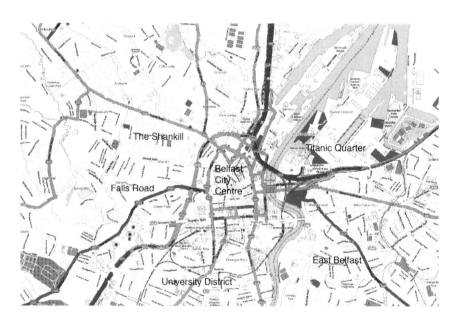

Figure 8.2 Belfast's neighbourhoods, August 2015.

Source: Author, based on OpenStreet map. CC BY-SA ©OpenStreetMap contributors.

city's comeback. *Lonely Planet*, for example, proclaimed that 'once lumped with Beirut, Baghdad and Bosnia as one of the four "Bs" for travelers to avoid, Belfast has pulled off a remarkable transformation from bombs-and-bullets pariah to a hip-hotels-and-hedonism party town' (Davenport and Berkmoes 2012: 551).

Tourism as a tool of conflict transformation?

From their onset, these regeneration strategies were jointly conceived as conflict management tactics. Politicians used the prospect of an economic 'peace dividend' to encourage paramilitary disarmament, arguing that the cessation of violence would be met with financial rewards and communal prosperity brought about by increased tourism and inward investment (Murtagh and Keaveny 2006; Nagle 2010; O'Hearn 2008). O'Hearn (2008) argues that this prospect of a peace dividend – made more attractive by the economic boom brought about by FDI in the Republic of Ireland in the 1990s – was an influential factor in decision of the Irish Republican Army (IRA) decision to announce a 1994 ceasefire. In addition, politicians hoped that a remade, neoliberal Belfast would engender the cultivation of non-sectarian identities based on personal interest and expressed primarily through consumerist and/or entrepreneurial practices. Nagle (2010: 37) states:

> By supporting indigenous free-market entrepreneurs to produce wealth through tourism, this would reduce the polarizing strategies of ethno-national leaders seeking to foment interethnic discord. By encouraging individualism and wealth creation facilitated by tourism, locals would no longer be encumbered by their affiliations to the respective ethnic 'tribes'.

Spatially, this would take place in the 'neutral' consumerist districts of the city centre. It was also hoped that new branding strategies would increase civic pride and the salience of superordinate identities (Northover 2010).

Despite these intentions, Belfast's rapid and radical transformation has provoked socio-political tensions, both exacerbating old problems and instigating new ones. In addition to the strengthening of segregation patterns, the city now faces the new polarization of the city between a thriving centre and wilting working-class districts – socio-economically deprived areas where the majority of the fighting took place and the potential for recurrent conflict still lies (Shirlow and Murtagh 2006; Murtagh and Keaveny 2006). The concentration of new enterprise in the city centre has prevented tourism revenue from reaching working-class neighbourhoods and has thereby reinforced centre/periphery divisions. High price points have placed the new attractions and commercial offerings of the city centre outside the reach of working-class communities (Neill 1993, 2007; Bairner 2003). In addition, few have found jobs in the new service sector, as these jobs either require educational levels or skill sets that the unemployed do not possess, or the jobs are difficult to reach given the city's disjointed layout and poor public transit (Shirlow and Shuttleworth 1999). Communities protest that they have seen nothing of the promised 'peace dividend', and people have grown increasingly resentful of the polarization of the city, which sees them further barricaded from the prospering city centre and trapped in 'sink estates' (Murtagh and Keaveny 2006: 188) characterized by poverty, chronic unemployment and societal aliena- tion. Nor do working-class communities see themselves represented in the narra- tives and images of the new cosmopolitan Belfast. Spatial, economic, symbolic and psychological boundaries have therefore combined to create a profound cleavage between what O'Dowd and Komarova term 'Consumerist Belfast' and 'Troubles Belfast' (O'Dowd and Komarova 2011: 2016).

Community leaders interpret the imbalanced promotion of tourism and the uneven distribution of its benefits as indicative of state indifference and negli- gence. They see the exclusion of their group narratives and cultural traditions as a failure of the government to offer recognition and support cultural parity of esteem. This dissatisfaction with the performance of state functions is deeply problematic in societies such as Northern Ireland, where the very legitimacy of the state remains tenuous. Growing class divisions, moreover, are intensifying sectarian divisions. Rather than framing their problems as a class issue common to both parties, Belfast's working-classes tend to blame their economic difficul- ties on outgroup favouritism (O'Hearn 2008). The Catholic community attributes social deprivation and immobility to the legacy of institutionalized anti-Catholic discrimination by the Protestant ethnocratic state. Protestants, in turn, frame the hardships of their communities in light of the Catholic community's growing financial and political influence. On both sides then, socio-economic exclusion has stimulated feelings of victimization and sectarianism. As Baker (2014) states, 'if there is one thing that can be said for sectarianism, it gives meaning to one's life and it is free at the point of entry.' Boredom and resentment stemming from disenfranchisement can provoke interface violence and rioting; moreover, unem- ployed youth left behind by the new economy can become 'easy prey' for recruiting paramilitaries (Murtagh and Keaveney 2006: 187; Nolan 2014). The economic growth that was supposed to undermine ethnic tension has become a driver of the old conflict in a new form.

Challenges to official tourism policy through alternative forms of tourism development

The growth of political tourism: protesting the official image of the New Belfast

An alternative tourism industry first developed in nationalist West Belfast, where already during the Troubles 'political tourists' were coming to learn about the conflict and to show solidarity by participating in parades and demonstrations. Curious to see the sites of conflict known to them through news reports and films, more conventional tourists began trickling into the area following the 1994 cease- fire. Groups from schools, prisoner services, NGOs, political organizations and research institutes also arrived to tour the area and meet individuals involved in the conflict and the peace process. West Belfast locals quickly jumped on this interest and began creating products and services catering to these new visitors. Sites and artefacts related to the Troubles, such as graves, political murals, watch-towers and sites of clashes, were framed as attractions and interpreted through bus and taxi tours, maps and guidebooks and other touristic 'markers' (MacCannell 1999). These attractions and services formed the basis of a tourism sub-industry, concentrated along the Falls Road in West Belfast and referred to as 'political tourism' (Figure 8.3, left) – or, for those wishing to disparage the practice, 'Troubles tourism.'

Although some saw the potential for profit, this form of tourism provision was more a political than an economic enterprise. Many involved were community workers, political activists, politicians, even former prisoners and ex-combatants, nationalists who saw tourism development as a means of securing international support for their political cause (Nagle 2010). The internationalization of repub-licanism in Northern Ireland was a political tactic long used by Sinn Fein, the IRA, and the wider nationalist community (Miller 2010). Thanks in part to the British broadcasting ban, nationalists were particularly adept at finding crea-tive means of disseminating messages abroad. Tourism development, the very nature of which entails the repackaging and circulation of select images and narra-tives (MacCannell 1999), was a natural forum for the dissemination of state-silenced discourses. Artists painted a factory wall at the entrance to West Belfast with murals celebrating the Republican cause and linking it with nationalist move-ments elsewhere in the world. The 'Solidarity Wall', as it has come to be known, is now the area's most iconic sight. Black taxi drivers, many of whom came from a political or paramilitary background, began offering tours, where they would provide nationalist commentary on the conflict and seek political sympathizers. Sinn Fein opened their headquarters on the Falls Road as an information and souvenir shop, selling a host of materials related to Irish nationalism. Thus, in its early form, West Belfast tourism constituted a form of political protest against British direct rule and Northern Ireland's position in the United Kingdom.

In the late 1990s and 2000s, West Belfast's tourism industry expanded, and a wider array of agents (including private entrepreneurs, political associations, cultural groups and community organizations) became involved in its execution. In 1998, tourism development was partially integrated into the statutory system when a local tourism bureau, Fáilte Feirste Thiar (FFT), was inaugurated and nestled under the West Belfast Area Partnership, a community-level organization sponsored by the DSD. However, the relationship between the FFT and Belfast's main tourism departments – the BCC, the NITB and the BVCB – has not always been harmonious, as the different agencies have mismatched ideas about the role of political tourism in Belfast's regeneration.

Neighbourhood tourism has similarly diversified in its motivations and prod-ucts. Political sites remain a major draw, but have been augmented by services and products based on Irish heritage and culture (Figure 8.3, right). As Sinn Fein's position has shifted from dissent to active participation in governance (Tonge 2006), and as issues of cultural identity have moved to the centre of Northern Ireland's political stage, the promotion of Irish cultural heritage has

Figure 8.3 Political and cultural tourism in West Belfast. Mural advertising political walking tour and mural promoting Irish cultural heritage, June 2015.

Source: left: Author; right: Claire Colomb.

become an increasingly central part of Sinn Fein's political project (Nic Craith 2003). Since 2003, the party has supported a community-led initiative to rebrand West Belfast as a Gaeltacht Quarter, a cultural district based on the Irish language and traditions. The Gaeltacht Quarter Board has increased Irish language signage in the area, commissioned murals celebrating Irish heritage, and facilitated the refurbishment of *Cultúrlann McAdam Ó Fiaich*, a multi-use space featuring Irish language classes, Irish music and theatre performances, and a tourism information point for West Belfast. Such initiatives, although pursued for multiple motivations, seek to legitimize the Irish cultural identity in Northern Ireland.

In addition, increasing importance is being placed on tourism as a tool to combat socio-economic deprivation, by creating jobs, spurring urban renewal and attracting further investment. The idea for the Gaeltacht Quarter, for instance, originated from a task force charged with 'bringing forward recommendations aimed at reducing poverty and unemployment' (White and Simpson 2002: 7). Although the hope is in part that the Quarter will bring cultural recognition and educational funding, as one board member declared – pointing out that the four wards included in the initiative are among the most deprived areas in Northern Ireland – 'the Gaeltacht Quarter is about wealth accumulation.'[4]

Contentions between district tourism and state agencies

Although tourism in West Belfast has expanded since the 1990s, it still lags significantly behind the rest of the city.[5] Problematically for local tourism providers, the majority who do come tend to do so as part of a guided bus tour, quickly photographing the murals and peace lines and returning to the city centre without patronizing local businesses.[6] Locals have even attacked tour buses. One reason such tourism continues to predominate is that the district lacks basic infrastructure, such as hotels or sit-in eateries, that would encourage guests to linger or more deeply explore the area. Moreover, safety assurance remains a hurdle; although some visitors are attracted by the neighbourhood's conflict history, and some are even enthralled by its dangerous feel, most find the 'roughness' of the area off-putting and are scared to enter unaccompanied (Tourism Development International 2001). Community tourism officers have struggled to overcome this image problem within the past few years, mainly by publishing information booklets, maps, brochures and websites framing West Belfast as a safe, desirable tourist destination. Their efforts, however, are impeded by the NITB's and the BVCB's policy of not actively promoting tourism in the area, leaving West Belfast to appear as a frontier, enter-at-your-own-risk destination.

Those working in West Belfast's tourism sector attribute the limited success of their endeavours to the unwillingness of the state to fund services or infrastructure and to include West Belfast in promotional material. Community leaders, district councillors and party MPs pontificate about the disproportionate amount of public investment allocated to regeneration in the city centre, particularly in the Titanic Quarter, which many consider a massive over-expenditure to build premises doomed to fail. Questions of representation are also contentious, as community members see the state's refusal to help combat West Belfast's image problem as crucial to its own perpetuation. In response to a tourist publication highlighting the yet-to-be-built Titanic Quarter, but excluding West Belfast, a columnist for the *Andersontown News* wrote, 'It was a throwback to the days when Vasco de Gama, Columbus, and Galileo explored the world, "civilizing" territories which had previously been marked on the map as unexplored or "Here be dragons"'(Ó Liatháin 2003).

State inaction is combated through multiple, simultaneous strategies. At one end of the spectrum is a 'go-it-alone' approach: tourism developers trudge forward, building structure and services with any and all available resources, funding initiatives themselves (even through door-to-door collections) and often coming up with innovative schemes that require little initial investment. For example, FFT headed a creative initiative to turn West Belfast into a Eurozone, getting area shopkeepers to accept the currency in an effort to attract Republic and mainland tourists (*Andersontown News*, 21 May 2005, p. 16). The area's biggest draw is the murals and locals have continued to paint new ones in an effort to create attractions and brand the neighbourhood. Murals are even used to advertise tourism products and services.

Developers position their work as the most recent episode in a long history of Catholic self-sufficiency, citing the community's past self-provision of housing and infrastructure in the face of government neglect and antipathy. Even the advertising for the Black Cab tours emphasizes that the taxis are the legacy of a self-provided transport system designed when city buses stopped servicing West Belfast (Taxi Trax 2015). Whether consciously or not, this attitude manifests in spatial and discursive forms that reinforce the geographic split between West Belfast and the rest of the city (see also McDowell 2008). For all of their talk about integrating West Belfast with the rest of the city, whether as 'West Belfast, site of the Troubles' or 'The Gaeltacht Quarter', the Falls Road is in fact marketed as a distinct space at odds with greater Belfast.

DIY development has its limitations, however, and developers are aware that their visions for West Belfast will not materialize without public investment. Sinn Fein councillors therefore fight for increased funding from both the city council and the National Assembly. Leaders of other organizations responsible for tourism continue to put pressure on government departments through letter writing and lobbying. Another strategy has been to find funding piecemeal from other sources. The Gaeltacht Quarter Board has been particularly adept at this, applying to the BCC's Renewing the Routes arterial route regeneration programme for money for Irish language signage, to the Arts Council and Foras na Gaeilge (the all-island council for Irish Language) for funds for a public sculpture celebrating the Irish language, and to DCAL and DSD for the refurbishment of the cultural centre An Chultúrlann. Groups are also attempting to circumvent state constraints by seeking investment from international organizations such as the European Union or the International Fund for Ireland. Widening the field necessitates the mobilization of discourse, i.e. the ability to frame tourism as a driver for whatever the application calls for: culture, equality, employment, regeneration, even – as explained in detail below – social reconciliation.

Intercommunal competition[7]

However stymied the Catholic community may see their tourism ventures, the Protestant community views these initiatives as resounding successes, and many feel threatened by the sympathy and clout these efforts have brought to the nationalist side. The proliferation of nationalist narratives and symbols through tourism has been read by some as a symbol of the Catholic community's increasing power and, by extension, evidence of diminishing Protestant influence. Unionist politicians fight funding for political tourism. When Sinn Fein councillor Paul Maskey proposed that DETI support political tourism as a means of assisting deprived neighbourhoods, Unionist politicians dismissed his proposal as an attempt to push Republican propaganda and argued that political tourism would prove detrimental to the attraction of inward investment. This opposition not only shot down Maskey's proposed amendment, but the Unionists also successfully passed a counter-amendment removing all mention of political tourism and decreeing that DETI should 'seek to promote Northern Ireland in a positive manner' (Northern Ireland Assembly 2008; see also Nagle 2010).

Seeking to claim their share of the perceived tourism benefits, in the mid-2000s, working-class Protestants in the neighbourhoods of East Belfast, the Shankill and later Sandy Row began constructing their own tourism offer (Figure 8.4). Expressing anxiety about exclusion as well as defamation, one Protestant tourism officer says, 'There is a need for a Protestant story to be told. Not a very positive Protestant story is being told at the moment' (personal communication, 10 April 2011). Less focused on the Troubles, tourism in these areas has focused on cultural traditions and historical events important to the Protestant community, such as the Loyal Orders, Ulster-Scots, the signing of the Ulster Covenant and the Battle of the Somme.

As working-class communities compete against the city centre for visitors and revenue, this 'district' or 'community tourism', as it is sometimes known, has become a playing field for intercommunal competition over resources as well as over structural and symbolic power. Most evident is the role of tourism as an arena of symbolic contest (Harrison 1995), in which groups endeavour to proliferate their own symbols and/or denigrate the outgroup symbols as a means of accumulating social and political capital. Irish cultural festivals are met with calls for showcases of Ulster-Scots music and dance. The Orangefest parades become a counterpart to St Patrick's Day festivities. Competition also exists for the 'correct' retelling of the conflict narrative, a project which finds its expression primarily in competing Protestant and Catholic guided tours (McDowell 2008; Wiedenhoft Murphy 2010; Nagle 2010).

In this tug of war, the state has come to play the role of legitimizing force, with the distribution of money interpreted as a decree of authorization and approval. The scarcity of public funds available to support tourism ventures leads to perpetual wrangling over resource allocation, with each group claiming preferential treatment for the other. When unionist DUP's Nelson McCauseland blocked an amendment supporting the Gaeltacht Quarter initiative, Sinn Fein's

Figure 8.4 The development of the Protestant 'Shankill Quarter', March 2010.
Source: Author.

Eoin Ó Broin responded, 'The Gaeltacht Quarter would provide jobs and attract tourists to the city. Clearly these parties cannot contemplate anything that supports the development of the Irish language in the city, and the decision was purely sectarian' (*Andersontown News*, 5 December 2003, p. 2). Upon the launch of the Progressive Unionist Party's manifesto, which included calls for a unionist 'Orange Quarter', party member Ken Wilkinson said, 'At present, everything red, white and blue [unionist] is sectarian and everything green, white and gold [nationalist] is culture' (Connolly 2011). Community newspapers, such as the (Catholic) *Andersontown News* and the (Protestant) *Shankill Mirror*, frequently run exposés regarding the disproportionate allotment of funds alongside editorials linking these numbers to sectarian discrimination.

Given the hearsay involved, it is impossible to accurately determine the degree of influence that sectarianism or group favouritism plays in resource allocation. However, it can be assumed that politicians fight for initiatives that benefit their constituents while blocking initiatives that would anger them. The success of community tourism initiatives is therefore linked to the political sympathies of relevant department heads. For instance, money from the Integrated Development Fund allocated for the Shankill tourism was delayed for years, before a unionist minister pushed the money through to delivery. Similarly, the Gaeltacht Board complained that McCauseland was blocking support for the Gaeltacht Quarter while he was head of DCAL, the lead government agency for the project. Regardless of the factuality of this claim, as soon as a Sinn Fein councillor became department head, she signed a charter of full support (Northern Ireland Executive 2013).

Cooperation and mitigation

Paradoxically, while tourism has sparked conflict, it has also provided institutional and dialogic space for unprecedented levels of intercommunal cooperation. In particular, the more community workers of disparate backgrounds have come to regard tourism as a vehicle of economic development, the more they have worked collectively. Members of the West Belfast Partnership Board, for instance, have shared grant writing tips with less-experienced officers working in Protestant communities, acting on the belief that improving district tourism in one area will benefit all socio-economically deprived communities in Belfast. Certain moments are therefore evident of a solidarity based on collective exclusion.

The commitment of the BCC and the Northern Ireland Office to promoting 'good relations' and 'shared space' means that initiatives supporting interaction between or benefits across communities are more likely to receive financing than projects engaging only one community. Many funding proposals therefore purposely foreground cross-communal components, seeking support for joint mural projects, marketing initiatives, service provision, etc. This effort occurs in spite of the fact that many involved are not yet interested in, or prepared for, cross-communal work. Combining tourism with cross-communal work also enables organizations to access both local and international funding streams intended for conflict transformation activities. *Coiste na n-iarchimí*, an organization of former Republican prisoners offering Republican walking tours of the Falls Road since 2003, has used European PEACE money to develop joint tours with EPIC, the organization of former Loyalist prisoners.

Tourism has also promoted the mitigation of contentious symbols. In order to increase support for the Gaeltacht Quarter, for instance, the project board has gone to great lengths to depoliticize the Irish language. Given the strong association of Irish with the Republican struggle (O'Reilly 1997), the board was aware that state agencies would hesitate to support the regeneration initiative. In order to increase buy-in for the Quarter, the board has actively worked to disassociate the language from Republicanism, and to reposition the language as a shared cultural resource and as such, one capable of uniting the two communities and promoting reconciliation. To this end, the board has stressed prominent Protestant Irish speakers and the role of Protestants in the language's twentieth-century revival in its marketing materials, exhibitions and press releases, and has helped establish Irish classes in Protestant neighbourhoods.

These processes of competition and cooperation are occurring concurrently. Moments and patterns of cooperation are increasing, but contestation and competition have by no means disappeared. Even within collaborative projects, conflict continues: an initiative to create a joint tourism map of the Falls Road and the Shankill has faced numerous delays due to disagreement about content and language use. Likewise, some Protestants see the Gaeltacht Quarter Board's overtures to the Protestant community as insincere ploys for money, aimed at furthering the Catholic community alone.

Conclusion: whose story is the 'Belfast Story'?

The BCC's 2003 strategy document, *Cultural Tourism: Developing Belfast's Opportunity*, concedes 'Troubles Tourism – Belfast needs to come to terms with this,' adding that 'formalisation and contextualisation and better presentation might help' (BCC 2003: 46). This statement indicates the city council's coming to terms with political and community tourism, and their intent to repackage it in the best possible light, i.e. as non-sectarian.

Indeed, a tentative willingness to incorporate district tourism into official promotional materials is evident. Murals and political tours appear on the pages of the city's website and printed visitor guides with increasing frequency. However, these sites and services are still mostly sidelined, often buried in laundry lists of more acceptable attractions, e.g. 'from traditional music sessions to political murals, from Milltown and City Cemeteries to Clonard Monastery and St Peter's Cathedral, West Belfast certainly has lots to see' (BVCB 2011: 15). Community tourism based on cultural heritage has been more warmly received. Since 2007, the BVCB has included the Gaeltacht Quarter as an official city quarter in their annual visitor guides, and the council is experimenting with the branding theme 'Belfast City of Quarters' as a means of providing representational space for the city's multiple – and ever-splintering – narratives and identities (Carden 2012).[8] It is unsurprising that city officials are more open to culture than politics – even if in Belfast the two are often one and the same – and it is to be expected that communities will continue to mitigate their narratives under the rubric of cultural heritage in order to gain state approval and resources. The most recent tourism strategy, the 2010–14 Belfast Integrated Tourism Framework, gives a small indication of the direction of future convergence between community and state tourism. Overall, the strategy recommendations remain strongly focused on the city centre. However, one of six 'visionary drivers' is the 'Belfast Story', the theme under which the NITB and the BCC have selected to incorporate the city's conflict and community history and described as follows (BCC and NITB 2011: 23):

> The Belfast Story: This is a thread which should run through all that is done to develop tourism – to reflect the brand values of the city. It should embrace: Heritage – the story of the city through the ages – its people, its buildings, its conflicts; Tradition & Community – the legacy of the city's recent history needs to be accessible to visitors. It should include the character and charac- ters of Belfast and cross-cutting our cultural offering. This is where we belong, edgy, different, cool, etc. This also presents an opportunity to embrace our culture and identity.

Here, conflict history is grouped under one heading along with culture, identity, heritage, tradition and community. The language used is vague, and it is impossible to determine any concrete plans from the text. The action plan ambiguously states, 'Identify innovative ways to communicate the Belfast Story across the city and at key strategic locations' (ibid.). The framework does suggest that 'conflict resolution can be a focus' (ibid.), suggesting the possibility of a future effort to incorporate community tourism's conflict narrative with the city council's Renaissance narrative. Such a turn would support recent moves made by the government – thus far only in the sphere of international politics – to establish Northern Ireland as a potentially exportable model of conflict resolution.

The Belfast Story might indicate a continuum with regard to the presentation of conflict heritage: the further in time the relevant events have receded, the less state actors are hesitant to engage with a contentious past. On the other hand, the appearance of the Belfast Story in the latest policy document may signify the state's confidence to address the conflict under an acceptable rubric. Its appearance does indicate that communities' demands for greater representation are being heard by the council and the tourism board, even if the response to date has been minimal. However, whether representation will grow to significant levels or translate into significant investment is more questionable. Belfast's tourism growth since 1998 has been remarkable; yet as stated, numbers have dropped in the past two years and the damage done to the city's reputation and the economy by the flags protest has made politicians wary. For these reasons, state agencies are likely to continue to shy away from community tourism, in spite of the fact that offering support could potentially offset some of the very problems they are trying to hide.

The substantial link with and impact of tourism on Belfast's ethnic conflict underscores a fundamental issue witnessed pervasively throughout the chapters of this book: whether it is gentrification in Berlin, poverty and exclusion in Rio de Janeiro or structural urban transformation in Prague, tourism is deeply embedded in key socio-spatial processes – and likewise, transforms their manifestations. By extension, protests and challenges to tourism development overlap with other, even seemingly unrelated interests and issues. As this volume has shown, protest against tourism policy can take many different forms. Belfast's political/district tourism industry exemplifies how tourism *itself* can serve as a form of protest, in this case against dominant narratives of place identity and urban development (see Luger on Singapore in this volume). However, tourism initiatives pursued in opposition to state visions face strong limitations, and developers must proceed creatively in order to circumvent obstacles arising from a lack of public support. The most successful tactic in Belfast has been the engagement of third-party actors, whether private investors, international funders, non-local journalists or the tourists themselves. International attention forces governments to recognize that there is a compelling demand for new types of tourism which may be economically profitable and socially beneficial. This can lead the state to accept or co-opt such forms of tourism. In the end, tourism development and its contestations unfold across different types of actors (public, private and civil society) and scales (local, national and international), with conflict and cooperation between them occurring not along fixed lines, but changing dynamically as interests and alliances shift.

Notes

1 The term 'post-conflict' designates the period following the political resolution of conflict. The term, however, misleads by implying an end to the conflict, i.e. peace. In spite of an absence of violence (negative peace), most 'post-conflict' societies, such as Northern Ireland, are still dominated by conflict structures and mindsets and are far from a state of positive peace.
2 The two communities are commonly referred to using the terms Catholic/Nationalist/ Republican and Protestant/Unionist/Loyalist. The use of these terms is inconsistent and all six terms are problematic in their misrepresentation of the complexity of social and political identities in Northern Ireland. Moreover, communities are heterogeneous; therefore, not all Catholics are Republicans, nor are all Unionists Protestants, etc. While acknowledging that the terms may be used differently elsewhere, within this chapter the two communities are commonly designated by 'Catholic' and 'Protestant'. The terms 'Nationalist' and 'Unionist' are used when emphasizing a political position concerning Northern Ireland's membership of the United Kingdom. 'Republican' and 'Loyalist' are used when referencing those involved in or supportive of military action.
3 Out-of-state business tourists who spent at least one night in Belfast numbered 583,000 in 2012, indicating that business tourists are no longer the city's predominant market (BCC 2012).
4 The Board Member was citing Northern Ireland Statistics and Research Agency, Northern Ireland Multiple Deprivation Measure 2010.
5 No accurate statistics of visitors to West Belfast exist. The 2012 Belfast Tourism Monitor shows that 8 per cent of overnight visitors and 4 per cent of day visitors visited the city's political murals. Given that most of the murals are in West Belfast coupled with the fact that there are no other major attractions in the area, we can assume these figures are a representative percentage.
6 This complaint was repeated in numerous interviews with community workers, private tour providers, city representatives and in informal conversations with area residents.
7 In the context of Northern Ireland addressed in this chapter, the term intercommunal is used to refer to relations between the two major ethnic communities in Belfast, i.e. the Catholic and Protestant communities.
8 The Shankill Quarter, a designation sought by the Greater Shankill Partnership following the Council's recognition of the Gaeltacht Quarter, exists in strategy documents but has yet to appear in promotional materials.

References

Andersontown News (2003) 'City councillor vote against Gaeltacht Quarter', *Andersontown News*, 5 December, p. 2.
Andersontown News (2005) 'West gets set for tourist flow', *Andersontown News*, 21 May, p. 16.
Bairner, A. (2003) 'On thin ice?', *American Behavioral Scientist*, 46(11): 1519–32.
Baker, S. (2014) 'Belfast: new battle lines in a post-conflict city', *New Left Project*, blog post, 11 March. Online. Available at http://www.newleftproject.org/index.php/site/article_ comments/belfast_new_battle_lines_in_a_post_conflict_city (accessed 30 October 2014).
Bar-Tal, D. (2000) 'From intractable conflict through conflict resolution to reconciliation: psychological analysis', *Political Psychology*, 21(2): 351–65.

BCC (Belfast City Council) (2000) *Belfast Tourism Monitor 1999*. Belfast: BCC.

BCC (Belfast City Council) (2003) *Cultural Tourism: Developing Belfast's Opportunity*. Belfast: BCC.

BCC (Belfast City Council) (2012) *Belfast Tourism Monitor 2012*. Belfast: BCC.

BCC and NITB (Belfast City Council and Northern Ireland Tourism Board) (2011) *Belfast Tourism: Gateway to the Future. An Integrated Strategic Framework for Belfast Tourism 2011–2014*. Belfast: BCC & NITB.

Boyd, S. (2013) 'Tourism in Northern Ireland: before, during, and post war', in R. Butler and W. Suntikul (eds), *Tourism and War*. London: Routledge.

BVCB (Belfast Visitor and Convention Bureau) (2011) *Belfast Visitor Guide 2011*. Belfast: BVCB.

Cairns, E. (2010) 'Intergroup conflict in Northern Ireland', in H. Tajfel (ed.), *Social Identity and Intergroup Relations*. Cambridge: Cambridge University Press.

Carden, S. (2012) 'Making space for tourists with minority languages: the case of Belfast's Gaeltacht Quarter', *Journal of Tourism and Cultural Change*, 10(1): 51–64.

Connolly, M. (2011) 'PUP wants Orange Quarter on the Shankill to attract tourists', *Irish News*, 22 April, p. 16.

Davenport, F. and Berkmoes, R. V. (2012) *Lonely Planet Ireland*, 10th edn. Footscray, Vic. and Oakland, CA: Lonely Planet.

Harrison, S. (1995) 'Four types of symbolic conflict', *Journal of the Royal Anthropological Institute*, 1(2): 255–72.

Jarman, N. (2008) 'Security and segregation: interface barriers in Belfast', *Shared Space*, 6: 21–34.

McCabe, C. (2013) *The Double Transition: The Economic and Political Transition of Peace*. Belfast: Irish Congress of Trade Unions & Labour After Conflict.

MacCannell, D. (1999) *The Tourist: A New Theory of the Leisure Class*. Berkeley, CA: University of California Press.

McDowell, S. (2008) 'Selling conflict heritage through tourism in peacetime Northern Ireland: transforming conflict or exacerbating difference', *International Journal of Heritage Studies*, 14(5): 405–21.

McKeown, S. (2013) *Identity, Segregation and Peace-building in Northern Ireland*. Basingstoke: Palgrave Macmillan.

Miller, D. (1994) *Don't Mention the War: Northern Ireland, Propaganda and the Media*. London: Pluto Press.

Murtagh, B. and Keaveney, K. (2006) 'Policy and conflict transformation in an ethnocratic city', *Space and Polity*, 10(2): 187–202.

Nagle, J. (2010) 'Between trauma and healing: tourism and neoliberal peace-building in divided societies', *Journeys*, 11(1): 29–49.

Needham, R. (1998) *Battling for Peace: Northern Ireland's Longest-Serving British Minister*. Belfast: Blackstaff Press.

Neill, W. J. V. (1993) 'Physical planning and image enhancement: recent developments in Belfast', *International Journal of Urban and Regional Research*, 17(4): 595–609.

Neill, W. J. V. (2007) *Urban planning and Cultural Identity*. London: Routledge.

Neill, W. J. V., Murray, M. and Grist, B. (eds) (2013) *Relaunching Titanic: Memory and Marketing in the New Belfast*. London and New York: Routledge.

Nic Craith, M. (2003) *Culture and Identity Politics in Northern Ireland*. Basingstoke: Palgrave Macmillan.

NITB (Northern Ireland Tourism Board) (2010) *NITB Brand in Your Hand*. Belfast: NITB.

Nolan, P. (2014) *The Northern Ireland Peace Monitoring Report: 3*, Belfast: Northern Ireland Community Relations Council.

Northern Ireland Assembly (2008) *Parliamentary Debate on Tourism in the Northern Ireland Assembly*, 19 February. Online. Available at http://www.theyworkforyou.com/ni/?id=2008-02-19.5.1&s=travel+industry (accessed 8 October 2011).

Northern Ireland Executive (2013) *The Big GQ Plan to Map Future for the Gaeltacht Quarter*, 20 September. Online. Available at http://www.northernireland.gov.uk/news-dcal-200913-the-big-gq (accessed 30 October 2014).

Northover, J. (2010) 'A brand for Belfast: how can branding a city influence change?' *Place Branding and Public Diplomacy*, 6: 104–11.

Ó Liatháin, C. (2003) 'West Belfast: here be dragons!', *Andersontown News*, 3 February, p. 22.

O'Dowd, L. and Komarova, M. (2011) 'Contesting territorial fixity? A case study of regeneration in Belfast', *Urban Studies*, 48(10): 2013–28.

O'Hearn, D. (2008) 'How has peace changed the Northern Irish political economy?' *Ethnopolitics*, 7(1): 101–18.

O'Reilly, C. (1997) 'Nationalists and the Irish language in Northern Ireland: competing perspectives', in A. Mac Póilín (ed.), *The Irish Language in Northern Ireland*. Belfast: Ultach Trust.

Ruane, J. and Todd, J. (1996) *The Dynamics of Conflict in Northern Ireland: Power, Conflict, and Emancipation*. Cambridge: Cambridge University Press.

Selwyn, T. (1996) *The Tourist Image: Myths and Myth Making in Tourism*. New York: John Wiley.

Shirlow, P. and Murtagh, B. (2006) *Belfast: Segregation, Violence and the City*. London: Pluto Press.

Shirlow, P. and Shuttleworth, I. (1999) '"Who is going to toss the burgers"? Social class and the reconstruction of the Northern Irish economy', *Capital and Class*, 23(3): 27–46.

Short, J. (2006) 'The competitive city', in J. Short (ed.), *Urban Theory: A Critical Assessment*. Basingstoke: Palgrave Macmillan.

Taxi Trax (2015) *About Taxi Trax*. Online. Available at http://www.taxitrax.com/about/ (accessed 1 December 2015).

Tonge, J. (2006) 'Sinn Fein and the "New Republicanism" in Belfast', *Space and Polity*, 10(2): 135–47.

Tourism Development International (2001) *Fáilte Feirste Thiar/Welcome to West Belfast: A Strategic Review of Tourism in West Belfast*, Report prepared for the West Belfast Partnership. Belfast: TDI.

Urry, J. (1990) *The Tourist Gaze: Leisure and Travel in Contemporary Societies*. London: Sage.

White, P. and Simpson, J. (2002) *The Joint West Belfast/Greater Shankill Task Force Report*. Belfast: Joint West Belfast/Greater Shankill Task Force.

Wiedenhoft Murphy, W. A. (2010) 'Touring the Troubles in West Belfast: building peace or reproducing conflict?' *Peace and Change*, 35: 537–60.

Wilson, D. (1993) 'Tourism, public policy and the image of Northern Ireland since the Troubles', in B. O'Connor and M. Cronin (eds) *Tourism in Ireland: A Critical Analysis*. Cork: Cork University Press.

9 The *No Grandi Navi* campaign

Protests against cruise tourism in Venice

Michele Vianello

When the latest annual tourism statistics were issued by the city of Venice in November 2014, there was an outcry in the local media: Venice had welcomed an unprecedented amount of 25 million annual visitors in 2012, and not all commentators deemed this a reason to celebrate.[1] Venice's alarmingly high tourist pressure has, in recent years, attracted a great amount of public attention, but the interest in Venice as an object of analysis for tourism studies is older. The city's unique spatial, historical and environmental features have inspired researchers for decades and Venice has served as a case study for addressing various issues central to tourism studies, ranging from the 'disneyfication' of heritage (Cosgrove 1982) to the application of the concept of 'tourism carrying capacity' (Canestrelli and Costa 1991) and the sustainability of tourism in heritage cities (van der Borg *et al.* 1992) as well as broader concerns with tourism management (van der Borg 1998).

Nevertheless, despite being a central feature in the city's economy, tourism was not quite as central in local public and political debates on planning and urban policies until the 1990s. A comparative study on planning and tourism in Venice and Florence by Lombardi (1992) shows that the municipal government of Venice from the 1950s to the early 1990s largely refrained from discussing, let alone setting, specific long-term objectives to control or direct tourism flows. Instead, tourism regulation was rather limited. Even the oppositional political forces in Venice – for the most part of its recent modern history an industrial city – only marginally addressed tourism. Social and political controversies revolved primarily around labour conditions and collective consumption issues, e.g. the shortage of affordable housing (Lombardi 1992), and it was only in recent years that tourism, in particular cruise ship tourism, emerged as an issue in local political discourses and struggles.

This chapter focuses on the formation and activities of the *Comitato No Grandi Navi – Laguna Bene Comune* (*No Big Ships – Lagoon as a Common* Committee), a local social movement that has challenged the city government's and harbour authorities' approach to cruise ship tourism and has campaigned to ban giant cruise liners from the entire Venetian Lagoon. The opposition to this type of tourism is not unprecedented (Johnson 2002). The targets of Venetian protests are partially comparable to developments in other contexts, including in particular in

Australia and Northern and Central America (London and Lohmann 2014; Dredge 2010; Diedrich 2010; Lester and Weeden 2004). In Venice, a number of locally specific factors have led to the formation of the campaign and more broadly to a growing public opposition against the city's official tourism policies: the city government's turn towards urban entrepreneurialism in the 1990s, which included the privatisation of several public assets (involving parts of the harbour activities through Law 84/1994), the growing number of ever-bigger cruise ships mooring in Venice since the mid-2000s (Tattara 2013) and more recently a series of corruption scandals which have marred local politics, as will be explained in the first part of this chapter.

The chapter will then show how social mobilizations questioning the impact of cruise tourism on Venice have started to emerge, before analysing the composition of the *No Grandi Navi* protests as a social movement.[2] We focus here on the two types of groups which have taken a central role in the Committee: *social centres* and associations, and argue that the modes of organization and action of the movement match the features of a new generation of (urban) social movements identified by Italian scholars such as Daher (2012). Particular attention is then paid to how the movement has used legal windows of opportunities to pursue its objectives, and how the movement's agenda has adopted the concept of the 'Commons' to broaden its claims. Finally, the conclusion will discuss how the movement has influenced local politics in recent years and what role the movement might have in future developments.

The shift to entrepreneurial urban governance, tourism policy and the rise of cruise ship tourism in Venice

The number of tourists in Venice has been increasing steadily over recent decades. While official statistics refer to around 9.7 million overnight guests in official accommodation in 2013 (Comune di Venezia 2013), the methodology devised to calculate the number of 'city users for leisure activities' (COSES 2009) estimated 21.6 million visitors in 2007, based on the number of people accessing the city's main transport hubs on a daily basis such as the airport, stations, bus terminals and ship terminals. At the same time, the population of the Old City (the central municipality of Venice, excluding Murano and Burano), has seen a major decrease from about 175,000 inhabitants in 1951 (COSES 2009) to about 56,000 in 2015 (Comune di Venezia 2015). This decrease has been mostly connected to structural factors, such as deindustrialization and the increase in real-estate values (Gasparoli and Trovò 2014), which were never countered by effective policies for the retention of resident population (e.g. by intervening through the taxation of holiday/second homes or providing incentives for resident first buyers). Touristic uses, both formal (e.g. hotels) and informal (e.g. unregistered bed and breakfasts), have today taken over a large part of the Old City's built environment and social fabric (Settis 2014).

In this context, a turn towards urban entrepreneurialism in Venetian local politics happened during the first tenure of Massimo Cacciari, one of Venice's longest-serving mayors (1993–2000 and 2005–10).[3] This turn involved, among other things, the privatization of parts of major public assets such as the passenger terminal, the Biennale foundation, several historical palaces and the Arsenale compound. It was also characterized by a shift towards property- and event-led development as a means to assert and increase Venice's role as a tourism destination and support urban economic development. Even during the mandate of a supposedly more 'progressive' mayor – Paolo Costa (2000–5) – who, prior to his tenure, had promoted the idea of applying 'tourism carrying capacity' assessment techniques to control visitor numbers (Canestrelli and Costa 1991) – the city's policy orientations remained virtually unchanged. Private initiative was supported unrestrainedly and, as a result, emerged as a central force in the reconfiguration of the city for tourism purposes (Judd and Fainstein 1999).

This reconfiguration received further traction with the growth of cruise ship tourism in the mid-2000s. Cruise line traffic has seen a constant increase in the harbour of Venice, with 650,000 cruise tourists in 2004 and almost 1.8 million in 2011, an increase of over 100,000 visitors per year (Tattara 2013). This growth has to be seen against the backdrop of the rise of the cruise ship industry as a global tourism industry during the same time span (Soriani *et al.* 2009; Véronneau and Roy 2009). It was also owed to local political decisions which turned the city into an attractive home port for cruise companies, e.g. the conversion of a major shipyard in Marghera, an industrial suburb, into a construction and maintenance site for cruise liners in the mid-1990s, alongside with the organization of a platform for the handling and supply of ships in the Old City, with three new cruise terminals completed between 2003 and 2009.

Policies to regulate tourism flows appeared in the late 1990s and sought to respond to, and reconcile, two contradictory issues: a demand for regulation of the flows and concentrations of visitors accessing the Old City as well as for policies to retain local residents, and a demand for enhanced accessibility to the Old City, in particular for cruise tourists. This contradiction was, however, not explicitly recognized, because the parallel rise of tourism and the decline of the Old City's social fabric following deindustrialization processes were for the most part kept on separate agendas by the city government. This disconnect in the political agenda was mirrored in local social movements: no relevant protest addressed the issues of urban economic and demographic decline and of tourism simultaneously. With the exception, perhaps, of *Italia Nostra*, a national conservation organization that was established in 1955 to preserve Italy's cultural and natural heritage, the handful of protests that attempted to look at these two issues together before the year 2000 did not go beyond some meetings and written exchanges.

The main novelty of the protests against cruise tourism which have arisen in Venice in recent years rests on the successful mobilization of a wide range of citizens and their engagement with issues that had not been addressed by local social movements before. The reasons are to be found in the increased visibility of the impacts of cruise tourism, but also in a growing discontent with the city authorities' approach to urban and economic development which characterized the turn to urban entrepreneurialism referred to above. Additionally, the protests have to be read within the context of a series of dramatic corruption scandals. The mayor of Venice, Giorgio Orsoni (2010–14), was overthrown in 2014 after a series of corruption allegations related to the highly controversial MOSE project, a system of mobile barrages separating the Venice Lagoon from the open sea in case of exceptional high tides (*acqua alta*) that has been under construction since 2003. The scandals led to the arrest of the mayor and several city council members and culminated in the dissolution of the city council in June 2014. A central government official, Vittorio Zappaloroto, was appointed to oversee the city's administration, and it was only in June 2015 that municipal elections were held. This scandal – alongside the resulting void in power as Venice was left for a year without a democratically elected decision-making body – helped the Committee *No Grandi Navi* to take on an important role in shaping public opinion and push for a new agenda linking the issue of tourism to that of the Old City's decline.

Questioning the impact of cruise tourism

The constant growth in the size and number of cruise ships (in 2012, 48 per cent of cruise liners docking in Venice were above 70,000 gross tonnage – Tattara 2013) had already worried the general public in Venice for several years,[4] but it was only in January 2012 that a variety of activists from different social and professional backgrounds and local associations formed the Comitato *No Grandi Navi – Laguna Bene Comune* (No Big Ships – Lagoon as a Common Committee, henceforth referred to as the Committee). Its foundation coincided with the *Costa Concordia* disaster near Giglio Island on 13 January 2012. Significantly, however – and contrary to what some commentators have argued – it occurred not after, but prior to the tragic accident off the Italian coast that claimed 32 victims and sparked international debates on the costs and risks of the rapidly growing cruise ship industry (UNESCO 2012). Apart from the risks posed to the vulnerable ecosystem of the Venice Lagoon by a potential accident involving a cruise liner, the Committee from the onset drew attention to a number of other adverse effects of cruise ship tourism, including the solid waste, waste waters and air pollution which cruise ships generate (Caric 2010); the environmental, hydraulic and geological effects of digging canals in the lagoon; as well as the economic and social impacts of cruise ship passengers, such as the very limited duration of their visit to the city or their propensity to spend less and on lower-quality items and services (Tattara 2013).

Furthermore, the Committee raised critical questions about a series of large-scale infrastructure projects which public authorities had realized or were planning to realize to accommodate the needs of cruise ship tourism, e.g. an automated tram built to connect the passenger terminal with parking areas and the city's train station and the proposed redevelopment of industrial land adjacent to the terminal for tourism and leisure purposes (Autorità Portuale di Venezia 2013). Such projects were portrayed by the Committee as indicative of an approach to urban and tourism development that prioritized mass tourism and short-term growth at the expense of more sustainable forms of development and long-term visions.

In order to challenge and ultimately change the city's approach to cruise ship tourism, the Committee developed a multifaceted campaign within which the legal framework regulating cruise ship traffic would soon take on a particularly important role. With respect to the latter, it is important to understand the political and legal consequences that came out of the above-mentioned *Costa Concordia* disaster. In response to the strong public pressure over environmental concerns which followed the accident, the Italian Ministry of Infrastructure and Transport issued a ministerial decree in March 2012 to limit or ban ships above 500 gross tonnage from sensitive marine areas (Ministero delle Infrastrutture e dei Trasporti 2012a, 2012b), namely Marine National Parks, and introduced a limitation of up to 40,000 gross tonnage for ships entering the San Marco Basin and the Giudecca Canal in Venice. Political commentators (Vitucci 2012; Petricca 2013) interpreted the government's decision to respond to the disaster with a ministerial decree as an attempt to demonstrate that it understood its ramifications and was determined to act accordingly. At the same time, they also pointed to two controversial aspects of the chosen instrument: the fact that ministerial decrees are not subject to parliamentary debate and approval, and the fact that their statutory power is limited to the amendment of existing legislative provisions.

In addition, a number of inconsistencies, loopholes and lacunas were soon identified. With respect to the Venice Lagoon, the decree only proposed the protection of the San Marco Basin and the Giudecca Canal (a very small area of the Lagoon at the centre of the Old City) from ships of more of 40,000 gross tonnage, for instance, and refrained from regulating the traffic in the wider lagoon area. Moreover, the regulation was from the outset made conditional on the designation of an alternative shipping lane by the local branch of the Maritime Authority (which is under the control of the Ministry of Infrastructure and Transport) for ships to access the docking area adjacent to the Old City, which effectively postponed its implementation in Venice *sine die*. As a result, the decree was soon derided as inefficient and criticized for leaving the responsibility for acting upon it to the Maritime Authority. However, by leaving the implementation responsibility to the local level, the 2012 decree also created a significant window of opportunity for action by local social movements – a window of opportunity seized by the Committee.

Moreover, the waterways that are the object of contestation (San Marco's Basin, Giudecca Canal and the opening towards the sea) fall under the competence of the Port Authority (the public-private organization that manages the port). The policies and objectives for their development and use are not set out in the city's strategic planning document (discussed below), but in a specific harbour plan that is prepared under the auspices of the Port Authority. Issues concerning cruise ship regulation are currently not addressed in it, as the plan's latest version was adopted in 1965, way before the cruise ship industry made its mark upon the city. To many activists and observers, it was clear from the start that a new harbour plan was required to effectively deal with the regulation of the industry and settle questions of cruise ship passage and docking, as well as the infrastructure necessary to accommodate such ships.

Analysing the composition of the *No Grandi Navi* protests in Venice as a social movement

In order to analyse the Committee's structure and operation, it is important to first contextualize it within the particularities of Italian social movements. A social movement is defined for this purpose as a voluntary unitary mobilization organizing a concerted action in favour of a cause (Neveu 2001; della Porta and Diani 1997; Farro 1998; Daher 2002). The impact of social movements on the Italian political system has been widely researched. Scholars have in particular investigated whether specific legislative changes addressing big national issues which occurred in the 1960s and 1970s in Italy were the direct result of the demands and protests organized by particular social movements of the time, or whether such changes had more complex causes that were only partly catalysed by social movements (Daher 2012: 8). Scholars mostly concentrated on protests connected to class struggles, such as the mobilizations for advancing workers' rights (enshrined in Law 300/1970) – or to identity struggles (e.g. the feminist movement which led to the introduction of legal abortion with Law 194/1978). In both cases, scholars argued that a strong sense of collective identity and/or a sharing of life-styles and cultural codes, as well as the use of common slogans, discourses and collective symbols among local groups across the nation, were central to the success of social movements (Beccalli 1994; Bedani 1995).

In line with the international evolution of social movements discussed in the introduction of this book, many Italian social movements began from the 1980s onwards to broaden their composition and turn from confrontation with the government towards negotiation and compromise to achieve their objectives (Diani 1999; della Porta and Diani 2004). Italian researchers have analysed how the nature of social movements has changed (Daher 2012), *inter alia* through the deployment of more fluid and complex sets of practices that are not simply rooted in an identifiable form of collective identity, but rely on more flexible forms of identification and participation (Diani 2008: 58), as well as new strategies. Daher (2012) suggests that contemporary Italian social movements have relied upon a combination of three types of strategies – of *institution*, *association* and *lobby* (2012: 56–70). The notion of *institution* entails that movements assume characteristics of predictability and stability similar to those of formal institutions (e.g. in terms of functioning, organization, aims and long-term objectives), and that they can – from the very beginning – mobilize within formal arenas, alongside or as a substitute for other more traditional forms of protests such as demonstrations. The concept of *association* is used to indicate the fact that pre-existing associative forms take a prominent role within movements: members of existing associations whose objectives are in line with those of a social movement have an increasingly strong motivation to take part in such collective mobilization. As will be discussed below, the concept also refers to the fact that social movements can take on strategies that connect and create networks between very different associations. Finally the concept of the *lobby* (or *pressure group*) understands new social movements as interest groups focused on a specific issue (which can be part of a wider demand for change), which they seek to advance by influencing policies through pressures on institutions based both on threats (e.g. street protests, blockages, strikes) or on rewards (e.g. contributing to electoral success). Traditional forms of protests are thus used as tools for lobbying initiatives.

The *No Grandi Navi* Committee is composed of at least three types of active participants: activists connected to so-called *centri sociali* (social centres); associations, i.e. registered non-profit advocacy organizations and their members; and private individuals of different social and political backgrounds. Furthermore, representatives from formal institutions, such as some councillors of the municipality of Venice Old City-Murano-Burano, or the city council of the neighbouring town of Mira, gravitate around the Committee and take part in its work. The structure of the Committee takes the form of a loose association of otherwise autonomous groups and individuals. It uses a group mailing list as an organizing device which is open to all, the acceptance to which is scrutinized by active members. This instrument is used to convene bi-monthly assemblies in which the Committee's activities and positions are discussed, decided upon and planned. Significantly, the Committee is organized non-hierarchically. There are no leaders and hierarchical positions. Instead, it only has one spokesperson who deals with the press and issues public announcements that are approved by the assembly through a deliberative democracy approach.

The Committee thus relies upon fluid, Internet-based bonds among individuals: all participants have equal rights to propose ideas and actions for discussion, and cooperate with other committee members by elaborating shared concepts and motions before meetings. The importance of sharing lifestyles, cultural codes and collective symbols within the social movement – which were central to the movements of the 1960–70s – are not erased but are confined to smaller units/groups within the movement which seek to work together for common goals. This enhances the ability of participants to deploy their differences and make them coexist productively, marking the novelty of this form of organization. This is illustrated by the two types of groups which have taken a central role in the Committee, which both display a strong mobilizing capacity, while being very different in their structure, goals and the characteristics of their members: the *centri sociali* and the associations.

We now turn to look at the different roles and modes of action of two representative components of the Committee: the *centro sociale* Laboratorio Morion, located in Venice's Old City, heir to a radical approach to contestation typical of the 1970s and thus exemplifying the historical continuity and evolution of protests in terms of discourses and actions; and the association Ambiente Venezia, representative of the role of more formal groups in attracting and activating new forms of loose engagement around common objectives, thus widening the impact of the protests.

Centri sociali can be described as collectively self-managed community spaces used for cultural, social and political purposes in a non-commercial setting. Most of them are located in squats or former squats, and are still run according to principles aligned with the squatting traditions of the 1970s when the first *centri sociali* were set up – collectivism, autonomy and self-reliance. Unlike political parties or classic voluntary associations, they do not require formal affiliation – instead membership to them is built on direct participation. There is a comprehensive body of research on *centri sociali* and their multifaceted nature in different cities in Italy (Consorzio Aaster *et al*. 1996; Caniglia 2002; Bugliari Goggia 2007; Branzaglia *et al*. 1992). Several studies (e.g. Becucci 2003; Veltri 2003) have focused on their democratic forms of deliberation and the strong role of informal leadership within structures which are in theory marked by an absence of hierarchy. In Venice, the *centro sociale* Laboratorio Morion (founded as a local group at the end of the 1980s and permanently squatting a venue since the early 1990s) has around 20 core active members working in the squat, and over 40 in wider circles of sympathizers who regularly take part in its initiatives. Its members have all played a vital role in the protests against cruise ships and are mostly young people in precarious employment situations, between 20 and 40 years of age, with no formal engagement in political parties, but with individual stories of involvement in anti-globalization movements, world social forums, environmental local mobilizations, etc. The *centro sociale* has no formal statute: members belong to it by the mere act of attending meetings, taking part in the organization of political and cultural activities, and contributing to the collective management of the space.

The significance of Laboratorio Morion in the *No Grandi Navi* struggle can be attributed to different factors: on the one hand, it has kept a strong and constant spatial presence in the city and a visibility among local people, conducting several struggles for many years – e.g. for housing rights, immigrants' rights and insurgent cultural practices – through forms of activism that left a tangible mark in the city, such as building occupations. On the other hand, it has maintained the capacity to mobilize a consistent number of people and gather financial support through volunteers' subscriptions, in part by adopting a more open attitude departing from the at times inward-looking behaviour often associated with this type of activism, e.g. by organizing concerts and public events. Laboratorio Morion has also been instrumental in providing 'manpower' for the staging of spectacular protest actions by the Committee, such as the collective dives and canal blockages reported in the media. This is due to the fact that the Laboratorio Morion's activists are young and well versed in staging such kind of protest activities. While Laboratorio Morion lacks many of the characteristics of elastic and discontinuous forms of mobilization attributed to contemporary social movements, it has a very strong inertia and capacity of providing continuity to the struggle.

The formal associations taking part in the Committee are, by contrast, indicative of a new form of resistance, one that coalesces around the catchword of the 'Commons' (*Beni Comuni*), as will be explained further below. The most prominent of them, Ambiente Venezia – officially registered as a non-profit organization – counted at the time of research (September 2014) an active core of about 20 people and circa 40 additional members. Its members have played a vital role in the protest against cruise ships. They are all above 50, mostly retired from formal jobs, and with a history of political engagement either in left-wing political parties or in social movements of the 1970s (e.g. the feminist movement). The association focuses mainly on the environmental deterioration of the Lagoon of Venice and its consequences. It employs a number of strategies, among which monitoring, research and advocacy activities around a wide spectrum of environmental, legal and policy issues. These activities and the skills that the association's members possess to carry them out have proven to be instrumental to the Committee's work. The association's expertise and insight significantly informed the Committee's positions and proposals and greatly enhanced its ability to challenge official narratives and governmental power. In addition, Ambiente Venezia has enabled the Committee to build numerous contacts with important civil society actors and the academic community. The association's members are significantly older and more socially established than the activists of Laboratorio Morion and have on several occasions used their connections to advance the Committee's cause.

The activities of Ambiente Venezia thus contributed to one of the distinctive features of the protest movement: the collective production of knowledge to advance the Committee's agenda. The collection and dissemination of data, the production of reports and studies on the effects of cruise line tourism on the Lagoon of Venice, and the drafting of alternative projects for cruise ship docking were carried out as a constitutive part of opposition to cruise tourism, with the help of academics. This effort was a political statement in itself, advocating a strong role for social movements in data-informed and evidence-based planning processes. This was a novelty in the Venice context, which matches a global trend towards alternative scientific knowledge production on the part of social movements as a way to support their cause. This shift was accompanied by a reconsideration of the role of 'scientific information' as an important basis for supporting the movement's demands, in opposition to the vision often held by older social movements of scientific knowledge as inherently connected to 'oppressive state-centric politics' (Wyly 2011). This brings back to the fore an often neglected aspect of the Lefebvrian concept of the right to the city: the use of (non-technocratic) scientific knowledge production as a keystone to support emancipatory political projects, alongside insurgence and informality (Lefebvre 1996).

The differences between Laboratorio Morion and Ambiente Venezia thus form one of the defining characteristics of the Committee: the heterogeneity of its members. It was formed as a deliberately broad and flexible alliance between diverse sets of actors, who would harness their respective energy, creativity, skills and knowledge. Protests staged in public spaces were colourful and spectacular events, such as the physical blockage of big ships in the Giudecca Canal carried out on 16 September 2012 by protesters who swam and used dinghies and small boats (Figure 9.1). Such actions served two purposes: making rallies visually attractive, open to broad public participation and raising support for the cause, while enhancing the media exposure of the Committee to support its other activities, i.e. lobbying. The Committee can thus be described as an alliance that combines long-tested forms of social struggles with the newer tactics described by Daher (2012) to gather support and consensus, produce scientific and thematic knowledge and widen the participation to protests. This alliance is not a merger

Figure 9.1 Protest event organized by the *No Grandi Navi* campaign: blockage of the Giudecca Canal, 16 September 2012.

Source: Comitato No Grandi Navi – Laguna Bene Comune, photographer: Stefano Fiorin.

of different entities into one body, but rather a strategic form of cooperation that enables each member to maintain its specificity.

The Committee's modes of action: using legal windows of opportunity

The Committee, in the course of its existence, has sought to influence and change policies and regulations related to cruise tourism, its infrastructure and its impacts on the Venetian Lagoon at least at three overlapping levels: planning regulations at the municipal level, in particular the structural plan of Venice (PAT: *Piano di Assetto del Territorio*); harbour-related regulations coordinated by central state bodies through the harbour plan (PRP: *Piano Regolatore Portuale*); and national legislation on the preservation and management of the Lagoon of Venice (i.e. the 'Special Laws for Venice' 366/1963, 171/1973, 798/1984, 360/1991, 139/1992 and 206/1995).[5]

The following section analyses what is new in the modes of action of the movement compared to previous generations of Italian social movements. The purposefully and collectively established open structure of the Committee included very different groups of protesters which had different approaches, experiences and feelings about political confrontation. Its actions have thus taken different forms and typically involved a combination of *associative*, *lobbying* and *institutional* tactics of protest, to use Daher's (2012) concepts. This combination became particularly evident in one particular case: the public participation process accompanying the preparation of the *Piano di Assetto del Territorio* (PAT), Venice's development plan which sets the general objectives of the city's spatial management and transformation and forms the basis for the city's regulatory zoning plan (*Piano Interventi*). In the course of 2012 the Venice City Council debated, through a complex process of deliberation, the approval of a new PAT (Comune di Venezia 2012a). This process became the occasion for the Committee to deploy a mix of tactics including the organization of street demonstrations to exert pressure on the work of the City Council, as well as the use of *association* (i.e. of coordinated action among the different groups belonging to the Committee), *institutionalized participation* and *lobbying* techniques.

The Committee gathered the most relevant knowledge produced by the associations belonging to the network and submitted extensive observations and objections on the draft version of the PAT during the official public consultation process, but their observations were dismissed as irrelevant and rejected in the official report on the submitted public observations. In parallel, through a steady stream of public protests during the days of the final approval of the amendments to the plan (20 and 21 December 2012), the Committee members convened with two city councillors of a local political group named *In Comune* (In Common) to propose an amendment (known as 35 bis) to the proposed plan that subsequently received the support of the majority of the Council. The amendment involved the inclusion of a new article in the written regulations (*Norme Tecniche*) of the PAT. It contains an official commitment to banning 'incompatible' cruise liners from the Lagoon, in the context of the future task of better coordinating city planning (the PAT and PI) with harbour planning (the PRP). This commitment does not specify the terms of the ban on cruise liners, nor a time frame, but binds the municipality to carry out several studies on the environmental, health, socio-economic, employment and morphological impacts of cruise tourism and port activities within 18 months to inform the future preparation of effective regulations. These studies have not been carried out to date.

The achievement of this modification of the PAT forced the municipal government to take a stance on the issue of harbour planning and thus encouraged further protests. Over the following year and a half, new protest events were staged in public space, such as another blockage of the Giudecca Canal on 9 June 2013 and of the Cruise Terminal on 7 June 2014 (in which many protesters dressed up as beach-goers), or the 'Lagoon Festival' on 21 September 2014, a collective boat trip organized by the Committee in order to raise awareness of the impact of cruise tourism on the lagoon environment. In parallel, additional expertise and knowledge was developed, e.g. the Committee's *Libro Bianco* (White Book) which provided a comprehensive account of the environmental deterioration of the Lagoon and put forward suggestions for moving cruise activities outside the Lagoon (Fabbri 2015).

However, as mentioned earlier, the regulation of the waterways which are the object of contestation fall under the competence of the Port Authority and thus are subject to a specific harbour plan that is prepared under its auspices, not to the city's strategic plan – PAT. This is why the amendment of the PAT referred to the need for a new harbour plan, on which a definitive solution to the problem of cruise ship regulation is pending. The drafting of a new harbour plan has not started yet. The Port Authority had two options to put forward a vision for the harbour and its future infrastructural projects: either by preparing a new harbour plan, in cooperation with the government and citizens of Venice and surrounding municipalities, or by essentially bypassing local democratic procedures with the help of the 'Special Laws for Venice' and the controversial use of a national law on infrastructural development (Law 443/2001).[6] This enables the Port Authority to nominate infrastructure projects for funding and fast-forward approval by the national government, skipping important parts of the local planning procedures. In the summer of 2014 the Venice Port Authority chose the second option and presented a project to dig a new gigantic canal in the Lagoon, the Contorta Canal, to the Italian Ministry of the Environment for environmental impact assessment.

The proposed canal would enable cruise liners to approach, and dock in, the Old City without passing through the San Marco Basin and the Giudecca Canal. It represents a very ambitious undertaking involving the construction of several kilometres of underwater barriers and dykes, pushing further the transformation of the Lagoon into a highly artificial, engineered water body. By adopting a purely technical approach to solve the problem posed by the increase in large ships, rather than pursuing a deliberative, participatory process as demanded by the protesters – the Venice Port Authority not only ignored established international principles of environmental decision-making (such as those articulated by the Aarhus convention (UNECE 1998)), but also effectively imposed its vision of the city as a cruise tourism destination. No public discussion on the Contorta Canal was proposed, and the project's designation as a strategic national project under Law 443/2001 meant that its environmental impact assessment was fast-tracked. Significantly, this did not prevent members of the public from making use of the few opportunities available to air their views: 281 observations were submitted to the Ministry, of which a significant amount accused the Port Authority of failing to comply with the long-term objective to ban incompatible cruise liners from the lagoon expressed in the above-mentioned article 35 bis of the PAT. In spite of this, the digging of the new canal was approved by an inter-ministerial committee through the procedure envisaged by Law 443/2001, although a complaint to the Administrative Tribunal of the Veneto Region filed by Ambiente Venezia and the city government managed to delay its realization. The tribunal ruled, in July 2015, that no other alternative had been thoroughly considered and therefore that the Contorta Canal could not be realized before other options were evaluated. The Port Authority appealed to the Italian Council of State (the highest administrative court) against this ruling. In November 2015 the Port Authority, in agreement with the new government of the City of Venice, proposed a slightly different project for another canal (named Tresse Nuovo) aiming at getting it approved through Law 443/2001 while the Contorta project was still blocked in court.

From protests against large cruise ships towards the defence of the Commons

The story of the protests organized by the Committee *No Grandi Navi* in Venice provides a complex example of the restructuring of urban social mobilizations from movements involving identifiable social groups sharing a lifestyle, cultural codes and ideals, into more diverse and flexible coalitions using wider modes of action and including multiple actors characterized by significant differences. In opposition to the deployment of cruise tourism as a main driver for the economic restructuring of the city of Venice, the protests aimed at reframing the problem of cruise tourism in Venice as a collective decision problem regarding long-term social and environmental objectives, specifically the use of the shared resource of the Lagoon water body. This marked a difference from the demands advanced by previous political mobilizations and discourses, which were primarily focused on a fairer social redistribution of the income generated by economic activities and by the existing use of shared resources. This was achieved by resorting to the concept of the Commons (*Beni Comuni*) as a mobilizing slogan. The concept of the 'Commons' (Ostrom 1990) refers to traditional, complex systems of use of resources that set rules of mutual control and cooperation within a community, by designing arrangements capable of reproducing resources and incorporating externalities as part of the process of use and appropriation.

The notion of the Commons was used occasionally and in an uncoordinated way in several Italian local environmental and social struggles since the mid-2000s. It was inspired by an aborted Civil Code reform proposal (Ministero di Grazia e Giustizia 2007) which aimed at introducing the category of 'Commons' as a property regime. When the reform failed, the concept began to be used as a political slogan by various associations in different contexts. Their struggles shared characteristics of the 'new' forms of protests identified by contemporary social movement theorists (Melucci 1996; Castells 1997; Daher 2012). In 2011, national mobilizations involved hundreds of thousands of people against the planned privatization of water supply services, adopting the term 'Commons' as a slogan to call for local collective action and a revision of the legal framework to manage shared resources (Mattei 2011). A number of associations were largely responsible for the success of the two referenda which took place on the issue, by mobilizing citizens around specific interests (e.g. environmental concerns, health and civil rights), establishing new forms of cooperation, and framing a new discourse on the management of collective assets and resources (Bersani 2011).

In Venice, the first recorded use of the term 'Commons' in Venetian local protests was in 2007, in a document which proposed the formation of a 'forum [. . .] for the defence of the Commons' (Associazione Ambiente Venezia 2014) which were then defined as 'land, water, air'. That forum was to include environmental associations, later active in the above-mentioned referendum campaign on the privatization of water supplies and forming part of the Committee, with Ambiente Venezia among them. Individual members of Laboratorio Morion also referred to the term 'Commons' as part of their political struggle in support of the referendum on water, and some understood the idea of Commons as a parallel to Ocalan's ideas on 'Democratic Confederalism' (Ocalan 2011), i.e. a form of radical grassroots democracy.

It is allegedly through the environmental associations' initiative that the term Commons was included in the name of the Committee *No Grandi Navi*. The accent put on privatizations by city officials since the 1990s (Bonomi 1995) as the panacea for solving complex governance issues in Venice pushed the Committee to embrace this multifaceted concept. It was subsequently used in meetings and discussions as a vague but powerful narrative aimed at congealing efforts in favour of a stronger and more democratic control over public institutions in the collective management and control of the Lagoon's shared space and resources. It helped structure a discourse which did not fall into the trap of a simplistic opposition between 'tourists' and 'locals'. The notion of the Commons has thus been used in Venetian protests in the sense suggested by Marcuse in his idea of 'Commons planning' (2011), i.e. as a way to challenge currently prevailing economic and political paradigms and re-think current forms of governance and urban development. The opposition to cruise tourism has been used by the Committee as a vehicle to support a wider objective, that of linking the regulation of tourism to a comprehensive strategy for the conservation of the city's heritage, the improvement of environmental policies, and the use of comprehensive planning for these purposes (Casson 2014), after decades in which tourism had been surprisingly secondary in planning strategies (Lombardi 1992). This is illustrated by several alternative projects presented by the Committee to propose a viable and up-to-date logistic and docking platform for cruise ships, in harmony with the delicate nature of the city (Fabbri 2015).

Conclusion: the influence of the Committee on the local political agenda and the future of the campaign

The concerted action against cruise tourism in Venice has acted as a catalyst for the convergence of different actors and mobilization efforts and as a focal point to address broader issues related to Venice's decline as a 'lived city': depopulation, industrial decline, political corruption, etc. In the Venice context, it is worth reflecting on whether the mobilization against cruise tourism has displayed some of the preconditions described by Lefebvre (1996), Marcuse (2011), Soja (2010) and Wyly (2011) as necessary for the construction of a political front claiming the 'Right to the City'.

The Committee potentially represents the opinion of a relevant part of the local electorate with over 1,000 people – out of a population of 57,000 in the Old City – attending some of the protests it staged. The use of a decree to establish the agenda for the use of the Lagoon for cruise tourism (a procedure skipping democratic debate), the rejection of observations made on the PAT and the use of a special procedure to fast-forward the Contorta Canal project in the absence of an updated harbour plan – i.e. the absence of a truly democratic and transparent process for deciding on the future of the port and of cruise tourism in Venice – have resulted in rising public distrust of the institutions. This has also led to the suspicion that the local public institutions' recalcitrance in using standard institutional procedures was due to hidden agendas to favour opaque private interests in the management of cruise harbour activities and infrastructure construction and bring about misconducted privatization policies, a suspicion confirmed by the explosion of corruption scandals in 2014 related to the management of the MOSE project.

In this context, what has been the influence of the Committee on the local political agenda? The mayoral and city council elections of May 2015 were preceded by local primary elections where the mayoral candidate for the left-wing, progressive coalition was chosen through a public consultation process, according to the rules of the main party which led this coalition, the Democratic Party (the party involved in the corruption scandals of 2014). Although the Committee refused to openly support any candidate in the race, the debates in the city created the right preconditions for the candidate who showed more support to the protest movement's agenda, Felice Casson, to win the primaries. The candidate's programme displayed complete adherence to the Committee's demands about cruise tourism, which shows the ability of the movement to gradually push its agenda into the (progressive) local political arena, something that was made possible by the political crisis initiated by the corruption cases of the recent past.

In the mayoral election itself, Casson lost against Luigi Brugnaro, the candidate of the conservative coalition. Casson secured a majority of votes in the Old City-Murano-Burano constituency, where the Committee had been most active, but failed to do so in the other constituencies. Political commentators attributed Casson's loss to the failure to connect the problems of the Old City with an overall vision for the broader urban area, and to his lack of appeal to voters other than the core electoral base of the parties of the progressive coalition. Brugnaro, on the other hand, presented himself as an outsider, belittling the connection to the conservative coalition supporting him, while making as a main point of his programme the unconditional support to cruise tourism and cruise liners' docking in the Old City. The Committee's refusal to directly support the candidate of the progressive coalition was meant to mark a distance from recent corruption scandals. Yet its ability to influence the progressive coalition's political agenda on the issue of cruise tourism did not translate into an ability to make the coalition win.

At the time of writing (autumn 2015), many of the Committee's individual groups and members intended to pursue their campaigns and protests, including broadening their focus to oppose new initiatives taken by the newly elected conservative city council (e.g. a ban on children's books representing homoparental families in the city's schools or cuts in local welfare policies). As the current ruling coalition – the first openly reactionary coalition in 22 years to rule the city – announced the reinforcement of cruise ship tourism activities in the Old City as one of its first strategic objectives, protests continued but have partly changed. The Committee symbolically protested over the revocation of a public venue for a photo exhibition denouncing the environmental damage done by big ships. Opposition against the Tresse Nuovo and Contorta canals have remained a goal of the Committee, with some successful and well-attended protests, but the new local political conditions seem to rule out some of the tactics described in this chapter in the near future, such as lobbying, which partially frustrates the perspectives of success of the Committee.

As happened in other contexts (e.g. Bruhn 2008), the coming to power of an adverse local government seems to have weakened – at least temporarily – the scope and strengths of the protest, paradoxically making the Committee – whose *raison d'être* is the coalition against cruise tourism – lose momentum and face the need for some reorganization. The movement might evolve into a more structured and unitary political project, mobilizing its different groups into a comprehensive alternative political proposal for the city, able to run for elections as an independent platform or actively bargaining for political programmes with traditional parties – something along the lines of what happened in the Barcelona municipal elections of 2014, which saw the coming to power of a progressive mayor supported by a platform of citizens and social movements, *Barcelona en Comù*. This option, which has been discussed by some (marginal) parts of the Committee, would imply a stronger process of formalization and eventually some degree of institutionalization that are at odds with the Committee's modes of action to date and success in mobilizing very different actors. In the meanwhile, the volume of cruise traffic and cruise tourists and the size of cruise ships are expected to grow steadily in the harbour of Venice – along with their negative externalities.

Notes

1 This figure was calculated using data from the main access points to the city in addition to estimating the number of daily city users visiting for leisure activities, according to a methodology used by the research centre of the city and province of Venice (COSES 2009). This methodology was used again in 2014 with data of 2012, but although the general results were presented in a press conference, the study was never made public and was classified for the internal use of policy-makers of the city of Venice.

2 This chapter is based on a research project carried out between 2012 and 2014 as part of a doctoral dissertation at the IUAV University of Venice. A total of seven non-structured interviews with members of the social movement were carried out: four with members of the Laboratorio Morion social centre, three with members of the association Ambiente Venezia. The interviews were in-depth repeated conversations aimed at reconstructing the recent oral history of the movement (Nagy Hesse-Biber and Leavy 2006). Interviews were complemented by participant observation in eight Committee's assemblies and four informal meetings of the Laboratorio Morion and Ambiente Venezia. The dissertation was defended in April 2015.

3 The city of Venice, similar to other regional capitals in Italy, is divided into five *municipalità* (municipalities) each with an elected Area Council. One of them is the Old City-Murano-Burano (Murano and Burano are two small islands). The other four municipalities are Chirignago-Zelarino, Favaro Veneto, Lido-Pellestrina, Marghera and Mestre-Carpenedo. These have limited budgets and decisional powers on local planning and mostly serve administrative purposes. Most of the power is actually exerted by the City of Venice, its mayor and city council, which deliberate on key policies and planning. Its territory is comprised of the above-mentioned municipalities. Recently, national Law 56/2014 established Metropolitan Area Councils in Italy. The new Venice Metropolitan Area comprises a wider area of 2,467 square kilometres inhabited by roughly 850,000 people.

Its statute and organization was, at the time of writing, in the process of being decided through a deliberative process including the involved municipalities and councils.

4 The records of the preliminary public debates held in 2007 in the framework of the preparations for the drafting of the structural plan of Venice (PAT) show this worry. In the thematic discussions, the number of public observations on big ship traffic amounts to seven (Comune di Venezia 2009: 20, 27, 45, 56, 80, 87, 92).

5 The 'Special Laws' for Venice (Laws 366/1963, 171/1973, 798/1984, 360/1991, 139/1992 and 206/1995) are a series of laws through which the Italian state recognizes the preservation of Venice as an objective of national importance and sets special objectives, provides special funding and establishes fast-track procedures to facilitate its achievement. In particular, Law 798/1984 envisages a procedure for direct funding and approval of projects done by an ad hoc body composed of six government officials and five representatives of local city councils and of the Veneto region, rather than through normal planning procedures decided upon locally.

6 Law 443/2001 aims at fast-tracking infrastructural projects declared 'strategic' for national economic development. One of its most prominent aspects is the simplified procedure it puts forward for the shorter and faster evaluation of the environmental impacts of new infrastructure.

References

[Unless otherwise stated, all URLs were last accessed 1 December 2015.]

Associazione Ambiente Venezia (2014) *Materiali d'informazione, Febbraio 2014, la nostra storia e le nostre lotte, Grandi Navi fuori dalla Laguna*. Venice: Ambiente Venezia.

Autorità Portuale di Venezia (2013) *P. O. T. Piano Operativo Triennale*. Venice: APV. Online. Available at http://www.port.venice.it/files/document/documenti-istituzionali/2013/pot2013-2015.pdf.

Beccalli, B. (1994) 'The modern's Women Movement in Italy', *New Left Review*, 2: 86–112.

Becucci, S. (2003) 'Disobbedienti e centri sociali fra democrazia diretta e rappresentanza', in P. Ceri (ed.), *La Democrazia dei Movimenti, Come Decidono i no Global*. Soveria Mannelli: Rubbettino.

Bedani, G. (1995) *Politics and Ideology in the Italian Workers' Movement*. Oxford: Berg.

Bersani, S. (2011) *Come Abbiamo Vinto il Referendum*. Rome: Edizioni Alegre.

Bonomi, A. (ed.) (1995) *Privatizzare Venezia, il Progettista Imprenditore*. Venice: Marsilio.

Branzaglia, C., Pacoda, P. and Solaro, A. (1992) *Posse Italiane: Centri Sociali, Underground Musicale e Cultura Giovanile degli Anni '90 in Italia*. Florence: Tosca Editore.

Bruhn, K. (2008) *Urban Protest in Mexico and Brazil*. Cambridge: Cambridge University Press.

Bugliari Goggia, A. (2007) *Outsiders Metropolitani: Etnografia di Storie di Vita Sovversive*. Rome: Armando Editore.

Canestrelli, E. and Costa, P. (1991) 'Tourist carrying capacity: a fuzzy approach', *Annals of Tourism*, 18(2): 295–311.

Caniglia, E. (2002) *Identità, Partecipazione e Antagonismo nella Politica Giovanile*. Soveria Mannelli: Rubbettino.

Caric, H. (2010) 'Direct pollution cost assessment of cruising tourism in the Croatian Adriatic', *Financial Theory and Practice*, 34(2): 161–80.

Casson, F. (2014) *Ordine del Giorno*, in *Resoconto Stenografico, Allegati – Assemblea 185° seduta (antimerid.) giovedì 6 febbraio 2014*. Senato della Repubblica: Roma, p. 90. Online. Available at: http://www.senato.it/service/PDF/PDFServer/BGT/745534.pdf.

Castells, M. (1997) *The Power of Identity*. Oxford: Blackwell.

Comune di Venezia (2009) *Partecipazione e Concertazione 2. Interventi e contributi alla definizione degli obiettivi e delle scelte individuate dal Documento Preliminare*. Online. Available at http://www.comune.venezia.it/flex/cm/pages/ServeBLOB.php/L/IT/IDPagina/3490.

Comune di Venezia (2012a) *Portale dei Servizi, PAT – Piano di Assetto del Territorio*. Online. Available at http://portale.comune.venezia.it/pat.

Comune di Venezia (2012b) *PAT, Allegato B, relazione*. Online. Available at http://portale.comune.venezia.it/utilities/delibereconsiglio/files/2012/DC_2012_104_ALL.%20B_.pdf.

Comune di Venezia (2013) *Annuario del Turismo 2013*. Online. Available at http://www.comune.venezia.it/flex/cm/pages/ServeAttachment.php/L/IT/D/4%252Ff%252F3%252FD.4fa6b6ee5679683c2e54/P/BLOB%3AID%3D53175/E/pdf.

Comune di Venezia (2015) *Mappa della Popolazione Residente al Giorno Precedente*. Servizio Statistica e Ricerca – Comune di Venezia 2015. Online. Available at http://www.comune.venezia.it/flex/cm/pages/ServeBLOB.php/L/IT/IDPagina/27082.

Consorzio Aaster, Centro Sociale COX 18, Centro Sociale Leoncavallo and Moroni, P. (1996) *Centri Sociali: Geografie del Desiderio*. Milan: Shake.

COSES (2009) *Rapporto 141.0, Turismo Sostenibile a Venezia, studio per il coordinamento delle strategie turistiche del Comune di Venezia*. Online. Available at http://www.comune.venezia.it/flex/cm/pages/ServeAttachment.php/L/IT/D/D.fe155294363b8b944ed1/P/BLOB%3AID%3D28868/E/pdf.

Cosgrove, D. (1982) 'The myth and the stones of Venice: a historical geography of a symbolic landscape', *Journal of Historical Geography*, 8(2): 145–69.

Daher, L. M. (2002) *Azione Collettiva, Teorie e Problemi*. Milan: Franco Angeli.

Daher, L. M. (2012) *Fare Ricerca sui Movimenti Sociali in Italia: Passato, Presente e Futuro*. Milan: Franco Angeli.

della Porta, D. and Diani M. (1997) *I Movimenti Sociali*. Rome: NIS.

della Porta, D. and Diani M. (2004) *Movimenti Senza Protesta*. Bologna: Il Mulino.

Diani, M. (1999) 'La società Italiana: protesta senza movimenti? Presentazione', *Quaderni di Sociologia*, 43(21): 3–13.

Diani, M. (2008) 'Modelli di azione collettiva: quale specificità per i movimenti sociali?', *Partecipazione e Conflitto*, 1: 43–66.

Diedrich, A. (2010) 'Cruise ship tourism in Belize: the implications of developing cruise ship tourism in an ecotourism destination', *Ocean and Coastal Management*, 53: 234–44.

Dredge, D. (2010) 'Place change and tourism development conflict: evaluating public interest', *Tourism Management*, 31(1): 104–12.

Fabbri, G. (ed.) (2015) *Venezia, la laguna, il porto e il gigantismo navale, Libro Bianco sul perché le grandi navi debbano stare fuori dalla laguna*. Venice: Moretti & Vitali.

Farro, A. L. (1998) *I Movimenti Sociali. Diversità, Azione Collettiva e Globalizzazione della Società*. Milan: Franco Angeli.

Gasparoli, P. and Trovò, F. (2014) *Venezia Fragile, processi di usura del sistema urbano e possibili mitigazioni*. Florence: Altralinea Edizioni.

Johnson, D. (2002) 'Environmentally sustainable cruise tourism: a reality check', *Marine Policy*, 26(4): 261–70.

Judd, D. R. and Fainstein, S. (1999) *The Tourist City*. New Haven, CT: Yale University Press.

Lefebvre, H. (1996), 'Right to the city', in H. Lefebvre, *Writings on Cities*. Oxford: Blackwell.

Lester J.-O. and Weeden, C. (2004) 'Stakeholders, the natural environment and the future of Caribbean cruise tourism', *International Journal of Tourism Research*, 6(1): 39–50.

Lombardi, F. (1992) *Città Storiche, Urbanistica e Turismo: Venezia e Firenze*. Florence: Mercury Edizioni.

London, W. and Lohmann, G. (2014) 'Power in the context of cruise destination stakeholders' interrelationships', *Research in Transportation Business and Management*, 13: 24–35.

Marcuse, P. (2011) 'From justice planning to Commons planning', in P. Marcuse *et al.* (eds), *Searching for the Just City: Debates in Urban Theory and Practice*. London: Routledge.

Mattei, U. (2011) *Beni Comuni, un Manifesto*. Bari: Laterza.

Melucci, A. (1996) *Challenging Codes: Collective Action in the Information Age*. Cambridge: Cambridge University Press.

Ministero delle Infrastrutture e dei Trasporti (2012a) 'Decreto 02 marzo 2012: Disposizioni Generali per Limitare o Vietare il Transito delle Navi Mercantili per la Protezione di Aree Sensibili nel Mare Territoriale', *Gazzetta Ufficiale*, 56: 39–41.

Ministero delle Infrastrutture e dei Trasporti (2012b) 'Decreto 30 aprile 2012, Modifiche al Decreto 2 marzo 2012, n. 79 Concernente Disposizioni Generali per Limitare o Vietare il Transito delle Navi Mercantili per la Protezione di Aree Sensibili del Mare Territoriali', *Gazzetta Ufficiale*, 104: 7.

Ministero di Grazia e Giustizia (2007) *Commissione Rodotà – per la modifica delle norme del codice civile in materia di beni pubblici (14 giugno 2007) – Relazione*. Online. Available at http://www.giustizia.it/giustizia/it/mg_1_12_1.wp?contentId=SPS47617.

Nagy Hesse-Biber, S. and Leavy, P. (2006) *The Practice of Qualitative Research*. Thousand Oaks, CA: Sage.

Neveu, E. (2001) *I Movimenti Sociali*. Bologna: Il Mulino.

Ocalan, A. (2011) *Democratic Confederalism*. London: Transmedia.

Ostrom, E. (1990) *Governing the Commons*. Cambridge: Cambridge University Press.

Petricca, M. (2013) 'Grandi Navi in centro, "legalità sospesa"', *Il Manifesto*, 10 May.

Settis, S. (2014) *Se Venezia Muore*. Torino: Einaudi.

Soja, E. W. (2010) *Seeking Spatial Justice*. Minneapolis, MN: Minnesota University Press.

Soriani, S., Bertazzon, S., Di Cesare, F. and Rech, G. (2009) 'Cruising in the Mediterranean: structural aspects and evolutionary trends', *Maritime Policy and Management*, 36(3): 235–91.

Tattara, G. (2013) *È Solo la Punta dell'Iceberg. costi e ricavi del crocerismo, Note di Lavoro, Dipartimento di Economia*, 2. Venice: Università Ca' Foscari di Venezia. Online. Available at http://www.unive.it/media/allegato/DIP/Economia/Note-di-lavoro-economia/nl_2013/NL_DSE_tattara_02_13.pdf.

UNECE (1998) *Convention on Access to Information, Public Participation, in Decision-Making and Access to Justice in Environmental Matters*. Online. Available at http://www.unece.org/fileadmin/DAM/env/pp/documents/cep43e.pdf.

UNESCO (2012) *UNESCO Calls for Restrictions on Cruise Line Traffic in Venice Following Costa Concordia Disaster*, UNESCO Media Service, 23 January. Online. Available at http://www.unesco.org/new/en/media-services/single-view/news/unesco_calls_for_restrictions_on_cruise_line_traffic_in_venice_following_costa_concordia_disaster/.

Van der Borg, J. (1998) 'Tourism management in Venice, or how to deal with success', in D. Tyler, Y. Guerrier and M. Robertson (eds), *Managing Tourism in Cities. Policy, Process and Practice*. Chichester: John Wiley & Sons.

Van der Borg, J., Costa, P. and Gotti, G. (1992) 'Tourism in European heritage cities', *Annals of Tourism*, 23(2): 306–21.

Veltri, F. (2003) 'Non si chiama delega, si chiama fiducia', in P. Ceri (ed.), *La Democrazia dei Movimenti, come Decidono i no Global*. Soveria Mannelli: Rubbettino.

Véronneau, S. and Roy, J. (2009) 'Global service supply chains: an empirical study of current practices and challenges of a cruise corporation', *Tourism Management*, 30: 128–39.

Vitucci, A. (2012) 'I colossi del mare e la laguna. Decreto Grandi Navi: senza alternativa niente divieti', *La Nuova Venezia*, 29 February.

Wyly, E. (2011) 'Positively radical', *International Journal of Urban and Regional Research*, 35(5): 889–912.

10 Favela tourism

Negotiating visitors, socio-economic benefits, image and representation in pre-Olympics Rio de Janeiro

Anne-Marie Broudehoux

As an emerging global power, Brazil has recently experienced one of the highest rates of economic growth in the world. Tourism is a key sector of the Brazilian economy, which has also enjoyed a steady growth since the 2008–9 economic crisis (UNWTO 2014). While in 2006 direct employment in the tourism sector reached 1.87 million people, this number rose to 8.5 million jobs in 2014, making Brazil the fifth greatest tourist nation in terms of direct employment (Embratur 2014). In 2013, the World Travel and Tourism Council ranked Brazil sixth in the world tourism economy, identifying it as the nation with the greatest growth potential in terms of tourism (UNWTO 2014). Experts link this tourism boom to the global visibility that mega sporting events like the 2014 FIFA World Cup and the 2016 Olympics afforded Brazil on the world stage. They also cite a stable currency and the pacification of Rio de Janeiro's favelas among the main reasons behind this increase (Oliveira 2012). Rio de Janeiro is Brazil's primary tourist attraction and one of the most visited cities in the southern hemisphere (Tavener 2012). It receives more visitors than any other South American city, with an average of 2.82 million international tourists a year (UNWTO 2014). Rio also represented the most popular destination for national visitors in 2012 (Embratur 2014). According to a 2012 World Travel Market Industry Report, almost two-thirds of tourism industry observers believed that Rio de Janeiro would benefit from a tourism boost until and after the 2016 Olympics (WTM 2012).

This chapter details the emergence of a new phenomenon in the Brazilian tourism landscape, that of 'slum' or 'favela tourism', with a particular focus on the city of Rio de Janeiro, host of the 2014 FIFA World Cup and 2016 Summer Olympics.[1] The chapter pays particular attention to the source and nature of conflicts, tensions and resistance movements that have appeared in Rio de Janeiro as favela tourism expands. The development of favela tourism has been at the root of frictions within local communities, especially when those perceived to be the main beneficiaries of tourism are not local residents. Tourism-related investments, which appear to serve outside visitors to the detriment of community members or which threaten people's quality of life, intimacy, accessibility or security of tenure, are increasingly condemned. Diverse forms of resistance movements to tourism expansion within favela territories are taking form, especially when tourism is imposed without the residents' consent.

The chapter begins with an overview of the historical rise of 'poverty tourism' around the world, contextualising the emergence of this phenomenon and discussing the motivations driving its development. The chapter examines in more detail the emergence of favela tourism in Rio de Janeiro and discusses its drivers, its appeal and the ways in which it is perceived within and outside the favelas. The chapter then presents a typology of different forms of favela tourism, based on different management structures, and examines the relationship between visitors, residents and intermediary agents. The final part of the chapter focuses on the conflicts generated by the growth of favela tourism and details some of the critiques and modes of resistance developed by local residents. The chapter concludes with an early assessment of the impacts and benefits of such a form of tourism, underlining the possibility of future areas of conflicts and resistance related to the growing 'touristification' of the favela and suggesting directions for further research.

Slum tourism as a global phenomenon

As one of the world's fastest growing service industries, tourism is constantly trying to diversify its products and expand into new, increasingly segmented markets. Alternative forms of tourism that go off the beaten track have emerged as part of this segmentation (Lew 2015). They answer a desire for the acquisition of symbolic capital and the search for new modes of distinction (Bourdieu 1979) that help uphold class differentiation and maintain a social distance with main-stream forms of tourism. New trends in global sightseeing are also fed by a grow-ing demand for intense, unconventional or 'extreme' experiences, a phenomenon witnessed in the rise of extreme sports and thrill-seeking adventure travel. They respond to a quest for a real, authentic and unique experience that departs from the artificiality of packaged tourism products (Jaguaribe and Hetherington 2006). More than the simple search for authenticity described by Dean MacCannell (1976), these alternative forms of tourism are the product of a fast-growing obsession for reality, for the direct, first-hand experience of the real: what I would call *extreme authenticity*.

This quest for raw reality and thrilling experiences has given rise to a range of new forms of tourism that take people far from the mainstream to places on the margin. For one, 'disaster tourism' (Robb 2009), also termed 'dark tourism' (Lennon and Foley 2000), offers so-called reality tours of sites that have acquired a historical and political significance for their association with natural or man-made disasters. This practice is highly controversial, and denounced as a commodification of human tragedy that feeds upon a morbid fascination for pain and suffering (Veissiere 2010; Lisle 2004).

Another controversial form of tourism on the rise is 'poverty tourism'. Specialists distinguish between *volunteer tourism*, also known as 'pro-poor tour-ism', which claims a more humanistic, altruistic and educational mission with a participatory approach, and *slum tourism*, derogatively branded *poorism*, described as mere sightseeing without the intent of alleviating local conditions and lacking a humanitarian motive (Rolfes 2010; Scheyvens 2013; Steinbrink 2012). Recent years have seen an explosion in the popularity of visits to impoverished areas, starting in the mid-1980s with South African township tours, closely followed by jeep tours of Rio de Janeiro's favelas (Freire-Medeiros 2008). Today, tour operators take tourists to garbage dumps in Cairo, Delhi's railway underworld and some of the world's most notorious slums.

Poorism has been compared to 'slumming', a trendy elite pastime practised in nineteenth-century London, Paris and New York, which was driven by a mix of philanthropy, curiosity and voyeuristic titillation (Parker 2003; Koven 2009; Parker 2003). Like faraway colonies, seedy neighbourhoods were seen by artists, intellectuals and parts of the gentry as places of freedom and danger, of missionary altruism and of social, personal and sexual liberation. For Henry James, slumming was a passion driven by a desire to cross opposite universes, from the rich to the poor, the clean to the dirty, the virtuous to the depraved (El-Rayess 2014). Charles Baudelaire also enjoyed mingling with the masses. In *Les Fleurs du Mal* (2003 [1857]: 93), he writes: 'In murky corners of old cities, where everything – horror too – is magical, I study, servile to my moods, the odd and charming refuse of humanity.'

For many contemporary experts, poverty tourism falls into what MacCannell (1976) defined as *negative sightseeing*, and is critiqued as an unethical trivialisation of poverty for socio-voyeuristic or self-promotional motives (Rolfes 2010; Whyte *et al.* 2010). At the onset, the idea of poverty tourism was thus regarded as highly offensive (Lancaster 2007). The premise was that visits were motivated by a morbid desire, on the part of predominantly bourgeois thrill-seekers, to witness human suffering up close. Poverty tourism was also condemned by critics and academics as a transnational desire for the consumption of Third World poverty, a commodification of power inequality and of human misery (Frenzel *et al.* 2012; Sellinger and Outterson 2010). Some authors denounce the 'theme-parkification' of the slum, repackaged as a product to be consumed by an international clientele (Zeiderman 2006).

The development of favela tourism in Rio de Janeiro: background, drivers and perceptions

Rio de Janeiro's favelas in historical context

The favela has long been a characteristic feature of the city of Rio de Janeiro and a central part of its urban reality. Resulting from the illegal occupation of hills and marshlands by poor and often black residents in search of affordable housing, favelas came to be viewed as *special* territories, located on the margin of the formal city (Valladares do Prado 2005). Favelas were feared as a threat to authority, order and stability and their inhabitants despised for refusing to conform to established rules. Defined in radical opposition to the formal city, they were construed as a negatively connoted landscape, associated with illegality, disorder and decline (Perlman 2010). Their residents paid no taxes, received few public services and were deprived of the same civil rights as other Brazilians (Zaluar and Alvito 1998). Having been all but abandoned by the state, these territories began attracting criminal groups, and by the 1990s, many were left to the cruel domination of violent drug gangs and militias.

Throughout most of their history, favelas were desired as an absence in Rio's urban landscape and subjected to many measures of invisibilisation and silencing, from bulldozing and evictions, widely practised until the 1980s, to more subtle measures of beautification (Valladares do Prado 2005). They did not exist in the formal imaginary and did not appear on official city maps (Johanson 2013). The term favela itself, being too negatively connoted, suffered a similar invisibilisation process, replaced by the euphemistic 'hill' (*morro*) or 'community' (*communidade*). Although the local media continues to depict favelas as places of crime and violence and as the natural habitat of the 'dangerous classes', after 118 years of existence, perceptions are changing and the stigma towards Rio's favelas is waning. Since the late 1990s, public policies have tended towards the recognition of favelas as urban neighbourhoods and favoured their integration into the formal city (Riley *et al.* 2001). In 2014, one in five residents of Rio de Janeiro lived in a favela (IBGE 2014).

Historical development of favela tourism in Rio de Janeiro

Favelas have long been an object of fascination for visitors to Rio. However, they were generally observed from a safe distance (from the *asfalto* or street level) as an oddity in the urban landscape. Among the first foreigners who dared enter this forbidden world were social scientists, eager to understand its peculiarities, or members of non-governmental organisations working on poverty alleviation. But tourists also accessed the favela on special occasions, especially to visit samba schools in the weeks before Carnival, as an important part of the Carnival experience. Earliest initiatives at touring the favelas can be traced back to the mid-1970s and were led by NGOs (Rodrigues 2014).

But it would take almost twenty years for the first formal tours of Rio's favelas to be conducted. During the 1992 United Nations Summit on the Environment, delegates reportedly asked to visit a favela and were taken by jeep to Rocinha, then known as Latin America's largest slum (Freire-Medeiros 2012). Favela tourism was thus demand-based, and developed in response to the request of curious visitors, even though no formal tourist product was on offer. It was only later that local entrepreneurs and residents, ultimately aided by the government, would capitalise upon this initial interest by multiplying tour offers and developing attractions. While favela tours steadily expanded over time, the phenomenon experienced an unprecedented boom in the years preceding the 2014 World Cup and the 2016 Olympics. This expansion has been attributed to state programmes for the pacification of favelas, initiated in 2008. Preparation for Rio's mega-events has included the permanent occupation of key settlements by a specially trained police force, with the disarmament and expulsion of drug traffickers and armed militias. The arrival of these Police Pacification Units prompted a series of rapid transformations in the favelas, bringing peace and security to the residents while making them safer for tourism-related activities (Freeman 2012).

Motivations of favela tourists

Paradoxically, part of the attraction of the favela has long rested in its association with violence, idealised in recent feature films (Jaguaribe 2004). The global popularity of Brazilian 'reality' movies such as *City of God* (2002)[2] and the use of the favela as a backdrop in mainstream Hollywood films,[3] a trend that was branded *slumsploitation* (Gilligan 2006), has attracted hosts of thrill-seeking visitors. Interest in the favela was also stimulated by its glamorisation in the global mass media, especially as an exotic stage set for music videos by African-American pop stars. First popularised by Michael Jackson in *They Don't Care About Us* (1996), directed by Spike Lee, the favela is now featured in videos by Beyoncé Knowles, Alicia Keys and Snoopdog. The favela is also becoming a fashionable site for international art projects, such as the Dutch artists Haas and Hahn's 2010 *favela painting* project, or the French artist JR's 2008 *Women are Heroes* installation.

Since the turn of the millennium, the favela has acquired a sort of cult status in the global geographical imaginary, where it occupies a unique position as both a hot, fashionable commodity and a trendy trademark (Freire-Medeiros 2008). There are Favela Chic nightclubs in London, Paris, Glasgow, Montreal and Miami (Sterling 2010). Two Brazilian-Italian designers, Umberto and Fernando Campana, have created the *favela chair* out of rough pieces of plywood (at a price of $5,185). For Tom Philips (2003), the word 'favela' now stands as a tropical prefix capable of turning the most diverse products into something exotic. The favela even represents a state of mind, as suggested by a 2005 photo exhibition held in a Paris subway station, titled *Favélité*. The vast production, reproduction and diffusion of images of the favela testifies to its fetishisation as a 'cultural object' that goes beyond Western fascination with the exotic 'Other' but suggests a vaster consumption appeal (Zeiderman 2006).

The favela therefore carries a strong evocative power, with multiple connotations, ranging from the strange and mysterious, to the forbidden, amoral and violent all the way to the rickety, haphazard and chaotic. It exerts a secret fascination for outsiders, symbolising the dark, the low, the unknown, onto which the most lurid fantasies can be projected (Steinbrink 2012; Zeiderman 2006). The favela is imagined as a kind of forbidden underworld, the evil twin of formal society, liberated from rigid social norms, propriety and morality, where licentiousness, libidinal freedom, and unbridled depravity can be found (Steinbrink 2013). For anthropologist Bianca Freire-Medeiros (2012), the perception of danger remains one of the favela's most seductive aspects, attractive not only for its adrenaline rush appeal but also for its capacity to enhance the symbolic capital that can be gained from a visit.

As favela tourism develops, it becomes clear that visitors are driven by a complex host of motives that are often contradictory and difficult to disentangle. While the notion of poverty tourism implies that poverty alone is what is being sought out, the desire to see and experience raw human misery up close is not always the main motive. Visits to neighbourhoods like Harlem (in New York City) or Brazil's favelas are also driven by curiosity about a different way of life and by the promise of a close encounter with radical forms of alterity. Such motives betray a heroisation of the poor, idealised not for their lack of material wealth, but for their resilience in the struggle against adversity and their capacity to turn oppression into cultural vibrancy. This attraction suggests a conceptualization of poverty as a pure and primitive state, closer to raw human nature, as if material deprivation had made the poor more authentic representatives of mankind and beholders of true values.

My own research suggests that poverty tourism is motivated by a natural attraction for the unknown, doubled with a yearning to experience compassion for the suffering of others. The experience can be at once reassuring in one's own material comfort while fulfilling a desire for empathy. Visitors are also attracted to these steep hillside communities out of curiosity for the human ingenuity and capacity for survival that is embedded in their self-built environment: the feat of building such elaborate neighbourhoods on precarious land with limited resources and skills is a source of great admiration. It is therefore not so much poverty per se that motivates many visits but the resilience, resourcefulness and determination of a community of hard-working people who managed to carve out an existence for themselves in spite of their difficult circumstances. My research also suggests that part of the favela's attraction also rests upon the great social capital that can be gained from having 'been' to a favela. Just as early researchers and NGO workers gained an aura of respectability for having 'lived among the poor', tourists are seeking out similar 'bragging rights' that testify to their own courage, altruism and selflessness. Artists who use the favela as the locus of their art projects similarly capitalise upon the sympathy capital that a great social cause can confer. Other travellers, especially those described as 'anti-tourists' (Miller and Auyong 1998), may also be motivated by a search for distinction and seek to distantiate themselves from ordinary tourists by sojourning in the favela.

Brazilian perception of favela tourism

Inside Brazil, the notion of favela tourism was met by resistance and opposed by those who still believe in the illegality of these settlements and the necessity of their eradication. Local authorities long condemned the association between favela and tourism, through fear it would tarnish Brazil's international image. In 1996, the filming of Michael Jackson's music video was widely opposed by the state, who argued that its display of local poverty could damage the local tourism industry and ruin Rio's chances to get the 2004 Olympics (Schemo 1996).[4] But this attitude is changing, as testified by Rio's tourism board's 2010 decision to include Rocinha on its official website as one of the city's top attractions.

In the favela, attitudes towards tourism vary. Many welcome the practice as an opportunity to replace drug trafficking as an income-generating activity. They believe that tourism will stimulate the development of local businesses and create new jobs. Favela tourism is also widely perceived as a path to change, to promote social inclusion, alter perceptions and reverse stereotypes. Many believe that it is only through first-hand knowledge that outsiders will understand the challenges faced by *favelados* and overcome the stigma that has isolated them for years. Daily encounters with foreign visitors are also seen as beneficial for the young, helping develop alternative visions of their future.

A survey conducted in 2013 by Catalytic Communities, a Rio de Janeiro-based NGO, demonstrates the potential of direct contact with favela residents in affecting perceptions (Sinek 2013). Based on 750 interviews made in Rio de Janeiro, San Francisco, Brisbane and London, the survey made clear that people who had actually visited a favela held dramatically more positive views of these settlements. The survey also demonstrated how violent and sensationalist representations of the favela in film and the media contributed to their negative image. Among the top keywords used to describe the favela by people who had visited one, words like *community, misunderstood* and *vibrant* stood out while for those who only knew of the favela through the media, top key words included *dangerous, cramped, poverty, crime* and *ghetto* (Sinek 2013).

Still, many favela residents have reservations towards what is often perceived as an invasive practice. The growing presence of outsiders in the favela's dense urban fabric can be problematic, since the limited transitional space between the private and the public realms provides few filters for the preservation of intimacy. Ironically, from the residents' point of view, tourists are seen as a potential source of danger and crime. Many residents expressed reservations towards the idea that their children could run into strangers on the streets of their hitherto isolated community.

Local perception of tourism thus varies greatly depending on who is promoting it, how it is conducted and for whose benefit. The following section provides a panorama of different forms of favela tourism that currently exist in Rio de Janeiro and helps ascertain differences in their acceptation and impacts.

The multiple manifestations of favela tourism: a typology

Initial research conducted between 2009 and 2014 helps trace a portrait of the current state of favela tourism initiatives in Rio de Janeiro, which can be divided into four broad categories: private, for profit initiatives from outside the favela; community-based, non-profit initiatives; local commercial initiatives; and state-led favela tourism. Each category is defined and analysed below to reveal areas of success, friction and resistance.

Private, for profit initiatives from outside the favela

The oldest and still predominant form of favela tourism in Rio de Janeiro is based on professionally conducted tours by private companies, which often have little ties to the community. Packaged tours generally include a visit in jeeps, on motorcycles or on foot, with stops at community centres, crafts markets and scenic lookouts. They are conducted by guides who may or may not be from the favela. Although many companies claim to reinvest part of their profits in community projects, research shows that it is seldom the case (Freire-Medeiros 2012).

There now exists a well-established commission-based cooperation between tour operators and local shops and restaurants in the favelas. Each month, up to 3,000 tourists are taken to Rocinha alone, by ten different agencies whose names evoke a range of experiences from an adventure in the urban wilderness to a more authentic, less voyeuristic tour.[5] Since the beginning of the pacification process in 2008, the number of competing operators has grown dramatically, with dozens of new tourism agencies seeking to exploit these newly opened territories.

Favela tourism was long dominated by this kind of operation, which favour visits to favelas with easy road access, especially in Rio's elite South Zones, with great views of the city's famous landscape. These tours were founded on the premise that foreigners were more interested in 'having been' to the favela than in interacting with locals. Long tolerated by local community members, these outside initiatives are increasingly the objects of scorn. Motorised tours are despised because they prevent contact between visitors and residents, especially when tourists stay inside their air-conditioned vehicle for the duration of the visit, without setting foot in the favela. Locals are offended by the attitude of visitors who photograph residents without their consent, like animals in a zoo. They experience a lack of respect, a violation of their privacy and an affront to their dignity. Non-motorised tours are perceived as less intrusive and more respectful, allowing a greater level of interaction. Most residents interviewed believe that tours should be conducted by local guides. They resent the position of cultural authority that outside guides have over the interpretation of their community. They accuse this kind of tour of reproducing stereotypes about the favela rather than helping overcome them. To meet the expectations of international tourists, some private tour operators have been known to purposely take visitors through some of the most derelict parts of favelas and to stage some dramatic encounters to boost the adrenaline content of their visit (Frisch 2012).

Community-based initiatives

A second type of tourism that is quickly developing in Rio de Janeiro is community-based, not-for-profit tourist initiatives. Local groups capitalise upon growing interest for their settlement by developing local attractions, including interpretation centres, open-air museums, eco-trails, belvederes, art projects and cultural events. In the favela complex of Pavão-Pavãozinho-Cantagalo, the Museu de Favela (Favela Museum) was founded in 2008 to promote community development (Moraes 2010). It gained visibility after pacification and the construction of the new elevator in 2010, linking Cantagalo to Ipanema and its main subway station. The open-air museum, which comprises the entire favela, tells the story of the settlement through a series of murals signed by Acme, a local artist. The murals immortalise local heroes and depict the community's many historical struggles: against water shortages, faulty infrastructure, exclusion and exploitation. More than a mere tourist attraction, the murals serve as instruments of storytelling that help foster community pride, collective identity and shared memory. Tours sometimes include a samba show, drinks and cake from the baking coop, and visits to artist workshops. Considered to be Brazil's first 'territorial museum', the Museu de

Favela was an initiative of Rio Arte Popular, a local tourism cooperative founded in 1998. It was funded by the federal Programme for the Acceleration of Growth (PAC) and its Social Insertion Base (BISU) (Moraes 2010). The stated goal of this initiative was to develop community-managed tourism and to attract tourists to the favela without the use of middlemen. Revenues generated by guided tours are used to fund community-training programmes in tourism (Moraes 2010).

Community-based initiatives take various forms. In the twin favelas of Babilonia-Chapéu Mangueira, guides from local tourism cooperatives, Babilonia Coop and Chapéu Tour, take visitors through the jungle on a community-maintained 'eco-trail' to the top of the hill for spectacular views and point to the filming locations of Marcel Camus' award-winning *Black Orpheus* (1959). In Maré, an indoor museum created in 2005 traces the history of this bayside favela complex through photos and artefacts. While serving the community's need for collective memory and legitimacy by establishing its long occupation of the site, the museum also addresses an outside audience, invited to shop in its crafts cooperative.

Many residents view these initiatives as opportunities to debunk misrepresentations of their community and to bolster collective self-esteem by showing a more positive side of the favela. Community-led tourism gives residents the chance to 'speak' for themselves and to control the way they are represented. By advocating visits on foot, in small groups and with a local guide, encouraging local consumption and limiting unauthorised photography, community-based tourism helps mitigate the perverse asymmetry that exists between the tourist and the object of his gaze. The main impediment for this kind of community-led development is language, as few residents speak foreign tongues. But tourism has stimulated interest in new state programmes for the acquisition of language skills.

Hospitality tourism and local for-profit initiatives

A third form of favela tourism concerns private, for-profit businesses catering to tourists inside the favela. Since the late 1990s, long before pacification, individual entrepreneurs began buying lots or transformed abandoned mansions to accommodate hostels, bars or art galleries. These early pioneers, often foreign expatriates, wanted to benefit from cheap land, great views and proximity to elite beach neighbourhoods, while experiencing another urban reality. They also lacked the deeply rooted prejudice towards the favela that many middle- and upper-class Brazilians harbour. Their businesses cater mainly to members of the backpacker crowd, who cannot afford Rio's expensive accommodations, often settle for long time periods and are open to different ways of life. Many large mansions abandoned by their owners after drug trafficking drastically reduced their real estate value have been converted into hostels. Located along paved streets, at the transition point between the *asfalto* (asphalt, i.e. formal city) and the *morro* (hill, i.e. favela), these affordable accommodations have rendered porous the psychological barrier that long separated these two antagonistic worlds. As foreign tourists began venturing into favelas and consumed locally in small shops and eateries, they helped break down this virtual border, helped change mentalities and contributed to local economic development. Their presence made the favela increasingly safe and accessible for other visitors and paved the way for entrepreneurs, from both within and without the community. Since pacification, many residents have thus converted part of their homes into hostels and small shops, also wishing to benefit from the tourism boom linked to Rio's mega-events. One example is Favela Inn, a youth hostel managed by a local couple, high up in the hills of Chapéu-Mangueira. A survey of entries left by travellers in their visitors' book reveals feelings of fear and anxiety at residing in the favela, mixed with excitement at the rare opportunity to live such a truly 'authentic' experience. Recurring keywords found in these testimonies include *community*, *typical*, *real*, *genuine*, *authentic*, *anxiety* and *danger*.

Residents claim not to mind the presence of these establishments but some have reservations about businesses owned by outsiders who seek to benefit from a combination of cheap real estate and exotic appeal. The gradual and rather limited nature of this ongoing transformation has contained some of the negative effects of tourism development seen elsewhere, especially regarding gentrification. However, the recent arrival of larger commercial institutions is more problematic and is causing tensions inside the favelas. Not only do residents fear rising prices and speculation, but they also resent newcomers who profit from a land that long-term residents have developed with their own labour, without contributing their share. Locals fear that their hard won and already overstretched infrastructure will be monopolised by these newcomers. In Vidigal, residents are blaming a new designer hotel for clogging the limited transport system with their wealthy guests, forcing labourers to waste their limited free time waiting for the shuttle that would take them home. Local resentment against this business has taken diverse forms, from graffiti to petty theft, indicating that its presence is not welcome.

State-led favela tourism

A last form of favela tourism in Rio de Janeiro concerns public sector initiatives, as favela tourism is increasingly embraced, funded and even promoted by the state. Undoubtedly related to Rio's mega-events, this phenomenon marks a radical change in attitude on the part of local authorities and betrays a desire to reassure the world about the safety of Brazilian cities, by enhancing the visibility of the state in long-neglected favelas and improving security and access. State investment in tourism can take the form of individual infrastructure projects, such as cable cars, elevators, and funiculars linking hillside favelas to public transportation networks. They also follow a more comprehensive approach, as in the case of Santa Marta, presented below.

The first and most extensive experiment with state-led favela tourism was Rio Top Tour, a pilot project that sought to help provide guided tours of pacified favelas. The programme was financed by a special fund dedicated to community-based tourism, at the initiative of Brazil's Ministry of Tourism, Sports and Leisure in 2006 (Rodrigues 2014). The pilot project was inaugurated in 2010, by President Lula himself, as one of his last legacies before leaving office, and lasted until the end of 2012. It aimed to provide alternative sources of employment after the departure of drug trafficking and was to become a model to be replicated in other favelas (Rodrigues 2014). It is in Santa Marta, a favela often used as a testing ground for several state programmes, that the pilot programme was implemented. The favela was selected because of its relatively small size, housing some 5,000 souls; its location in the middle-class neighbourhood of Botafogo at the foot of the Christ the Redemptor statue; and its great visibility and easy access. Santa Marta was the first favela to be pacified in December 2008, and received Rio's first Police Pacification Unit a few months after the inauguration of the funicular, also a first in the city.

The favela benefited from a great tourism potential, thanks to its privileged views of the Corcovado and close association with global pop star Michael Jackson. As the film location of his 1996 music video, the favela had gained a kind of cult status among Jackson fans. In 2010, a rooftop featured in the video, which had become a popular tourist attraction, was renovated by the state and rebranded Michael Jackson Square. On the first anniversary of his death, a statue of the star was unveiled along with a mural by a close friend of Jackson, world-renowned artist Romero Britto (Figure 10.1). The same year, the favela was blessed with another world-class attraction, with Dutch artists Haas and Hahn's *Favela Painting*, covering 34 houses in a stunning kaleidoscopic fresco.

Figure 10.1 Statute of Michael Jackson in Santa Marta favela, 2016.

Source: Author.

The pilot project included a free technical course in tourism offered at a nearby state college to train local guides. Workshops and micro-loans were made available to those residents wishing to develop tourism-related enterprises. With the participation of residents, 34 points of interest were selected and identified with plaques, in both English and Portuguese. Free bilingual maps featuring points of interest were offered to visitors, who were also given the opportunity to hire a local guide. A total of 60,000 visits were conducted during the two years of the pilot project, with an average of 2,000 per month, 60 per cent of which were from Brazil, thereby debunking the myth that favela tourism was for 'gringos' (Rodrigues 2014). All visitors were accompanied. At the end of the pilot project in 2012, newly trained guides from Santa Marta founded their own agency, renamed Rio Favela Tour.

Overall, the project was successful, allowing residents to control how and when their neighbourhood could be toured and creating a few jobs. However, problems are emerging. The existence of an organized agency has hindered independent visits, with tourists complaining of harassment from local guides, who pressure them to take a paying tour even on repeat visits. The multiplication of tourist shops near the favela's main attractions (Figure 10.2) is giving the area the feel of a 'tourist trap'. Some visitors disliked being hassled by local vendors and saw their tourist experience as less authentic compared to other, more 'open' favelas. This experience poses a dilemma between integration and turning the favela into a regular neighbourhood, and self-segregation by restricting admittance. In its efforts to control the tourist experience and to discourage independent visits, the community has turned itself into a paying attraction, thereby denaturing the experience of the 'real' sought by visitors. While this approach may ensure a steady revenue for tour guides, it also gives the favela an exclusive character and can lead to its negative branding as 'touristified'.

Conflicts and resistance to favela tourism

As it develops, favela tourism has become a source of conflict between residents, entrepreneurs, civic authorities and visitors. More than mere tensions between 'hosts' and 'guests', these disputes reflect wider struggles over the socio-spatial transformations that are restructuring the urban landscape as the city prepares to host the 2016 Olympics. The main points of friction concern a generalized lack of public consultation in the decision-making process regarding tourism development and project implementation, coupled with a total disregard for community needs or what is often perceived as prioritising tourists over residents. Anger is not only directed at local authorities but also at private actors in the tourism industry. Those without direct ties to tourism resent bearing the cost of its development – in terms of the invasion of privacy, the strain on infrastructure and rising prices – without reaping the benefits.

Residents increasingly see infrastructure improvement and pacification as part of a wider state project to transform the image of the favela for the benefit of outsiders. State interventions are often perceived as a means of displacing the poor to facilitate the reclaiming of valuable territories by private capital. People

Figure 10.2 Self-made billboard attracting tourists to a souvenir shop near Michael Jackson Square in Santa Marta, 2014.

Source: Author.

see state-led tourism in the favelas as part of a civilising process that seeks to tame, regulate and control the favela and make it safe for foreign visitors and investors. In recent years, the most notable tourism-related conflicts have been linked to the construction of transportation infrastructure in Rio's favelas, especially cable cars, presented by the state as public transportation initiatives but denounced as a misuse of welfare funds to serve tourism.

The cable car wars

In 2012, the first in a series of new favela cable car systems built in the years leading to the coming mega-events was erected in the Complexo do Alemão. The location of this infrastructure clearly responded to a desire, on the part of local authorities, to counter negative perceptions of this particular favela, whose violent invasion by Brazilian armed forces in 2010 had made global news. While some residents welcomed the project, especially those with reduced mobility or living near the five cable car stations, many accused the city of diverting federal funds intended for much needed sanitation, education and road repair (Broudehoux and Legroux 2013). Additionally, people knew that such an

204 Anne-Marie Broudehoux

expensive, sophisticated, European-made system would never have been built for them alone. Trilingual signage throughout the system, in Portuguese, English and Spanish, supports the theory that, under the pretence of a public service, the cable car was built for tourists (Broudehoux and Legroux 2013). Residents thus deride the infrastructure as an 'image project', ill-suited for local mobility needs. They complain that the cable car, which links the five hilltops of the favela complex, is difficult to access for most residents who do not live near those summits. Furthermore, it does not allow for the transport of merchandise. According to 2014 statistics, after an initial boom in ridership due to novelty, resident use fell to a mere 10 per cent. On weekends, up to 60 per cent of users are tourists, local residents having reverted to using moto-taxis and other alternative modes of transport, rather than the inefficient cable car (Broudehoux and Legroux 2013).

It was with the implementation of a second cable car, in Providência, a highly emblematic favela located at the heart of Rio de Janeiro's old harbour, that more vocal and organised resistance started to emerge. Investments in access roads, cable cars and historical preservation were denounced as serving Porto Maravilha, a vast port revitalization project launched with the Olympic deadline in mind. These projects would require massive demolition and the displacement of up to one-third of Providência's community. In 2011, a series of well-organized protests were held to save Praça Americo Blum, the favela's main square, where the cable car station was to be erected. By joining forces with other community groups, protestors increased their leverage against state authorities and succeeded in attracting the attention of local media and international observers. A few victories were made: demolitions were postponed and many tourism-related projects were abandoned, especially the sanitised renovation of Cruzeiro, the favela's historical district. The controversial cable car could not be stopped, but it would take almost two years after its realisation before it was finally put into operation in July 2014. The great fanfare, media attention and timing of the inauguration, in the middle of the FIFA World Cup, were taken as yet another proof of the touristic motives of the project.

Who benefits from favela tourism?

In spite of growing discontent over tourism-related investments, resistance rarely spills outside the limits of the favela. However, in June 2013, as people all over Brazil held demonstrations to denounce excesses related to mega-events,[6] people in Rocinha took to the streets of the upmarket neighbourhood of São Conrado to protest the planned construction of a cable car in their community. They castigated the project as a tourist-oriented white elephant. Protestors also condemned outside tourist agencies for painting a superficial and stereotyped portrait of the community and for pocketing the benefits from favela tours without giving anything back. In July 2013, residents from Santa Marta also marched on the streets of the middle-class area of Botafogo to complain about tourism. They railed against the multiplication of jeep tours, denounced as a violent invasion of their territory. People reviled the promotion of favela tourism by the state and complained of the growing number of visitors flocking to their community.

Resistance to favela tourism was not only aimed at large-scale, state-led initiatives but it was also waged against new businesses, such as recently established hotels and restaurants. Initially perceived as a potential source of employment, these businesses soon became a cause of anxiety for residents, who feared losing what precious little they had gained through hard work and perseverance. Uncertainty was palpable during a series of public debates held in Vidigal in May 2014, organised by the NGO Catalytic Community in collaboration with local community groups. Entrepreneurs who had recently settled in the community were invited to answer questions from residents about their concerns over the rapid transformation of the favela, especially with regard to real-estate speculation. Residents' testimonies revealed growing suspicion towards these potential new 'invaders'. The Mirante do Arvrão Hotel built at the top of Vidigal in 2013 was accused of having taken advantage of an elderly couple, who sold their home for R$2,000, without knowing it would be replaced by a million dollar hotel. The new art school built by world-renowned artist Vik Muniz was also charged with exploiting the favela as a source of social capital, gained on the back of poor people. While the school's manager insisted on the benevolent character of the institution, concerned with the well-being of the community, residents expressed resentment against the arrogance of outsiders who come uninvited and pretend to know their needs. *Favelados* were obviously tired of being used as a 'social cause' by well-intentioned people wanting to feel good about 'giving back'.

Across Rio, residents have started to realise how their favela is becoming a resource for all sorts of capital gain: not only are outsiders extracting economic capital from new businesses in the form of cheap land and new markets, but the favela is also used as a source of symbolic capital. After academics, researchers, designers and NGOs, artists are taking on philanthropic projects to polish their image in the eye of the global public, a trend that has been called *humanitarian* or *compassion branding* (Vestergaard 2008). For locals, tourists are only adding to the lot of intruders who come and help themselves in the favela as if at an open buffet.

In this light, Santa Marta's unique tourism experience as a state-led tourist project could be seen as a different form of resistance, a resistance to the banalization of the favela as a mass tourist destination, and a refusal to give in to self-help tourism, where outsiders just walk into their neighbourhood as if it were an open house. Paradoxically, maintaining control over access and demanding that paid local guides accompany visitors is beginning to impact the favela's attractiveness as a tourist product.

Conclusion

This chapter traced a portrait of favela tourism in Rio de Janeiro, a practice still in its infancy and undergoing rapid transformations. Already, over the six-year study period, several changes could be noted. Motivations for visiting favelas are evolving, moving away from stereotypes of crime, violence and the eroticisation of poverty towards a true experience of favela life. The hosting of the World Cup greatly improved knowledge of Rio's favelas and drastically altered perceptions: many recent visitors ignored the fact that favelas were once forbidden territories. In Brazil, media coverage of the favela is becoming more positive, covering cultural practices and gastronomy as much as violence and crime.

While thorough impact studies of favela tourism still need be conducted, it is possible to evaluate some of the early outcomes of such practices. The chapter suggests that favela tourism is both an opportunity and a threat: it could contribute to these settlements' integration and economic development as much as it could take away from them. The pressure exerted on local real estate can make favela tourism a promoter of gentrification, splitting up communities and exacerbating socio-spatial segregation. This phenomenon is already visible in several favelas located near the city's most famous beaches, where a recent rise of more than 400 per cent in house values has triggered the departure of many residents away from the South Zone towards the Northern periphery. The boom in tourism linked to the hosting of mega-events such as the 2014 World Cup and 2016 Olympics is directly responsible for this phenomenon.

On the other hand, the growing attention and increased visibility given to the favela in the global media thanks to tourism development has been beneficial, resulting in a greater level of attention and care towards these settlements on the part of local authorities. In the future, the challenge will be to find a balance in the way favela tourism is conducted, one that will warrant dignity for residents and income generation while limiting its adverse effects.

Overall, the most positive favela tourism initiatives are those that have been conducted in collaboration with local communities, which limit the feeling of intrusion and disturbance, respect their need for privacy and yield clear benefits for the collectivity. Most offensive have been those initiatives imposed without consultation and which appear disrespectful and exploitative to the locals. Low-impact, small-scale, community-led initiatives such as resident-managed eco-trails and crafts cooperatives are successful examples. Other tourist activities, either individual commercial initiatives or state-led infrastructure projects, must be developed in consultation with local groups, include transparent impact assessment studies and propose innovative ways for the favela to benefit from such projects or to compensate residents for perceived losses and nuisances.

Future studies of favela tourism will have to address key questions. Will the favela retain its appeal now that the danger has gone? Will its rising popularity be the source of its demise, as interest for favelas dwindle once they become accessible to mass tourism? Will pacification, integration and gentrification transform the favela's unique territorial identity, turning it into a working-class neighbourhood with a view? As favela tourism expands and develops, it will also be interesting to see how it impacts local self-representation. Will *favelados* alter their behaviour to fit outside expectations and meet outsiders' criteria of authenticity, however staged? Will they 'perform' a version of their 'culture' for the tourists? Will the continuous expansion of favela tourism fuel more tensions and conflicts over its benefits for favela residents? These questions and many more will have to be investigated in the future to deepen our understanding of this emerging phenomenon.

Notes

1 This chapter is based on repeat visits conducted between 2009 and 2014 to ten squatter settlements, or favelas, in Rio de Janeiro. The favelas studied include: Rocinha, Complexo do Alemão, Providência, Pavão-Pavãozinho-Cantagalo, Babilônia-Chapéu-Mangueira, Santa Marta, Complexo da Maré, Trabajaras y Cabrito, Tavares Bastos and Vidigal. These favelas were identified as those with the greatest level of tourism development. Multiple semi-directed interviews with residents, tour operators and visitors (both local and foreign), community representatives and other local actors like NGO workers and entrepreneurs were conducted to better understand their views on this phenomenon, to document its diverse manifestations and to evaluate its impacts on local communities. Research sites and informants were visited every year to measure progress and map out changes. Whenever possible, community meetings, festive gatherings and other key community events were attended, including public protests, to take the pulse of the community and elicit discussions about tourism development. Guest books at various hospitality sites were consulted to survey visitors' comments and measure satisfaction levels. This information was supplemented by a continuous review of the local press and surveys of secondary sources and of the growing literature on the subject.
2 Other feature and documentary films include *Favela Rising* (2005), *Elite Squad* (2007), *City of Men* (2007), *City of Favelas* (2010) and *Five Times Favelas* (2011).
3 *The Hulk* (2008), *Fast and Furious* 5 (2011) and *Rio* (2011).
4 According to a 2007 survey published in the *Folha de São Paulo*, 78 per cent of people interviewed were against the idea of favela tourism (Freire-Medeiros 2009: 141). The idea of touring a favela was qualified as absurd, insane, risky, disrespectful and indecent. Many participants worried that the global dissemination of images of gross inequality could bring shame to Brazil.
5 Companies include Exotic Tour, conducted on foot; Jeep Tours, by jeep; Favela Adventure, on motorcycles; Indiana Jungle Tour, by jeep; and Be a Local, on motorcycles.
6 In June 2013, a demonstration against a rise in public transportation fares in São Paulo turned into a nationwide protest movement that widely denounced Brazil's excessive public spending on the hosting of the 2014 World Cup and 2016 Olympics.

References

[Unless otherwise stated, all URLs were last accessed 8 April 2015.]

Baudelaire, C. (2003) [1875] *The Flowers of Evil*, trans. Richard Howard. Jaffrey, NH: David R. Godine.

Bourdieu, P. (1979) *La Distinction: Critique Sociale du Jugement*. Paris: Éditions de Minuit.

Broudehoux, A.-M. and Legroux, J. (2013) 'L'option téléphérique dans les favelas de Rio de Janeiro: conflits d'intérêts entre méga-événements, tourisme et besoins locaux', *Téoros*, 32(2): 16–25.

El-Rayess, M. (2014) *Henry James and the Culture of Consumption*. Cambridge: Cambridge University Press.

Embratur (Brazil Institute of Tourism) (2014) 'Brasil e o 6 no mundo em economia do turismo'. Online. Available at http://www.embratur.gov.br/piembratur/opencms/salaImprensa/noticias/arquivos/Brasil_e_o_6_no_mundo_em_economia_do_Turismo.html.

Freeman, J. (2012) 'Neoliberal accumulation strategies and the visible hand of police pacification in Rio de Janeiro', *Revista de Estudos Universitários*, 38(1): 95–126.

Freire-Medeiros, B. (2008) 'And the favela went global: the invention of a trademark and a tourist destination', in M. Valença Marico, E. Nel and W. Leimgruber (eds), *The Global Challenge and Marginalisation*. New York: Nova Science.

Freire-Medeiros, B. (2009) *Gringo na Laje: Produção, Circulação e Consumo da Favela Turística*. Rio de Janeiro: Fundação Getúlio Vargas.

Freire-Medeiros, B. (2012) *Touring Poverty*. London: Routledge.

Frenzel, F., Koens, K. and Steinbrink, M. (2012) *Slum Tourism: Poverty, Power and Ethics*. London: Routledge.

Frisch, T. (2012) 'Glimpses of another world: the favela as a tourist attraction', *Tourism Geographies*, 14(2): 320–39.

Gilligan, M. (2006) 'Slumsploitation: the favela on film and TV', *Metamute*. Online. Available at http://www.metamute.org/en/Slumsploitation-Favela-on-Film-and-TV.

IBGE (Instituto Brasileiro de Geografia e Estatisticas) (2014) *Rio de Janeiro. Estimativa da População 2015*. Online. Available at http://www.cidades.ibge.gov.br/xtras/temas.php?l ang=&codmun=330455&idtema=130&search=rio-de-janeiro|rio-de-janeiro|estimativa-da-populacao-2014-.

Jaguaribe, B. (2004) 'Favelas and the aesthetics of realism: representations in film and literature', *Journal of Latin American Cultural Studies*, 13(3): 327–42.

Jaguaribe, B. and Hetherington, K. (2006) 'Favela tours: indistinct and mapless representations of the real in Rio de Janeiro', in M. Sheller and J. Urry (eds), *Mobile Technologies of the City*. London: Routledge.

Johanson, M. (2013) 'Why Rio's favelas disappeared from Google Maps', *International Business Times*. Online. Available at http://www.ibtimes.com/why-rios-favelas-disappeared-google-maps-1185455.

Koven, S. (2009) 'The queer politics of slumming', *History Workshop Journal*, 68(1): 259–66.

Lancaster, J. (2007) 'Next stop, squalor. Is poverty tourism "poorism", they call it exploration or exploitation?', *Smithsonian Magazine*, 1 March. Online. Available at http://www.smithsonianmag.com/people-places/next-stop-squalor-148390665/?no-ist.

Lennon, J. J. and Foley, M. (2000) *Dark Tourism: The Attraction of Death and Disaster*. London: New York: Continuum.

Lew, A. A. (ed.) (2015) *New Research Paradigms in Tourism Geography*. London: Routledge.

Lisle, D. (2004) 'Gazing at Ground Zero: tourism, voyeurism and spectacle', *Journal for Cultural Research*, 8(1): 3–21.

MacCannell, D. (1976) *The Tourist: A New Theory of the Leisure Class*. Berkeley, CA: University of California Press.

Miller, M. L. and Auyong, J. (1998) 'Remarks on tourism terminologies: anti-tourism, mass tourism, and alternative tourism', in M. L. Miller and J. Auyong (eds), *Proceedings of the 1996 World Congress on Coastal and Marine Tourism*. Seattle, WA: University of Washington and Oregon State University.

Moraes, C. (2010) 'Os Caminhos do Pavão, Pavãozinho e Cantagalo', *Intratextos*, número especial 01: 32–46.

Oliveira, N. (2012) 'Brazil shatters tourism records', *Infosurhoy.com*, 17 February.

Parker, J. (2003) 'Not slumming it: City of God and the Latin American continuum', *American Prospect*, 14(3): 35–6.

Perlman, J. (2010) *Favela. Four Decades of Living on the Edge in Rio de Janeiro*. Oxford: Oxford University Press.

Phillips, T. (2003) 'Brazil: How favelas went chic', *Brazzillog*. Online. Available at http://www.brazzillog.com/2003/html/articles/dec03/p105dec03.htm.

Riley, E., Fiori, J. and Ramirez, R. (2001) 'Favela Bairro and a new generation of housing programmes for the urban poor', *Geoforum*, 32(4): 521–31.

Robb, E. M. (2009) 'Violence and recreation: vacationing in the realm of dark tourism', *Anthropology and Humanism*, 34(1): 51–60.

Rodrigues, M. (2014) *Tudo junto e misturado: O almanaque da favela, turismo na Santa Marta*. Rio de Janeiro: Mar de Ideas.

Rolfes, M. (2010) 'Poverty tourism: theoretical reflections and empirical findings regarding an extraordinary form of tourism', *Geojournal*, 75(5): 421–42.

Schemo, D. J. (1996) 'Rio frets as Michael Jackson plans to film slum', *New York Times*, 2 November, p. 3.

Scheyvens, R. (2013) *Tourism and Poverty*. London: Routledge.

Selinger, E. and Outterson, K. (2010) 'The ethics of poverty tourism', *Environmental Philosophy*, 7(2): 1–22.

Sinek, W. M. (2013) 'Perceptions survey', *Catalytic Community*. Online. Available at http://catcomm.org/perceptions/.

Steinbrink, M. (2012) '"We did the slum!" Urban poverty tourism in historical perspective', *Tourism Geographies*, 14(2): 1–22.

Steinbrink, M. (2013) 'Festifavelisation: mega-events, slums and strategic city-staging. The example of Rio de Janeiro', *Die Erde*, 144(2): 129–45.

Sterling, B. (2010) 'Favela chic as a Brazilian cultural tourism issue', *Wired*, 19 August, p. 3.

Tavener, B. (2012) 'Brazil reports record tourism', *Rio Times*, 5 May, p. 5.

UNWTO (United Nations World Tourism Organisation) (2014) *Tourism Highlights, 2013 Edition*. Washington, DC: UNWTO.

Valladares do Prado, L. (2005) *A invençao da favela: Do mito do origem a favela.com*. Rio de Janeiro: Fundaçao Getulio Vargas Editora.

Veissiere, S. P. L. (2010) 'Making a living: the Gringo ethnographer as pimp of the suffering in the late capitalist night', *Cultural Studies, Critical Methodologies*, 10(1): 29–39.

Vestergaard, A. (2008) 'Humanitarian branding and the media: the case of Amnesty International', *Journal of Language and Politics*, 7(3): 471–93.

Whyte, K., Selinger, E. and Outterson, K. (2010) 'Poverty tourism and the problem of consent', *Journal of Global Ethics*, 7(3): 337–48.

WTM (World Travel Market) (2012) *2012 Industry Report*. Online. Available at http://www.wtmlondon.com/files/6335_wtm_industry_report_v10_lo.pdf.

Zaluar, A. and Alvito, M. (1998) *Um seculo de Favela*. Rio de Janeiro: Fundaçao Getulio Vargas Editora.

Zeiderman, A. (2006) *The Fetish and the Favela: Notes on Tourism and the Commodification of Place in Rio de Janeiro, Brazil*. Stanford, CA: Stanford University Press.

11 Politics as early as possible

Democratizing the Olympics by contesting Olympic bids

John Lauermann

Urban 'mega-events' like the Olympics are frequently used to spur tourism flows and pursue urban development goals in the process. They are defined as events with 'dramatic character, mass popular appeal and international significance' (Roche 2000: 1).[1] These events stimulate temporary tourist economies, but they may also crowd out other tourism activity as non-event tourists avoid temporarily inflated costs and crowds (Porter and Chin 2012; Zimbalist 2015). For example, the London Olympics attracted 11 million visitors (LOCOG 2012: 32), but the United Kingdom's international tourist count decreased by 5 per cent during the two months of the Games (ONS 2012). Thus rather than relying only on short-term tourism gains, event promoters highlight the role of mega-events as catalysts for local investment. Usually promoted as offering the potential for 'legacy', Olympic investments are said to regenerate communities (Smith 2012), to facilitate social inclusion (van Wynsberghe *et al*. 2013; Pillay and Bass 2008) and to deliver innovations in sustainable infrastructure (Mol 2010).

However, boosterish claims about the potential for Olympics to produce positive legacies are routinely challenged by researchers from across the political spectrum. Critics note that mega-events are more likely to experience cost overruns than most other types of urban mega-projects (Preuss 2004; Flyvbjerg and Stewart 2012), that evidence of net positive impacts on the regional economy is suspect (Porter and Chin 2012), that long-term and 'trickle-down' development effects are often smaller than promised (Pillay and Bass 2008; Zimbalist 2015) and that Olympics are institutionally structured to allocate risk to city governments and profits to sports federations and their business partners (Boykoff 2014b).

Mega-events represent a prominent tool of urban tourism policy and are symptomatic of broader tourism politics in neoliberal urban contexts. Planning for mega-events introduces what I term a 'democratic displacement' in the politics of the tourist city, by which debate over urban policy and public finance circumvents the participatory protocols expected of many urban mega-projects. This displacement derives from the timelines required of event planning: decisions made at the early stages of bidding and planning establish path dependencies which displace subsequent deliberation. This is not to say that cities should never host the Olympics nor that Olympic planners intentionally seek to disenfranchise urban residents. There are certainly mega-event development success stories (e.g. in Pillay *et al.* 2009; Smith 2012), and taxpayers are sometimes willing to pay for the intangible benefits of hosting (Atkinson *et al.* 2008). Rather, the decision to host an Olympics is often not subjected to the same standards of participatory review and deliberation which are expected of other urban mega-projects, and this ultimately diminishes the legitimacy of and public support for mega-events as a tool of (tourism-led) urban development.

In this chapter I analyse the urban politics of mega-events by tracing the process of democratic displacement to its source: the bidding process. After reviewing the relationship between mega-events and urban tourism, I empirically assess the extent of democratic displacements and the impact of anti-bid social movements. I argue that mega-events and other 'temporary' event-led initiatives should not be viewed as *ad hoc* instances in urban politics, but rather as embedded in long-term agendas by particular stakeholder groups in the city (cf. Lauermann 2015). The politics of the event happen long before it; in this sense bids are a key site and moment in the politics of the Olympic city. I demonstrate this with a study of social movements which protest Olympic bids, documenting how democratic displacements are accomplished in urban politics.[2] The chapter also seeks to evaluate how they might be avoided.

The chapter contributes to debates about the 'post-political' dimension of urban governance in the case of the tourist city. Critical analysts view contemporary urban governance as a form of techno-managerialism which leaves space for debate over the 'how' of governance but forecloses discussion over the 'why' (Dikeç 2007; Swyngedouw 2009; Davidson and Iveson 2015). In Olympic cities there is significant debate over managing and mitigating Olympic projects, but as I demonstrate in the following discussion, debates over if and why a city should host the event are less common. This latter form of contestation is often limited to a temporary 'moment of movements' (Boykoff 2014a: 26) in which activists mobilize in response to the impacts of Olympic planning after the project is underway. However, a number of recent movements have formed to contest Olympic bids at earlier planning stages. These anti-bid movements have caused significant disruption within the Olympic industry. For instance, in the most recent round of bidding for the 2022 Winter Olympics, anti-bid protests derailed plans for the Games in Krakow, Munich, Stockholm, St Moritz (Switzerland) and Oslo, leaving only two cities (Almaty and Beijing) in the applicant pool.[3]

Mega-events and the tourist city

Previous scholarship highlights three relationships between the tourist city and mega-events like the Olympics. All are concerned with the impact of using a temporary event to increase visitor flows and catalysing local development. Debates over post-event 'legacy' are central to each approach. First, there is a contentious debate over the economic impact of temporary tourist events (see reviews in Preuss 2004: ch. 6; Smith 2012: ch. 8). Event tourism can generate a temporary increase in demand for local services (Chalip 2004; O'Brien 2006), and mega-events can produce a 'signal effect' which improves consumer and employer confidence (Rose and Spiegel 2010). Willingness-to-pay surveys have shown that taxpayers value the intangible benefits of a mega-event (e.g. community pride, global exposure) but not always enough to match the costs of hosting (Atkinson *et al.* 2008; Ahlfeldt and Maennig 2012). Economic impact assessments are hotly contested: most rely on input-output models which fail to account for the fact that by definition a 'mega'-event shifts the parameters of the regional economy – and thus the multipliers which should be used in an economet-ric model (Porter and Chin 2012; Zimbalist 2015). Specifically, claims that mega-events generate net positive economic impacts often neglect to account for crowding out effects (Olympic tourists displacing other tourists) and substitution effects (tourists spend more on Olympic activities but less at other local busi-nesses) (Baade and Matheson 2004; Whitson and Horne 2006; Maennig and Richter 2012). *Ex post* studies based on more reliable data (like tax receipts) are much less optimistic than *ex ante* impact studies, which are often commissioned by bid promoters (Dwyer *et al.* 2005; Baumann and Matheson 2013). Scholars from across the political spectrum have demonstrated instead a pervasive over-optimism in bidders' cost-benefit projections (Flyvbjerg and Stewart 2012; Boykoff 2014b).

Second, there is a debate on post-event 'legacy tourism' and the broader role of Olympics in place marketing (see reviews in Getz 2008; Gold and Gold 2008). Enhanced destination brands have been described as intangible but significant tourism legacies, especially when iconic venues becomes tourist attractions in their own right (Chalip and Costa 2005; Gratton and Preuss 2008). Others signal to the geopolitical role that this place branding portends, as mega-events are used not only for marketing cities but also to re-brand ambitious national states (Zhang and Zhao 2009; Black and Peacock 2011; Müller 2011). This tourism legacy sometimes extends outside the city, as various 'sport for development' programmes use revenues for national and international development programmes (Pillay and Bass 2008; Levermore 2011).

Third, there is a debate over how mega-events and other tourist spectacles are used in urban politics, especially the politics of the neoliberal/entrepreneurial city. These commentators debate the role of mega-events in market-led develop-ment strategies, especially when public funds are used to subsidise private-sector projects (Boykoff 2014b; Zimbalist 2015). Analysts drawing on urban regime theory (Cochrane *et al.* 1996; Burbank *et al.* 2002) have pointed to the role of tourism in legitimating and maintaining a city's governance elite; a 'mega-event strategy' uses global media exposure to promote local projects (Andranovich *et al.* 2001). A related argument points to the role of tourist spectacles in urban growth politics: tourist events enable 'selectively transnationalized' growth coali-tions which use global relationships and expertise to promote local growth poli-tics (Surborg *et al.* 2008: 327), e.g. by rhetorically linking real-estate projects to broader imperatives for globalizing cultural industries in the city (Hiller 2000a; Hall 2006).

Protest and contestation in the Olympic city

While these three approaches present compelling narratives about the (positive and negative) impacts of mega-events on the city, relatively little has been written about protest in the Olympic city (though note studies like Lenskyj 2008; Cottrell and Nelson 2011; Boykoff 2014a). Contestation is typically framed as a debate over the scope and limits of legacy narratives: boosters highlight the impact of Olympic projects while critics deconstruct it and challenge the claims of the boosters. Thus contestation is often relatively narrow in scope: debating how to ameliorate impacts or improve project outcomes, rather than broader questions about opportunity costs and whether the Olympics should be pursued at all. This is due in part to democratic displacements at the bid stage, hampering public debate and oversight at later planning stages.

Within the urban politics and social movements literatures, Olympic protest is typically framed in two ways. The first describes mega-events as temporary but exceptionally problematic projects in urban politics. They are interpreted as producing 'states of exception' (Agamben 2005) in which typical standards of governance legitimacy are suspended. The state of exception induces a temporary legal and institutional climate which diverges from conventional forms of urban politics. Boykoff (2014b) concisely summarises this approach, describing Olympic urban politics as a form of 'celebration capitalism', the 'affable cousin' of disaster capitalism (Klein 2007): 'Both occur in states of exception and both allow plucky politicos and their corporate cohorts to push policies they wouldn't dream of during normal political times' (Boykoff 2014b: 3). However, 'rather than disaster we get spectacle . . . the Olympics become an alibi for forging spaces of political-economic exception where authoritarian tendencies can more freely express themselves' (ibid.: 11).

In this framing, mega-events are viewed as interventions in urban politics which induce temporary relaxations of the normal rule of law, to the benefit of corporate sponsors and real-estate investors. Such states of exception temporarily allow for tax-free profits (Louw 2012), for extraordinary security laws and the use of military-grade weapons for policing (Giulianotti and Klauser 2011), or for the displacement of disadvantaged residents (Greene 2003; CHORE 2007). These 'temporary' states of exception can have long-term impacts as they permanently displace residents, redistribute public funds or create path dependencies in urban policy (e.g. around the militarization of policing practices).

Given the 'mega' dimensions of Olympic projects, impacts are widespread and protests are common. But protest against states of exception tends to be reactive rather than proactive. In a rare comparative study of anti-Olympic activism, Boykoff (2014a: 26) explores anti-Olympic social movements in Vancouver, London and Sochi and describes this temporality as a 'moment of movements' during which 'extant activist groups come together using the Olympics as their fight-back focal point'. This type of momentary protest is temporally circumscribed, occurring when planning produces negative impacts rather than at earlier phases when the entire project could be contested. It is also highly localised, organised to contest specific impacts of an individual Olympics (e.g. securitisation in London, slum demolitions in Rio de Janeiro) rather than against the mega-events industry as it migrates from one city to the next.

The second framing describes mega-events as bound up in neoliberal urban politics. That is, the Olympics are discussed as one part of broader governance strategies which favour market-led approaches to governing the city. In such forms of governance, bids for mega-events are interpreted as part of a 'mega-event strategy' for local development, in which even unsuccessful bids for the Games are 'enough to warrant media exposure and provide some claim to Olympic symbols to unify disparate stakeholders, however transitory these claims might be' (Andranovich *et al.* 2001: 127). Thus mega-events are viewed as a global-local strategy for profit and political legitimation: they are planned by 'selectively transnationalized' growth coalitions whose 'primary function is to balance the traditional political power of locally-based growth coalitions with the need to respond to extra-territorial actors and coalitions – a growth machine diaspora' (Surborg *et al.* 2008: 324).

In this second framing, contestation is analysed as part of protest against neoliberal governance tactics like austerity or municipal speculation. For mega-event planning, urban decision-makers often turn to global networks of expertise by recruiting consultants (Lauermann 2014a; Müller 2014), sending municipal staff to learn from peers in other cities (Cook and Ward 2011; González 2011) and directly adopting the technical standards requested by the sports federations (Eick 2010; Klauser 2011; Kassens-Noor 2013). Much of the scholarship on those processes critiques the top-down relationships reproduced between cities and the international sponsor/federation/consultant networks. Forms of contestations and activism targeting these relationships have denounced corruption and lack of transparency in the governance of sport federations (Girginov 2010; Horne and Whannel 2012), although the networks of consultants and real-estate firms which undergird those relationships receive less attention (Lauermann 2014a; Müller 2014).

One common argument in both lines of interpretation is that Olympic bidding displaces or circumvents public debate over urban policy. Bid proposals are contingent on winning a contract and are by definition speculative, but if a bid succeeds the logistical challenge of delivering the project on time creates substantial political pressure to solidify the proposal quickly (and foreclose future debate). Hiller (2000b: 193, original emphasis) summarises this displacement:

> Since the foundation of the plan is laid in the bid phase, there is always a tendency for urban residents to see the exercise as only hypothetical and, therefore, not to take it seriously. When citizens do take it seriously, it can be countered that this is only an early plan. But the problem is that, when and if the bid is successful, something conceived by others as only a conceptual idea takes on a life of its own as *the* plan.

But it is perhaps too simple to blame hapless citizens; this abrupt transition from contingent proposal to contractual obligation produces 'celebratory states of exception' (Boykoff 2014b: 11). Writing on this transition from a contingent plan to a contractually obligated 'delivery imperative' in the case of the London 2012 Games, for instance, Raco (2014: 191) documents how

> responsibility for policy has been handed over to project managers, with the delivery of the Games converted into a technical programme of action adhering to specifications and decisions outlined in the contractual phase of the development, and therefore subject primarily to technical challenges and adaptations, rather than significant policy objections. It represents a clear example of how decisions become frozen at a particular point in time to facilitate the development process.

The consequence is that contestation over Olympic planning has historically focused on ameliorating impacts and improving legacies after a city commits to hosting (see discussions in Lenskyj 2008; Boykoff 2014a). But Olympic impacts are only felt years after plans are finalised and contracts are signed. Olympic boosters officially launch their bids to host the Games 8–10 years before the event, and some unofficially start earlier by bidding for the Olympics multiple times and hosting a variety of smaller events along the way (Lauermann 2015). Thus democratic debate over the role of mega-events in urban development can be displaced as contract negotiations are completed long before local movements mobilize to contest the project.

Olympic bids and the democratic displacement

Both of these critical interpretations – protesting states of exception, or contesting the neoliberalisation of urban politics – converge around a shared understanding of the political dynamics of mega-events. Both signal the use of mega-events as a means for depoliticising urban governance. States of exception take place at the final stages of a long-term political process, in which questions about the opportunity cost of hosting – and about whether an Olympics should be pursued at all – are already moot. Similarly, the post-political dimensions of neoliberal urban politics are well documented (see reviews in Kiel 2009; MacLeod 2011), and mega-events can be read as a tool for facilitating market-led forms of urban development policies (Raco 2014). In short, both interpretations discuss the politics of mega-events as symptomatic of broader post-political trends in urban politics.

The notion of the 'post-political' or the 'post-democratic' has emerged as a prominent framework for interpreting the contemporary city (see reviews in Dikeç 2007; Swyngedouw 2009; Davidson and Iveson 2015), often as an outgrowth of entrepreneurial governance practices (MacLeod 2011). This concept refers to a form of governance which allows, and even encourages, participatory forms of decision-making within an established governance paradigm, but avoids and excludes systemically disruptive conversations about alternative paradigms (Rancière 1999, 2006; Mouffe 2005). That is, there is a place for participation in discussions over 'how' the city is governed within an existing paradigm (e.g. how do we ameliorate Olympic impacts or increase legacies?) but not normative debates over 'why' the city should be governed as such (e.g. why should the city host an Olympics in the first place?). As Davidson and Iveson (2015: 546) put it:

> The presence of contestation and/or difference does not mean that it is incorrect to characterise urban governance as 'post-political' or 'post-democratic'. In any given city there may indeed be scope for debate about which policies might help that city to become more competitive, more global, more sustainable, more secure, and so on. But challenging the underlying necessity and legitimacy of these visions is far more difficult.

Olympic urban politics are a case in point: contestation often develops over how the city might be governed (ameliorate the negatives, add to legacy funds, compensate the displaced, etc.). But there is less conversation about the 'underlying necessity and legitimacy' (*ibid.*) of event-led governance models. This displacement is institutional and temporal. The institutional displacement is a familiar one in neoliberal urbanism: profit-oriented transnational networks are able to plug into local urban politics and provide a set of business-friendly practices for delivering the Games (Hall 2006; Whitson and Horne 2006; Surborg *et al.* 2008; Eick 2011; van Wynsberghe *et al.* 2013). While they are promoted as apolitical and pragmatic, these practices can also 'manipulate state actors as partners, pushing us toward economics rooted in so-called public-private partnerships . . . [which are] lopsided: the public pays and the private profits' (Boykoff 2014b: 3). More specifically, the local state (usually a municipal government) pays and consultants, sponsors, sports federations and real-estate firms profit.

The temporal displacement occurs when temporary interventions induce states of exception in urban politics. A state of exception implies that it is too late to contest the origins of that exception: the fundamental political question as to whether a city should host the Olympics at all. The early stages of planning, especially the bidding process, are the origins of a state of exception. For example, the IOC's former director of marketing (Payne 2006: 191) went so far as to praise this as a form of top-down planning led by transnational experts. He suggested imposing a 'strict brand discipline' at the bid phase:

> The danger, otherwise, is that the local politics get in the way. A city that is one of several on a shortlist is altogether easier to deal with than the same city once it is confirmed as the next Olympic host.

After a bid has been approved, the moment for that normative debate is quickly supplanted by project management issues, subcontracts and a 'delivery imperative' (Raco 2014). Thus broader normative debates over the opportunity costs of the mega-event are displaced by project deadlines and relatively narrow debates over impact and legacy.

The analysis which follows shows that mega-events are an important site for analysing the urban post-political condition. This offers broader insight into the role of urban post-politics in tourist cities. The post-political (despite its 'post' prefix) is not so much an end state where 'politics' no longer exists. Rather it refers to an ongoing process of separation – often but not always led by policy-making elites (Rancière 2006; Swyngedouw 2009) – between the 'how' of governance and contesting the 'why'. In the case of Olympic cities this is a process by which decision-making about the city's future mega-event is relegated to technical debates over how to manage or mitigate the impacts of the Games, rather than normative debates over if and why hosting is a wise policy agenda. In the discussion which follows, I show how this displacement process occurs, and how urban social movements have sought to contest it.

Olympic urban politics: contesting the bid

While the impacts of a mega-event are most likely to elicit protest, the core institutional inequalities which produce those impacts are designed earlier during the bid phase. Bids are the site and moment when normative dimensions of urban development visions might be debated. They define who has a voice in how policy will incorporate new priorities, how investments will be financed, how urban space will be planned and, most fundamentally, if a city will host the Games at all.

Most Olympic bid corporations claim some form of local political legitimacy when representing 'their' city. Yet their representativeness can be questionable. A sample of polls on Olympic bids over the last 20 years highlights this trend.[4] Since the early 1990s most bid corporations have surveyed public opinion on the bid. Bidders have significant incentives to overstate public support for their projects, and the level of support claimed in some cities is high enough to be suspect (on average, bidders claimed 72.7 per cent of residents in their cities were in support). Cities in non-democratic states present particularly suspect examples: for instance, the original Beijing bid (written in 1993 for a 2000 Olympics) claimed that 92.6 per cent of citizens strongly supported the Olympic project, and noted ominously that 'neither now nor in the future will there emerge in Beijing organisations opposing Beijing's bid' (Beijing 2000 1993: vol. 1, p. 24).

As a counterweight to this tendency the IOC has funded separate surveys in each bid city since 2000 (finding levels of support which are, on average, 4.1 percentage points lower than the bid corporation surveys) (IOC 2000). But authoritarian outliers and questionable survey techniques distract from the broader limits to public participation in Olympic bids: out of the 81 sampled bids (for Summer and Winter Games between 2000 and 2020), only 12 were subject to a formal referendum and 56 bids claimed to have no knowledge of any local opposition at all. While bidders' claims of 'no discernible opposition' (Moscow, 2012), 'no organized opposition' (London, 2012; PyeongChang, 2018) or 'no major movement against' (Tokyo, 2020) seem strategically myopic, this also signals to the relatively limited scale and visibility of anti-bid protest.

Contesting a bid requires activists and critics to be proactive. With one exception (Denver), no city has withdrawn from an Olympic contract after winning a bid.[5] Post-award contestation lacks an institutional mechanism for demanding concessions from Olympic planners: recalling the previously quoted IOC marketing expert, bidding negotiations are a way to make decisions 'before local politics get in the way' (Payne 2006: 191). The host city government is contractually obligated to provide the capital investments detailed in the bid, because the bid document forms the legal basis for a city's contract with the IOC. Recalling Raco (2014: 191), 'decisions become frozen at a particular point in time to facilitate the development process.' In contrast, anti-bid politics often involve proactive, normative contestation: highlighting the opportunity costs of an Olympics (Figure 11.1) and contesting whether the Olympics should be pursued at all

Figure 11.1 Questioning the opportunity costs of hosting the Olympics: *No Boston Olympics* activists highlight how public funds might be spent on other local investment priorities, May 2015.

Source: Author.

(Figure 11.2). As one anti-bid activist (protesting the Boston bid for the 2024 Games) put it:

> We wouldn't have been working on this as volunteers . . . if it were just about some of the factors in the deals, or about getting to the table for negotiating and then going away [after we were heard]. So I think we should be very clear about one thing: we are not 'maybe Boston'. We are 'no Boston' and we have no intention of changing that.[6]

There are relatively few historical examples of large-scale anti-bid protests. But these protests often had the effect of slowing or stopping the bid outright. Voters

Figure 11.2 Playing on a marketing campaign which promoted a potential Berlin bid for the 2024 Olympics, an anti-Olympics poster reads: 'We do not want the Games! IOC not welcome. Against militarization and surveillance', February 2015.

Source: Emily Bereskin.

successfully demanded a referendum on a Quebec bid to host the 2002 Winter Games (the bid failed before the referendum occurred) and voters in Berne rejected a 2010 Olympic bid (Bramham 2002). An 'Anti-Olympia-Komitee' organized a movement against the Berlin 2000 bid, damaging the brand value of the bid and prompting opposition parties in local and national government to launch corruption investigations (Colomb 2012: ch. 4). A 'Bread not Circuses' social movement failed to prevent Toronto's 1996 and 2008 bids for the Games, but it did produce enough negative publicity to undermine the bid corporations' proposals (Lenskyj 2008). A movement in Paris had a similar negative publicity effect on bids for the 2008 and 2012 Games (Issert and Lunzenfichter 2006). Recent movements have achieved more success in halting Olympic bids. For example, in the competition to host the 2022 Winter Games, local activists were successful in halting bids – sometimes by successfully demanding and winning referendums – in Krakow, Munich, Stockholm, St Moritz (Switzerland) and Oslo (Clarey 2014).

But stopping a bid outright is not necessarily the only or optimal outcome of contesting an Olympic project. Rather, contesting bids is a way to call for accountability and transparency from Olympic planners. For example, anti-bid protests partially inspired an institutional review at the IOC, summarised in the *Olympic Agenda 2020* strategic planning exercise (IOC 2014). Munich's anti-bid activism played a significant role: after voters narrowly approved a bid for the 2018 Olympics, they rejected a second bid for the 2022 Games. IOC president Thomas Bach had participated in the 2018 bid in his previous role as chairman of the national *Deutscher Olympischer Sportbund*, and blamed the subsequent anti-bid referendum on voters 'being wrongly informed about quite a number of issues' (quoted in Hula 2013). But regardless of his critique, reforming the bid process became a dominant theme in Bach's promotion of the 2020 strategic plan.[7]

Anti-bid activism helped trigger a collapse in institutional confidence with the concept of 'legacy'. The legacy concept provides a political rationale for linking temporary events to claims about urban development, and by extension a justification for unequal partnerships between host cities and sports federations. It is at the core of the IOC's two-budget event management model: the model involves an operational budget which is funded with event revenues, and a capital/infrastructure budget which is funded from non-Olympic sources, often public funding. This is intended to prevent the Olympic 'brand' from being extended to marginally relevant land investments, and to allow cities flexibility in designing infrastructure that will have legacies after the Games (Lauermann 2014b). But in practice this can result in an infrastructure subsidy for the bid corporation, in which 'the public pays and the private profits' (Boykoff 2014b: 3).

The legacy concept has been critiqued extensively by academic analysts from across the political spectrum, especially for the role that it plays in legitimizing expenditures of public funds on private real-estate projects (see reviews in Preuss 2004: ch. 11; Horne and Whannel 2012: ch. 10; Smith 2012: ch. 3; Zimbalist 2015: ch. 4). What is new is a growing uncertainty about it among consultants, planners and other Olympic industry stakeholders (e.g. the *Olympic Agenda 2020* reforms). A former director of legacy planning at the London Olympics described the justification of two-budget accounting through references to legacy as allowing 'a tendency to systematically under-cost the event' by bid boosters.[8] The head of an urban design firm (who has worked on mega-events in over a dozen cities) noted that 'the word legacy is such a tired, overused word . . . I'm very critical of it and I think it really needs definition . . . "legacy" is just a buzzword for people to justify their salaries.'[9] And one consultant – whose firm advises city governments on mega-event planning – summed up this loss of confidence within the Olympic industry, noting that 'I have never heard a politician or people working in city administration using the term "legacy" . . . it's a term invented by rights holders [sports federations like the IOC], and that's one of the reasons why people do not vote for it.'[10]

The long-term outcome of these trends remains to be seen. However, this does indicate that contesting the bid – rather than the event – provides a way to counteract democratic displacements. Anti-bid activists focus on two strategies. First, they may call for participatory governance over the bid process. As discussed above, launching a direct referendum is a high-profile victory for social movements in part because these referendums are so rare. Second, a more widespread strategy involves broader demands for accountability and transparency in Olympic planning: calling for bidders to provide realistic cost projections and economic impact assessments (or commission independent assessments). For example, Games Monitor (gamesmonitor.org.uk) activists used a freedom of information request to secure and publish host city contract documents in advance of the London 2012 Games. These documents define the specific responsibilities of a host city but are usually embargoed by Olympic organizers. Likewise, using more reliable metrics and more participatory practices can allow normative debate about the opportunity costs of devoting public funds to Olympic infrastructure. For example, *No Boston Olympics* activists recruited academic experts and government officials into their coalition as a way to deconstruct legacy claims made by the bidders, a messaging strategy which had some success: independent polling found that the more information voters had about the specifics of the bid, the less favourable their opinion of it became (WNEU Polling Institute 2015).

Conclusion

This chapter has explored a form of 'democratic displacement' in urban politics. Discussions over the role of mega-events in urban tourism and development – and of anti-Olympic activism in response – focus on the temporary dynamics of these events as they produce short-term economic benefits and anti-democratic 'states of exception' in urban politics. The role of Olympics in the broader neoliberalisation of urban policy is a similarly dominant theme in scholarship and in activist circles. Historically, however, anti-Olympic activism has been reactive and localised as social movements protest particular impacts of Olympic planning

(Boykoff 2014b). That form of contestation may not engage broader normative debates over whether an Olympics should be hosted in the first place, a point which a subgroup of anti-bid activists have focused upon by calling for votes on the bids before they are approved and for more transparency and accountability in the early-stage planning process.

Some cities may benefit from hosting the Olympics, and the goal of this chapter is not to discourage their hosting but to make recommendations for their planning. Events and other temporary tourist projects are embedded in long-term local development politics, for instance as mega-events draw on interrelated projects associated with other mega-events and failed Olympic bids (Lauermann 2015; Oliver 2014). Thus Olympic urban politics need to be proactive: the stakeholders who promote the bids start their work a decade preceding the event, and Olympic protest is most likely to succeed before the bids are approved, the funding is promised and the contracts are signed. Protest in Olympic cities has been most effective when targeted toward normative debate over the process (e.g. why should the city pursue an Olympics?) rather than issue-specific debate over the project (e.g. how can Olympic impacts be minimized or mitigated?). Critical analysis of boosterish claims about legacy is a particularly effective strategy: demonstrating that the event would likely cost more and produce less than bidders claim is an effective tactic for improving public debate. While social movements are starting to share this expertise, there is still much opportunity for building city-to-city alliances among Olympic protest movements. A clearer picture of the institutional and legal nuances of mega-events planning identifies openings for contestation.

Notes

1   Müller (2015) defines mega-events based on ticket sales, the value of television broadcast contracts, event costs and investment impact on the urban environment. This is a composite definition which varies based on all four variables, but most 'mega' events sell 1–3 million tickets, earn US$2–3 billion in broadcast revenues and include US$5–10 billion in costs and investments.
2   The chapter draws on a comparative analysis of Olympic bid protests through archival analysis and a field study of the Boston bid to host the 2024 Summer Olympics. The comparative data are based on a sample of bids to host the Olympics between 2000 and 2020 (bid dates 1991 to 2012 and n = 67), drawn from bidding documents prepared by each city (obtained from the archives of the Olympics Studies Centre in Lausanne, Switzerland). That project also involved interviews with 30 key informants in the mega-events planning industry (see Lauermann 2014a, 2014b, 2015). The Boston field study was ongoing at the time of writing in early 2015, and has tracked the urban politics of bidding since the beginning of the bid process in 2013. It is based on participant observation at meetings held by local governments, the bid corporation and activist groups, and on interviews with these same stakeholders.
3   The following discussions of protest movements is based on archival research drawn from mega-events trade journals (*Around the Rings*, *Inside the Games* and *Sportcal*) and a search of the LexisNexis newspapers database (cross-referencing each bid name with key terms like 'protest', 'activism' and 'referendum').
4   The following metrics are based on a sample of bids to host the Olympics between 2000 and 2020; bid dates 1991 to 2012 and n = 67.

5 Voters in Denver terminated a contract to host the 1976 Winter Olympics, two years after the city had won its bid (Boykoff 2014a: ch. 1).

6 Co-chair of *No Boston Olympics*, at a community meeting in May 2015.

7 Press conference and presentation notes circulated to media for an event titled *Olympic Agenda 2020: 126th IOC Session* (5 February 2014).

8 Interview with former executive in the British Department for Communities and Local Government, November 2013.

9 Interview with head architect at a Qatar-based architecture firm, May 2014.

10 Interview with CEO of a Swiss mega-event consultancy, June 2014.

References

Agamben, G. (2005) *State of Exception*. Chicago: University of Chicago Press.

Ahlfeldt, G. and Maennig, W. (2012) 'Voting on a NIMBY facility: proximity cost of an "iconic" stadium', *Urban Affairs Review*, 48(2): 205–37.

Andranovich, G., Burbank, M. and Heying, C. (2001) 'Olympic cities: lessons learned from mega-event politics', *Journal of Urban Affairs*, 23(2): 113–31.

Atkinson, G., Mourato, S. and Szymanski, S. (2008) 'Are we willing to pay enough to "back the bid"? Valuing the intangible impacts of London's bid to host the 2012 Summer Olympic Games', *Urban Studies*, 45(2): 419–44.

Baade, R. A. and Matheson, V. A. (2004) 'The quest for the cup: assessing the economic impact of the World Cup', *Regional Studies*, 38(4): 343–54.

Baumann, R. and Matheson, V. A. (2013) 'Estimating economic impact using ex post econometric analysis: cautionary tales', in P. Rodríguez, S. Késenne and J. García (eds), *The Econometrics of Sport*. Northampton: Edward Elgar.

Beijing 2000 Olympic Games Bid Committee (1993) *Beijing 2000 Olympic Candidature File*. Lausanne: Olympic Studies Centre Archives.

Black, D. and Peacock, B. (2011) 'Catching up: understanding the pursuit of major games by rising developmental states', *International Journal of the History of Sport*, 28(16): 2271–89.

Boykoff, J. (2014a) *Activism and the Olympics: Dissent at the Games in Vancouver and London*. New Brunswick, NJ: Rutgers University Press.

Boykoff, J. (2014b) *Celebration Capitalism and the Olympic Games*. London and New York: Routledge.

Bramham, D. (2002) 'Bern voters give a resounding "No" to Winter Games bid: it's likely Vancouver voters would say the same thing about our Olympic campaign', *Vancouver Sun*, 24 September, p. A1.

Burbank, M. J., Andranovich, G. and Heying, C. H. (2002) 'Mega-events, urban development, and public policy', *Review of Policy Research*, 19(3): 179–202.

Chalip, L. (2004) 'Beyond impact: a general model for sport event leverage', in B. Richtie and D. Adair (eds), *Sport Tourism: Interrelationships, Impacts and Issues*. Clevedon: Channel View Publications.

Chalip, L. and Costa, C. A. (2005) 'Sport event tourism and the destination brand: towards a general theory', *Sport in Society*, 8(2): 218–37.

CHORE (Center on Housing Rights and Evictions) (2007) *Fair Play for Housing Rights: Mega-events, Olympic Games and Housing Rights – Opportunities for the Olympic Movement and Others*. Geneva: CHORE.

Clarey, C. (2014) 'Bidders for 2022 Winter Games are melting away', *New York Times*, 28 May.

Cochrane, A., Peck, J. and Tickell, A. (1996) 'Manchester plays games: exploring the local politics of globalisation', *Urban Studies*, 33(8): 1319–36.

Colomb, C. (2012) *Staging the New Berlin: Place Marketing and the Politics of Urban Reinvention Post-1989*. London: Routledge.

Cook, I. R. and Ward, K. (2011) 'Trans-urban networks of learning, mega-events and policy tourism', *Urban Studies*, 48(12): 2519–35.

Cottrell, M. P. and Nelson, T. (2011) 'Not just the Games? Power, protest, and politics at the Olympics', *European Journal of International Relations*, 17(4): 729–53.

Davidson, M. and Iveson, K. (2015) 'Recovering the politics of the city: from the "post-political city" to a "method of equality" for critical urban geography', *Progress in Human Geography*, 39(5): 543–59.

Dikeç, M. (2007) *Badlands of the Republic: Space, Politics and Urban Policy*. Malden, MA: Blackwell.

Dwyer, L., Forsyth, P. and Spurr, R. (2005) 'Estimating the impacts of special events on an economy', *Journal of Travel Research*, 43(4): 351–9.

Eick, V. (2010) 'A neoliberal sports event? FIFA from the Estadio Nacional to the fan mile', *City*, 14(3): 278–97.

Flyvbjerg, B. and Stewart, A. (2012) *Olympic Proportions: Cost and Cost Overrun at the Olympics 1960–2012*, Saïd Business School Working Papers. Oxford: Oxford University Press.

Getz, D. (2008) 'Event tourism: definition, evolution, and research', *Tourism Management*, 29(3): 403–28.

Girginov, V. (2010) *The Olympics: A Critical Reader*. Abingdon and New York: Routledge.

Giulianotti, R. and Klauser, F. (2011) 'Introduction: security and surveillance at sport mega events', *Urban Studies*, 48(15): 3157–68.

Gold, J. and Gold, M. (2008) 'Olympic cities: regeneration, city rebranding and changing urban agendas', *Geography Compass*, 2(1): 300–18.

González, S. (2011) 'Bilbao and Barcelona "in motion": how urban regeneration "models" travel and mutate in the global flows of policy tourism', *Urban Studies*, 48(7): 1397–418.

Gratton, C. and Preuss, H. (2008) 'Maximizing Olympic impacts by building up legacies', *International Journal of the History of Sport*, 25(14): 1922–38.

Greene, S. J. (2003) 'Staged cities: mega-events, slum clearance, and global capital', *Yale Human Rights and Development Law Journal*, 6: 161–87.

Hall, C. M. (2006) 'Urban entrepreneurship, corporate interests and sports mega-events: the thin policies of competitiveness within the hard outcomes of neoliberalism', *Sociological Review*, 54: 59–70.

Hiller, H. H. (2000a) 'Mega-events, urban boosterism and growth strategies: an analysis of the objectives and legitimations of the Cape Town 2004 Olympic Bid', *International Journal of Urban and Regional Research*, 24(2): 449–58.

Hiller, H. H. (2000b) 'Toward an urban sociology of megaevents', *Research in Urban Sociology*, 5: 181–205.

Horne, J. and Whannel, G. (2012) *Understanding the Olympics*. Abingdon and New York: Routledge.

Hula, E. (2013) 'Exclusive – Bach, Bokel: "Extremely difficult time" for German Olympic bids', *Around the Rings*, 21 November. Online. Available at http://www.aroundther-ings.com/site/A__45111/Title__Exclusive----Bach-Bokel-Extremely-Difficult-Time-for-German-Olympic-Bids/292/Articles (accessed 22 November 2013).

IOC (International Olympic Committee) (2000) *Report by the IOC Candidature Acceptance Working Group*. Lausanne: IOC. Online. Available at http://www.olympic.org/host-city-elections/documents-reports-studies-publications (accessed 16 August 2012).

IOC (International Olympic Committee) (2014) *Olympic Agenda 2020: Recommendations*. Lausanne: IOC.

Issert, P. and Lunzenfichter, A. (2006) *Malheureux aux jeux: pourquoi, depuis vingt ans, Paris ne parvient pas à obtenir l'organisation des jeux olympiques d'été*. Issy-les-Moulineaux: Prolongations.

Kassens-Noor, E. (2013) 'Transport legacy of the Olympic Games, 1992–2012', *Journal of Urban Affairs*, 35(4): 393–416.

Keil, R. (2009) 'The urban politics of roll-with-it neoliberalization', *City*, 13(2–3): 230–45.

Klauser, F. (2011) 'The exemplification of "Fan Zones": mediating mechanisms in the reproduction of best practices for security and branding at Euro 2008', *Urban Studies*, 48(15): 3203–19.

Klein, N. (2007) *The Shock Doctrine: The Rise of Disaster Capitalism*. New York: Metropolitan Books/Henry Holt.

Lauermann, J. (2014a) 'Competition through inter-urban policymaking: bidding to host megaevents as entrepreneurial networking', *Environment and Planning A*, 46(11): 2638–53.

Lauermann, J. (2014b) *Legacy After the Bid? The Impact of Bidding to Host Olympic Games on Urban Development Planning*. Lausanne: International Olympic Committee and Olympic Studies Centre.

Lauermann, J. (2015) 'Temporary projects, durable outcomes: urban development through failed Olympic bids?', *Urban Studies*. Online preview at DOI: 10.1177/0042098015585460.

Lenskyj, H. (2008) *Olympic Industry Resistance: Challenging Olympic Power and Propaganda*. Albany, NY: State University of New York Press.

Levermore, R. (2011) 'The paucity of, and dilemma in, evaluating corporate social responsibility for development through sport', *Third World Quarterly*, 32(3): 551–69.

LOCOG (London Olympic Organizing Committee) (2012) *A Legacy of Change: London 2012 Post-Games Sustainability Report*. London: LOCOG.

Louw, A. (2012) *Ambush Marketing and the Mega-event Monopoly*. The Hague and Berlin: TMC Asser Press & Springer-Verlag.

MacLeod, G. (2011) 'Urban politics reconsidered: growth machine to post-democratic city?', *Urban Studies*, 48(12): 2629–60.

Maennig, W. and Richter, F. (2012) 'Exports and Olympic Games: is there a signal effect?', *Journal of Sports Economics*, 13(6): 635–41.

Mol, A. P. J. (2010) 'Sustainability as global attractor: the greening of the 2008 Beijing Olympics', *Global Networks*, 10(4): 510–28.

Mouffe, C. (2005) *On the Political*. London and New York: Routledge.

Müller, M. (2011) 'State dirigisme in megaprojects: governing the 2014 Winter Olympics in Sochi', *Environment and Planning A*, 43(9): 2091–108.

Müller, M. (2014) 'The topological multiplicities of power: the limits of governing the Olympics', *Economic Geography*, 90(3): 321–39.

Müller, M. (2015) 'What makes an event a mega-event? Definitions and sizes', *Leisure Studies*, 34(6): 627–42.

O'Brien, D. (2006) 'Event business leveraging the Sydney 2000 Olympic Games', *Annals of Tourism Research*, 33(1): 240–61.

Oliver, R. (2014) 'The legacies of losing: rethinking the "failure" of Toronto's Olympic Games bids', *Sport in Society*, 17(2): 204–17.

ONS (Office of National Statistics) (2012) *London 2012 Olympic and Paralympic Games Attracted 680,000 Overseas Visitors*, 15 November. Press release. London: ONS.

Payne, M. (2006) *Olympic Turnaround: How the Olympic Games Stepped Back from the Brink of Extinction to Become the World's Best Known Brand*. Westport, CT: Praeger.

Pillay, U. and Bass, O. (2008) 'Mega-events as a response to poverty reduction: the 2010 FIFA World Cup and its urban development implications', *Urban Forum*, 19(3): 329–46.

Pillay, U., Tomlinson, R. and Bass, O. (2009) *Development and Dreams: The Urban Legacy of the 2010 Football World Cup*. Cape Town: HSRC Press.

Porter, P. K. and Chin, D. M. (2012) 'Economic impact of sport events', in W. Maennig and Zimbalist, A. (eds), *International Handbook on the Economics of Mega Sporting Events*. Cheltenham: Edward Elgar.

Preuss, H. (2004) *The Economics of Staging the Olympics: A Comparison of the Games, 1972–2008*. Cheltenham: Edward Elgar.

Raco, M. (2014) 'Delivering flagship projects in an era of regulatory capitalism: state-led privatization and the London Olympics 2012', *International Journal of Urban and Regional Research*, 38(1): 176–97.

Rancière, J. (1999) *Disagreement: Politics and Philosophy*. Minneapolis, MN: University of Minnesota Press.

Rancière, J. (2006) *Hatred of Democracy*. London and New York: Verso.

Roche, M. (2000) *Mega-events and Modernity: Olympics and Expos in the Growth of Global Culture*. London and New York: Routledge.

Rose, A. and Spiegel, M. (2010) 'The Olympic trade effect', *Finance and Development*, March, pp. 12–13.

Smith, A. (2012) *Events and Urban Regeneration: The Strategic Use of Events to Revitalise Cities*. London and New York: Routledge.

Surborg, B., VanWynsberghe, R. and Wyly, E. (2008) 'Mapping the Olympic growth machine', *City*, 12(3): 341–55.

Swyngedouw, E. (2009) 'The antinomies of the postpolitical city: in search of a democratic politics of environmental production', *International Journal of Urban and Regional Research*, 33(3): 601–20.

van Wynsberghe, R., Surborg, B. and Wyly, E. (2013) 'When the Games come to town: neoliberalism, mega-events and social inclusion in the Vancouver 2010 Winter Olympic Games', *International Journal of Urban and Regional Research*, 37(6): 2074–93.

Whitson, D. and Horne, J. (2006) 'The glocal politics of sports mega-events: underestimated costs and overestimated benefits? Comparing the outcomes of sports mega-events in Canada and Japan', *Sociological Review*, 54: 71–89.

WNEU Polling Institute (2015) *Western New England University Polling Institute Finds Voters Lean Against Boston Olympic Bid. 17 April Polling Report*. Springfield, MA: Western New England University.

Zhang, L. and Zhao, S. X. (2009) 'City branding and the Olympic effect: a case study of Beijing', *Cities*, 26(5): 245–54.

Zimbalist, A. (2015) *Circus Maximus: The Economic Gamble behind Hosting the Olympics and World Cup*. Washington, DC: Brookings Institution Press.

12 Attracting international tourism through mega-events and the birth of a conflict culture in Belo Horizonte

Lucia Capanema Alvares, Altamiro S. Mol Bessa, Thiago Pinto Barbosa and Karina Machado de Castro Simão

Tourism has become an increasingly key sector of the Brazilian economy over the past decade, although in 2012 the country only occupied the 38th place on the global scale in terms of international tourist receipts (i.e. tourist international expenditure in the country), and tourism only accounted for 0.3 per cent of the country's GDP (WTO 2014). The state of Minas Gerais occupies the ninth position among the 14 Brazilian states with international airports in terms of international tourist arrivals in Brazil, despite official efforts to boost this activity (Ministério de Turismo 2014). In Belo Horizonte (BH), the capital of Minas Gerais, the process of urban transformation for the creation of an international tourism destination began in the late 1980s and has become the main goal of the metropolitan administration, supported by state and national policies. The attraction of mega-events has been a key element of that strategy, but until 2012 the city only managed to attract 'second-class' events. With the FIFA[1] Confederations Cup 2013 and World Cup 2014, and the Olympic Games Rio 2016 (which will use training centres in many Brazilian cities), the BH city government found a new impetus for its strategic initiatives, and a number of large-scale construction projects have been built allegedly to host activities as part of those mega-events. FIFA events require host cities to fulfil a long list of demands and recommendations, which comprise technical issues related to the hosting stadia and their surroundings, as well as other infrastructural and budgetary issues. In all 12 World Cup host cities, urban governments have used the construction works allegedly justified by mega-events to evict thousands of citizens and boost the real-estate market.[2] Due to their social, economic, cultural and urban impacts, such large-scale projects have thus triggered the resistance of Brazilian social movements involved with urban issues, which have organised themselves, in BH, into the Popular Committee of the people affected by the FIFA World Cup (COPAC-BH, *Comitê Popular dos Atingidos pela Copa – Belo Horizonte*). This committee joined the National Coordination of the World Cup Popular Committees (ANCOP, *Articulação Nacional dos Comitês Populares da Copa*) and was one of the major players in the organization of the large-scale demonstrations of 2013 in the city (referred to later on in this chapter). Urban social movements have received the help of a number of academics, who have been studying the impacts of large-scale projects and tourism-led urban development on the socio-economic, environmental and cultural urban realms.[3]

This chapter briefly introduces the role of urban tourism and mega-events as a (contested) strategy of urban development in Brazilian cities and focuses on the large-scale development projects which have been launched in BH in the run-up to the 2014 FIFA World Cup. These projects, and the impacts and conflicts they have generated, are analysed in detail, as well as the composition of the social movements and coalitions which have risen against them. While the megacities of Rio and São Paulo are already well known in the tourism trade, mid-size metropolises are struggling to be recognized as tourism destinations. The case study of BH exemplifies the strategy adopted in mid-size metropolitan areas in Brazil to attract more visitors.[4]

Urban tourism and mega-events as a (contested) strategy of urban development in Brazilian cities

Urban governance in Brazilian metropolises has gone through paradigmatic changes in the last three decades: as Harvey (1989) first observed in advanced capitalist countries, the managerial approach of the 1960s was replaced in the 1970s and 1980s by an entrepreneurial stance in a post-Fordist and neoliberal context. The economic and political deterioration of nation states in a global world, together with the transnationalization of monetary flows, encouraged local governments to try and attract private investments and international capital without resorting to national channels (Harvey 1989; Maricato 2003; Jessop 1997; Mascarenhas 2014). In Brazil, the Federal Constitution of 1988 decentralized planning competences and transferred more responsibilities and taxes to municipalities, setting the legal ground for the adoption of an entrepreneurial governance model at the local scale. With still fragile structures and finances, local governments felt urged to attract investments through city marketing strategies and through selling their city's image (Câmara 2006). Due to the earlier centralized system, Brazilian cities turned to urban entrepreneurialism with considerable delay in comparison to First World local administrations, which made the process more aggressive. As such, they adopted – following their Northern counterparts – a set of urban intervention strategies which have included: (1) the insertion of architectural icons; (2) the requalification of urban structure and infrastructure; (3) interventions in the built heritage; (4) urban marketing; (5) the construction of strategic partnerships; (6) the formulation of legal, *ad hoc* instruments; and (7) the attraction of mega-events (Bessa and Capanema Alvares 2014). Vainer (2009) notes that the notion of strategic planning has become central in Brazilian urban governance to pursue the creation of a 'modern city' image, in which elements associated with the notion of backwardness should not be on display. This is especially the case in cities where poverty is distinctly visible in the urban landscape, as is the case in most Brazilian cities.

All 12 host cities across Brazil saw the FIFA mega-event as an excuse to dust off plans for mega-projects: using the World Cup's global dimension and 'urgent' character as a legitimizing argument, local governments sought to build political and public 'consensus' around new projects. As Mascarenhas (2014) observes, the mega-event approach to local governance in Brazil must be understood within the current national neo-developmentalist model, firmly tied to the political clout of construction companies and real-estate developers, who are highly interested in structural and infrastructural works, the construction of architectural icons and the refurbishment of historical neighbourhoods through public-private partnerships (Bessa and Capanema Alvares 2014). The role of the federal government in this process is key. Besides discursively backing the mega-event industry, Brazil's Federal government spared no efforts to support the FIFA mega-event financially, launching the so-called World Cup Growth Acceleration Program (PAC – Copa) to support urban mobility projects in the host cities. In the 12 cities alone, a total of US\$70.33 billion were invested in infrastructure between 2011 and 2013 (PAC 2014). All in all, it was the most expensive and, to FIFA's pockets, most lucrative soccer cup in history (Associated Press 2014).

The case of Rio de Janeiro is emblematic and has been studied by several scholars (e.g. Capanema Alvares *et al.* 2008; Vainer 2009; Silvestre and De Oliveira 2012; Sánchez and Broudehoux 2013; Mascarenhas 2014). Besides hosting the 2013 FIFA Confederations Cup, the 2014 FIFA World Cup and the 2016 Summer Olympic Games, the city has also staged a number of other international events in recent years, such as the 2007 Pan American Games, the 2011 Military Games and the 2013 World Youth Day. Legitimized by the alleged necessities associated with the hosting of the FIFA World Cup and Olympic Games 2016, Rio's urban structure has been totally renewed and works executed in the whole city, from the port area to the South and West Zones in particular, where there are more positive externalities to capture and sell on the real-estate market. A number of architectural icons have been under construction; strategic partnerships have been established and new city marketing strategies have been adopted (Capanema Alvares *et al.* 2008). The government of Rio overtly embraced the Barcelona example, hiring Catalan consultants for the numerous mega-projects in preparation for the mega-events and other related interventions and measures (Ferreira 2010).

The process of trying to displace or erase the features which do not fit in a marketable image of Brazilian cities – such as favelas, the homeless and prostitutes (Harvey 2014; Vainer 2009) – has generated a lot of tensions, conflicts and dissent. Mega-event related investments caused a number of negative social and structural impacts, as the detailed dossier on 'Mega-events and Human Rights Violations in Brazil' (ANCOP 2012) shows. The strategies employed by the authorities generally entailed persecution and harsh constraints against street sellers and forced evictions leading to gentrification. The latter especially impacted informal settlements and frequently disrespected both Brazilian laws and international treaties concerning human rights, as many families were brutally evicted without prior notice or adequate compensation. Approximately 170,000 families in the host cities were undergoing eviction processes by 2012 due to the FIFA

World Cup and the Olympics (ANCOP 2012). One of the strategies adopted by city governments backed by state and national forces in Brazil has been the fragmentation of steps towards eviction into different phases: at first, governments spread misinformation and rumours, which are followed by threats and, in a third phase, by brutal evictions. Most construction projects implying evictions are unknown by the general public until governments start the third phase of action, meaning that projects can only be denounced on the basis of rumours or threats.

Hence, the urban development agenda in Brazil has become widely challenged. From 2010 onwards, different groups which identified themselves as affected by the FIFA mega-event and its construction projects raised their voices against such an agenda. In each of the host cities, affected groups organized themselves into Popular Committees of the FIFA World Cup, all 12 together forming the ANCOP. The Popular Committee of BH was composed of a diverse social spectrum, including favela dwellers, evicted people, the prostitutes' association, street dwellers' organizations, NGOs, human rights activists, students, scholars and an association of street sellers who were forbidden to continue their traditional food market in the surroundings of the soccer stadium. Besides networking and organizing conferences and protests, one of the main strategies of these committees was to denounce the local government's arbitrary actions to local and general attorneys, to the media and to the broad public. This work might have been decisive for raising public awareness about the issue, which proved to have an explosive potential.

In 2013, general public discontent over mega-event preparations became loud and clear. Over two weeks during the FIFA Confederations Cup in Brazil, the country was shaken by the largest demonstrations in twenty years. Triggered by a brutally repressed protest against the rise in public transport fares in São Paulo and by the Confederation Cup context, hundreds of thousands of citizens took to the streets across the whole country, achieving more than a million protesters on the main demonstration day. The discontent with the ever-growing expenditures on mega-event related projects was one of the main slogans, with recurrent claims such as 'FIFA-standard public schools and hospitals'. Signs asking 'How many schools are worth a stadium?', 'World Cup for whom?' or referring to evictions were also displayed at the protests, which often occupied the surroundings of the stadia in the host cities. Most protests were brutally repressed by military police forces.

Belo Horizonte, tourism and the FIFA World Cup 2014

The city of BH was founded in 1897 to be the capital of the State of Minas Gerais and designed to provide shelter for 200,000 inhabitants mostly involved in state administrative activities. It began its economic life as a service provider but soon acquired a function as a distribution centre. Its social life was characterized by forms of social exclusion since its foundation, when the former rural village dwellers were evicted from the city's construction site. In the 1950s the city went through an industrialization process attracting migrants from other parts of Minas

Gerais and neighbouring states. Reflecting the national and international economic crises, BH faced two economic problems in the 1970s: stagnation and relocation of activities from the central area to its fringes and to nearby cities (PBH 1996).

From the 1990s until the beginning of the 2000s the city's GDP decreased and successive local administrations began to see the business and event tourism industry as a panacea for economic renewal. The administrations of Mayors Pimentel (2001–8) and Lacerda (2009 onwards) – with substantial support from the administration of the state of Mina Gerais (under the government of Aécio-Anastasia (2003–14)) – have adopted tourism development strategies including city marketing, urban infrastructure renewal, heritage refurbishment, the insertion of iconic architecture (e.g. Latin America's highest skyscraper project), the formulation of legal *ad hoc* instruments (e.g. Law 9952/10 that 'institutes the Development Urban Project for Culture, Health, Tourism and Business Infrastructure in BH in order to meet the FIFA World Cup 2014 demands'),[5] the creation of a municipal secretariat for international relations in 2005 and, last but not least, the attraction of mega-events. Such strategies were clearly promoted through official broadcasts on national TV and other media. However, up to 2010 the city only managed to attract 'second-class' events. This explains why the possibility of raising land values and making immense profits through the attraction of the FIFA World Cup 2014 and of some training sites for the Olympic Games 2016 has been frantically pursued by the city government, to the detriment of other policies, such as the delivery of quality services to all citizens, infrastructure improvements or land tenure grants to favela squatters.

The fulfilment of FIFA's demands and recommendations comprised technical issues related to the hosting stadia and their surroundings (e.g. easy road access and public transportation to nearby hotels and airports), telecommunications and budgetary issues. The BH municipality, the state and the federal governments, the Brazilian Soccer Federation and the state soccer federations had to commit to all the infrastructural expenses. A new institutional design was put forth with the creation of a new super-secretariat at the federal level, aggregating recently created secretariats and committees organized at all three governmental levels with private sector partners. Finally, the 'Belo Horizonte Strategic Plan for 2030' approved in 2010 is in tune with the mega-event hosting role and proposes various 'development strategies' for the next twenty years. It envisions turning BH into an internationally projected metropolis, economically attractive, enhanced by a 'dynamic and less bureaucratic business environment' promoting, attracting and maintaining private investments. It foresees the need to transform the city into a 'clean and organized' one (PBH 2010: 13–23). In order to meet these goals the document highlights that 'the materialization of the Development Strategy will require [. . .] strong consensus and social cohesion concerning the desired future' (ibid.: 26).

But the development agenda of the city government has not been unchallenged. In particular, many social movements and residents have identified themselves as affected by the FIFA World Cup and its construction projects, organizing themselves into the COPAC-BH and integrating ANCOP. In June 2011, different groups making up COPAC-BH protested in downtown BH against the social impacts caused by the preparations for the mega-event, asking for an end to forced evictions (Figure 12.1) and for the construction of housing for the poor instead of hotels, in what came to be known as the 'Freedom March'. The city government's arbitrary actions have been also denounced on the COPAC-BH Internet blog. A number of highly recognized social movements and organizations such as COPAC-BH, *Polos Cidadania* at the Universidade Federal de Mina Gerais (UFMG) (a free legal advice service offered by the university), *Movimento de Luta pela Moradia* (a housing struggle movement), and *Brigadas Populares* (Popular Brigades), have accused the city government of misguided 'poverty cleansing' in different parts of the city in relation to the World Cup and its induced real-estate speculation (Correio do Brasil 2011). According to members of COPAC-BH, numerous poor citizens have reported threatening situations related to urban development and real-estate processes enacted by the city government and driven by its city marketing agenda which demand, as previously

Figure 12.1 'The [FIFA World] Cup for whom?' Protest mural in Belo Horizonte referring to 170,000 Brazilians threatened with eviction as a result of the construction works for the FIFA World Cup as well as to underfunded schools and hospitals, June 2013.

Source: COPAC-BH (*Comitê dos Atingidos pela Copa – Belo Horizonte*), https://www.facebook.com/copacbh/photos/pb.150997365089667.-2207520000.1450633383./150999551756115/?type=3&theater.

mentioned, a 'clean and organized' city (PBH 2010: 23). For example, in a COPAC-BH meeting and at the public hearing on the Word Cup's social impacts, representatives of the National Centre for the Defence of the Human Rights of the Homeless (*Centro Nacional de Defesa dos Direitos Humanos da População em Situação de Rua*), of the Recyclable Materials' Collectors Association (*Associação dos Catadores de Materiais Recicláveis*) and street dwellers complained about being violently evicted from downtown areas by policemen and inspectors from the city government.

Protests and conflicts around the reshaping of the city

In this section, we discuss the conflicts surrounding the projects officially presented by the BH city government as part of the 2014 FIFA World Cup, as well as a number of related projects on which one can only get contradictory and imprecise official information. In so doing we focus on public infrastructure and facilities, transportation and mobility projects, sports facilities, urban design projects, and commercial and tourism-related projects. The main official projects related to mega-events in BH are the renewal of Magalhães Pinto Stadium (Mineirão) (Figure 12.2, number 1); the International Airport expansion (number 2);

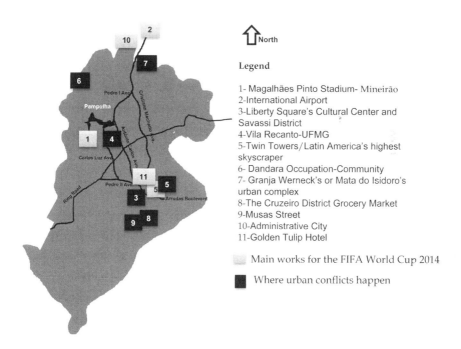

Figure 12.2 Large-scale projects backed by the city government and related conflicts in Belo Horizonte.

Source: Authors' mapping.

the Liberty Square's Cultural Centre and revitalization of the Savassi District (number 3); two Bus Rapid Transit (BRT) paths and one transit corridor; the new roads 210 and 710; the revitalization/construction of the Arrudas-Tereza Cristina Boulevard; the construction of 'Latin America's tallest skyscraper' (number 5); and the construction of the Golden Tulip Hotel (number 11).

Transportation and mobility projects and related conflicts

Most structural works in BH were related to roads and transportation, of which the federal Growth Acceleration Programme (PAC) World Cup Urban Mobility, totalling U$0.5 billion, financed a number. The first finished project was the intersection viaduct connecting Antonio Carlos and Abrahão Caram avenues – the two main roads giving access to the football stadium. The viaduct area previously housed 65 families in a settlement called Vila Recanto UFMG, built in the mid-1990s, when its dwellers occupied an abandoned plot in front of the university (Figure 12.2, number 4). Since 1999 the dwellers of the Vila had been facing eviction threats through a long judicial and political struggle. Finally, in 2009 a state court decision – based on Google satellite photos and, as the judge put it, with the goal of 're-establishing social peace' – ruled that the plot should be restored to its former owner, ignoring the dwellers' rights under Brazilian laws.[6] After expropriating that piece of land for public utility, the city government of BH became its owner and pursued the eviction of the 65 families. Tense negotiations between the city government and the families took place for many months; dwellers complained about the government's lack of dialogue and transparency and were especially dissatisfied with the amount offered as compensation for the eviction (which was based on the value of construction materials alone). The evicted families moved to the Metropolitan Region's fringes, where they could bear the costs of new housing but barely had access to basic public services (Barbosa 2011). During the 2013 protests, the dealership store of Hyundai (one of the FIFA World Cup's sponsors) – which now occupies part of that plot – was a target for break-ins and bomb explosions.

Other urban mobility projects financed by the World Cup PAC have caused and might still cause severe impacts: the BRT system to be installed in Dom Pedro II Avenue entails the eviction of 15 families, according to the Federal Public Prosecutor, while the Cristiano Machado Avenue BRT entails the displacement of an unknown number of residents near the São Gabriel neighbourhood, in a typical process of road expansion in BH. Between March and August 2014, the BRT lines and stations started operating; since then, protests questioned the system's security and quality. The new MG 210 road, now in operation, meant the forced eviction of 200 people without previous notice or due compensation (Cruz 2013), whereas the new MG 710 road, which was taken out of the FIFA obligations' matrix in 2013, is projected to start operations by the end of 2016 following an eviction process affecting 413 families (Alves 2014). The expansion of Pedro I Avenue and the implementation of the BRT Pedro I/Antonio Carlos forcibly evicted 86 families in 2013 and another 250 houses were in the process of being evicted in early 2015 (ABONG 2014). Works included the construction of a viaduct that collapsed shortly after its opening, killing two people and hurting 23 during the FIFA World Cup. In order to reconstruct the viaduct, 186 families were removed in August 2014, leaving the evicted to demonstrate in the nearby streets. According to a local newspaper (Malta 2011), all those eviction processes are characterized by dwellers' complaints about the lack of information concerning the expropriations and the low amounts offered as compensation.

Another transportation project that has gained new momentum since BH was confirmed as a FIFA World Cup host city was the expansion of the city's outer ring road. In 2010 a federal transportation agency notified dwellers around the ring to leave their houses within 15 days; no housing alternative was offered. At least 2,600 families living in the two main communities along the road would be affected, which prompted the Public Prosecutor to look into the case. A federal court stopped the public bidding process, pointing out a number of financial irregularities in the project, such as a €110 million overpricing. According to press reports (G1 2001), the project was reshaped and the bid procedure was again authorized at the end of 2011. By 2014, there was no agreement over resource transfers between the federal and the state governments, and as of 2015 works had not started. Meanwhile residents continued to protest against expropriations in the affected favelas.

Sports facilities and related conflicts

Interventions in the Mineirão stadium (Figure 12.2, number 1) began as early as February 2010 to deliver the final product in February 2013. At COPAC-BH meetings and in a public hearing promoted by the Federal Public Prosecutor in 2011, members of the Mineirão Street Vendors Association presented a list of 150 families, who depended on their daily work in the stadium vicinity to make a living and had been evicted, facing severe financial difficulties. Despite their protests such prohibitions prevailed during the World Cup, when all products commercialized in the stadium surroundings had to be FIFA-licensed (ABAEM 2013). On the occasion of the public bid for inspection of the contractors involved in the works, the National Association of Architectural and Consulting Engineering Companies brought legal proceedings against the bidding process, arguing that it favoured certain groups. Despite all evidence, construction works went on.

In the same public hearing, representatives of the Dandara Occupation Community (Figure 12.2, number 6) revealed rumours of a training centre and hotel project in the plot they had occupied since 2009 – a 315,000 square metre vacant plot home to 1,000 families who have been struggling for their housing rights ever since. In September 2010 dwellers of Dandara, Torres Gêmeas and other communities organized a protest camp in front of the City Hall. They wanted to discuss evictions and housing conditions, demanding a stake at the negotiation table with local, state and national government representatives. When setting up the camp, protesters were violently threatened by the police, who injured some of the participants with pepper spray (Passa Palavra 2010).

Large real estate and urban design improvement projects and related conflicts

This section specifically focuses on projects aiming at enhancing the city's ability to attract business and tourism through landscaping, street redesigning, and public realm improvements in general, as well as at opening new real-estate fronts through rehabilitation projects in the city's central areas designed to make BH more attractive nationally and internationally. In order to pursue these purposes and to meet FIFA's urgent demands, the BH City Council diligently approved Bill 1692 in October 2011. Elaborated as 'exceptional legislation' by the executive, the 'Development Urban Project for Culture, Health, Tourism and Business Infrastructure in Belo Horizonte' relaxed urban planning parameters and urban-environmental legislation, thereby facilitating urban development.

The biggest real-estate development project planned in the 'World Cup city' era was the Granja Werneck – or Mata do Isidoro – urban complex (Figure 12.2, number 7). Part of the projected buildings were supposed to be ready by 2013 and were to be called the 'World Cup Village', as they would initially serve as accommodation for delegations, journalists and tourists during the 2014 mega-event (Franco 2011). However, not a single athlete or journalist were hosted and the village was never built. The project was later modified and geared towards the construction of luxury housing and office buildings. According to municipal law 3106/1993, this is an environmentally protected area, therefore subject to a number of construction and land use constraints, and is publicly owned. It has, however, been leased out for a number of years,[7] raising another set of legal issues over its ownership. Nevertheless, as published in a regional newspaper:

> Belo Horizonte's last green frontier is about to lose a bit of its colour and gain tons of concrete. Cut by the Isidoro river, part of the Velhas river basin, the immense forest in the capital's North Region might soon receive 300,000 inhabitants. [. . .] The Municipality aims to transform the territory – known as Isidoro and the last big non-occupied plot in the city – into the city's newest district, opening the doors for the construction of 72,000 apartments, shopping malls, supermarkets, schools, health centres, among other facilities. The proposal alters urbanization patterns in the 10 km² surface of the area.
>
> (Werneck and Ayer 2010)

The land use changes approved by municipal law 1692/2011 also go against the federal Forestry Code. In a public hearing on the project organized by the City's Environmental Commission in April 2010, many architects expressed their concern about the project, pointing out that although developers had been asked to spend 370 million for infrastructure provision as a condition for being granted the development rights, 90 per cent of this sum would go back to them in tax breaks. During the preliminary environmental licensing process, another public hearing on the project was held and the residents of surrounding neighbourhoods expressed their concern about its unlawful proposals and impacts. In October

2011, 24 houses of the Zilah Sposito's occupied settlement located in the area were demolished and the families evicted without any court order. The Catholic Land Commission denounced the case of Ricardo, his wife and their four-year-old asthmatic son. As the family resisted leaving their house during the night, police troops fired pepper spray into the house through every slit and below the door, asphyxiating the child. The mother then passed the child over to a municipal inspector outside the house, who ordered the policemen to 'fire pepper spray at the child so the parents will come out'. The policemen did so and the parents gave up. Witnesses reported that due to the pepper spray, inspectors could not go inside the house to get the family's belongings out so they broke everything down (CEDEFES 2011).

Also located in the Isidoro area, the Mangueiras *quilombola*[8] community has been threatened by eviction as well. The process of recognition by federal institutions of that community's heritage is in its final stage, which will grant it special land rights to the plot (GESTA 2013). In August 2014 the state attempted to recover possession of the Isidoro area with 2,000 police officers trying to forcibly evict 8,000 residents in the Rosa Leão, Esperança and Vitória settlements, without respect for any of their rights. This caused demonstrations in the central areas of the city (ANPG 2014) and the assassination of a local leader (GESTA 2015). In June 2015 residents organized a protest against the evictions, but police forces repressed the movement. Shortly afterwards, the state and community representatives reached an agreement postponing evictions from the plot (Estado de Minas 2015a).

Tensions over evictions also arose in the central area of BH, where other large-scale development projects were planned. The Campo do Pitangui community has been struggling for over fifty years to achieve legitimization in the central area of BH. Located close to a soccer field, its dwellers were notified that the local government was interested in locating a World Cup-related project in the field's vicinity. In the same public hearing, a representative of the Minas Gerais Prostitutes Association (*Associação das Prostitutas de Minas Gerais*) protested against the insecure labour conditions experienced by prostitutes in the city's traditional red light zone, caused by rumours of revitalization projects in the area. As Dip pointed out:

> With the beginning of the preparations for the World Cup in the city women fear for their work place; they fear repression and losing their jobs. The downtown area already shows what social movements call 'hygienization' (or 'cleansing') of its poor. Big real estate projects have caused poor communities, street vendors and sex workers to be removed. 'We are all interested in revitalization. Working in a better, safer place would be nice. The problem is that nobody knows nothing.'
>
> (Dip 2012: 1)

Commercial and tourism-related projects and related conflicts

Crowning its efforts to support real-estate projects, the city government managed to attract an iconic five-star Golden Tulip Hotel project signed by architects Farkäsvolgyi & Armentano in the traditional red-light district, which caused land speculation in the area, threatening small shops and hotels, street vendors and prostitutes. Back in 1995, the squatters' community 'Twin Towers' (Figure 12.2, number 5) took over two unfinished and vacant apartment buildings (Figure 12.3, left) on the now refurbished Arrudas Boulevard, only eight minutes away from the Golden Tulip project. After a fire broke out in one of the apartments in 2011, police troops evacuated the whole building and blocked its entrance for months. Over 300 dwellers were banned from accessing their homes or personal belongings and were precariously lodged in tents in front of the building or at friends' and relatives'. After a local court decision, the twin buildings were evacuated and they were both auctioned to the private sector (O Tempo 2013). In June 2012, the remaining 171 families occupying the Twin Towers were removed under the promise of being relocated. The business plan is to transform the buildings into a hotel and an office building, forming a commercial complex which includes Latin America's 'tallest skyscraper' with an estimated cost of U$970 million (Ferreira 2012). As of 2015, construction plans are still pending on official approval and earlier residents continue to demonstrate against them.

The Cruzeiro District Grocery Market (Figure 12.2, number 8) was another target for the city government. The project included the demolition of the forty-year-old market and the eviction of its vendors to make way for a shopping mall, two hotels and a parking lot. Most local residents protested against the project not only because of its demolition, but also because of its likely environmental and traffic impacts, as was expressed at the public hearing on the World Cup social impacts. Market vendors, neighbours and the local branch of the Institute of Brazilian Architects organized a project competition for the market's revitalization, but the mayor refused to attend the September 2011 ceremony in which results were presented to the city. The project for the market demolition was not implemented since there was not enough private interest. In September 2014, the city government opened a bidding process for the revitalization of the market, stating that the building's characteristics must be preserved. The market's concession will be auctioned in 2016 (Estado de Minas 2015b).

After approving the privatization of part of Musas Street in the Santa Lúcia neighbourhood (Figure 12.2, number 9), the city government put the street up for sale in a public bid in 2012, despite strong opposition by surrounding residents and users. According to members of the 'Save the Musas Street' movement (http://www.salveamusas.com.br/), the privatization of the street paves the way for a thirty-storey high luxury hotel with 500 apartments to be constructed on two plots on both sides of the street. Local news corroborated this, reporting that a consortium of local developers would build a hotel to be leased to the US Hyatt hotel chain (Flávia Gussen 2013). In a public hearing on this issue in August 2011, dwellers strongly protested, not accepting any compensation such as the installation of security cameras in the neighbourhood's streets, as proposed by one city councillor. Dissatisfied with the lack of clarifications, the neighbourhood association reported the case to the State Court.

Figure 12.3 Worlds apart: the formerly squatted 'Twin Towers' and the neighbouring Boulevard Shopping Mall.

Source: Authors.

On Liberty Square (Figure 12.2, number 3) – until recently the state's historical administrative centre (Figure 12.2, number 10) – the heritage listed buildings were conceded to large conglomerates such as TIM, Banco do Brasil and the mining companies Vale and MMX. They have transformed the historical buildings into museums or leisure spaces for short-term event rental, transforming the square into what is now called 'Liberty Square Cultural Centre' and modifying the buildings' heritage characteristics. This process symbolizes the privatization policies adopted by the city government and the state of Minas Gerais regarding public buildings and heritage. On the same square, the state government vacated a Social Services government building, leasing it to the luxury Fasano hotel chain, through a suspicious public bid process which favoured one single bidder with personal connections to the then governor. The hotel chain was offered a lease for less than R$15,000 per month to use the high-value building for 35 years. In the 'Freedom March' protests of June 2011, COPAC-BH, Brigadas Populares and other social movements occupied the building, denouncing the illegality of the bid and demanding more affordable housing projects instead of hotels for the World Cup (Brigadas Populares 2011). Subsequently, the State Court declared the bidding process null.

The previous examples have shown how the FIFA World Cup momentum was used by the city government to legitimize many large-scale interventions in BH, at great social costs for existing communities. This has generated social mobilizations and protests which eventually began to coalesce into a broader movement.

Challenging the tourism- and event-led redevelopment of the city: citizen movements come together

As houses on occupied land and public spaces gave way to public works and private developments, precluding people from their housing, mobility and work rights, protests got more and more organized throughout the years 2012 and 2013. Favela associations created in the pre-dictatorship era in the 1950s, lower- and middle-class neighbourhood associations from the 1970s and 1980s, anti-hegemonic civil movements from the 1990s and 2000s and more recent movements like COPAC-BH all united against the tourism- and event-led redevelopment strategy of the city government. In June 2013 – when the FIFA Confederation Cup began – the world watched, in surprise, Brazil's population rising in upheaval against the federal, state and local governments and their policies contradicting the majority's will. More than 20 million people were out in the streets all over the country. In BH, more than one million protested in the streets, clearly positioning themselves against mega-events and related projects. The leading organization involved in the city's demonstrations was COPAC-BH, which called most events.

Although the alliance of social movements and its protests went unnoticed to most observers, the prairie was dry and ready to catch fire, in Mao Tse-tung's words. Based on data gathered by the Observatory of Urban Conflicts for one year, taking June 2013 as the midpoint, it is possible to see two fairly different patterns in the evolution of protests: between the months of December 2012 and

May 2013, there was a steady growth in the number of protest events, totalling 69. Events were mostly organized by residents' associations (15) and their focus was mostly on health and security (16 each) and multiple issues (11); only 14 per cent of the demonstrations involved closing streets or occupying plots and buildings. As time went by, protests concerning the entire city grew significantly (at the 99 per cent level of certainty) while groups of professionals such as professors, public sector workers, bus drivers and construction workers together with social movements in general took the organization of events into their own hands.

From June to November 2013, there were 197 protest events, with a loss of momentum in November. They were mostly organized by groups of professionals (63) and by social movements and residents (31 each); their issues were mostly multiple. As time went by, protests concerning the entire city shrank significantly (at the 99 per cent level of certainty) and included a number of demonstrations in Pampulha and Regional Norte (foci of construction works related to mega-events). While 'multiple-issue' demonstrations lost momentum, closing streets or occupying plots and buildings, together with going on strike, became routine strategies (used in 47 per cent of the protests), demonstrating a more hard-hitting and planned activity pattern. Protests were targeted at federal, state and local governments, particularly in July, when the Confederations Cup was still going on. The most remarkable difference between the two periods is the correlation among their descriptive variables: from June 2013 on, 'timeline', 'organizers', 'location', 'raised issues' and 'targeted institutions' were all somehow interconnected (correlations found at the 99 per cent level), implying better networked and more robust protests.

Mainly led by the COPAC-BH initiatives, the 2013 protests in BH strengthened popular struggles against the hegemonic interests imposed by the different tiers of government through urban development and renewal policies aimed at selling the city in the global tourism, event, business and leisure markets. The protests offered a vivid example of the social potential of conflicts when they receive support from a number of sectors and movements.

Conclusion

Paradigmatic changes in urban governance in Brazil have meant that city governments, including mid-sized metropolitan areas, have entered a fierce race among cities to become international business centres and tourism destinations. Local governments have tried to attract investments at all costs and have planned a set of urban intervention strategies to that end, including hosting mega-events. This chapter showed how the strategies adopted in BH sought to position the city in the tourism map through the attraction of the 2014 FIFA World Cup. The construction works and projects bearing the World Cup stamp were mostly directed towards the city's Northern rim, opening new accesses and facilities in a previously undeveloped and mostly natural region, the Mata do Isidoro, where a real-estate mega-project will forcibly remove at least 8,000 poor families to make way for 72,000 luxury apartments. As a complement to the scheme, centrally located plots (some of which with historical buildings) have also been put on the real-estate market for the development of hotels and shopping facilities but have received relatively little private interest to date. All those strategies used public funds in order to revalorize targeted areas and extract surplus value through public-private partnerships to the detriment of the local population.

Evidence of public administration mismanagement can be identified not only in new pieces of exceptional legislation that contradict municipal and federal laws in order to 'relax' urban planning and environmental criteria, but also through exclusionary practices evident in thousands of forced eviction processes and cleansing of the poor in downtown public spaces. Protests, public hearings or compulsory environmental and neighbourhood impact assessments have not proven effective against technocratic arguments and local political arrangements. The 'urgency' discourse constructed on the basis of the FIFA's 'needs' list served as a justification for the abuses, while more and more citizens engaged in the struggles. Favela associations, lower- and middle-class neighbourhood associations, anti-hegemonic civil movements and more recent movements mutually reinforced themselves in a 'dialogical construction of diversity', to use Paulo Freire's terminology (Freire 2002), especially among those movements related to housing. Together and under the COPAC-BH leadership, they massively contributed to the 2013 protests and were able to expose the insidious governmental behaviour while strengthening their planning, organizing and networking capabilities. Demonstrations in 2014 were fewer than in 2013, however, which can be explained by the heavy police repression that took place in the aftermath (especially on World Cup match days) and by the frequent attempts to criminalize social movements through the adoption of *ad hoc* prohibitions and laws (e.g. the prohibition of the use of masks by protesters so that they can be identified and subjected to a police record). As of 2015, COPAC-BH still exercises a strong leadership in demonstrations against increases in bus fares and the eviction of occupied urban land such as Isidoro. It has also questioned the World Cup's legacy and contractors' overbilling practices demonstrated in official accounts.

Regardless of the highly exclusive character of the FIFA event, BH fared reasonably well during the event itself: six out of eight urban mobility projects were completed on time, despite delays ranging from six months to two and a half years. According to official numbers, 355,000 tourists visited the city, generating direct revenues of about R$451 million (Portal da Copa 2014). Looking at the big picture generated by the FIFA 2014 mega-event in BH, a few conclusions seem to be warranted: as much as the event itself might have been somewhat successful according to official appraisals, it did not work as the main strategy to sell the city in the international tourism and business market. The main objective of the whole project – to bring the biggest undeveloped area within the city limits to the development and real-estate market – has not been accomplished yet, as the 'urgency discourse' was not sufficient to pull the necessary strings. Eight thousand poor people have resisted eviction and still live in the area. Elsewhere, the construction industry and developers were privileged, mainly through mobility projects which led to the eviction of more than 1,000 families from their houses. As far as tourism goes, BH went back to its historical track: a mid-sized city with few attractions, suitable for hosting second-class events. On the other hand, the mega-event acted as the missing glue which brought together various social movements despite fierce police repression and *ad hoc* legislation to hinder protests. The Brazilian economic scenario is now one of slow growth, which means less construction and urban development, a reduction in job creation and a decrease in public investment in health, education, social security, etc. In democratic regimes this situation usually leads to dry prairies ready to catch fire.

Notes

1   Fédération Internationale de Football Association.
2   The 12 cities hosting the 2014 FIFA World Cup were Rio de Janeiro, Porto Alegre, Curitiba, São Paulo, Manaus, Cuiabá, Salvador, Natal, Fortaleza, Recife, Brasília and Belo Horizonte.
3   The data presented here were collected within the context of two research projects: the *Observatório de Conflitos Urbanos de Belo Horizonte* (Belo Horizonte Observatory of Urban Conflicts) at the Universidade Federal de Minas Gerais (UFMG), which is the local branch of a nationwide project, and the *Construção das Paisagens Turísticas de Belo Horizonte* (Construction of Belo Horizonte's Touristic Landscapes). Other studies undertaken by the *Grupo de Estudos em Temáticas Ambientais* – GESTA (Study Group on Environmental Themes) at the UFMG and by the *Comitê Popular dos Atingidos pela Copa* (COPAC-BH) are also used. All translations of original quotes from Portuguese into English are the authors' own.
4   BH is a good representative of the latter group insofar as it averages Brazilian metropolises in terms of population, income, education and a number of other social indices.
5   Prefeitura Municipal de Belo Horizonte, Law no. 9952 from 5 July 2010.
6   According to the Brazilian Civil Code, urban land tenure may be acquired through continuous possession of a plot, exercised in a calm and peaceful manner for a period of ten years, reducing this period by half in case the property has been acquired against payment and has served the housing purpose of its occupants.
7   In Brazil, privately and publically owned land can be 'granted in possession' (i.e. leased – somewhat similar to granting rights of way) to a third party without granting it full land ownership. But that possibility has brought a number of legal cases to the courts.
8   Brazilian term for traditional black communities formed by runaway slaves. Such groups have special land rights.

References

[Unless otherwise stated, all URLs were last accessed 5 August 2015.]

ABAEM Associação dos Barraqueiros da Área Externa do Mineirão (2013) *Associação dos Barraqueiros da Área Externa do Mineirão*. Blog. Online. Available at http://abaem.blogspot.de/.

ABONG (Associação Brasileira de Organizações Não Governamentais) (2014) *Copa 2014, Olimpíadas 2016 e megaprojetos – remoções em curso no Brasil*. Online. Available at http://www.abong.org.br/final/download/dossiemegaeventos.pdf.

Alves, L. (2014) 'Via 710 só deve ser concluída no segundo semestre de 2016', *Hoje em dia*, 18 September. Online. Available at http://www.hojeemdia.com.br/horizontes/via-710-so-deve-ser-concluida-no-segundo-semestre-de-2016-1.269011.

ANCOP (Articulação Nacional dos Comitês Populares da Copa) (2012) *Dossiê Megaeventos e Violações de Direitos Humanos no Brasil*. Online. Available at http://www.apublica.org/wp-content/uploads/2012/01/DossieViolacoesCopa.pdf.

ANPG (Associação Nacional de Pós-Graduandos) (2014) *Nota de Repúdio ao despejo das Ocupações Rosa Leão, Vitória e Esperança na região do Isidoro em Minas Gerais*. Online. Available at http://www.anpg.org.br/?p=5983.

Associated Press (2014) 'World Cup set to be most lucrative ever', *Associated Press*, 23 May. Online. Available http://www.espnfc.com/fifa-world-cup/story/1830732/2014-world-cup-set-to-be-most-lucrative-ever.

Barbosa, T. P. (2011) *A Copa, a Cidade e a Vila: Um estudo de caso sobre a Vila Recanto UFMG*, Bachelor's thesis. Belo Horizonte: Universidade Federal de Minas Gerais, Faculdade de Filosofia e Ciências Humanas.

Bessa, A. S. M. and Capanema Alvares, L. (2014) *A construção do Turismo: megaeventos e outras estratégias de venda das ciudades*. Belo Horizonte: C/Arte.

Brigadas Populares (2011) *Copa sim! Despejo não!*, 5 May. Online. Available at http://brigadaspopulares.blogspot.com.br/2011/05/copa-sim-despejo-nao.html.

Câmara, B. P. (2006) *Insegurança pública e conflitos urbanos na cidade do Rio de Janeiro (1993–2003)*, MSc thesis. Rio de Janeiro: Universidade Federal do Rio de Janeiro.

Capanema Álvares, L. *et al.* (2008) *Políticas Urbanas para o Turismo e suas consequências nas paisagens e culturas locais: O caso recente do Rio de Janeiro*. Paper presented at 9o Encontro Nacional de Ensino de Paisagismo em Escolas de Arquitetura e Urbanismo no Brasil, 22–25 October, Curitiba.

CEDEFES (2011) *Despejo no Zilah Sposito em Belo Horizonte*, 20 October. Online. Available at http://www.cedefes.org.br/afro_print.php?id=7201.

Correio do Brasil (2011) 'Copa de 2014 impulsiona desocupação de terrenos em BH', *Correio do Brasil*, 8 November. Online. Available at http://correiodobrasil.com.br/noticias/brasil/copa-de-2014-impulsiona-a-desocupacao-de-terrenos-em-belo-horizonte/324858.

Cruz, L. (2013) 'MPF recomenda que PBH indenize moradores retirados para obra da Via 210', *Estado de Minas*, 20 May. Online. Available at http://www.em.com.br/app/noticia/gerais/2013/05/20/interna_gerais,391102/mpf-recomenda-que-pbh-indenize-moradores-retirados-para-obra-da-via-210.shtml.

Dip, A. (2012) 'As prostitutas de BH perguntam: e a gente, como fica?', *Pública, Agência de Reportagem e Jornalismo Investigativo*, 18 September. Online. Available at http://apublica.org/2012/09/gente-como-fica/.

Estado de Minas (2015a) 'Após reunião, reintegração de posse das ocupações do Isidoro é suspensa', *Estado de Minas*, 22 June. Online. Available at http://www.em.com.br/app/noticia/gerais/2015/06/22/interna_gerais,660745/apos-reuniao-reintegracao-de-posse-da-granja-werneck-e-suspensa.shtml.

Estado de Minas (2015b) 'Licitação para obras do Mercado do Cruzeiro deverá ser aberta apenas em 2016', *Estado de Minas*, 3 August. Online. Available at http://www.em.com.br/app/noticia/gerais/2015/08/03/interna_gerais,674823/licitacao-para-obras-do-mercado-do-cruzeiro-devera-ser-aberta-apenas-e.shtml.

Ferreira, A. (2010) 'O projeto "Porto Maravilha" no Rio de Janeiro: inspiração em Barcelona e produção a serviço do capital?', *Revista Bibliográfica de Geografía y Ciencias Sociales*, XV(895). Online. Available at http://www.ub.es/geocrit/b3w-895/b3w-895-21.htm.

Ferreira, P. (2012) 'Vizinhos das Torres Gêmeas festejam remoção da última família que ocupava imóvel', *Estado de Minas*, 19 July. Online. Available at http://www.em.com.br/app/noticia/gerais/2012/07/19/interna_gerais,306868/vizinhos-das-torres-gemeas-festejam-remocao-da-ultima-familia-que-ocupava-imovel.shtml.

Flávia Gussen, A. (2013) 'Antiga rua Musas em BH pode não receber hotel previsto', *Hoje em Dia*, 30 July. Online. Available at http://www.hojeemdia.com.br/noticias/politica/antiga-rua-musas-em-bh-pode-n-o-receber-hotel-previsto-1.152060.

Franco, A. (2011) 'Última área livre de Belo Horizonte terá Vila da Copa', *Hoje em Dia*, 15 March.

Freire, P. (2002) *Pedagogia do Oprimido*, 32nd edn. Rio de Janeiro: Paz e Terra.

G1 (2011) 'Edital de licitação para obras no Anel Rodoviário é autorizado, diz PBH', *G1*, 25 August. Online. Available at http://g1.globo.com/minas-gerais/noticia/2011/08/edital-de-licitacao-para-obras-no-anel-rodoviario-e-autorizado-diz-pbh.html.

GESTA (2013) *Mapa dos Conflitos Ambientais em MG*. Online. Available at http://www.sites.google.com/site/copacbh/home/gesta-ufmg---mapa-dos-conflitos-ambientais-em-mg.

GESTA (2015) *Por não permitir venda de lotes em ocupação, militante é assassinado*, 5 April. Online. Available at http://conflitosambientaismg.lcc.ufmg.br/noticias/por-nao-permitir-venda-de-lotes-em-ocupacao-militante-e-assassinado.

Harvey, D. (1989) 'From managerialism to entrepreneurialism: the transformation in urban governance in late capitalism', *Geografiska Annaler B*, 71(1): 3–17.

Harvey, D. (2014) *Cidades rebeldes. Do direito à cidade à revolução urbana*. São Paulo: Martins Fontes.

Jessop, B. (1997) 'The entrepreneurial city: re-imaging localities, re-designing economic governance, or re-structuring capital?', in N. Jewson and S. MacGregor (eds), *Realising Cities: New Spatial Divisions and Social Transformation*. London: Routledge. Online. Available at http://bobjessop.org/2013/12/02/the-entrepreneurial-city-re-imaging-localities-re-designing-economic-governance-or-re-structuring-capital/.

Malta, H. (2011) '260 remoções no caminho das obras da Copa em BH', *Hoje em Dia*, 2 June.

Maricato, E. (2003) 'As idéias fora do lugar e o lugar das idéias: planejamento urbano no Brasil', in O. Arantes, C. Vainer and E Maricato (eds) *A cidade do pensamento único: Desmanchando consensos*. Petrópolis: Vozes.

Mascarenhas, G. (2014) 'Cidade mercadoria, cidade-vitrine, cidade turística: a espetacularização do urbano nos megaeventos esportivos', *Caderno Virtual de Turismo*, 14(1): 52–65. Online. Available at: http://www.ivt.coppe.ufrj.br/caderno/index.php?journal=caderno&page=article&op=view&path[]=1021.

Ministério de Turismo (2014) *Tourist Arrivals in Brazil, by Access and States, 2012–2013*. Online. Available at http://www.dadosefatos.turismo.gov.br.

O Tempo (2013) 'Segundo prédio das Torres Gêmeas leiloado por quase 4 R$ milhões', *O Tempo*, 29 May. Online. Available at http://www.otempo.com.br/cidades/segundo-pr%C3%A9dio-das-torres-g%C3%AAmeas-%C3%A9-leiloado-por-quase-r-4-milh%C3%B5es-1.654713.

PAC (Programa de Aceleração do Crescimento) (2014) *Conheça os investimentos do PAC nas 12 cidades-sede da Copa do Mundo*, 11 June. Online. Available at http://www.pac.gov.br/noticia/acc7b92b.

Passa Palavra (2010) *Comunidades ameaçadas de despejo montam acampamento na prefeitura de BH*, 30 September. Online. Available at http://www.passapalavra.info/2010/10/29737.

PBH (Prefeitura Municipal de Belo Horizonte) (1996) *Plano Diretor*. Belo Horizonte: PBH.

PBH (Prefeitura Municipal de Belo Horizonte) (2000) *Anuário Estatístico de Belo Horizonte 2000*. Belo Horizonte: PBH.

PBH (Prefeitura Municipal de Belo Horizonte) (2010) *Planejamento Estratégico de Belo Horizonte 2030*. Belo Horizonte: PBH. Online. Available at https://bhmetaseresultados.pbh.gov.br/content/planejamento-estrat%C3%A9gico-2030.

Portal da Copa (2014) *Balanço: Belo Horizonte contabiliza receita direta de R$ 451 milhões com turistas durante a Copa*, 15 July. Online. Available at http://www. copa2014.gov.br/pt-br/noticia/balanco-belo-horizonte-contabiliza-receita-direta-de-r-451-milhoes-com-turistas-durante-a.

Sánchez, F. and Broudehoux, A.-M. (2013) 'Mega-events and urban regeneration in Rio de Janeiro: planning in a state of emergency', *International Journal of Urban Sustainable Development*, 5(2): 132–53.

Silvestre, G. and De Oliveira, N. G. (2012) 'The revanchist logic of mega-events: community displacement in Rio de Janeiro's West End', *Visual Studies*, 27(2): 204–10.

Vainer, C. B. (2009) 'Pátria, empresa e mercadoria: notas sobre a estratégia discursiva do Planejamento Estratégico Urbano', in O. Arantes, C. Vainer and E. Maricato (eds), *A cidade do pensamento único: Desmanchando consensos*. Petrópolis: Vozes.

Werneck, G. and Ayer, F. (2010) 'Granja Werneck. De última fronteira verde a 10ª regional de BH', *Estado de Minas*, 28 March. Online. Available at: http://www. em.com.br/app/noticia/gerais/2010/03/28/interna_gerais,153363/de-ultima-fronteira-verde-a-10-regional-de-bh.shtml.

WTO (World Tourism Organization) (2014) *Yearbook of Tourism Statistics: Compendium of Tourism Statistics and Data Files*. Online. Available at http://data.worldbank.org.

13 The right to Gaudí

What can we learn from the *commoning* of Park Güell, Barcelona?

Albert Arias-Sans and Antonio Paolo Russo

PROLOGUE: Crying for Park Güell

Since Gaudí's famous salamander was damaged with an iron bar in February 2007, the sword of Damocles has been hanging over Park Güell, threatening its condition as public open space. After several failed attempts, on 25 October 2013 the municipal government's plan to regulate the access to one of the most visited tourist attractions in Barcelona became operational. Part of the park, designed by Catalan architect Antoni Gaudí and acquired by the city in 1922 after the failure of the original residential project, is no longer publicly accessible. Through the enclosure and control of its central area, Park Güell officially became an open-air museum with restricted access.

From a classical liberal perspective, this decision may look justified. Some of the arguments in support of the closure can hardly be contested: the pressure on a fragile space with high cultural and heritage value; the nuisances produced by mass tourist flows in the neighbourhood; the hassle of informal activities and petty criminality taking place in the park; the high costs of conservation . . . It could be said – as did the hegemonic discourse – that success killed Park Güell, and that the only way to manage this situation was to establish a quota of visitors per hour and regulate their entrance through ticketing and queuing, as has been done in many other World Heritage sites, like the Machu Picchu complex, the Kew Royal Botanical Gardens or the Galapagos natural park. The closure of Park Güell could be considered an example of the 'tragedy of the commons' (Hardin 1968), in which the over-exploitation of a common resource dooms it to subsequent enclosure. It could be argued that this decision was thought to create a *lesser evil* scenario (Hardt and Negri 2009) concerning the management of an urban commons threatened by tourism pressure: a palliative solution to regulate overcrowding through the enclosure of an area tagged as 'touristic'.

Nonetheless, challenging the hegemonic discourse legitimating the enclosure and regulation, a group of citizens, the *Plataforma Defensem el Park Güell* (Platform Let's Defend the Park Güell, hereafter referred to as PDPG) voiced its discontent with this decision. Under no circumstances, they claimed, can tourist overcrowding lead to the privatisation and regulation of a park which would prevent public and free access for everyone. Without denying the unique value of the site and while acknowledging the effects of it being one of the most visited places in the city, the PDPG argued that the park has to remain a public space. And here comes the main paradox of the contestation: by advocating the right to access the park for *everyone*, with no distinctions, the claim also includes tourists – the very ones whose mass presence justified the regulation. While being fully aware that such mass appropriation is widely seen as the main problem to be solved, the 'cry and the demand' for the right to the city (Lefebvre 1968) made by the PDPG transcends the boundaries which frame the tragedy. Thus, proposing an exercise of *commoning* beyond the place-based community's interests, the PDPG assumed a *relational* and *compositionist* approach (Latour 2010) in order to defend the right to public space. The commoning process is not understood as a claim for historical accumulation rights (Linebaugh 2008), but as the right to participate in and negotiate – and so to produce – urban space with all the inhabitants, without excluding tourists. What we term here the 'Right to Gaudí' has become a struggle against the urban strategies of privatising and enclosing public space due to tourist overcrowding. At the same time, the discourse of the PDPG has unwittingly turned into an opportunity to redefine the position of local community groups and urban social movements with regard to tourism issues, shifting the question from 'how to protect the city from tourism' into 'how do we compose the city along with tourism', and thus eschewing a logic of dualism (tourists vs locals) in the production of tourist places.

Leaving many of the details of the struggle surrounding the enclosure of part of the Park Güell aside for the sake of brevity, this chapter – structured as a Greek tragedy – will focus on the learning process (McFarlane 2011) which has emerged through the enclosing and commoning process. Following this brief *Prologue*, the *Parode* presents a short explanation of the park's tragedy prior to the execution of the regulation plan. The tragedy then continues with three *Episodes* and three related *Stasima* illustrating the *enclosing-commoning* process of the park. Following the analytical approach proposed by Jeffrey *et al.* (2012), the process has been addressed in its multiple dimensions, through the intertwining of materiality, spatiality and subjectivity. In the final chapter – the *Exode*, after the unfolding of the tragedy – some concluding remarks are made on the opportunities to learn from the process, i.e. how to claim the 'right to the tourist city'.

PARODE: Something must be done

The tragedy of the Park Güell must be understood within the context of the decade-long strategy of turning Barcelona into one of the most popular urban tourism destinations in the world. The Olympic Games of 1992 and the subsequent transformation of Barcelona's cityscape put the city on the global tourist map; since then, the city has hosted millions of tourists, with the visitor count growing from 2.4 million in 1993 to 7.5 million in 2013 on the basis of hotel occupation alone (Barcelona Turisme 2013). When all types of accommodation are considered and day visitors included, tourism flows in Barcelona were estimated at around 27 million visitors in 2013 (Ajuntament de Barcelona 2014), in a small, dense city of 100 square kilometres and 1.6 million inhabitants. Beyond any discussion of the costs and benefits involved, tourism-related activities have become consolidated as one of the leading forces in the economy and in the production of the city. In the context of the acute economic recession of the late 2000s, the tourism sector has continued to be one of the main foci of public and private investment. It is only at the beginning of the 2010s that the increasing pressure provoked by tourism on the everyday life of residents in certain neighbourhoods has triggered critical voices denouncing the development of 'tourist bubbles' (Judd and Fainstein 1999). Many of the expressions of popular discontent and demands have been channelled by the traditional neighbourhood associations.[1] A wide array of claims have emerged in relation to the citizens' discontent with issues such as traffic problems related to tourist flows, illegal short-term holiday rentals or the misbehaviour of tourists in public space. The defence of the Park Güell against its enclosure has been one of the mushrooming local mobilizations around the impacts of mass tourism upon the city's neighbourhoods and residents.

In order to frame our case study, it is also important to highlight a dual process made of two highly interconnected dimensions. Firstly, the increase of visitors to the Park Güell has been initiated by the public sector-driven marketing strategy 'Gaudí's Year' in 2002. Conceived to commemorate the 150th anniversary of Antoni Gaudí and intended to give a new value to the artist and his work in Barcelona through new activities and facilities, this promotional branding exercise turned all of Gaudí's heritage sites into major urban attractions: the *Gaudí effect*. Before 2002 the Park Güell was not unknown. But the steady promotion of the park, marketed through the visual icon of the Salamander – a powerful metonymic object reproduced everywhere – together with the improvement of accessibility to the park (located on the top of a steep hill) through sightseeing buses, private coaches' parking lots and outdoor escalators – turned the park into one of the most visited free attractions in the city.

Secondly, in parallel, as the park was getting more crowded, local activities were disappearing from its spaces. Public events and festivals that once took place in the park were cancelled and programmed elsewhere; community activities such as traditional dance gatherings were banned from the park; children's activities were circumscribed to specific playground areas; and mundane everyday practices, although persistent, became invisible in the central space of the park at peak visiting hours. Touristic practices thus became dominant through a threefold process encouraged by the local administration: place promotion, restrictions of local uses and practices, and a decline in the critical mass of local users' activities.

Unfortunately, there has been no regularly published data to give evidence of the growth of visitors' numbers in the park. In 2006 a newspaper estimated a quantity of 2,000 to 3,000 visitors per day (Brodas 2006). In 2009, the first version of the regulation plan increased this estimate to 14,400 visitors per day. The last published count, accompanying the last version of the regulation plan in

2013, raised the figure to 25,000 visitors per day – although it was calculated during the peak period of the summertime. However, despite the unreliability of such estimated accounts, the overcrowding of the park was both a fact and a concern. Local newspapers frequently denounced an 'unsustainable situation' and the 'need for regulation', reporting any noteworthy incident in the park. In the mid-2000s, some local residents started to voice concerns about the lack of maintenance, the insecurity of the park and its overcrowding. But the attack on the Salamander in February 2007 by two people armed with an iron bar, which damaged its mouth, was the turning point for the City Council to embark on the preparation of a regulation plan. After a few meetings with a number of local stakeholders, a first version of the *Integrated Action Plan* was presented by the municipal government in July 2009. Conceived as a broad management plan, it proposed, among other things, to control and limit the access of visitors in order to diminish the impact of 'uncontrolled tourist visits' (Ajuntament de Barcelona 2013). Such control of visitors was to be implemented in the area of the park declared a World Heritage Site by UNESCO in 1984, that is 17 hectares out of the total surface of the park, including a public school. This space, surrounded by other public and private facilities, is used by local residents not only as a space of leisure but also as a connecting corridor with the surrounding areas.

However, this first plan failed because of the complete lack of support from relevant local stakeholders. No residents' associations, no collectives, no political parties except those in the government coalition endorsed the Plan. During this first period, from 2009 to 2011, an assembly of existing neighbourhood associations was created under the label *Coordinator of Park Güell*, and became the most active collective opposing the regulation plan. Its mission statement was clear: avoiding the closure and the privatization of Park Güell. The *Coordinator* platform collected more than 20,000 signatures; organized rallies; alerted international consulates denouncing the City Council's plans; and obtained the support of other broader collectives such as the Federation of Neighbourhood Associations of Barcelona (FAVB) and the Public Gardeners' Union Committee,[2] among others. Due to this political failure, the idea of regulating entry to the park was temporarily put aside, although refurbishment works were carried out. But the tragedy was still there, and the local public opinion periodically expressed itself against the 'degradation' and the 'insecurity' of the park – an unsustainable situation represented by photographs of half-naked bodies sunbathing on shattered benches, illegal sellers displaying cheap plastic souvenirs or visitors taking photographs of their friends riding the back of the Salamander. 'Something must be done.' And so was it.

EPISODE I: The lesser evil scenario

After the local elections of May 2011, a new political party (from the centre-right) ruled the City Council until May 2015. Although some members of that party had, in previous years when still in the opposition, assured that they would not close the park, a discussion process was set in motion to prepare a new plan to regulate the impact of visitors on the Park Güell. The new plan's objectives displayed some crucial differences from the previous one's. First, the new proposed regulation affected a smaller area, the most attractive (and visited) part involving 8 per cent of the total park area. Ignoring the delineation of the UNESCO designated area, and with the legitimation of the History Museum of Barcelona, the City Council arbitrarily declared the regulated zone as the 'monumental' one. Such a regulation was proposed without fencing the zone, but by setting up removable ribbons and checkpoints and contracting a security team to control access. The monumental heritage would be thus preserved and the rest of the park would remain freely accessible so as to allow functional and leisure uses in it. According to the official discourse (Ajuntament de Barcelona 2013: 6), the Regulation Plan aimed 'to preserve the right of neighbours to enjoy their space' and 'to recover the park for the city'. Secondly, the plan fixed a maximum quota of 800 visitors per hour and an entry fee. To avoid paying a fee, neighbouring residents and the school community inside and around the park could apply for a free access card. Moreover, any EU citizen, living or not in Barcelona, could fill in a public register and, after a week, be allowed to book a visit in the 'monumental area', limited to 100 such visitors per hour. By limiting the access to a fixed number, the City Council aimed, on the one hand, 'to conserve and protect a unique heritage' and 'to optimize the experience of the visit' (ibid.). On the other hand, by making *tourists* pay but allowing *neighbouring residents* to enter for free, they aimed 'to improve the quality of life of residents, reverting the benefits generated by tourist activities' (ibid.). Thus the plan proposed to enclose the 'monumental zone' to take the pressure off the rest of the park, while generating funds to sustain the preservation of the park's heritage. The park was converted officially into an 'open-air museum'.

This new 'lesser evil' scenario changed the framework of the negotiation process with respect to the previous plan. A formal top-down 'participatory process' was set up *ad hoc* by the District government, consisting of five sessions aimed at generating consensus among the various stakeholders. The first meeting was announced publicly, and more than 50 people participated. However, the District Council rapidly announced the need to reduce this number by half, by cutting out representatives of the entities from outside the five neighbourhoods surrounding the park, but retaining many people with no clear representative mandate. From that point onwards, the meetings were no longer publicized. During the five meetings – from September 2011 to October 2013 – nothing was ever negotiated nor decided jointly with the attendees in a public discussion. Some of the relevant stakeholders did not join in the expected 'consensus', showing dissent from the beginning of the process; other critical voices emerged during the process. The implementation of the regulation plan, moreover, was formally initiated while the participatory process was still taking place, with the approval of a 2 million euro contract in December 2012 for the infrastructural works necessary to put the regulation system in place: demarcation wires, ticket offices, street pacification measures, etc. This debate did not serve to 'reveal the truth about the controversy to the audience', as Walter Lippmann wrote many years ago, but to 'identify the partisans' (Lippmann 1993 [1927]: 129). In this respect the *Coordinator* platform, which had opposed the previous plan, showed its inconsistency when some of the leading actors agreed to the new conditions referred to below. Moreover, the political parties with representation in the District Council did not mobilize against the new plan, and either agreed with the enclosure or avoided any positioning in the face of such controversy. It was in this context that the PDPG emerged to catalyse the voices of contestation against the enclosure plan.

The PDPG was officially constituted in July 2012 to pursue the opposition against the enclosure in a very different way from the previous *Coordinator* platform. Instead of being driven by the traditional neighbourhood associations, the PDPG was the result of an assemblage process, with its core coming from the neighbourhood assembly of the *15M Indignados* movement[3] (see Corsín Jiménez and Estalella 2011), joined by former members of the disbanded *Coordinator* platform, people from other local collectives, members of marginal political parties, artists, craft sellers working in the park and individuals who just wanted to 'do something' against the plan. Thus a heterogeneous collective of groups and individual with different trajectories was assembled through 'temporary, contested and partial practices of articulation' (Featherstone 2011: 141).

The PDPG was created with a clear orientation towards a single issue with a simple and unchanging objective in its foundational manifesto: 'to keep Park Güell public and free for everybody' (PDPG 2012), a claim in tune with the idea of the 'right to the city', but remote from the hegemonic opinion in the media and city government's discourse. Thus the PDPG rejected the idea of enclosing the central part of the park as the lesser evil solution and stood firm on that position. At the same time, it also emerged as a response to the opaque practices of the traditional residents' associations which were rooted in a local frame of reference, prioritizing their own partial interests over a broader, more general interest. The PDPG thus started a 'commoning process' against the imminent enclosure of Park Güell.

STASIMON I: Enclosing and commoning

There has been a resurgence of interest and discussions on the concept of the *commons* within critical or radical perspectives on neoliberal practices of dispossession, destruction and commodification of *common* social and spatial resources (Brenner and Theodore 2002; de Angelis 2003, 2007; Hardt and Negri 2004, 2009; Harvey 2003, 2012). These perspectives question the liberal idea of the *enclosure* as the unavoidable solution to address the tragedy of the commons (Hardin 1968) and broaden the notion of the 'nested' governance of common pool resources (CPR) proposed by Ostrom (1990). This renewed approach 're-envisions the *commons* outside of the public-private dichotomy and introduces the social, cultural and political practices that allow new possibilities, thus reconstituting the commons as an object of thought' (Eizenberg 2012: 766). Thus the *commons* here are not merely a matter of property regimes but 'an effect of a social practice of commoning' (Harvey 2012: 73) constructed through the relational process within and between a group (a community) and an existing or yet-to-be-created heterogeneous (common) resource.

From a spatial perspective, *commons* have been tackled in closed connection with three main interrelated ideas. First, the idea of 'accumulation by dispossession' (Harvey 2003) explains neoliberal enclosure practices in urban space in relation to the need for capitalism to solve the permanent cycles of over-accumulation through an analogy with Marxian 'primitive accumulation'. Second, the idea of *commons* as a practice of interaction, cohabitation and cooperation is related with a biopolitical mechanism – that is, one in which what is directly at stake is the production and reproduction of life itself, and which refuses 'to let the bodies be eclipsed, and insists instead on their power' (Hardt and Negri 2009: 38). Finally, the Lefebvrian idea of *oeuvre* and the principle of 'the right to the city' have been crucial to translate both the concept of the *commons* – the whole city as a resource permanently under construction – and the *commoning* process as a political horizon, to the urban sphere without losing sight of spatial production (Lefebvre 1968).

Many recent works engage with what has been termed *urban commons* (Blomley 2008; Chatterton 2011; Hodkinson 2012) through the analysis of processes of enclosing and commoning public spaces (Foster 2011), community gardens (Eizenberg 2012) or infrastructure (Corsin Jiménez 2014). Nevertheless, such critical perspectives have barely been introduced in tourism studies, which mostly address the question of the *commons* in a liberal or institutional frame of analysis. The main articles on this subject have been focused on exploring the economic values of communal property land (Bostedt and Mattsson 1995), on analysing how the property regime determines the structure and evolution of tourist destinations (Russo and Segre 2009), on evidencing the challenges of managing natural resources threatened by overuse and a lack of investment incentive (Healy 1994, 2006), or on enhancing the value of the tangible and intangible resources to assure their sustainability as tourist products (Briassoulis 2002). Although not explicitly mentioning the issue of the *commons*, some authors have evidenced the effects of the priority given to tourist activities on urban communities, mainly focusing on marketing strategies and tourism-related urban redevelopment processes (Colomb 2011; Fox Gotham 2005; Fainstein and Powers 2006; Novy and Huning 2009), or calculating the impacts of tourism on a community and its quality of life (Hoffman *et al.* 2003; Pearce *et al.* 1996; Uysal *et al.* 2012).

The following episodes aim to explain the *enclosing-commoning* process of the Park Güell in order to understand the tragedy as a 'generative spacing' by identifying 'how it produces specific materialities, spatialities and subjectivities' (Jeffrey *et al.* 2012: 3). Such an approach allows us to move beyond grand narratives of dispossession triggered by neoliberalism – the prevailing discourse from a political economy perspective – and to explain the phenomena in a more situated, heterogeneous, complex and embodied way. By doing so, it makes it easier to identify singularities about, and gather the knowledge emerging from, each specific enclosing-commoning process (Hardt and Negri 2009).

EPISODE II: Mobility and maintenance come first

In between the failure of the first plan in October 2010 and the local elections in May 2011, many enhancement works were carried out in the park for a total of approximately 10 million euros, including the design of internal pathways, the erection of railings alongside the inner viaducts, the improvement of drainage pipes, wood maintenance, the improvement of surrounding streets, the redesign of the coach parking lot, the replacement of the fences surrounding the whole perimeter of the park, and the construction of new escalators to access the park. In spite of such huge investments, a number of neighbouring residents continued to denounce a lack of maintenance, problems of mobility and insecurity in the park.[4] Even the *Coordinator* platform, whose main focus was against the enclosure of the park and its privatization, spoke out against the 'degradation' of the park and denounced the lack of policing and the declining number of public garden workers. Many things were done, but they were not enough: tourists were still overcrowding the place, jumping over the Salamander and having picnics on the famous Jujol benches. Informal sellers were still displaying their blankets full of one-euro souvenirs. Traffic jams were still affecting the neighbourhood every weekend.

In September 2011, the District Council started the above-mentioned participatory process. New players entered the game with new intentions and a shift in politics, practices and discourses took place. The central issue remained the fact that the park heritage was at risk due to overcrowding, an issue against which public opinion and the media made constant claims. Nonetheless, the city government's priorities were now the priorities of others: 'mobility and maintenance first, then the enclosure' (Balanzà 2011: 6). Plainly put, heritage could wait – until the problems identified by the neighbouring residents were solved. Apart from giving local residents and the local school community a free pass, increasing police presence in the park and expanding the garden maintenance team, there were still things to be done by the public authorities in order to gain legitimacy and reach consensus with previously critical stakeholders. Hence, in parallel to the participatory process, the District Council organized a number of separate closed meetings with different actors in order to discuss their requests on a face-to-face basis. Such tactics allowed the Council to propose a number of bilateral agreements on problems beyond the enclosure, mainly related to mobility and maintenance. Some issues, like the nuisances generated by sightseeing bus stands, remained unresolved, but for others – like the position of the taxi rank or the regulation of the coach parking lot – new solutions were found. When there were no technical problems to be solved, the Council awarded public recognition to the leaders of the residents' associations or granted them the organization of events such as the festival to commemorate the centenary of the park. Myriad small tactics, difficult to trace yet very effective, served to dismantle and fragment the main critical issue – heritage protection and the enclosure plan – into small manageable 'pieces', allowing the government to build up consensus for the new enclosure plan.

After witnessing how the *Coordinator* platform had lost force in the confrontation against the plan, the PDPG, was constituted as a very issue-oriented collective with the aim of maintaining Park Güell as a public and free space for everybody (Figure 13.1). The closed and opaque nature of the above-mentioned 'participatory process' led the PDGD to publicly denounce such divisive meetings and co-opted agreements between parties. Their position against any enclosure was very firm, supported by complex and diverse arguments summarized by the following four principles (PDPG 2012). First, the enclosure will definitely wipe the community uses out of the park, transforming it into a 'tourist container'. Second, the problems of the park do not originate within the park, thus the enclosure will not solve anything. Third, the alternatives to avoid the enclosure are

Figure 13.1 Contesting the enclosure of Park Güell: 'Let's defend public space' – graffiti on a wall near the park and protest gathering by the PDPG on the first day of the enclosure, October 2013.

Source: Albert Arias-Sans.

more complex, but also much more just and sustainable for everybody. Fourth, the enclosure will create a precedent for future action in other overcrowded spaces in the city.

The PDPG was standing, on the one hand, for a highly ideological – not necessarily symbolic – 'cry and demand' for the 'right to the park', which had to remain public and free. On the other hand, it was responding to the complexity of the situation with a very hybrid and practical approach: claiming a shared responsibility, asking for heterogeneous solutions, advising against the risks which the enclosure would have beyond the park, even beyond the neighbourhoods surrounding the park, i.e. trying to argue that the closure and subsequent segregation of uses would not only leave the problems of the park unsolved but would produce other problems elsewhere. Such a practical translation of the 'right to the city' was neither welcomed by policy-makers nor by the local stakeholders or the media.

The complex position held by the PDPG was clearly going beyond the scope of their actions and involved many issues which the regulation plan could not control. The PDPG aimed too high: managing the park fairly implied revisiting, among other thing, the overall tourism promotion policies of the City Council – a challenge in a city where tourism has, in recent years of economic recession, been the goose that lays the golden egg. Local stakeholders felt that their face-to-face bilateral agreements with the District and their political capital were under threat when confronted with an approach that combined broad claims about the right to the city with incremental enhancements of the place. The media did not value the practical proposals of the PDPG and recurrently criticized what they perceived as the ideological nature of the 'right to the city' position, keeping the focus mainly on the visual impacts of overcrowding and quantifiable issues such as the number of visitors, investments and costs. Divisive tactics were winning the battle. Complex approaches did not convince anybody. Alliances were not strong enough to bear influence. The only opportunity left to the PDPG was the mobilization of public opinion, but this was not an easy task.

STASIMON II: Thinking the park beyond the park

The PDPG was dealing with the *common* as 'a kind of gathering of multiplicities through the political work of assembly' (McFarlane 2011: 212). Two crucial questions emerge from the previous episode. The first has to do with how to deal with a 'politics of place beyond the place' (Massey 2007: 188) and, consequently, how to face responsibilities in an utterly place-based political scenario. This has to do with the assumption of a relational ontology of space. According to Massey (2005), space is the product of interrelations, the sphere of the possibility of multiplicity and heterogeneity, and it is always under construction. In this perspective, there *is* no Park Güell in essence. The park is much more than a 'Catalan Arcade'[5] or an 'open-air museum': it is also a recreational site replete with mundane, everyday practices. Thus the park can be conceptualized in relational terms as configured by translocal and mobile trajectories, interactions and technologies that perform and produce the space. Tourists, elderly residents, children, dogs, sellers, policemen, maintenance vehicles, images, postcards, souvenirs, cameras, policies, plants – all of them configure the space with different rhythmical patterns over time. This approach to the park allows us to unearth the *translocal* character of the heterogeneous agencies producing the place through space and time. Moreover, a relational approach allows us to think of a 'politics of place responsibility' (Darling 2009) in a dual way: on the one hand, as an account of the tensions of negotiating the multiplicity of elements that construct contemporary spaces; on the other, as a demand to take responsibility for the global flows and connections that help to constitute such a spatial multiplicity. This relational approach helps to challenge what Purcell (2006) has called the *local trap*, that is the assumption that the local scale – the five neighbourhoods surrounding the park in this instance – is always the most democratic option to frame the decision-making process. In this case, it was showed that the neighbourhood scale allowed certain tactics of control to develop.

The second question, closely intertwined with the first, can be formulated as how to play up the issue in order to ensure the political involvement of the public in the controversy (Marres 2007), understanding the public as 'all of those who arc affected by the indirect consequences of transactions to such an extent that it is deemed necessary to have those consequences systematically cared for' (Dewey 2012: 16). The fragmentation of the issue into a series of individual solvable problems confronted the PDPG with the need to engage as many voices as possible in the debate, in order to shift the discussion back to the broader, city-wide effects of the enclosing. However, this double movement of publicizing the issue and decentring the urban object – the park – to outline distributed responsibilities was one of the crucial limits the PDPG faced during the *commoning* process. Apart from the difficulty of negotiating the space through everyday or community practices and the incapability of dealing with the divisive tactics of technical and participatory arrangements charged with 'moral and political capacities' (Marres and Lezaun 2011: 495), the attempted mobilization of the public found another limit: the difficulty to enrol subjects who have been detached from the *commons* even before the enclosure.

ESPISODE III: Making tourist things public

The PDPG was created with the agenda to widen both representation and participation in the debate beyond the geographic limits of the surroundings of the park. This can be explained, on the one hand, because of the previous experience with the *Coordinator* platform, which shifted position when direct benefits were offered to the participating actors, as outlined earlier in the chapter. On the other hand, there was an attempt to convert the 'Real Democracy Now!' slogan which drove the mobilizations of the *Indignados* movement of May 2011 into an issue-oriented claim for the park as an *urban commons*. Nevertheless, the alliances forged with many local and regional institutions (such as the FAVB) and minor political parties – such as the CUP (*Candidatura d'Unitat Popular*, a radical left-wing Catalan independentist party) – were not sufficient to allow the PDPG to influence the decision-making process. This situation forced the PDPG to start seeking support beyond the local scale and to try to enlist new solidarities by calling to the wider public. In March 2013, an online petition against the enclosure was set up, and more than 50,000 signatures were collected in two weeks. Rallies, festivals and a documentary were prepared in a very short period of time to raise awareness about the effects of the imminent enclosing.

However, in order to keep the public away from the controversy – once the support of place-based stakeholders had been assured by solving 'their' localized problems – the City Council set up a three-pronged strategy aiming at alienating the park from the community and the public. Firstly, all programmed festivals and events planned in the park were cancelled some years prior to the controversy over the enclosing.[6] The park, once the centre of many cultural and community activities, was erased from the city's public cultural map. Secondly, there was a clear discursive strategy to label the area to be regulated under the 'touristic' category. In an arbitrary way, there was suddenly a *touristic* area and a *touristic* schedule referred to in many official publications: not a *public* park, but a *touristic* park. Such a label was accompanied with a new, highly questionable visitors count estimate, carried out over four days in July 2012, which increased the total reported amount from 4.5 to 9 million annual visitors. This allowed, thirdly, public authorities to give visitors the responsibility to take care of the park by paying a fee, which owed public legitimacy to the city government through the statement 'Tourists will pay, residents won't'. But only the people with a registered domicile in the surrounding neighbourhoods and the school community had the privilege to freely access the park whenever they wanted. In order to avoid paying the entrance fee, the remaining 85 per cent of Barcelona residents, as well as European citizens, would have to sign a register in person and later would be able to book a pass and visiting time to enter the enclosed 'monumental' area. The efforts of the PDPG to dismantle such a system came too late, and the impact of its claim that 'everybody but a minority is treated as a tourist' was very weak. The argument of the city's ombudswoman, whom the PDPG asked to evaluate the legality and legitimacy of the enclosure, was crucial. Despite her criticism of the visitor numbers accounting method, the lack of public communication about crucial information and the lack of democratic guarantees during the debate, and while in favour of re-scaling and widening the issue, her sentence ended with an acceptance of the closure as a 'reasonable solution' (Síndica de Greuges de Barcelona 2013: 15).

STASIMON III: New subjects, old forums

After showing the impossibility for the opposition to the enclosure to escape from the orchestrated *local trap*, and how the issue was purposely blurred and dismantled by public authorities, it is worth reflecting about two processes which ensured the success of the enclosure. First, there was a *subjectification* of the enclosure process (Jeffrey *et al.* 2012) towards what Ong (2007) called a 'market criteria citizenship' setting a 'new mode of political optimization' in which the state – the City Council in this case – injects into citizens the idea of co-responsibility for the municipal budget. In a moment of sharp economic crisis, the evocation of the opportunity to make *others*, the 'tourists', pay for the maintenance was very effective in order to disenfranchise the public from the issue and 'normalize' it. The formation and the further action of PDPG was a response to such an enclosure process through *subjectification*: it sought to shift representation patterns and advocate a translocal scenario of alliances (Featherstone 2009) between the constellation of agents implicated in the production of the space in order to address the enclosure. Nonetheless, there were serious difficulties in making such alliances effective. None of the achieved enlistments of new agents were powerful enough to shift things. There was no support from larger political parties and other more widely representative institutions to mobilize a broader public opinion against the enclosure. Moreover, tourists had no institutional representation to defend their options, but on the contrary were treated as clients and pushed out of the political debate as the main guilty actors in the tragedy. Many of the residents agreed with this situation which was supported by the discourses and actions of the public administration.

The second process has to do with the lack of political spaces in which to deal with the complexity of urban tourism-related issues. Using Latour's (1993) terms, the park suffered a double process of *purification* in the public sphere by being turned into a *tragic* touristic place refuting all other multiple realities and, at the same time, by seeing its *hybrid* composition used in a very tactical way in order to dismantle both ideological and practical critiques. The techno-political mechanisms of control discussed before were very difficult to challenge through communicative action alone within the terms of the political debate set by the local government. The greater the acknowledgement of the hybrid, mobile and translocal composition of the *commons*, and the more public was the distribution of responsibilities, the fewer chances the PDPG had to negotiate, confront or reverse the effects of such a messy reality in *hybrid forums* (Callon *et al.* 2009). Discursive action alone was not enough to confront entrenched positions and claims to deal with all the things at stake in the *commons*. All opportunities to acknowledge complexity and seek for a better balance between ideology and technology in the public debates were denied. Taxi ranks, sightseeing bus stops, escalators, security, heritage interventions or tourist promotion – among other issues – remained outside the participatory process and discussions about figures, budgets and ratios were confined to technical matters.

EXODE: The right to negotiate the tourist city

The park was finally enclosed on 25 October 2013. The PDPG lost their battle. There was no *deus ex machina* nor any miracle. The *pathos* was consumed with the enclosure and the erasure of practical opportunities to negotiate a space that turned from public space to a monumental tourist area. However, as in many

Greek tragedies, the death of the main character could be used as a *pharmakon*, a piece of moral advice, for the learning benefit of other protagonists in other places. In this sense, the 'cry for the right to the Park Güell' has helped us unearth new knowledge bases that could guide the empowerment of social and political actors in the search for the *commoning of the tourist city.*

It should encourage us to eschew the *local trap* by recognizing and assuming that 'inhabitants [not just enfranchised citizens] have the right to participate centrally in the decisions that produce urban space' (Purcell 2002: 104), including tourists. Dealing with tourism irrevocably forces us to assume an *outward-looking* perspective on our cities (Massey 2007), which are simultaneously the result of, and the sphere of possibility for, translocal mobilities. Tourists could not be singled out as the guilty party in this story without the risk of legitimizing the enclosure of this public space. The delimitation of *tourist spaces* may induce the segregation of the space precisely because of its *touristic character.* Labelling places as *touristic* and enacting them as such may erase the chance to negotiate the space through the mundane practices and performances beyond tourism. Multiplicity, here, is treated as a political achievement – beyond an ontological assumption: the one that maintains the chances for the enactment of different multiplicities *in* and *through* the space. On the contrary, if one limits and encloses tourist places, the result is often regulated and controlled spots where nothing but tourism can happen.

If another *common world* has to be built, we have to think about places beyond the representational approach – transcending the notion of what is 'touristic' or 'authentic' and what is not – and focus on how decentred, related and neglected the constituting parts of any urban controversy are. The right to the city cannot be an essentialist stance, but the effect of a heterogeneous assemblage process that has to be 'constantly shifting and sifting [of] spatial imaginaries of networks, hierarchies, and scales' (McFarlane 2009: 564). The challenge is how the inhabitants of a city can think of the right to the tourist city *with* and *through* the agency of tourism, not relegating tourists to enclosed spaces, since by doing so, they would be enclosing themselves too.

Notes

1   Neighbourhood associations are rooted in Spain's urban social movements of the 1960s–70s created by residents to demand improvements in the living conditions in their neighbourhoods under the Franco regime. They continued to be very active after the transition to democracy in the 1980s and in Barcelona in particular they remain powerful residents' pressure groups, federated into the FAVB (Federation of Neighbourhood Associations of Barcelona).
2   The trade union of the employees of the Institute of Municipal Parks and Gardens, the public company in charge of the maintenance of green spaces in the city of Barcelona.
3   The '15M' or 'Indignados' movement was a social movement similar to the Occupy Movement. In Spain it emerged through a large-scale protest on 15 May 2011 and the subsequent occupation of the main squares of many Spanish cities. Very liquid and with multiple slogans, the protests were related to the consequences of the real-estate crisis, the public expenditure cuts, the public debt and claims for a 'real democracy'.

4   After the investments in maintenance works in the park were publicized, two very small rallies were held in the neighbourhood surrounding the park: one against the taxi rank (10 April 2011) and the other against the coach parking lot (1 July 2011).
5   The *Coordinator* platform evoked this nationalist metaphor many times in order to stress the social and identitarian value of the park.
6   In 2008 the City Council banned the Annual Festival of *Sardanes* (a traditional Catalan dance) after 53 years of it taking place in the main square of Park Güell, on the grounds of security arguments.

References

[Unless otherwise stated, all URLs were last accessed 4 July 2015.]

Ajuntament de Barcelona (2013) *Park Güell, un museu obert. Inici de la regulació d'accés de la zona monumental en horari turístic*, 19 July. Barcelona: Ajuntament de Barcelona.

Ajuntament de Barcelona (2014) *Pla de mobilitat turística de Barcelona*. Barcelona: Ajuntament de Barcelona.

Balanzà, A. (2011) 'Mobilitat i manteniment, eixos inicials de debat a Park Güell abans que l'accés', *L'Independent de Gràcia*, 403, 16 September.

Barcelona Turisme (2013) *Barcelona Receives 100 million Tourists in 20 Years*. Press release, 13 November. Online. Available at http://professional.barcelonaturisme.com/files/8684-1031-pdf/Barcelona%20receives%20100%20milion%20tourists%20in%20 20%20years_Press%20ang.pdf.

Blomley, N. (2008) 'Enclosure, common right and the property of the poor', *Social and Legal Studies*, 17(3): 311–31.

Bostedt, G. and Mattsson, L. (1995) 'The value of forests for tourism in Sweden', *Annals of Tourism Research*, 22(3): 671–80.

Brenner, N. and Theodore, N. (2002) 'Cities and the geographies of "actually existing neoliberalism"', *Antipode*, 34(3): 349–79.

Briassoulis, H. (2002) 'Sustainable tourism and the question of the commons', *Annals of Tourism Research*, 29(4): 1065–85.

Brodas, J. (2006) 'El Park Güell mejora su seguridad y rehabilita sus puntos turísticos', *La Vanguardia* [*Vivir* supplement], 21 October, p. 5.

Callon, M., Lascoumes, P. and Barthe, Y. (2009) *Acting in an Uncertain World. An Essay on Technological Democracy*. Cambridge, MA: MIT Press.

Chatterton, P. (2010) 'Seeking the urban common: furthering the debate on spatial justice', *City*, 14(6): 625–8.

Colomb, C. (2011) *Staging the New Berlin. Place Marketing and the Politics of Urban Reinvention Post-1989*. London: Routledge.

Corsín Jiménez, A. (2014) 'The right to infrastructure: a prototype for open source urbanism', *Environment and Planning D*, 32(2): 342–62.

Corsín Jiménez, A. and Estalella, A. (2011) '#spanishrevolution', *Anthropology Today*, 27: 19–23.

Darling, J. (2009) 'Thinking beyond place: the responsibilities of a relational spatial politics', *Geography Compass*, 3(5): 1938–54.

De Angelis, M. (2003) 'Reflections on alternatives, commons and communities or building a new world from the bottom up', *The Commoner*, 6. Online. Available at http://www.the*commoner.org.uk/deangelis06.doc.*

De Angelis, M. (2007) *The Beginning of History: Value Struggles and Global Capital*. London: Pluto Press.

Dewey, J. (2012 [1927]) *The Public and Its Problems: An Essay in Political Inquiry*. New York: Pennsylvania State University Press.

Eizenberg, E. (2012) 'Actually existing commons: three moments of space of community gardens in New York City', *Antipode*, 44(3): 764–82.

Fainstein, S. S. and Powers, J. (2006) 'Tourism and New York's ethnic diversity: an underutilized resource?', in J. Rath (ed.), *Tourism, Ethnic Diversity and the City*. London and New York: Routledge.

Featherstone, D. (2009) *Resistance, Space and Political Identities: The Making of Counter-global Networks*. Oxford: Wiley-Blackwell.

Featherstone, D. (2011) 'On assemblage and articulation', *Area*, 43(2): 139–42.

Foster, S. R. (2011) 'Collective action and the urban commons', *Notre Dame Law Review*, 87(1): 57–134.

Fox Gotham, K. (2005) 'Tourism gentrification: the case of New Orleans' Vieux Carré (French Quarter)', *Urban Studies*, 42(7): 1099–121.

Hardin, G. (1968) 'The tragedy of the commons', *Science*, 162 (3859): 1243–48.

Hardt, M. and Negri, A. (2004) *Multitude*. New York: Penguin.

Hardt, M. and Negri, A. (2009) *Commonwealth*. Cambridge, MA: Harvard University Press.

Harvey, D. (2003) *The New Imperialism*. Oxford: Oxford University Press.

Harvey, D. (2012) *Rebel Cities: From the Right to the City to the Urban Revolution*. London: Verso Books.

Healy, R. G. (1994) 'The "common pool" problem in tourism landscapes', *Annals of Tourism Research*, 21(3): 596–611.

Healy, R. G. (2006) 'The commons problem and Canada's Niagara falls', *Annals of Tourism Research*, 33(2): 525–44.

Hodkinson, S. (2012) 'The new urban enclosures', *City*, 16(5): 500–18.

Hoffman, L., Fainstein, S. and Judd, D. (eds) (2003) *Cities and Visitors: Regulating People, Markets, and City Space*. Oxford: Blackwell.

Jeffrey, A., McFarlane, C. and Vaudevan, A. (2012) 'Rethinking enclosure: space, subjectivity and the commons', *Antipode*, 44(4): 1247–67.

Judd, D. R. and Fainstein, S. S. (eds) (1999) *The Tourist City*. New Haven, CT: Yale University Press.

Latour, B. (1993) *We Have Never Been Modern*. Cambridge, MA: Harvard University Press.

Latour, B. (2010) 'An attempt at a "compositionist" manifesto', *New Literary History*, 41: 471–90.

Lefebvre, H. (1968) *Le Droit à la Ville*. Paris: Anthropos.

Linebaugh, P. (2008) *The Magna Carta Manifesto: Liberties and Commons for All*. Berkeley and Los Angeles: University of California Press.

Lippmann, W. (1993 [1927]) *The Phantom Public*. New Brunswick, NJ: Transaction Publishers.

McFarlane, C. (2009) 'Translocal assemblages: space, power and social movements', *Geoforum*, 40(4): 561–7.

McFarlane, C. (2011) 'The city as a machine for learning', *Transactions of the Institute of British Geographers*, 36(3): 360–76.

Marres, N. (2007) 'The issues deserve more credit. Pragmatist contributions to the study of public involvement in controversy', *Social Studies of Science*, 37(5): 759–80.

Marres, N. and Lezaun, J. (2011) 'Materials and devices of the public: an introduction', *Economy and Society*, 40(4): 489–509.

Massey, D. (2005) *For Space*. London: Sage.

Massey, D. (2007) *World City*. Cambridge: Polity Press.

Novy, J. and Huning, S. (2009) 'New tourism (areas) in the "New Berlin"', in R. Maitland and P. Newman (eds), *World Tourism Cities: Developing Tourism off the Beaten Track*. London: Routledge.

Ong, A. (2007) 'Neoliberalism as a mobile technology', *Transactions of the Institute of British Geographers*, 32(1): 3–8.

Ostrom, E. (1990) *Governing the Commons: The Evolution of Institutions for Collective Action*. Cambridge: Cambridge University Press.

PDPG (Plataforma Defensem el Park Güell) (2012) *El manifest*. Online. Available at http://defensemparkguell.wordpress.com/manifest/.

Pearce, P. L., Moscardo, G. and Ross, G. F. (1996) *Tourism Community Relationships*. Oxford: Pergamon.

Purcell, M. (2002) 'Excavating Lefebvre: the right to the city and its urban politics of the inhabitant', *GeoJournal*, 58(2–3): 99–108.

Purcell, M. (2006) 'Urban democracy and the local trap', *Urban Studies*, 43(11): 1921–41.

Russo, A. P. and Segre, G. (2009) 'Destination models and property regimes: an exploration', *Annals of Tourism Research*, 36(4): 587–606.

Síndica de Greuges de Barcelona (2013) *Decisió de la Síndica de Greuges en la investigación d'ofici endegada arran de manifestacions de diferents persones i grups veïnals en matèria de patrimoni històric artístic monumental i participación ciutadana (Park Güell), Barcelona, 20/09/2013*. Online. Available at http://sindicadegreugesbcn.cat/pdf/resolucions/res_131380881773.pdf.

Uysal, M., Perdue, R. and Sirgy, M. J. (eds) (2012) *Handbook of Tourism and Quality-of-life Research*. Vienna: Springer.

14 Of artisans, antique dealers and ambulant vendors

Culturally stratified conflicts in Buenos Aires' historic centre

Jacob Lederman

The year 2002 represented rock bottom for Argentina and its capital Buenos Aires. The country's embrace of structural adjustment policies advocated by the International Monetary Fund (IMF) had meant high-flying times during the 1990s. Investment flowed from around the world, with Argentina representing a major emerging market for institutional funds and savvy investors (Blustein 2006: ch.1). Large-scale urban redevelopment projects turned the city's derelict port into glittering new office space (Jajamovich 2012) while the former fruit market was converted into an urban shopping mall (Centner 2012a; Carman 2006) and new highways connected the city centre to rapidly expanding gated communities to the city's north and west (Libertun De Duren 2006; Torres 2001; Crot 2006). But by 2001, mired in recession and drowning in dollarized debt, the fragile nature of the country's open-market model was evident. In early 2002, the government of Argentina devalued its currency, defaulted on its debt, and sent 57 per cent of the country's urban population below the poverty line (Beccaria and Groisman 2008).

In the midst of images that were rare for a country that had come to think of itself as middle class – children begging in the street, formerly middle-class citizens searching through the trash – few would have imagined that the pillars of a new form of mass tourism were being laid. Yet the country's sharp currency devaluation transformed Argentina from one of the most expensive countries in the world, to one of the cheapest (Cohen 2012: 149). As the crisis subsided, the global media 'discovered' Buenos Aires, a more chaotic, grittier version of Milan, Paris or Prague according to many of these accounts (Dávila 2012: 137). The *New York Times* kicked off a decade of such stories with a paradigmatic headline in 2003: 'Buenos Aires, where glamour and chaos merge' (Luongo 2003). Importantly, media coverage and global travel patterns soon converged. Total visitors to Argentina increased from roughly two million in 1990, to just under three million in 2001 and nearly six million in 2011 (World Bank 2014).

The media's emphasis on urban 'chaos' referred in part to the city's still high levels of poverty and infrastructural decay. As the members of the *porteño*[1] creative class opened boutiques, galleries and restaurants catering to a greater flow of international visitors, many residents struggled to make ends meet. But the urban poor and 'newly poor' members of the middle class (del Carmen Feijó 2003) also began to carve out spaces of survival in the interstices of a thriving cultural and visitor economy. While the city government promoted international festivals for tango, jazz and film, and created new public agencies for studying the cultural – and later, creative – industries (Kanai and Ortega-Alcázar 2009; Lederman 2015), many residents took to informal scavenging or street vending (Perelman and Boy 2010; Whitson 2007; Lacarrieu 2007; Rullansky 2014). Some produced 'artisanal' souvenirs and small gifts while others sold mass-produced trinkets such as tango figurines or key chains to foreign tourists. Knowledge of tourist-friendly cultural forms became a scarce good and one that could result in concrete material advantages in a city battered by unemployment yet buoyed by new visitors.

Drawing upon qualitative fieldwork, this chapter examines the new forms of conflict that have arisen in the historic centre's long-standing outdoor market-fair, as crisis coincided with a sharp rise in tourism.[2] The connection between economic turmoil and the rise of the visitor economy is not unique to Buenos Aires. As has been pointed out in other contexts explored in this volume, from Berlin to Belfast and Rio, tourism is an especially seductive strategy for cities struggling with declining industries, or for neighbourhoods with few economic resources. Yet rather than examine conflicts between local residents and visitors, this chapter explores another theme noted in the introduction: how are the benefits of tourism distributed? Which kinds of local conflicts may arise from the uneven distribution of such benefits?

In analysing the touristic transformation of Buenos Aires' historic centre, this chapter asks how different social groups compete over the resources generated by the visitor economy. This competition does not emerge independently of existing inequalities. Local systems of stratification are transformed or solidified by the everyday political strategies, access to institutions of power and knowledge of recognized artistic forms that residents mobilize to benefit from the city's restructuring. Following a brief history of the touristic district of San Telmo, this chapter documents the strategies that street vendors ranging from artists to antiques dealers to trinket sellers attempt to utilize in a thriving tourist marketplace. It concludes with some insight into the way in which resources associated with the visitor economy are transformed by the dynamics of local inequality.

San Telmo: from historic quarter to tourist quarter

Following the economic crisis, informal vending increased throughout Buenos Aires, but especially in the public spaces of the city's most touristic neighbourhoods such as the historic district of San Telmo. San Telmo is a small neighbourhood located five blocks south of the city's central square, the Plaza de Mayo. Comprising mostly one- and two-storey houses built prior to an 1871 yellow fever outbreak, the area's elite population mostly abandoned the neighbourhood's many ornate dwellings, decamping to the north of the city following the epidemic. Residents and guidebooks point to this history as the reason for the neighbourhood's charm: its mansions became tenements for mostly European immigrants who began arriving soon after the neighbourhood's decline and infused the district with its special amalgam of crumbling elegance and immigrant folkways such as the tango.

The mid-twentieth century represented a key turning point in the neighbourhood's trajectory. A 1950s Corbusier-inspired plan for the redevelopment of the south of the city, the Plan Bonet, included San Telmo and cemented dynamics of disinvestment and outmigration that had begun in the prior decade (Molina y Vedia 1999: 203–233). With the government promising the total demolition and redevelopment of the neighbourhood, local owners and residents were reluctant to invest in the upkeep of their buildings. The redevelopment plan never progressed due to budget shortfalls, but by the 1960s a young architect working for the city government, José María Peña, 'discovered' the now run-down neighbourhood and its mix of old-time residents and newer arrivals from the rural countryside, a *mestizo* working class that had been streaming into Buenos Aires since the 1930s (Donghi 1975; Luna 1971), threatening dominant conceptions of Argentina as a nation of European immigrants (Garguin 2007).[3] Peña eventually pushed through the city's first preservation laws. He also created an antiques fair in 1970 that attracted other middle-class residents to a neighbourhood formerly avoided. These developments created a 'bohemian' revival in the neighbourhood. San Telmo attracted artists and antiques storeowners with its cheap but impressive housing stock.

By the 1970s, the local press was already abuzz with a 'return to the south'. Local magazines touted the neighbourhood's charming cobbled streets, quirky antiques dealers, and emerging nightlife. Erased from this history were the racialized migrants that had become a significant – if invisible – presence in the neighbourhood. Instead, the returning middle class of antique dealers and artists became the inheritors of the neighbourhood's European immigrant past. The Sunday fair's reputation grew throughout the 1980s and 1990s. Though tourism in the city picked up in the 1990s, San Telmo retained a fairly sleepy atmosphere, with antiques stores catering to deep-pocketed locals and tourists in the know. From the perspective of the owners of antiques stores, these were heady times. Buenos Aires was an expensive city and attracted well-heeled visitors. Tourists came to San Telmo specifically to buy pricey antiques rather than mass-produced souvenirs on the street.

With the local currency devalued by almost 75 per cent in 2002, this dynamic changed almost overnight. While at first this meant a surge of 'early adopters' – mostly North Americans and Europeans – following the global financial crisis of 2008, the demographics of tourism shifted. Latin Americans – especially newly flush members of Brazil's rapidly growing middle class – significantly increased their share of Argentina's tourism flows. Whereas in 2006 Europeans outnumbered Brazilian tourists to Argentina, by 2012 the situation was reversed, with Brazilians making up close to one quarter of all visitors entering the country (Secretaría de Turismo 2006, 2012).

Tourists were attracted to the vending of local gifts and souvenirs, an activity taking place in the street and thus largely unaffected by rising real-estate prices. In the streets of San Telmo, this generated new forms of conflict between antiques storeowners, ambulant artisans and everyday street vendors. Tourists no longer came to San Telmo to buy antiques priced in the thousands of dollars. Instead, the consumption needs of the majority of tourists were now met by artisans and handicraft makers, and, at the lowest end, mass-produced trinket and souvenir sellers. Souvenir stores and restaurants began to replace antiques stores, while the sidewalks in front of businesses became battlefields between storeowners protecting their turf and vendors making ends meet.

A 2008 plan by the local government to pedestrianize the neighbourhood's cobbled streets was opposed by antiques dealers who saw in it a tacit boon to the neighbourhood's street artists and restaurants who would fill more public space with tables and commerce (Kiernan 2008). Paradoxically, the most precarious informal workers saw their fortunes rise with the flood of tourism.

The art of value

As Harvey (2002) has pointed out, to the degree to which products are understood as unique, producers are able to capture monopoly rents, higher prices characteristic of a good's one-of-a-kind nature. Some products may be natural monopolies while others can achieve this status if they successfully produce a differentiated image. Culture is by its very ontology situated locally and provides a type of monopoly rent. In other words, it is never fully fungible despite its increasingly commercialized forms. For this reason, local culture has become a particularly valuable commodity in the global economy, mobilized in a competition for investment by a hierarchy of culturally differentiated urban 'brands' (Greenberg 2008).

For local governments, cultural forms that are most identifiably local are particularly attractive for branding efforts aimed at tourism. Forms such as tango in the case of Buenos Aires provide multi-directional opportunities for image production: a cultural form may become associated with an individual city, while the city itself gains a reputation for these cultural forms (Johansson and Kociatkiewicz 2011). Though urban governments may try to promote or develop cultural offerings using instrumental logics, at its core, culture is difficult to detach from the local identities, spaces and histories that produce it (Gotham 2005a, 2005b).

However, not all cultural products are equally valuable. The most readily marketable often are subject to strict forms of cultural gatekeeping. The knowledge necessary to produce these forms corresponds to higher social locations, valorising 'art for art's sake' orientations over commerce and individual production over standardization (Wherry 2012). On an everyday level, street performers or vendors often require permission from government institutions to engage in cultural production. Some vendors are considered artisans if they use established fine arts production methods or have formal artistic training. In this way they are legitimized in the eyes of the state or neighbourhood institutions.

Beyond the knowledge necessary to partake in institutionalized cultural forms, particular kinds of social networks may be used as strategic resources in cities undergoing tourism-based redevelopment. Those with access may associate with

institutions such as museums or local fairs, or obtain legal legitimacy from politicians or neighbourhood associations. But these associative forms are not distributed at random; they typically express existing forms of inequality, with higher
status individuals capable of mobilizing more beneficial networks (see, for example, Centner 2012b). Especially in cities with large informal sectors, the urban
poor and middle classes may attempt to insert themselves into new global flows
by commercializing the cultural forms and experiences that comprise the visitor
economy. However, state institutions and existing cultural hierarchies define the
cultural repertoires that are deemed representative of a city, providing artistic
legitimacy to some residents, while excluding others. The outdoor tourist market
explored in the next sections of this chapter shows how commercial activities that
appear to provide possibilities for all residents may in fact reproduce existing
forms of exclusion.

The production of value at a tourist market

It is 7 a.m. on a Sunday morning and the vendors in San Telmo are beginning to
set up their stands. Many of the structures are metal; tables standing on four legs
cresting a few feet above to create a canopy on which plastic can be placed in the
case of rain. Like much of the Sunday San Telmo fair, what appears to an outside
observer to be a singular form of vending is in fact a range of differentiated
organizations with varying levels of formalization and legality. Vendors range
from the city-ordained antiques fair in the centrally located Plaza Dorrego, to
semi-legal artisan fairs on the adjacent streets, to knick-knack, clothing and
perfume sellers further north on the Calle Defensa. Some rent tables while the
least privileged work with a towel or blanket on the sidewalk or street.

The Plaza Dorrego remains the heart of the fair, first organized in the 1970s
Figure 14.1). The vendors here are older and well regulated. Their stands have
plastic nametags and numbers. Many are hobbyists, with professions such as
architect, pensioner or civil servant. Some joined the fair as a hobby to later
become antiques storeowners in the neighbourhood. Unlike the other vendors in
the area, they have a monopoly on legal vending, as it is the only fair sponsored
by the Museum of the City and organized through the Ministry of Culture.

For this reason, they have aligned themselves with the antiques storeowners,
against the vendors who many regard as intruders who have diminished the fair's
genteel history. Many of these original members of the fair refer to the other
vendors generically as *manteros* ('blanketers' – those who lay their products on
blankets on the sidewalk), a term that deprives them of their status as artisans,
suggesting that they are merely sellers of wholesale goods.

A few blocks south on the Calle Defensa, David is a vendor in his early fifties
who organizes an artisan cooperative and is therefore not new to organizing. His
weathered face and conspiratorial laugh seem in keeping with his political beliefs
and life trajectory. He describes nostalgically his participation in Argentina's
Leftist guerrilla movement of the 1970s. David's cooperative, La Piedra, is near
the bottom of the fair's hierarchy and is made up of artisans and handicraft

Figure 14.1 The 'formal' vendors of the Museum of the City's antiques fair, June 2013.
Source: Author.

makers that organized in order to resist the criminalization of street vending. They do not have a permit to operate where they are, unlike those in many of the other streets, who gradually acquired temporary permission by city authorities eager to pacify needy residents in the aftermath of the 2001–2 crisis. The members of La Piedra are not, however, among the most precarious, who are often immigrants from other South American countries with few political ties. David and his co-organizer are politically savvy and tied to the social and political movements aligned with the national government, with deep knowledge of the legal system, strategies of collective representation and organizing.

Culture and economic crisis in urban artisanship

In the 1970s urban artisanal production made its debut in Buenos Aires. Stemming in part from artisanal traditions gaining ground in Europe, the original artisans in Buenos Aires saw themselves connected to a type of global 'hippy culture' (Rotman 2004: 17). The first established artisanal fairs took place in the Plaza Francia, in the upscale neighbourhood of Recoleta, inspired by the institutional arrangement of the antiques fair in San Telmo. But the strict protocols of the Museum of the City (which sponsors the fairs) did not last long. By 1973 a number of 'parallel' fairs had appeared adjacent to the original fair and lacked the institutional backing of the museum. This led artisans to seek institutional approval based on their *de facto* use of public space.

During the 1990s there was increasing institutional interest in the most professionalized forms of urban artisanship. This was a time when UN programmes highlighting local cultural heritage were being diffused on a worldwide scale. The new level of political and administrative autonomy obtained by the city of Buenos Aires in 1996 (De Luca *et al.* 2002) also contributed to a deepening concern for local identity, seen as a deficit during prior unelected municipal governments. In the late 1990s, the city government set up a programme for studying and promoting what it called 'urban artisanship'. While the programme sought to call attention to an artistic activity that had garnered little official interest in the realm of culture, in many respects it produced new hierarchies among vendors. The prizes awarded to artisans as well as the institutional backing in the form of museum exhibitions and edited volumes on the topic reinforced 'art for art's sake' criteria that divorced artistic recognition from the forms of labour precariousness and economic struggle that characterizes artisanal production in the city.

By 2001, however, the city government's interest in promoting non-traditional forms of cultural production would seem woefully inadequate. Far from creating a new realm of high-status artistic appreciation based on 'urban artisanship', the city was replete with various forms of semi-artisanal production. In many cases, newly impoverished residents created parallel fairs to those already regulated and were regarded as inauthentic interlopers among many of the established *feriantes*. They were no longer non-conformist members of the middle class, but in many cases were sectors of the urban poor and members of the so-called 'new poor' produced as a result of crisis.

As the economy worsened, new forms of ambulant vending appeared throughout the city. The hierarchies of vending – its legality, pricing and location – demonstrated the ways in which individuals made use of culture as an economic resource as they sought out new forms of survival. This search for value in the marketplace produced a dizzying array of distinctions between different kinds of vendors. There were fine artists, artisans, handicraft makers (*manualistas*) and those selling everyday goods on a blanket. The highest value-added activities generally required distinct repertoires of knowledge, training and tools. These included awareness of various artistic styles and language ability for interactions with tourists. These categories were particularly salient in San Telmo following the 2001–2 crisis. The restricted access to the established fairs catalysed organizing for the legalization of new fairs. Yet in order to position themselves as deserving subjects of state legalization, vendors had to claim the social identity of artisans, not ambulant vendors. After an intense campaign for legalization, including making contact with various local legislators and picketing streets in order to call attention to their cause, the city authorized a number of new fairs between 2002 and 2006.

The new fairs had distinct social origins and political themes. For example, the new 'Tango, Tradition, and First Peoples' fair was comprised of many formerly lower-middle- and middle-class residents whose political actions consisted mostly of petitioning the local government for legalization. On the other hand, other fairs were tied to broader social movements such as the Asamblea del Pueblo (Assembly of the People) social movement, a group oriented toward housing struggles in the city but with broader political intentions centred upon 'revolutionary struggle'.

The temporary granting of official permits for access to public space represented a new modality of governance in dealing with the effects of crisis. For example, the Asamblea del Pueblo had originally occupied a site underneath a highway, engaging in bartering, a practice that emerged during the most desperate days of the crisis. In order to remove them from this spot, they were offered access on Sunday to the Pasaje Giuffra in San Telmo, a single-block alley with high visibility from the Sunday fair. There they were allowed to sell handicrafts or collector items.

Blocks away, the 'Tango, Tradition, and First People's' fair also managed to eke out a tenuous form of permanence. For years these producers had sold artisanal products on the other side of the street, across from the Museum of the City's fine arts fair (Figure 14.2). After being subject to police harassment, however, they mounted a campaign for legalization. They framed their struggle within a

Figure 14.2 The stand of an artist at the 'Tango, Tradition, and First Peoples' fair, one of many fairs given semi-legal status in the aftermath of crisis, April 2013.

Source: Author.

broader narrative of economic struggle in the post-crisis period, connecting their cause to a local health centre and devising a plan to donate a small fee to the centre in exchange for the city's permission.

Tenuous belonging: informal and formal

Informal gatekeeping

The northern blocks of Defensa Street are the least attractive to vendors. They are far from the Plaza Dorrego, the centre of the original fair, and tourists are unlikely to walk so many blocks. Departing from the Plaza de Mayo, the city's central square, the first blocks of the fair are crammed with scarves, perfume, souvenir trinkets, DVDs and the occasional handicraft (Figure 14.3). According to many of the more privileged vendors, these stands are run by 'mafias', sellers of whole-sale goods that employ informal vendors, often immigrants, who are paid only a fraction of the sales made. Indeed many of the vendors here are Bolivian and Peruvian immigrants, who generally have legal status given Argentina's progressive immigration laws, yet are nonetheless subject to discrimination and police harassment (Grimson 2005, 2006).

Figure 14.3 Vendors selling socks and other wholesale items toward the north of Defensa Street, May 2013.

Source: Author.

Walking further toward the Plaza Dorrego, the fair becomes increasingly arti-sanal. Beatriz, a middle-class artisan in her late twenties sits on a block that represents one of the first of those displaying handicrafts and artisanal goods. Beatriz and her fellow artisans demonstrate the hidden mechanisms of symbolic ownership of the street. She proudly claims that the artisans here took over this block informally. These practices were particularly important prior to establish-ing an internal organization for the block. She explains that during this period, rules were made on the spot: "The rules aren't written, they're more tacit,' she says. "Here the city doesn't interfere. It's the street, it's free, we organize however we can . . . Now we have an internal organization', she explains, 'but before it was just like if someone came over here [trying to sell wholesale goods], you as an artisan would just be like, "excuse me, no, get up, here, you can't sell that, you'll have to leave, you can't be here".'

Beatriz's conception of 'the street' suggests the idea of a chaotic public sphere where individuals must create organization through informal negotiation, 'however they can'. Yet Beatriz and her group's symbolic ownership of this space shows how rights and belonging are not universally accessible, but strati-fied by claims to legitimate forms of cultural and artistic production. Beatriz and her block have now organized internally, with a street delegate who evaluates the appropriateness of the goods of any potential newcomer. Yet prior to this formal mode of boundary creation, the block was already inaccessible to those unable to conform to their standards of production.

Beatriz's block of artisans does not exclude non-artisans out of malice. They are, however, mindful of the value of their own work. The presence of non-artisans calls into question the authenticity of their production. Yet while many artisans frame their struggle within this context, expressing solidarity with the least privileged vendors, they too have internalized the hierarchies that systematically exclude some vendors from the most prized spaces of the street. Beatriz and others like her at the fair do not need to resort to force to protect the symbolic purity of their space. Rather, they have a much more powerful set of claims at their disposal. Their work blends a repertoire of privileged practices with a sense of belonging, the stakes of which are physical sites of the city (Centner 2008). Their artisanal work appeals both to the dominant cultural values of the neighbourhood, which have been produced by powerful public institutions and individuals, as well as an artistic identity that corresponds to these values. It is worth noting, however, that these artisans are deploying a particular set of cultural repertoires – a specific strategy or 'toolkit' to achieve commercial success and moral authority over this space. The contours of this toolkit may be creatively applied by individu-als yet it is not available to all. Rather, it is stratified by a set of social back-grounds and forms of cultural knowledge.

A block away from Beatriz is Daniel, a vendor in his early fifties who is selling handmade jewellery identified as 'indigenous' for its blend of metals with exotic multi-colour stones that are not easy identifiable. A book entitled *Mapuche Art* is sitting prominently on his table next to his jewellery, though when I ask Daniel if he is from the Mapuche community he says no. He is from outside Buenos Aires. Daniel buys sheets of metal and spends his week making his jewellery and sometimes selling at other fairs outside of the city, where he lives in a lower-middle-class western municipality. Daniel is not one of the most privileged vendors; he does not have a university degree, nor was he a formal full-time worker prior to the crisis, as many of the vendors are. Indeed Daniel says that he has done this for the last thirty years, sometimes taking up odd-jobs (*changas*) to get by.

Daniel, however, is not among the least privileged vendors either. His smaller pieces such as earrings sell for 50 to 100 pesos (about US$6–12 at the time of the interview), which in the local context is a meaningful sum. His cultural capital in terms of knowing other middle-class vendors and thus being able to achieve a place on this street of artisans allows him to avoid the value-deteriorating experience of selling with those at the beginning of Defensa who do not possess the proper repertoires of knowledge necessary for selling to tourists. Daniel also refers to these groups as 'Peruvian mafias', explaining to me that Peruvians will sell anything anywhere with no scruples. Ironically, those most likely to be of an indigenous identity to which Daniel's work appeals – such as the Bolivian or Peruvian vendors – are not able to commercialize this identity. They likely lack the institutionalized training, foreign language skills or political connections that would provide access to prominent spaces on the street or the artistic representations tourists demand. Instead, the wholesale goods of the least privileged vendors elicit far smaller margins and considerably less profit.

Formal politics: mobilizing networks

The first stretch of vendors recede into the Avenida Independencia, which separates an area legalized by a 2011 law from the blocks ceded to the antique galleries. But these blocks have not in fact been given over without conflict. The cooperative La Piedra, mentioned at the beginning of this chapter, has remained on these blocks, despite police harassment and the increasingly angry antique gallery owners and their business group, the Association of Antiquarians of San Telmo. Drawing mostly from lower-middle and impoverished middle-class residents of Buenos Aires and its outskirts, La Piedra's resistance to removal shows how cultural resources can be parlayed into social and political rights. La Piedra has deftly tapped into a discourse on artisanship, its members positioning themselves as artisans and not 'ambulant vendors' while appealing to San Telmo's creative vibe and bohemian history to legitimize their presence. They have also tapped into a current of economic nationalism that resonates in post-crisis Argentina. La Piedra is about creating workers (*trabajadores*) and not vendors. Workers in Argentina have rights and members cast their ability to sell their goods not as a form of the local government's munificence but as a right to a dignified existence.

La Piedra is led by David and Cecilia. Cecilia is an activist in her fourties with deep political ties and allegiances to the Evita Movement (*Moviemiento Evita*), a social movement connected to the national government. La Piedra is aligned with the Federation of Popular Economy Workers (CTEP), an organization that has attempted to organize informal economic sectors, a reality that it argues must be recognized rather than criminalized. The *cooperativistas* from La Piedra represent a broad section of lower-middle-class and working-class individuals. Few, however, are immigrants or from the very poorest backgrounds. Some live in the less expensive areas of the capital, while many live in the rust-belt municipalities surrounding the city. La Piedra must police the boundaries of members' behaviour and sales activity if the blocks where vendors sell are to be recognized as artisanal.

On the 1000 block of Defensa early on a Sunday morning Hilda approaches David. She too would like to sell on Defensa and has been told to speak with David about acquiring a spot. 'Not today,' she is told; 'Come back next week early in the morning to see if there is a spot available. What is it that you sell?' David asks. 'You know, these headbands like the one I'm wearing.' David looks sceptical. 'OK, well come back next week, but you know you have to make them yourselves, nothing from Once[4] can be sold on this block.'

Weeks later, at a meeting at the Confederation of the Popular Economy in the working-class neighbourhood of Constitución, María, a clothing designer, presents a capacity building programme that will provide members with assistance in marketing and merchandizing. Moments later, Cecilia enters the building and starts to explain current strategies of the cooperative. 'I have some good news, comrades (*compañeros*),' she says. The order to evict them from Defensa Street had been temporarily revoked by a judge. 'But we can't let down our guard,' Cecilia cautions, the city government can appeal, and according to her sources, the judge who will hear the appeal has a family member that is an antiques dealer. Cecilia proceeds to outline strategies for creating associations with local actors and institutions. In organizing for a day of publicity and a press conference meant to counter negative news coverage documenting 'chaos', 'scams' and 'threatening' vendors in San Telmo (see for example Ríos 2013), Cecilia notes that having the head of her political movement, known for his fiery class rhetoric, will not help their cause. Instead, she is trying to get the country's former Minister of Foreign Affairs and supporter of *Movimiento Evita*, to come and publicize the vendors' work. He is more acceptable to the middle-class residents, she says, well respected by people across the political spectrum, and will represent a more palatable figure for wooing local residents. Additional plans include handing out hot chocolate and putting on street shows for neighbourhood kids, as well as creating a catalogue of the *cooperativistas'* artisanal products in English, Spanish and Portuguese. Cecilia is thus appealing to the cultural values of the community and the potential ability of La Piedra to be a part of this community. Anything that will enhance local resident's impression of La Piedra enhances their legitimacy in a neighbourhood in which residents symbolize 'authenticity' against the sweeping tide of commercial gentrification and foreign tourism.

In order to mark the cooperative as legitimate in the neighbourhood, not all practices can be allowed on the street. Halfway through the meeting at the

Confederation for the Popular Economy, a woman in her forties makes a request. Her son is 16 and she is having trouble paying her rent. He has bought some T-shirts wholesale that he has altered with a new design and wants to sell on the street to help the family make some money. Her tone is pleading and everyone at the meeting seems moved. But surprisingly, Cecilia is firm and the other vendors agree. Her selling T-shirts on the street is a threat to the authenticity of all of them. If she starts with T-shirts, where will this end? Other members provide solidarity but remain unyielding. Her son can come to another artisan's leather studio, tell him to learn a trade. In this way, vendors collectively police their behaviour and that of other members to maintain the value of their products.

Cecilia and the cooperative thereby produce powerful forms of symbolism and create associations with multiple actors in order to further their economic aims. Yet it is worth pointing out that these actors and the cultural meanings invoked are not equally available to all. Access is based on a hierarchy of cultural knowledge. Cecilia is savvy at navigating this hierarchy: deploying certain symbolic strategies for some situations while recognizing that others require a different set of manoeuvres allows the cooperative to maintain a foothold in the lucrative tourist market. These strategies are multiple, situational and often creatively applied or ignored, yet they are not chosen at random. Creating a formal catalogue of their products in English and Portuguese, for example, requires a repertoire of knowledge that is socially patterned differently to the bilingualism in reach of Peruvian vendors at the northern end of the street. Access to English and Portuguese generates material benefits, but indigenous languages are positioned lower within a hierarchy of beneficial cultural tools.

The culture(s) of poverty: engaging cultural production at the margins

On a chilly day in August 2012, I approach the former Padelai orphanage, a stone building built in the nineteenth century at an important local intersection. The Padelai is an imposing construction that had been occupied by dozens of families since the 1980s. But in 2003, 128 families were evicted from the building with the city government citing structural problems and the risk of collapse. The site was later slated to become a Spanish cultural centre. The city subsidized the project by providing the Spanish government with a 30-year rent-free lease in exchange for the building's upgrade to create a new 'cultural pole' in the south of city. But Spain's economic crisis left the building in disuse and occupants reappeared in early 2012. A court case will decide the fate of those living in the building and in the meantime no new inhabitants are to enter. But Tomás, a short man in his fifties, encourages me to enter through a back gate and seems unconcerned with the police out front. Tomás has lived in the San Telmo neighbourhood on and off for some thirty years. Like many of the occupants of the Padelai he moved to Buenos Aires in the early 1980s from the impoverished northern province of Jujuy. In the late 1980s, Tomás and fellow residents petitioned the city government to be incorporated as a cooperative and to gain legal possession of the complex. Architectural renderings were created, funding was secured by the city and hopes were high among the *cooperativistas*. Tomás proudly shows me the twenty-year-old professional architectural blueprints. But hyperinflation and economic crisis, a change in city policy and increased land values from the redevelopment of the nearby waterfront scuttled plans for city funding.

Tomás believes the Padelai to be an important historical site in the neighbourhood. For Tomás, the cultural history of the orphanage as a place for marginalized children meant that the building should be preserved for marginalized ('popular') groups today. Tomás laments the partial destruction of the building that occurred as preliminary works began prior to the suspended plans for the Spanish cultural centre. Unlike the local state, which strove to frame redevelopment as a preservation policy contributing to the neighbourhood's revitalization through the building of a 'cultural pole', Tomás cast the use of the building for popular sectors without access to housing as representing an 'authentic' history of the building and neighbourhood.

While artisans generally present themselves as protecting the interests of the neighbourhood's popular sectors, the Sunday street fair provides few opportunities to members of the Padelai cooperative that may lack the connections and forms of knowledge, tools and capital that can be converted into material resources. Recently, however, this has changed. The Padelai cooperative has taken to organizing its own festival on Sunday on its sprawling premises, offering folk music and homemade food. This festival invokes a rather different set of symbolic forms than the rest of the market. It is called the 'Patio Provincial' (Provincial Patio), with folkloric music, dance and food from the country's rural provinces, such as Tomás' native Jujuy. The invocation of 'provincial' Argentina conjures a number of socially meaningful representations. The provincial culture being produced is not that of the wealthiest industrial centres of the country, but the mythic culture of the poorest, connected to the colonial creole past long mythologized in Argentina as untouched by modernity and the European immigration that characterized the development of cities like Buenos Aires (Prieto 1988; De Jong 2005; Sarlo 1982). In the Padelai's sprawling patio, there is dancing, drinking and a band playing Argentine folk music. Some international tourists look perplexed while the boldest join in the festivities. Yet when I ask three young women, all with light-brown hair and familiar accents about the band, I am told that they came down together with their friends from the large (and relatively prosperous) city of Rosario, some three hours away. Most of those attending are Argentine, from Buenos Aires. They appear excited at the prospect of a more authentic cultural experience. Some are politically aware of the Padelai's situation and keen to partake in popular offerings in the neighbourhood.

Here, then, culture is being used as a legitimation strategy as well. It is one that mobilizes culture for profit, yet contradicts the form of cultural instrumentalization produced by the city government in its urban policies in San Telmo. The 'cultural pole' the city sought to cement with the construction of a Spanish cultural centre and its proximity to the refurbished Museum of Modern Art a block away conflicts with the cultural strategies of the Padelai residents. The scenes of poverty and informality that characterize this site do not cohere with the dominant touristic image that city leaders sought to leverage in the neighbourhood's upgrade. Yet in recognizing the social power embedded in the *idea* of culture in the district, the cooperative residents have been able to mobilize cultural practices to their benefit. The residents of the Padelai appear to have skilfully constructed more than a spectacle of poverty. This is not a *favela* tour (see Broudehoux in this volume), but rather taps into the discourse of authenticity represented by the neighbourhood itself. What separates the members of the Padelai from the most precarious vendors at the market is their ability to combine the raw materials of a privileged space in the neighbourhood with linkages to actors with other forms of social and cultural capital.

Conclusions

All of these complex associational strategies suggest the ways in which cultural forms, global flows and urban spaces represent new sites of contention for cities undergoing processes of tourist-led redevelopment. In the case of Buenos Aires, the terms of struggle can be seen in conflicts over the definition of artisanal products, over what is the 'authentic' essence of the city's historic centre and who can embody it, and over the terms of access to the lucrative tourist market.

Cultural production is, of course, central to contemporary patterns of tourism. Visitors hope to see, experience and purchase elements of an authentic local culture. While studies of tourism in globalizing cities have tended to emphasize conflicts over rising rents and the impact of outsiders on local communities, less work has been done on understanding how existing forms of culture and inequality are reshaped by these global flows. On the one hand, the privileging of vernacular forms of culture, essential to the increased emphasis on 'authentic' experiences, might provide socially and economically marginalized groups access to new resources and labour markets. On the other, those with the ability to define the contours of authenticity often do so in ways that privilege their own forms of cultural production.

Debates over the value of particular artistic forms might appear to be obscure conflicts internal to local producers. But as the above cases make clear, they can also be central to establishing symbolic ownership over new sites of touristic development. Forms of gatekeeping may rely upon existing forms of stratification. But cultural producers must improvise new tactics, strategies of representation and associational linkages if they are to benefit from tourism-led dynamics of urban redevelopment.

What is clear in each of these struggles is the centrality of physical spaces of the city in the construction and maintenance of these boundaries. While access to repertoires of cultural knowledge may be stratified, public spaces of the city are purportedly accessible to all. Yet here too processes of social and cultural power reshape the ability of individuals to benefit from tourism. Some social connections, forms of knowledge and systems of representation may yield concrete benefits, while others prove of little assistance. While poor and working-class groups may be systematically disadvantaged in a struggle to claim belonging in urban space, the field of touristic production is hardly so straightforward. In an era characterized by claims to the authentic, less privileged residents may find themselves with the raw materials of culture that can be parlayed into economic benefit. Under a specific set of conditions, they may find creative strategies for reaping some of the benefits of the growing visitor economy.

Notes

1 *Porteños* ("of the port") are the residents of Buenos Aires.
2 Research for this chapter was conducted between July 2012 and September 2013. In addition to 17 semi-structured interviews with artisans and street vendors, it relied upon dozens of informal conversations conducted during participant observation at the fair itself, local political protests, community board meetings, and neighbourhood events. Pseudonyms are used throughout this chapter.
3 In many Latin American countries the term *mestizo* refers to the social groups that were descendants of Spanish colonizers and indigenous populations (see Mörner 1966 for a classic account of 'race' in Latin America). In Argentina, the term is rarely used in part because of an official discourse that stresses Argentina's roots in European immigration (Garguin 2007). However, as the country industrialized in the 1930s, the city of Buenos Aires and its outskirts became the site of the large-scale migration of darker-skinned migrants from the countryside. Alarmed by the presence of this racialized urban proletariat, much of Buenos Aires' middle and upper class scorned the presence of these rural migrants, dubbed '*cabecitas negras*' or 'little black heads' (Ratier 1972).
4 Once is a neighbourhood with a high concentration of wholesale businesses in which informal vending proliferates.

References

[Unless otherwise stated, all URLs were last accessed 4 August 2015.]
Beccaria, L. and Groisman, F. (2008) 'Informalidad y pobreza en Argentina', *Investigación Económica*, 266: 135–69.
Blustein, P. (2006) *And the Money Kept Rolling In (and Out): Wall Street, the IMF, and the Bankrupting of Argentina*. New York: Public Affairs.
Carman, M. (2006) *Las trampas de la cultura: Los 'intrusos' y los nuevos usos del barrio de Gardel*. Buenos Aires: Ediciones Paidos Iberica.
Centner, R. (2008) 'Places of privileged consumption practices: spatial capital, the dotcom habitus, and San Francisco's internet boom', *City and Community*, 7(3): 193–223.
Centner, R. (2012a) 'Moving away, moving onward: displacement pressures and divergent neighborhood politics in Buenos Aires', *Environment and Planning A*, 44(11): 2555–73.
Centner, R. (2012b) 'Microcitizenships: fractious forms of urban belonging after Argentine neoliberalism', *International Journal of Urban and Regional Research*, 36(2): 336–62.
Cohen, M. (2012) *Argentina's Economic Growth and Recovery, 2001–2008*. London: Routledge.
Crot, L. (2006) '"Scenographic" and "cosmetic" planning: globalization and territorial restructuring in Buenos Aires', *Journal of Urban Affairs*, 28(3): 227–51.
Dávila, A. (2012) *Culture Words: Space, Value, and Mobility across the Neoliberal Americas*. New York: NYU Press.

De Jong, I. (2005) 'Entre Indios e inmigrantes: el pensamiento nacionalista y los precursores del folklore en la antropología Argentina del cambio del siglo (XIX–XX)', *Revista de Indias*, 65(234): 405–26.

De Luca, M., Jones, M. and Tula, M. I. (2002) 'Buenos Aires: the evolution of local governance', in M. Del Carmen Feijó (2003) *Nuevo país, nueva pobreza*. Madrid: Fondo de Cultura Económica de España.

Del Carmen Feijó, M. (2003) *Nuevo país, nueva pobreza*. Madrid: Fondo de Cultura Económica de España.

Donghi, T. H. (1975) 'Algunas observaciones sobre Germani, el surgimiento del Peronismo y los migrantes internos', *Desarrollo Económico*, 14(56): 765–81.

Garguin, E. (2007) '"Los Argentinos descendemos de los barcos": the racial articulation of middle class identity in Argentina (1920–1960)', *Latin American and Caribbean Ethnic Studies*, 2(2): 161–84.

Gotham, K. F. (2005a) 'Tourism from above and below: globalization, localization and New Orleans's Mardi Gras', *International Journal of Urban and Regional Research*, 29(2): 309–26.

Gotham, K. F. (2005b) 'Tourism gentrification: the case of New Orleans' Vieux Carré (French Quarter)', *Urban Studies*, 42(7): 1099–121.

Greenberg, M. (2008) *Branding New York*. New York: Routledge.

Grimson, A. (2005) *Relatos de la diferencia y la igualdad: los Bolivianos en Buenos Aires*. Buenos Aires: Eudeba.

Grimson, A. (2006) 'Nuevas xenofobias, nuevas políticas étnicas en la Argentina', in A. Grimson and E. Jelin (eds) *Migraciones regionales hacia la Argentina: diferencia, desigualdad y derechos*. Buenos Aires: Prometeo.

Harvey, D. (2002) 'The art of rent: globalisation, monopoly and the commodification of culture', *Socialist Register*, 38: 93–110.

Jajamovich, G. (2012) 'Del parque España a Puerto Madero: circulación del urbanismo de los arquitectos y la planificación estratégica entre Argentina y España (1979–1993)', *Cuaderno Urbano*, 12(12): 7–25.

Johansson, M. and Kociatkiewicz, J. (2011) 'City festivals: creativity and control in staged urban experiences', *European Urban and Regional Studies*, 18(4): 392–405.

Kanai, M. and Ortega-Alcázar, I. (2009) 'The prospects for progressive culture-led urban regeneration in Latin America: cases from Mexico City and Buenos Aires', *International Journal of Urban and Regional Research*, 33(2): 483–501.

Kiernan, S. (2008) 'Una obra perfectamente inútil', *Página12*, 30 August. Online. Available at http://www.pagina12.com.ar/diario/suplementos/m2/10-1485-2008-08-30.html.

Lacarrieu, M. (2007) 'La "insoportable levedad" de lo urbano', *EURE*, 33(99): 47–64.

Lederman, J. (2015) 'Urban fads and consensual fictions: creative, sustainable, and competitive city policies in Buenos Aires', *City and Community*, 14(1): 47–67.

Libertun de Duren, N. (2006) 'Planning à la carte: the location patterns of gated communities around Buenos Aires in a decentralized planning context', *International Journal of Urban and Regional Research*, 30(2): 308–27.

Luna, F. (1971) *El 45: Crónica de un año decisivo*. Buenos Aires: Sudamericana.

Luongo, M. (2003) 'Buenos Aires: where glamour and chaos merge', *New York Times*, 29 April. Online. Available at http://www.nytimes.com/2003/04/29/business/business-travel-on-the-ground-buenos-aires-where-glamour-and-chaos-merge.html.

Molina y Vedia, J. (1999) *Mi Buenos Aires herido: planes de desarrollo territorial y urbano: 1535–2000*. Buenos Aires: Ediciones Colihue.

Mörner, M. (1966) 'The history of race relations in Latin America: some comments on the state of research', *Latin American Research Review*, 1(3): 17–44.

Myers, D. and Dietz, H. (eds) *Capital City Politics in Latin America: Democratization and Empowerment*. Boulder, CO: Lynne Reinner.

Perelman, M. and Boy, M. (2010) 'Cartoneros en Buenos Aires: nuevas modalidades de encuentro', *Revista Mexicana de Sociología*, 72(3): 393–418.

Prieto, A. (1988) *El discurso criollista en la formación de la Argentina moderna*. Buenos Aires: Sudamericana.

Ratier, H. (1972) *El cabecita negra*. Buenos Aires: Centro Editor de América Latina.

Ríos, H. (2013) 'La salada de San Telmo: vergüenza para Buenos Aires', *Noticias Urbanas*, 11 April. Online. Available at https://www.noticiasurbanas.com.ar/noticias/la-salada-de-san-telmo-verguenza-para-buenos-aires/.

Rotman, M. (2004) 'Ferias de Artesanías en la ciudad de Buenos Aires: memorias de una producción cultural urbana', in L. Maronese (ed.), *La artesanía urbana como patrimonio cultural*. Buenos Aires: Comisión para la Preservación del Patrimonio Histórico Cultural de la Ciudad de Buenos Aires.

Rullansky, I. (2014) 'Los manteros del microcentro porteño: la construcción de una presencia ilegítima en el espacio público', *Argumentos: Revista de Crítica Social*, 16: 286–314.

Sarlo, B. (1982) 'Vanguardia y criollismo: la aventura de "Martin Fierro"', *Revista de Crítica Literaria Latinoamericana*, 8(15): 39–69.

Secretaría de Turismo (2006) *Anuario estadístico de turismo 2006*. Buenos Aires: Secretary of Tourism of the Government of Argentina.

Secretaría de Turismo (2012) *Anuario estadístico de turismo 2012*. Buenos Aires: Secretary of Tourism of the Government of Argentina.

Torres, H. (2001) 'Cambios socioterritoriales en Buenos Aires durante la década de 1990', *EURE*, 27(80): 33–56.

Wherry, F. (2012) 'Performance circuits in the marketplace', *Politics and Society*, 40(2): 203–21.

Whitson, R. (2007) 'Hidden struggles: spaces of power and resistance in informal work in urban Argentina', *Environment and Planning A*, 39(12): 2916–34.

World Bank (2014) *International Tourism, Number of Arrivals*. Online. Available at http://data.worldbank.org/indicator/ST.INT.ARVL.

15 The abrupt rise (and fall) of creative entrepreneurs

Socio-economic change, the visitor economy and social conflict in a traditional neighbourhood of Shanghai

Non Arkaraprasertkul

During the mid-afternoon of a rather pleasant day in the autumn of 2013, no one expected a visit from more than two dozen officers from the Urban Management Bureau, especially not the residents of one of Shanghai's most famous traditional alleyway-house neighbourhoods. These officers, also known as *chengguan*, are not usually welcomed by the locals, as they are often the last resort of the city government in enforcing urban management regulations. Numerous media reports about how the *chengguan* abused their power in many large Chinese cities did not help to make their presence less fraught and contentious (Human Rights Watch 2012).[1] The residents of the Tranquil Light neighbourhood, a pseudonym I will use throughout this chapter,[2] were stunned by the number of officials gathered at the south gate of the neighbourhood, who eventually began marching into the main lane. Their blue and white uniforms, as well their white gloves, only added to the growing feeling of dismay among the residents who stood and watched as they dismantled informal structures, temporary tents and parts of buildings piece by piece, hurling the debris into the back of a garbage-collection truck that followed the procession of *chengguan* vehicles. A sizeable crowd gathered to observe the spectacle, and by four o'clock that afternoon it seemed that no one could focus on their work anymore, especially now that the noise from the dismantling process, as well as the shouting from the people whose belongings were confiscated, filled the alleyway.

What the visit of the *chengguan* illustrates is the escalation of a conflict long in the brewing and born out of the impacts of globalization and the rise of the tourism industry and the creative economy on urban space in Shanghai, which I hope to unpack in this chapter. Shanghai has arguably long been China's most well-known city in the eyes of foreign visitors thanks to its quasi-colonial history, primarily under British and French control from the end of the Opium Wars in the mid-nineteenth century until the end of the Second World War. Re-emerging from the socialist planned economy in the wake of China's reform and opening-up of economic policy (*gaigekaifang*) in the late 1980s, Shanghai in the twenty-first century is one of China's four so-called 'first-tier cities' (*yixian chengshi*) along with Beijing, Guangzhou and Shenzhen. Having been a major trading port in the mid-nineteenth century, Shanghai has regained its prominent economic status, and is one of China's most visited cities today. In 2013, the number of domestic and overseas tourists rose to 260 and 7.57 million respectively (HKTDC 2014). According to Reuters (2015), Shanghai ranked only second to Beijing for the number of tourists among all cities in China. What foreign tourists want to see in Shanghai is a combination of cultural and architectural heritage from the nineteenth century (as explained below), as well as physical evidence of China's re-emergence from the socialist shadow and displays of new forms of modernity (Larmer 2010). For domestic tourists, their motivation to visit Shanghai is rooted in a sense of pride and patriotism – citizens from all over China come to the city to have first-hand experience of the 'future of China' (HKTDC 2014).

Over the past decade, the city government of Shanghai has pursued a 'global city' agenda and attempted to put the city back on the map as Asia's most economically viable city (see the edited volume by Chen 2009) to attract customers for Shanghai's main industries (namely retail and wholesale, financial services and real estate). Achieving such status would also give Shanghai the all-round resources to compete head-to-head with the capital Beijing in terms of its symbolic importance to the 'New China' socio-economic programme (see Shin 2012; Wang and Li 2011; Yusuf and Nabeshima 2010). In its efforts, Shanghai's government has increasingly mobilized 'iconic' architecture (Sklair 2006), emulating other 'global' cities such as New York, London and Tokyo. It has also, as described in the next section, increasingly mobilized architectural heritage and the developing cultural and creative industries which have settled in various parts of the city in its place branding efforts. This chapter will investigate, through an ethnographic lens, the social conflicts which have arisen in the Tranquil Light neighbourhood in the face of a sharp increase in both the presence of creative entrepreneurs and of visitors in this traditional, dense neighbourhood of the city. The chapter shows how the emerging creative and visitor economy which has organically grown in this area is perceived in an ambivalent way by local authorities, and how its impacts have been uneven for different categories of local residents, thus paving the way for a conflict materialized by the dramatic entrance of the *chengguan* in the neighbourhood, further explained later in the chapter.[3]

The rise of heritage and creative industries in Shanghai's tourism development

The direct contribution of cultural industries to Shanghai's gross domestic product (GDP) is hard to measure, as it is subsumed within the tertiary sector, itself accounting for approximately two-thirds of the city's overall GDP of 2,160 billion RMB in 2013 (Deutsche Bank Research 2015). Cultural industries and their presence play a role in the decision-making process of potential entrepreneurs thinking about a potential business location in China (as reported by the Chinese Academy of Social Sciences, quoted in Chang 2015). In China, as elsewhere, cities with strong 'cultural brands' seem to be much more attractive to entrepreneurs than cities that only provide basic infrastructure for business such

Figure 15.1 Aerial view of a typical *lilong* neighbourhood, showing the rows of houses within the boundary of a block system, April 2014.

Source: Sue Anne Tay.

as buildings for rent and convenient public transportation system (Berg 2014; Fan 2014; Wuwei 2011; Zukin 1995). Across the world, the so-called 'city branding' process is a widely accepted strategy based on the recognition of the critical role that cultural industries and local cultural heritage play in the context of inter-urban competition. Since the 1990s, city branding has been a major part of Shanghai's urban development programme, and the preservation of historic monuments has increasingly been seen as integral to this process (see Levin 2010; Ren 2008; Tsai 2008). The underlying rationale for this is to protect 'cultural artefacts' that the local government considers appropriate for a city with global ambitions.

In Shanghai, as in many emerging global cities, there is, however, a palpable tension between the city government's growing preservationist ideals and the practical and economic needs of local communities. This is illustrated by the contestations surrounding the traditional alleyway-houses of Shanghai known as *lilong* – such as the 184 houses in the Tranquil Light. Literally meaning 'neighbourhood lane', the *lilong* houses are the legacy of Shanghai's Treaty Port era (1842–1946), representing the Chinese take on the British house row aesthetic (see Arkaraprasertkul 2009; Bracken 2013; Zhao 2004) (Figure 15.1). The *lilong* also constituted the primary housing stock found in Shanghai from the late nineteenth century when this particular building type became the most economical for mass housing up until the early 1980s, with several successive generations having occupied the same dwellings for over a hundred years. Historians, journalists and architects generally agree that *lilong* neighbourhoods are historically important and, therefore, must be protected in order to preserve and maintain the physical evidence of the city's memory so that it can be carried on to the next generation of Shanghainese residents (e.g. Guan 1996; Hammond 2006; Morris 1994; Sorkin 2008; Tsai 2008). In many ways, the attitude underlying this opinion has fuelled the local government's over-romanticization of Shanghai's neighbourhood life (a point which I have argued elsewhere, see Arkaraprasertkul 2011, 2012, 2013). As with the gradually disappearing courtyard family compound houses in Beijing (*hutong*), the *lilong* are now at the centre of a socio-political conflict over urban redevelopment because of their dual nature as both historical artefact and living community (see Wang and Chen 1987; Zhu 2002), as will be explained in the following sections.

Built between the late 1920s and the early 1930s, Tranquil Light was one of the few traditional alleyway-house neighbourhoods that were not torn down to make way for high-rise buildings during the first twenty years after China's economic opening up and reform in the early 1980s. It also survived the second wave of demolitions and new construction in the 1990s that paved the way for Shanghai to become another Special Economic Zone (SEZ), just like the handful of cities in the southern part of China that had hitherto enjoyed SEZ status. The earliest efforts to preserve historic buildings took place in the early 1990s by a few native Shanghainese architectural historians and conservationists. However, their efforts could only prevent a small proportion of historic buildings from being razed in the name of development (Peh 2014). It was not until the early 2000s that the Shanghai Municipal People's Congress passed the 'Shanghai Historical and Cultural Areas and Outstanding Historical Buildings Protection Ordinance', which is commonly hailed as one of the earliest regional laws in China on the preservation of urban historical features in the early 2000s (Information Office of Shanghai Municipality 2009).

The historian and native Shanghainese Qin Shao (2013) recounts the origin of this so-called 'heritage turn' as a series of events that began with the hyperbolic success of Shanghai's most famous luxury retail district Xintiandi, a former *lilong* neighbourhood in Shanghai's former French quarter that was revamped into a high-end commercial *quartier*. According to the urbanist Harry den Hartog (2010), Xintiandi played a crucial role in reinvigorating residents' cultural consciousness and changing how business owners and local government looked at old buildings in the city. Increasingly they were seen less as burdens, but more as assets upon which they could capitalize. The underlying rationale of the new preservation programmes throughout the city is summarized by the deputy chief engineer of the Shanghai Municipal Administration of Cultural Heritage, Tan Yufeng, himself: 'At first, preservation was subordinated to development, then it was seen as equal, and now preservation is seen as the premise of development' (as cited in Waldmeir 2013).

Since the early 2000s, the Shanghai Municipal Administration of Cultural Heritage has registered Tranquil Light as one of the city's important cultural relics to be protected, which made it impossible for anyone to change the way a building looked from the outside despite the fact that some of the houses' interiors had completely been revamped by the residents themselves. In some of the *lilong* neighbourhoods, usually the poorer ones, the government restored the exterior of the buildings, but left the job of upgrading the interior to the residents themselves. This was the case especially during the so-called 'beautification period' when the local government was preparing for the Shanghai Expo in 2010 (see Shao 2013; Weinstein and Ren 2009). Given the central location of Tranquil Light, its original residents were from the upper class, especially those who bought housing units and lived there during the 1930s. Since 1949, the Tranquil Light had been confiscated from these original residents by the CCP (Chinese Communist Party) and turned into public housing for working-class citizens who later populated the neighbourhood with four times more residents (which was then a typical pattern of housing redistribution and allocation across urban areas – see Junhua *et al.* 2001).

Although it is seen as traditional in contemporary Shanghai, the western architectural style that was chosen by the developer in the 1930s for the Tranquil Light project was considered at the time to be most modern and sophisticated. It was built in the British townhouse style with a touch of the classic London-styled crescent (a row of houses forming a uniformly beautiful arc). Archival blueprints and construction documents also show that the project was built with the finest craftsmanship, especially the European-styled metalwork and masonry, one could find outside of Europe. All of these were probably the reason why it had not been knocked down despite the fact that the buildings in the Tranquil Light were mostly three stories and had far less useable floor space than most of the buildings built after the 1990s. Famous film directors had also chosen this place to shoot, as did hundreds of tourists who came to the neighbourhood to have their portraits, photos and selfies shot against this rare backdrop.

But it is not simply visitors (domestic and international tourists) who have been attracted to the *lilong*. Young entrepreneurs, artists and professionals working in the cultural or creative industries were also drawn to the area and, from the early 2000s onwards, began to settle in its rows of houses (Li 2013; Yung *et al.* 2014). The transformation into a cluster for creative entrepreneurs took place over the course of a decade. A few local residents served as middlepersons (*zhongjie*) by putting up signs on behalf of residents who wanted to rent out or sublet their rooms and by showing potential renters around to pocket the 'middleperson's fee' (*zhongjie fei*). 'It was easy for me to get a room . . . The transformation from a typical senior citizen neighbourhood to a community of young creative entrepreneurs was gradual and peaceful, drawing a lot of attention from the media and young people,' said an informant who was one of the first foreigners to move into Tranquil Light and had witnessed the whole process. An internationally recognized online platform writes, 'Just one block down from one of Shanghai's most luxury shopping malls, Tranquil Light has preserved slices of "Old Shanghai" life alongside trendy cafés, indie handicraft stores, and art studios run by young hipsters.' At its peak around 2010, there were more than eighty small shops open in the Tranquil Light, and the neighbourhood was featured in both local and international media, attracting tourists from around the world.

On a typical weekday, there would be more than several hundred visitors in the lane, about half of whom were regulars who came for meals. On a busy weekend, the number of visitors could surge to a couple of thousand. With an area of just above 23,000 square metres and 3,000 residents, the neighbourhood began to feel overcrowded when thousands of visitors flocked onto its streets (Figure 15.2). There were increasing complaints from retired residents about the incursions of gawking tourists and the buzz of activity. 'One would have thought that it would have been the "new rich" types who felt they had paid for tranquillity and had been cheated of it, who complained,' said one of my informants. However, it was among the retired residents that there was a much stronger wish to see the neighbourhood 'remain purely residential as it had always been before the shops began to open'. Some retirees, whose lives were affected by the commercial activities (especially the ones that generated noise), began to write open letters to the neighbourhood committee (known locally as *juweihui*), the lowest level of government in charge of civil affairs, overseeing and enforcing micro-level policies such as family planning, mobile population management and crime prevention, to name but a few (Lieberthal 1995; Winckler and Greenhalgh 2005). These retirees were asking the *juweihui* to help maintain the peaceful environment of the neighbourhood.

Figure 15.2 A daily scene in a typical *lilong* neighbourhood lane, filled with visitors taking photos. July 2014.

Source: Author.

The urban management of a traditional neighbourhood in the globalizing city

Let's return to the *chengguan*'s visit to the Tranquil Light. The official reason for it had been made clear a few weeks earlier on the community's bulletin board: 'All unlicensed businesses in this neighbourhood must relocate within one month.' Although this notice was clearly written in official language and bore the local government's red stamp with a star in the middle of it, few residents thought that the *chengguan* would actually make good this implicit threat of a crackdown, knowing that Tranquil Light was centrally located in the busy, commercial spine of the city and not very far from the headquarters of a major local newspaper. 'The last thing that these *chengguan* officers want is news about their brutality appearing again in the news,' one of the residents told me when I was looking at the bulletin board with curiosity a few days earlier.

The full title of *chengguan* is Officer of the Urban Administrative and Law Enforcement Bureau. Their duty is to enforce laws and maintain social order in Chinese cities. To the CCP, maintaining urban order is key to social stability. Amid many scandals involving high-level officials, including the Communist Party chief of Shanghai himself (Watts 2006), government agencies like the *chengguan* were eager to avoid being seen as exerting unnecessary brutality against citizens when enforcing government orders in the central areas of the city. In the minds of those who opened illegal businesses in the Tranquil Light, there-fore, the notice was nothing more than a paper tiger. In Shanghai, there has been a sense of what some might call 'check and balance civility' – what the late politi-cal scientist and China observer Richard Baum (2007) would call 'the self-organizing civil society' – which means that while the residents are conscious of their place and their limited rights in a society governed by the CCP, they also know the limits within which such forms of governance could affect their lives. 'They wouldn't dare', said a cafe owner prior to the *chengguan*'s visit. She then continued: 'The most they could do is to come and knock on our door one-by-one, and then we will just close our shop down for the day, and then re-open it again the next day.'

Having studied this neighbourhood for more than two years before this dramatic visit by the *chengguan*, to my observer's eyes the neighbourhood did not appear in need of any urgent urban management. It never looked so disorderly that the city's government would need to call in the *chengguan*, who were most often spotted controlling illegal street food vendors on the sidewalks, as one of their jobs was to maintain the 'city's appearance, environment, sanitation, work safety, pollution control, and health' (South China Morning Post 2014). One can obviously see the link between street food vendors and the aforementioned concerns. This is the case especially when it comes to sanitation, as urban areas in China have become more vulnerable to various forms of food safety hazards, the most notorious recent case being the use of so-called 'gutter oil', an oil extracted from sewage and reused to cook food (see Ip 2009; Yan 2012). Tranquil Light was nothing close to that. The cafes and restaurants mainly served the middle class. Most of the cafes were 'rather hip', according to most of the customers who gave them four to five stars on multiple local online rating platforms, competing with large chains such as Starbucks. Some of them tried to capitalize on the 'historic' appearance of the area, with decor that offered patrons the experience of what the anthropologist Johannes Fabian (2014) calls 'going back in time'. Given the nature and standards of commerce in Tranquil Light, there was no basis for the *chengguan* to crackdown on a community that did not pose any threat to sanitation, safety or public peace.

In addition, based on my own and hundreds of customers' observations, both on the Chinese equivalent of the US-based Yelp online platform (*Dazhongdianping*) and in person, these shops were in fact much cleaner, friendlier and safer than most of the restaurants or shops elsewhere that had proper licences. The reason for that was simple: most of these shops were operating without proper businesses licences, in the grey area between legality and extra-legality, therefore they could not afford to gain a bad reputation online or elsewhere, let alone be inspected, which would often lead to them being permanently closed down. Thus, if it was not the obvious lack of professionalism and quality of the products and services on offer that were perceived to bring harm to the public, why then did the *chengguan* want to crackdown on the businesses in the Tranquil Light, knowing that their reputation was also at stake if the residents decided to resist in this particular location?

The scene in the Tranquil Light was most intense around 4:30 p.m., as the *chengguan* marched halfway through the main thoroughfare. At least a hundred objects – large and small – such as tables, chairs, umbrellas and tents and other merchandise were confiscated and taken away by the officers as they moved slowly through each of the lanes that branched out of the neighbourhood's north–south spine. Crowds gathered around them as they walked through, and the whole street was filled with shouting, yelling and unusually loud conversations in the local dialect – which, in a way, also implied some degree of resistance to central authorities that communicated with the residents using standard Mandarin. Reporters were there, so were a number of college students from journalism schools around the city, to observe the incident. The residents did not resist, neither did the owners of the shops, when the *chengguan* got a local construction worker to dismantle some of structures that were erected outside of the houses for unlicensed business activities. The *chengguan* also inspected the interior of all 183 buildings, looking at the gap between the gate and the wall, through the cracks in the walls, as well as through the windows to make sure that no one could escape the crackdown.

The tranquil 'rise' of the creative entrepreneurs

According to the Urban and Rural Planning Law of the People's Republic of China, no commercial activities are allowed in a residential neighbourhood such as the Tranquil Light. Exceptions are made for a few shops that receive licences owing to the nature of their business being deemed by the local government as 'beneficial' to the area such as a community barber, local canteen, paper recycling shops and local clinics. The entrepreneurs, artists and professionals working in the cultural or creative industries, who arrived at the Tranquil Light around the mid-2000s, said they found the convenient location as well as the affordable rent to be the main points of attraction (similar to the group of artists studied in Ren and Sun 2012). These entrepreneurs, whom I call throughout this chapter 'creative', were generally young (between their early thirties and early forties, with a few in their late twenties) and educated with at least a bachelor's degree. While acknowledging the critiques addressed to Richard Florida's notion of the creative class (e.g. Kotkin 2013; Malanga 2004; Peck 2005), I still use the adjective 'creative' to refer to a group of residents whose occupations are to create new ideas, new designs, new technology and content, which had not existed in the Tranquil Light area before their arrival in the mid-2000s. In fact, the Chinese concepts of 'creativists' (*chuangyizhe*) and 'people with creative capacity' (*you chuangzaoli de ren*) have been coined as identity markers by the media to refer to these resident entrepreneurs. These are 'flattering titles' that these entrepreneurs comfortably assume and with which they self-identify. What these entrepreneurs are engaged in might not be 'creative' in the strictest sense of the word, i.e. creating patents or new products. These entrepreneurs were, however, 'creative' because they were constantly looking for ways to improve their social and economic living conditions and standards by engaging in commercial, cultural and artistic activities rarely seen in Shanghai prior to their arrival. Different from workers in large service companies and inspired by their experiences abroad and in higher education, their commercial activities included alternative forms of artistic, entertainment and leisure activities, such as teahouses, 'hip' barista cafes and art schools (e.g. teaching Chinese calligraphy and painting), independent cinemas and specialized media libraries, as well as the sale of independently designed, non-corporate consumption goods such as clothing, furniture, porcelain and jewellery, to name but a few.

The condition of most of the houses in the Tranquil Light in the early 2000s was usually poor as a result of the lack of structural maintenance (as the regulations regarding historic preservation only prevent demolition but do not, in most cases, induce renovation). The assistance provided by the local government during the preparation for the Expo'10 was limited to the restoration of some of the buildings' exterior and the alleyways. Nevertheless, according to a number of shop owners, 'it made much more economic sense' to be there than elsewhere. Another contributing factor that had led young shop owners to settle in the Tranquil Light was also the sheer uncertainty of property development in the central business district. 'Everyone knows that this neighbourhood will be torn down, but no one knows exactly when, it's extremely difficult to speculate,' said one of the old residents who rented out the first floor of her house (she owned two rooms on the first and second floor) to a young local Chinese man who opened a small teahouse. On the owner's part, since she did not know when she would be asked to move out, the best strategy for her was to try to make as much money as possible when she still legally possessed the house. This benefited the tenants who were charged reasonable rents and were not asked to provide much proof of their income, status or a guarantor. Like artists and the creative classes in famous art districts elsewhere (see Li 2013; Tan 2005; Yung *et al.* 2014), these entrepreneurs and creative residents were operating on a small budget. Among the many who worked in the fashion business was a Shanghainese woman who had just returned from London with a degree in business management. She wanted to pursue her dream of owning a small boutique to sell ladies' shirts and dresses of her own design. For most of the young entrepreneurs like her, paying a large sum of money to get either the licence or certificate of standardization was not an option.

In fact, it would be impossible for the local government not to be aware of the fact that there were, at its peak, more than eighty shops open in the Tranquil Light. In theory, the 'extra-legal' businesses could have operated under the government's radar. In practice, however, such a closed neighbourhood watch system would not allow any social activities, let alone businesses, to operate by stealth. Among the most active members of the neighbourhood watch team were the elderly residents, who served as what Jane Jacobs (1961) called 'eyes on the street', by keeping track of what was going on in their micro-locality (e.g. lane) and transmitting information among each other through both formal and informal channels such as gossip, complaints and official reports to the neighbourhood committee.

At the same time, among these elderly watchmen there were some who also believed that the local government would see the benefits of turning a blind eye to these businesses and letting them stay in the neighbourhood for two reasons. First, the rents collected by the residents from these shops were important sources of income for many retired residents, many of whom were discharged from their local work units (*danwei*) and therefore did not have enough income to support their daily lives, let alone to support regular visits to the hospital as well as necessary medication. By allowing them to rent out the rooms they did not use, they could earn an income for themselves and therefore alleviate the financial responsibility of the local government for their welfare. In addition, the 'creative economy', while only accounting for a small portion of the city's income from tourism (World Cities Culture Forum 2014), had become increasingly recognized in the course of the late 2000s as offering potential for economic development and adding to the city's tourism product (Chang *et al.* 1996; McCain and Ray 2003).

The rationale of the crackdown on businesses

By 5 p.m., as the *chengguan* were preparing to leave, tensions were further ratcheted up when one of the shop owners, a senior resident who ran a small grocery store that had been selling cigarettes and confectionary for twenty years, passionately asked them for an explanation for why they wanted his shop to be closed after twenty years in operation. This senior resident had always been an important figure in the neighbourhood, especially when it came to the history of Tranquil

Light. More than three dozen reporters and journalists had photographed and written about his shop as one of the few remnants of Shanghai's 'nostalgic micro-economy' (for a deeper probe into the origin of this concept, see Tianshu 2011). The explanation that was given to him by the *chengguan* was, '*Laoshi* (lit. teacher, but a respectful pronoun commonly also used to address a senior citizen), we have no choice . . . We really have to do it across the board; otherwise, how could we tell those people whose merchandise we have already confiscated?'

There were two possible explanations for the crackdown. One was that the shop owners no longer kept a low profile in the neighbourhood, based on the mutual understanding between the renters and the landlords of the status of the extra-legal nature of their businesses. As the competition and concentration of shops grew, it was difficult for the local government to turn a blind eye to the extra-legal nature of these shops. For instance, after only a few months of profitable operation, one of the small cafes in the Tranquil Light had been transformed into a full-scale cafe and bar that was drawing more regular visitors than before. Apart from the fact that there is a difference between a cafe and a bar in terms of business licensing, the local government could not ignore the noise pollution as well as other forms of public disturbance that came as a result of the growing numbers of patrons the venue attracted.

Moreover, some entrepreneurs began to engage in rather speculative activities, as revealed by the case of the owner of a small handmade cookie shop. Once his business could generate enough profits, he began to look for other available rooms in the neighbourhood to rent from the original residents and then sublet them to others at much higher prices, thus acting as, what it was often called in Chinese, a 'second landlord' (*erfangdong*). There were a handful of these petty-shop-owners-turned-second-landlords in Tranquil Light. Such activity, though not illegal, had a profound impact both on the real estate market in the neighbourhood, as well as on the sentiment toward the creative entrepreneurs as a whole now that these shop owners had become landlords themselves. While the local government might have tolerated small-scale businesses in the area as a creative engine to be supported for the greater good of the small and medium-sized commercial atmosphere, problems arose when these shop owners became speculators at the expense of others, without compensating for the various forms of negative externalities they generated.

The structural inequalities among renters

The other explanation has to do with the structural inequality among the renters, as not all residents benefited from the economic opportunities brought about by the creative businesses and the visitor economy. The 'second landlord' phenomenon discussed earlier is one example of this inequality. Yet the agency of each individual renter also played a role in shaping the perceptions of inequalities. For example, while most of the residents were living in run-down rooms, most of the new residents were living in renovated spaces, some very fancy, as they could afford the rents, and in many cases they needed to renovate their places with 'fancy decoration' in order to attract customers. In addition, while many residents benefited from renting their places out, there was a strong sense of discontent among those who could not do so, either because they only had one single room for themselves to live in, or because their rooms had no mandatory amenities such as bathrooms, or desirable options like a courtyard (for an outdoor cafe) or a balcony (for a tea house) attached to it. These residents who were excluded from these new economic opportunities were thus extremely sensitive to any form of perceived 'public disturbances', which they could use as cases against those who benefited from such opportunities. Through this lens, the tension between the old and the new residents found its roots in jealousy between neighbours. The new tenants together with the original tenants who were able to sublet their rooms were the source of contention among the residents who lacked similar opportunities.

The structural inequality also extended to the national origin of the renters. Landlords often preferred foreigners because they had the reputation of being straightforward (i.e. 'not tricky'), 'cleaner', wealthier and friendlier. That said, there were also foreigners who, according to the tenants, 'partied all the time', to the extent that the neighbours filed noise complaints to the police. The presence of these foreigners often led to arguments among original residents, which the *juweihui* eventually had to step in to resolve the conflicts. Nevertheless, even when the same offer was made by foreign and Chinese individuals of equal socio-economic status, the tenants would still prefer to sublet the place to foreigners as, according to an interview with a well-known local community real-estate agent, the tenants would have more 'stories' to share with and would brag to their fellow neighbours and the *juweihui* about how important their houses were (see Kwong 1994; Economist 2012). 'See, even the foreigners want to live here', said one of the tenants who had been renting her best room to a foreigner. 'I don't mind giving up the best room in the house that even has a small balcony and the best view facing the desirable south side [referring to the Chinese belief in *fengshui* that the south is the best direction] of the lane to my renter; and that's because he's *laowai* (foreigner) – he pays the rent on time and is always friendly to us,' she gushed of her *laowai* tenant before going on at length to complain about her previous Chinese tenant who never treated her in any manner close to how her current tenant did. That is to say, by renting their room to a foreigner, the renters could implicitly claim access to much coveted symbolic capital.

One of the most vivid moments of my time in the field was when Ai, a fashionable, young Shanghai-born resident of Tranquil Light told me: 'I cannot understand why the neighbours hate me so much.' Just before that, we were at the local office of a governmental agency called the Trade and Commerce Bureau (*gong-shangsuo*) as Ai had been asked by the Bureau to 'come and have a tea' (*lai he cha*), a euphemistic expression that the authority often uses when an individual is summoned to report herself, in this instance, to discuss an issue with Ai's shop in the neighbourhood. 'We were informed by your neighbours that you have been conducting business activities in the neighbourhood, which is not allowed . . . and yes, someone called us; your neighbours called us,' said the Deputy Director of the *gongshangsuo*. Since she had begun to rent a room with both a large courtyard and full-scale kitchen attached to it a few months back, Ai, in fact, had been doing nothing but discretely conducting her own businesses: she displayed and sold her designer clothing, organized invitation-only parties and hosted private dinners. How did her neighbours know about her private activities and why did it matter to them? Her courtyard was considered a luxury and the adjacent rooms were highly prized. Ai paid a little above the market price to rent this courtyard from the previous renter, and as soon as she moved in she redecorated the courtyard with minimalist IKEA furniture with the purpose of turning it into her workshop and office space, as well as a multi-purpose room to be rented for rather expensive events, such as private dinners, parties, an exclusive speed dating club and so on.

During the first two months, the profits that she made were more than enough for her to operate the place with ease. The word soon got out that her business was doing well and that her clients had become her regular visitors. These guests, mostly middle-class young women, were by no means modest in their choice of clothing. Within the next two months, she sensed, in her own words, 'that my neighbours stopped being friendly to me, even though I bought them fruit almost every day'. There could be, needless to say, other factors that made her neighbours feel uncomfortable about her presence. 'I wouldn't want to ask Ai to close down her business if not for the constant reporting of the public disturbances caused by her by, mostly, her senior neighbours,' said the Deputy Director of *gongshangsuo*. 'But all my events never made any noise,' responded Ai, which was accurate, as I had witnessed some of her events to conduct participant observation. Although the Deputy Director of *gongshangsuo* did not share with us the written comments that she received, she did say that one of the persons who lodged a complaint wrote that the lamps in Ai's room were, simply, 'too bright'. In addition, a complaint from a resident claimed that 'what she cooked created too much smoke and an unpleasant smell', referring to the private dinners that she organized. Ai was speechless after she heard that it was the noise, smell and the light from her room that her neighbours were complaining about – as if she knew that no matter what she did, someone would come up with a reason to complain about her. 'They'd probably complain about the taste of my food and the roughness of my clothing too if they'd gotten to eat or touch it,' Ai said cynically. She was the object of jealousy owing to her foreign education and seemingly more comfortable lifestyle, along with the fact that she rented out the neighbourhood's largest room. After the visit to the *gongshangsuo*, it was clear that Ai had no choice but to be even more covert. 'The best would be that you stop doing your business here altogether,' said the Deputy Director of the *gongshangsuo*, who then continued, 'We understand you and want to support a young and aspiring native-Shanghainese [as the Deputy Director of the *gongshangsuo* is also a native-Shanghainese], but every time we hear a complaint, we would have to come and pay a visit.'

Ai was by no means the new kid on the block. By the time of her meeting with the Deputy Director of *gongshangsuo*, she had been living in Tranquil Light for almost three years. There were some quiet protests by the senior residents about the bars and shops that opened until late at night. The renters, including Ai, who knew about this brewing discontent collectively made some efforts both to appease the citizens by making less noise and closing earlier, and to resist the *gongshangsuo* by covertly opening their shops, especially those shops that did not need display windows such as cafes, restaurants and tea houses. Prior to renting a room with a large courtyard, Ai rented a small 12-square-metre showroom that was once a garage to display her designer shirts. According to Ai, this small shop was 'just for her to make extra income on the side', as she also had another full-time job elsewhere. Unfortunately for her, the prominent location of this 12-square-metre showroom at the north side of the lane behind uncovered gates attracted the attention of both the *chengguan* and *gongchangsuo*, resulting in a notice she received from both bureaus, followed by a personal note and visit from the *gongshangsuo*, that she had to close it down, which took place about two weeks before the crackdown. 'There's no point resisting, and I already have a backup plan,' said Ai, which turned out to be the plan to negotiate with the landlord of the new larger room with a courtyard which she then moved into. After the visit to the *gongshangsuo*, Ai continued to operate her showroom, but this time with an extremely low-key attitude: 'No outdoor party, alcohol, cigarette in the courtyard; no loud noise, bright light, cooking smoke from her room; no transaction to take place; and, finally, no evidence that would show that this place is doing anything commercial.'

By 6 p.m. in the evening, the *chengguan* lined up again at the south gate (through which they had entered earlier). They marched all the way to the north gate and back. The total distance was four hundred metres, which, according to a 72-year-old resident who walked back and forth in the lane everyday as exercise, usually only took about ten minutes. The march of the *chengguan*, however, took a full hour to complete, as they spent significant time taking down and confiscating 'illegal' objects as they moved. Resistance from the residents was not met with violence, but unusually gentle explanations from the *chengguan* that 'this had to be done'. One reporter said that the *chengguan* had prepared for this crackdown for weeks before they came in – as the last thing they wanted was more news about their brutality. On their way out, they put up another notice on the south gate, this time a much larger notice than the original warning that most people seemed to have ignored. With a long and meticulous explanation of their actions during the day's raid, the core message was simple: mission accomplished, Tranquil Light had returned to its original 'tranquil' state.

Conclusion

Through a detailed narrative of a story that lasted four hours – the crackdown on shops in a Shanghai alleyway by the Urban Management Bureau or the *chengguan* – I used ethnography to unpack the intertwined layers of conflicts around the structurally unequal distribution of benefits from the growing tourism and leisure industry in traditional neighbourhoods. This particular event is what anthropologist Sally Falk Moore (1987) called a 'diagnostic event', or the moment in which the ethnographer encounters a powerful contradiction in which both the deep cultural logics and the diversity of stakeholders in social conflicts are revealed in front of his/her keen senses. Moreover, a diagnostic event reveals socio-cultural, historical and political processes beyond what our senses can perceive. In this case, an event featuring two dozen district officers and powerless residents could potentially be read differently from the way it has been done in this chapter, without the knowledge of the genealogy of the conflict in the context of the wider socio-economic picture of Shanghai at large. The diagnostic event described here speaks to some very important issues affecting the sense of 'urbanity' in contemporary Shanghai, such as the impact of city branding, the rise of creative entrepreneurs, the ways in which 'place' has different meanings for different groups of residents and how these residents mobilize to protect their rights in such places. It was the resistance and resentment against some emerging and observable forms of inequality from within that brought down the whole heritage and creative tourism enterprise in the historic *lilong* neighbourhood called Tranquil Light. The paradox of this story is that it all began as a 'paradise' for the entrepreneurs and young creative returnees from overseas.

The picturesque quality of the 'tranquil' neighbourhood was an idea repeatedly invoked by both the original residents and the entrepreneurs who had lived in Tranquil Light since the mid-2000s. The former had seen how the neighbourhood had been transformed by the energy and the creativity of young minds into some-thing unprecedented, which, to many of my informants who were original resi-dents, 'was actually quite refreshing to see, after all of these years of only seeing each other's old faces'. Shanghai's local government first tried to give the crea-tive entrepreneurs some room to flourish and exercise their creativity – creativity that would be hampered under a stricter tax regime like that applied to established brands or corporations. Being aware of the Xintiandi as a successful model of architectural heritage tourism in the city, both locals and visiting foreigners alike valued such creative energy, which helped the neighbourhood to attract not only consumers to buy goods and services, but also potential tenants (especially foreigners and educated locals) who wanted to be part of the precious surviving cultural heritage before it eventually disappeared (see Levin 2010; Jian 2014). Local tourism flourished as a result. During the first years of co-existence between the new and the old tenants, it seemed that both of these groups benefited economically as well as financially from each other.

The peak of this 'honeymoon period' between the creative entrepreneurs, the long-standing residents and the local municipal government lasted for about five years. The tension between the various classes of tenants gradually built up with structural conflicts resulting from unequal access to the unprecedented range of opportunities which had emerged in the community. A sudden change occurred, however, when some of these entrepreneurs crossed the line and became, in the original residents' words, 'greedy capitalists' themselves. Yet it was not the local government who decided when enough was enough. As some of the residents themselves increasingly voiced their concerns about the impacts of the competition and concentration of shops to the local government, the latter, in turn, put pressure on law enforcement authorities to act – something the authorities had no prior intention of doing.

The sense of uneven benefit distribution that some residents felt is expressed by how the residents quarrelled with each other over the distribution of opportunities on which they could capitalize on a short-term basis. In the chapter, I specifically showed how 'residents' cannot be understood as a single homogeneous group. This is most vividly illustrated by how the original residents –those who lived in the neighbourhood before the economic reform and housing privatization of the 1980s – gradually came to see the arrival of creative entrepreneurs who capitalized on their alleyways after the early 2000s as an unjust process. What this story shows is how uneven access to economic opportunity arising from a combination of creative and visitor economy could be the source of local-to-local resistance that manifests itself in resistance against the perceived 'outsiders' – both business owners and tourists alike. In this case, what may appear on the surface to be a conflict between the locals and the non-locals, or the people and the local public authorities, is in fact a series of unfolding conflicts among the neighbours themselves. The conflicts, which may arise when not all residents benefit from the economic opportunities brought about by the cultural and creative industries and the visitor economy, echoes the story told by Lederman in this volume in the context of Buenos Aires. Both stories thus illustrate another form of resistance – one against the implications of the new creative activities (and the visitors they attract) in a historic residential neighbourhood, rather than one of protest against tourism as such.

Notes

1 As most Chinese nouns do not have the notion of 'singular' or 'plural' built into their meaning, the way in which I would like to refer to *chengguan* in this chapter is as a plural noun referring to a group of officers from the Urban Management Bureau, unless otherwise specified.
2 To protect the anonymity of the informants from whom I gathered the information which underpins the writing of this chapter, the specific names of the places mentioned (such as the name of the neighbourhood itself) and of the informants are pseudonyms. For the same reason, the descriptions of particular locations/venues are also limited.
3 This chapter draws on materials gathered in Shanghai over the course of almost two years during the summer of 2013 and 2015 through ethnographic data-gathering methods, such as participant observation, open-ended interviews and sensory ethnography (e.g. the use of photography and film in documenting social data) as part of a doctoral project in social anthropology at Harvard University under the dissertation title 'Locating Shanghai: Globalization, Heritage Industry, and the Political Economy of Urban Space'. This project has been generously funded by a Harvard-China Scholarship Council (CSC) Research Scholarship, the Harvard Asia Center Dissertation Research Grant for Chinese Studies, a Jens Aubrey Westengard Scholarship, a Fudan Fellowship at the Center for Studies of Chinese Civilization (ICSCC) of Fudan University in Shanghai, a Cora A. Du Bois Charitable Trust Anthropology Research Fellowship and a Global Postdoctoral Fellowship, New York University Shanghai. The author would like to thank these sponsors for their support. The author would like to thank Nicholas

Lawrence Caverly, Claire Colomb, Magnus Fiskesjö, Daniel Guttman, Matthew C. Gutmann, Barry Hashimoto, Erik L. Harms, Michael Herzfeld, Edward Akintola Hubbard, Jason D. Luger, Sean Mallin, Johannes Novy, Leo Pang, Xinyan Peng, Raymond Pun, Reilly Rabitaille, Sue Anne Tay, Qin Shao and Almaz Zelleke, for their careful reading, critical comments and excellent suggestions on earlier drafts of this chapter.

References

[Unless otherwise stated, all URLs were last accessed 1 December 2015.]

Arkaraprasertkul, N. (2009) 'Towards modern urban housing: redefining Shanghai's *lilong*', *Journal of Urbanism*, 2(1): 11–29.

Arkaraprasertkul, N. (2011) *Shanghai Urban Housing: A Planning Heritage or/and Nostalgic Obstacle?* Paper presented at the 11th International Congress of the Asian Planning Schools Association, University of Tokyo, Japan, 19–22 September.

Arkaraprasertkul, N. (2012) 'Moral global storytelling: reflections on place and space in Shanghai's urban neighborhoods', *Storytelling, Self, Society*, 8(3): 167–79.

Arkaraprasertkul, N. (2013) 'Traditionalism as a way of life: the sense of home in a Shanghai alleyway', *Harvard Asia Quarterly*, 15(3/4): 15–25.

Baum, R. (2007) *The Political Impact of China's Information Revolution*. Paper presented at the USC US-China Institute, 20 September. Online. Available at http://china.usc.edu/sites/default/files/legacy/AppImages/2007-baum-usc.pdf (accessed on 1/12/2015).

Berg, P. O. (2014) *Branding Chinese Mega-Cities*. Cheltenham: Edward Elgar.

Bracken, G. (2014) *The Shanghai Alleyway House: A Vanishing Urban Vernacular*. London: Routledge.

Chang, G. G. (2015) 'Move over, Hong Kong, Shenzhen now China's best city for business', *Forbes*, 17 May. Online. Available at http://www.forbes.com/sites/gordon-chang/2015/05/17/move-over-hong-kong-shenzhen-now-chinas-best-city-for-business/.

Chang, T. C., Milne, S., Fallon, D. and Pohlmann, C. (1996) 'Urban heritage tourism: the global-local nexus', *Annals of Tourism Research*, 23(2): 284–305.

Chen, X. (2009) *Shanghai Rising: State Power and Local Transformations in a Global Megacity*. Minneapolis, MN: University of Minnesota Press.

Deutsche Bank Research (2015) *Province: Shanghai*. Frankfurt am Main: Deutsche Bank.

Economist, The (2012) 'Foreigners in China: Barbarians at the gate, again', *The Economist*, 21 May. Online. Available at http://www.economist.com/blogs/analects/2012/05/foreigners-china.

Fabian, J. (2014) *Time and the Other: How Anthropology Makes Its Object*. New York: Columbia University Press.

Fan, H. (2014) 'Branding a place through its historical and cultural heritage: the branding project of Tofu Village in China', *Place Branding and Public Diplomacy*, 10(4): 279–87.

Guan, Q. (1996) *Lilong Housing. A Traditional Settlement Form*, MArch thesis. Montreal: McGill University, School of Architecture. Online. Available at: http://www.collection-scanada.gc.ca/obj/s4/f2/dsk2/tape16/PQDD_0001/MQ29850.pdf.

Hammond, P. H. (2006) *Community Eclipse and Shanghai's Lilong*. MA thesis, Columbia, MO, University of Missouri.

Hartog, H. den (ed.) (2010) *Shanghai New Towns: Searching for Community and Identity in a Sprawling Metropolis*. Rotterdam: 010 Publishers.

HKTDC (Hong Kong Trade Development Council Research) (2014) *Shanghai: Market Profile*. Hong Kong: HKTDC.

Human Rights Watch (2012) *'Beat Him, Take Everything Away': Abuses by China's Chengguan Para-Police*. Online. Available at https://www.hrw.org/sites/default/files/reports/china0512ForUpload_1.pdf.

Information Office of Shanghai Municipality (2009) *Preservation of City Historical Sites*. Official website of the Information Office of Shanghai Municipality. Online. Available at http://en.shio.gov.cn/topics-historical.html.

Ip, P. K. (2009) 'The challenge of developing a business ethics in China', *Journal of Business Ethics*, 88(1): 211–24.

Jacobs, J. (1961) *The Death and Life of Great American Cities*. New York: Vintage Books.

Jian, Y. (2014) 'Shikumen pledged extra protection after readers offer city suggestions', *Shanghai Daily*, 25 August. Online. Available at http://www.shanghaidaily.com/metro/entertainment-and-culture/Shikumen-pledged-extra-protection-after-readers-offer-city-suggestions/shdaily.shtml.

Junhua, L., Rowe, P. G. and Jie, Z. (eds) (2001) *Modern Urban Housing in China 1840–2000*. Munich and London: Prestel.

Kotkin, J. (2013) 'Richard Florida concedes the limits of the Creative Class', *Daily Beast*, 20 March. Online. Available at http://www.thedailybeast.com/articles/2013/03/20/richard-florida-concedes-the-limits-of-the-creative-class.html.

Kwong, J. (1994) 'Ideological crisis among China's youths: values and official ideology', *British Journal of Sociology*, 45(2): 247–64.

Larmer, B. (2010) 'Shanghai dreams: China's global city tries to recapture the glories of its past – this time on its own terms', *National Geographic*, 217: 124–41.

Levin, D. (2010) 'In Shanghai, preservation takes work', *New York Times*, 30 April. Online. Available at http://www.nytimes.com/2010/05/02/arts/design/02shanghai.html?_r=0.

Li, J. (2013) *Creating a Social and Cultural Space: A Continuation of Urban Memory: Opportunities and Obstacles for Developing Art Districts in the Process of Chinese Urban Revitalization – Three Case Studies in Shanghai, Beijing, and Xi'an*. Master's thesis, Muncie, Ball State University. Online. Available at: https://cardinalscholar.bsu.edu/handle/123456789/197833.

Lieberthal, K. (1995) *Governing China: From Revolution Through Reform*. New York and London: Norton.

McCain, G. and Ray, N. M. (2003) 'Legacy tourism: the search for personal meaning in heritage travel', *Tourism Management*, 24(6): 713–17.

Malanga, S. (2004) 'The curse of the Creative Class: Richard Florida's theories are all the rage worldwide. Trouble is, they're plain wrong', *City Journal*, Winter. Online. Available at http://www.city-journal.org/html/14_1_the_curse.html.

Moore, S. F. (1987) 'Explaining the present: theoretical dilemmas in processual ethnography', *American Ethnologist*, 14(4): 727–36.

Morris, D. L. (1994) *Community or Commodity? A Study of Lilong Housing in Shanghai*. Vancouver: Centre for Human Settlements, School of Community and Regional Planning, University of British Columbia.

Peck, J. (2005) 'Struggling with the Creative Class', *International Journal of Urban and Regional Research*, 29(4): 740–70.

Peh, C. (2014) *Politicizing Heritage: The Intangibility of Shanghai's Shikumens*. BA Hons thesis in History. Singapore: National University of Singapore.

Ren, X. (2008) 'Forward to the past: historical preservation in globalizing Shanghai', *City and Community*, 7(1): 23–43.

Ren, X. and Sun, M. (2012) 'Artistic urbanization: creative industries and creative control in Beijing', *International Journal of Urban and Regional Research*, 36(3): 504–21.

Reuters (2015) 'China says its gender imbalance "most serious" in the world', *Reuters* UK edn, 21 January. Online. Available at http://uk.reuters.com/article/2015/01/21/uk-china-onechild-idUKKBN0KU0V720150121.

Shao, Q. (2013) *Shanghai Gone: Domicide and Defiance in a Chinese Megacity.* Lanham, MD: Rowman & Littlefield.

Shin, H. B. (2012) 'Unequal cities of spectacle and mega-events in China', *City*, 16(6): 728–44.

Sklair, L. (2006) 'Iconic architecture and capitalist globalization', *City*, 10(1): 21–47.

Sorkin, M. (2008) 'Learning from the Hutong of Beijing and the Lilong of Shanghai', *Architectural Record*, 16 July. Online. Available at http://www.architecturalrecord.com/articles/6133-learning-from-the-hutong-of-beijing-and-the-lilong-of-shanghai?v=preview.

South China Morning Post (2014) 'Chengguan' [keyword search], *South China Morning Post*. Online. Available at http://www.scmp.com/topics/chengguan.

Tan, L. (2005) *Revolutionary Spaces in Globalization: Beijing's Dashanzi Arts District.* Paper presented at the 'Hybrid Entities' Intersections 2005 Annual Graduate Conference, York/Ryerson Programme in Communication and Culture, 18–20 March. Online. Available at http://etopia.journals.yorku.ca/index.php/etopia/article/view/36749/33422.

Tianshu, P. (2011) 'Place attachment, communal memory, and the moral underpinnings of gentrification in post-reform Shanghai', in A. Kleinman *et al.*, *Deep China: The Moral Life of the Person. What Anthropology and Psychiatry Tell Us about China Today.* Oakland, CA: University of California Press.

Tsai, W.-L. (2008) *The Redevelopment and Preservation of Historic Lilong Housing in Shanghai.* MSc thesis, Philadelphia, University of Pennsylvania. Online. Available at http://repository.upenn.edu/cgi/viewcontent.cgi?article=1115&context=hp_theses.

Waldmeir, P. (2013) 'Shanghai starts search for its heritage', *Financial Times*, 22 February. Online. Available at http://www.ft.com/cms/s/0/56a9ebf2-71d0-11e2-89fb-00144feab49a.html#slide0.

Wang, J. and Li, S. (2011) *The Rhetoric and Reality of Culture-led Urban Regeneration: A Comparison of Beijing and Shanghai, China.* New York: Nova Science Publishers.

Wang, S. and Chen, Z. (1987) *Lilong Jianzhu* [in Chinese]. Shanghai: Shanghai Kexue Jishu Chuban Shechuban.

Watts, J. (2006) 'Shanghai's Communist party chief sacked in corruption purge', *The Guardian*, 25 September. Online. Available at http://www.theguardian.com/world/2006/sep/25/china.jonathanwatts.

Weinstein, L. and Ren, X. (2009) 'The changing Right to the City: urban renewal and housing rights in globalizing Shanghai and Mumbai', *City and Community*, 8(4): 407–32.

Winckler, E. A. and Greenhalgh S. (2005) *Governing China's Population: From Leninist to Neoliberal Biopolitics.* Stanford, CA: Stanford University Press.

World Cities Culture Forum (2014) *Shanghai: City Profile.* Online. Available at http://www.worldcitiescultureforum.com/cities/shanghai.

Wuwei, L. (2011) *How Creativity Is Changing China.* London: Bloomsbury Academic.

Yan, Y. (2012) 'Food safety and social risk in contemporary China', *Journal of Asian Studies*, 71(3): 705–29.

Yung, E. H. K., Chan, E. H. W. and Xu, Y. (2014) 'Sustainable development and the rehabilitation of a historic urban district – social sustainability in the case of Tianzifang in Shanghai', *Sustainable Development*, 22(2): 95–112.

Yusuf, S. and Nabeshima, K. (2010) *Two Dragon Heads: Contrasting Development Paths for Beijing and Shanghai.* Washington, DC: World Bank. Online. Available at http://www-wds.worldbank.org/external/default/WDSContentServer/WDSP/IB/2010/01/15/

000333037_20100115001059/Rendered/PDF/527060PUB0Box345575B01Official0Us e0Only1.pdf.

Zhao, C. (2004) 'From shikumen to new-style: a rereading of lilong housing in modern Shanghai', *Journal of Architecture*, 9(1): 49–76.

Zhu, J. (2002) *Between the Family and the State: An Ethnography of the Civil Associations and Community Movements in a Shanghai Lilong Neighbourhood* [in Chinese]. PhD thesis in Anthropology, Honk Kong, Chinese University of Hong Kong. Online. Available at http://sunzi.lib.hku.hk/ER/detail/hkul/2679921.

Zukin, S. (1995) *The Cultures of Cities*. Oxford: Oxford: Blackwell.

16 The living versus the dead in Singapore

Contesting the authoritarian tourist city

Jason D. Luger

Singapore's 'unique selling point' is to be a . . . first world system in a complicated and non-first-world part of the world. We have new Casinos and a 'river safari', like the Amazon!

(Singapore Prime Minister Lee Hsien-Loong 'On the Record' at Chatham House, London, March 2014, as observed by author)

In summer 2015, two significant events occurred. Firstly, Singapore celebrated its 50th birthday, a year-long event marked by celebrations, speeches and much international publicity. Secondly, in July, UNESCO announced that the Botanic Gardens would officially become Singapore's first World Heritage Site – only the third botanical garden in the world to obtain that designation (after Kew Gardens, London, UK and Padua Gardens, Italy). The Botanic Gardens are one of Singapore's premier tourist attractions, featuring a 'national orchid garden' containing rare, vibrant orchids named for various visiting celebrities and dignitaries, such as Queen Elizabeth II. Originally established by the colonizing British powers during Victorian times, the gardens feature native and non-native tropical flora, meandering pathways through palm groves, ponds, and a scattering of restaurants, cafes and event venues such as a symphony bandstand.

About one mile away from the Botanic Gardens is Bukit Brown Cemetery, also dating back to the British colonial era but designated as a pan-Chinese cemetery – the largest outside of China, and the resting place for many of the nation's most prominent families (including the family of founding father Lee Kuan Yew). As the Botanic Gardens join the prestigious UNESCO family, the cemetery is slated for destruction and redevelopment into a new housing estate and underground station as part of one of Singapore's designated 'new towns'. The new town is planned by the Urban Redevelopment Authority (URA) and Land Transport Authority (LTA) to help Singapore absorb its expected population growth of up to 7 million by 2030 (Singapore Government 2013) and to ease transport congestion. Construction has begun on a portion of the site; by 2030 the entire cemetery is planned to be redeveloped.

'Save Bukit Brown' – the effort to preserve Bukit Brown Cemetery – has emerged as one activist movement with particular traction, as a disparate and loose network of residents, tourists and various affinity groups who contest the destruction of the site and, more broadly, the appropriation of the built environment for consumption-led urban development, in which tourism plays a major role. The *living* face off against the *dead* (and their allies) in one of the most hotly contested battles currently underway amid the reinvigorated activist milieu in a Singapore that is rapidly changing. The battle for Bukit Brown represents the type of alternative pathways (and narratives) that are being claimed by part of the local population, backed by (some) visitors, and the ways that such alternative narratives are performed in the built environment.

This chapter contrasts State-promoted tourist sites such as the Botanic Gardens with the grassroots-led battle to preserve Bukit Brown Cemetery, using empirical examples from field research conducted in Singapore[1] to paint a picture of grassroots activism in the *authoritarian tourist city*. I will suggest that the dominant narrative for tourism in Singapore is increasingly being challenged by a grassroots network of transgressive 'guerrilla tourists': I argue that this loose network, containing activists, artists and those 'just taking part', is rewriting Singapore's tourist script by going 'off the pathway' (De Certeau 1984) and forming a new tourist geography. This set of practices, which I term 'guerrilla tourism', takes place on foot (through the act of walking), but also occurs in/through narrative practices via social media, blogs, word of mouth and sites such as Tripadvisor. The resulting reshaping and reappropriation of the top-down, normative tourist script in Singapore represents a growing challenge to the entrenched power structure, its elite spaces and associated elitist policies that have defined Singapore's nation-building (but is increasingly disconnected from many Singaporeans). By envisioning Singapore's tourist landscape as catering to a particular international aesthetic (*colonial-chic* and monumental in scale) at the expense of more indigenous, unique characteristics, the state has alienated (and galvanized) the grassroots and traditional Singaporean 'heartland' (see Tan 2008).

Through 'guerrilla tourism', the public commons – heritage and the natural/ built environment – are being re-emphasized. The tourist city is being questioned and contested, rewritten and rescripted from the ground up, through practices which shake (and challenge) the authoritarian state's ability to plan, make and preserve urban space in the name of tourism development. Firstly, I will give a brief overview of how Singapore has seen a *tourism turn* in recent years, with major investments in globalized tourism landscapes. Next, I will briefly show how the prioritization of elite tourism spaces is emblematic of growing divides and schisms within Singapore, and how contestation and activism has been rising. I will then introduce the concept of 'guerrilla tourism' and use the case study of 'Save Bukit Brown' to demonstrate how grassroots efforts are seeking to reclaim and reappropriate the built and natural environment and increasingly question the dominant tourist narrative, before concluding with what the case of Singapore reveals about 'guerrilla tourism's ability to rewrite the urban pathway.

From 'staid' to 'sexy': the reimaging of Singapore through tourism and consumption-led urban development

Singapore has made a sweeping entrance into the first tier of world cities. From its colonial origins to today's sweeping, glitzy cityscape, the City-State has undergone a remarkable physical (and economic) transformation that is fairly unique in the world. In the words of the founding Prime Minister, Singapore has transitioned from 'Third World to First' in a single generation (Lee Kuan Yew 2000). Tourism has been central to this repositioning and reinvention and has represented a key economic strategy over recent decades (see Chang 2001, 2004, 2016; Chang and Huang 2009, 2014; Chang and Lim 2004; Chang *et al.* 2004). The City-State's *tourism turn* has seen the construction (and promotion) of a variety of attractions aimed at reimaging and reinventing Singapore from a (perceived) staid, conservative, tidy business centre and air-stopover to an 'all-in-one destination', capable of attracting tourists to stay (longer) and spend (more). As local author Neil Humphreys wrote (2012), the island got 'sexy', a stark departure from its squeaky-clean reputation.

Much of the new tourist infrastructure is spectacular in scale: the Moshe Safdie-designed Marina Bay Sands casino, hotel, shopping and entertainment complex, towering over Singapore harbour and featuring the world's largest (rooftop) infinity pool; the new Universal Studios Singapore at Sentosa Island; the Gardens by the Bay (including the enclosed and air-conditioned Flower Dome and Cloud Forest) and the River Safari and Night Safari – are just some of the many efforts carried out by state planning authorities in consortium with developers (some which are state-owned, such as Temasek Holdings) and multinational corporations (such as Universal Studios). With these 'experiential' attractions have come 'experiential' amenities (Chang 2016), like luxury shopping malls (such as the Ion Centre on Orchard Road), Michelin-starred restaurants, and upmarket hotels and spas (from the Mandarin Oriental on the harbour to chic boutique hotels ringing the City Centre). Flagship sports and cultural events such as the Singapore Formula 1 Night Race and the Art Biennale have also helped to elevate Singapore's international reputation as a destination among the global cultural and economic elite.

Singapore's years of investment in tourism infrastructure, branding and promotion have had tangible results. The Singapore Tourism Board (STB) has charted Singapore's meteoric rise as a visitor destination: tourism now accounts for some 160,000 jobs in Singapore and (at least) 4 per cent of the City-State's gross domestic product (STB 2013). Singapore's tourism promotion efforts have helped grow the number of visitors through the period which included the 2003 SARS[2] epidemic (in which visitor numbers to Asia tumbled) and the 2008–11 global financial crisis: international arrivals to Singapore grew from 7.6 million per year in 2002 to 14.4 million per year in 2012, while tourism receipts increased from SD\$8.8 million in 2002 to SD\$23 million in 2012 (STB 2013: 3). Policy efforts have sought to grow the numbers further, with plans to reach 17 million international visitors by 2015 (SMTI 2011). Meanwhile,

Singapore has gained on Macau as a major global gambling destination: in 2011, Singapore tied with Las Vegas (USA) as the world's second biggest gambling market by revenue (O'Keeffe 2014). This represented a stunning shift in a conservative City-State where gambling was banned until 2005, when Prime Minister Lee announced plans to develop two casinos during a Parliamentary session on 18 April (Arnold 2005).

Global press and media – from the *New York Times* to airline in-flight magazines – have frequently featured Singapore as a 'new' travel destination in recent years (e.g. Cohane 2011); the TV celebrity chef Anthony Bourdain has twice featured Singapore as one of his top food destinations on both of his TV shows ('No Reservations' and 'The Layover'). Language from all of these promotional efforts and feature stories focuses on the *new, relaxed, fun* Singapore – as contrasted with the *old, straitlaced, sterile* Singapore: 'Judging from the number of cranes that dot the skyline, Singapore is booming . . . and, best of all, sexy lounges and rooftop bars are helping the City-State shake off its staid image' (Cohane 2011).

The makeover of Singapore's urban landscape into a touristscape ready for global visitors (see Olds and Yeung 2004) has given rise to critical voices in the academic literature. Chang and Huang (2009), for example, explored the cultural makeover of Singapore's city centre into an homogenised, global geography of 'everywhere and nowhere' in which large-scale, commercialised art groups and art spaces were prioritized over smaller-scale, indigenous groups and spaces. The theatres by the Bay and the Esplanade, two new monumental performing arts venues, are highlighted as examples: smaller theatre companies and local artists have not featured as heavily in Singapore's new architecture of culture.

Such is the extent of the appropriation of, and state imagination of, the Singaporean touristscape. State planning authorities (the Urban Redevelopment Agency, URA; the Economic Development Board, EDB; and the Singapore Tourism Board, STB) along with state-development corporations (Jurong Town Corporation for example) have demarcated 'new' tourist spaces (the shopping malls of Orchard Road, the roller coasters and casinos of Sentosa Island) and 'old' tourist spaces (colonial-shop houses,[3] the posh verandas of the Raffles Hotel). Meanwhile, many spaces and places representative of Singapore's long, regional, vernacular past are not put forward (in the official script) as places worth visiting and often fall prey to bulldozers. These include spaces associated with the island's more traditional, less glitzy heritage, from older state housing estates[4] to religious sites.

A walk around Singapore's waterfront, with its massive financial buildings and palm-lined boulevards, brings to mind a host of cities around the world, from Miami to Dubai. The 'new' Singapore corresponds to Singapore's ascendancy into one of the world's most expensive places (Economist Intelligence Unit 2015) – a designation that has raised critical questions about the impacts of the decision to reorient Singapore to attract global wealth (visitors as well as expatriates). The increasing cost of living, as well as the appropriation of urban space for global tourism and high-end consumption, have corresponded with an increasing socio-cultural divide between 'cosmopolitan' and 'heartland' (Tan 2008). This divide has generated, in some cases, unease and mistrust between older, more traditional, working-class Chinese, Malay and Indian populations and cosmopolitan groups found circulating in the new 'sexy' touristscape (including wealthy mainland Chinese visitors). These schisms – between larger-scale, spectacular, globalized tourism landscapes and smaller-scale, more indigenous places, between wealthy visitors and poorer residents, and between Singapore's elite and lower-middle classes – cut across the tourist City-State and its micro-geographies.

In the context of this increased prominence attributed to tourism and consumption-led urban development, 'culture' plays three roles: a tool to appease, attract and retain the economically important 'cosmopolitans' (i.e. the so-called 'creative class' – see Florida 2002, 2004); a unifying, nationalistic ingredient that ties Singapore's multi-ethnic and polyglot population together (such as the annual 'National Day Song'); but also a potentially divisive wedge, destabilizing national unity in order to justify continued 'illiberal' authoritarian control by prioritizing some national visions and identities over others (see Yue 2007). In that context, tourism is developed as a tool to attract 'cosmopolitan' elements (e.g. wealthy visitors from around the world) while simultaneously serving nation-building purposes, all the while relying on low-paid migrant labour and pricing out many lower-income Singaporeans – thereby both destabilizing and stabilizing society. Like a Pandora's box, Singapore's 'tourism turn' has instigated new debates – and contestations – in the public sphere about the use and appropriation of the urban environment.

The years paralleling the 'tourism turn' have seen growing unrest and louder critical voices in Singapore. Political activism has grown as the City-State has increasingly embraced, and also felt, global capital, global ideas and global visitors (Tan 2008; Goh 2014). Singapore's status as an outwardly focused, global city is also a leading cause of societal discontent: ripples of the 2008 economic crisis, *Occupy* and the *Arab Spring* movements helped to give the opposition political party – the Workers' Party – its strongest electoral showing in decades in the 2011 general election. In 2012, the first labour strike in a generation occurred and, in December 2013, the first ethnic-related riot since the 1960s took place (in the 'Little India' district). It is no accident that the riot occurred in one of Singapore's designated tourist-spaces: such spaces are increasingly the sites where a variety of tensions play out on the street. In 'Little India', urban space is shared by tourists, by a long-standing ethnic community and by migrant workers from the Indian subcontinent. The riots demonstrated how this coexistence is not always peaceful and how tourist spaces can be a battleground.

Inclusions and exclusions in Singapore's official tourism narrative and promotion

The contrast between the 'official' version of Singapore's tourist narrative versus alternative versions is a theme that emerges in recent literature: sociologist Daniel

Goh (2014) used the example of a performance artist's subversion of an official walking tour of Singapore by 'walking backwards' (during the 2009 Art Biennale), while barefoot and holding her shoe in her mouth. Goh illustrates the subtle and complex ways that artists do their part to illuminate new possibilities and challenge the state's vision (for what tourists should or should not see or do). By walking backwards, the artist was going off-script, off-map and changing the tourist script, demonstrating what De Certeau (1984: 93) describes as a walker in a city stepping 'off the formal roadway, fashioning their own, uniquely personal pathways'. As such, the transgressive or 'guerrilla tourist' steps off the formal tourist roadway, fashioning something more personal and unique.

The contradictory images of an elite, global art fair (the Biennale) and a performance artist 'walking backwards' neatly encapsulates Singapore's tourism dichotomy, and sets the stage for an examination of two places in particular: the Botanic Gardens, Singapore's first UNESCO World Heritage Site, and the neighbouring Bukit Brown Cemetery, which faces demolition and redevelopment. In the gardens, the City-State's elites go for evening jogs past trees planted by British gardeners during the reign of Queen Victoria. In the cemetery, 'guerrilla tourists', activists, descendants of the buried and those Singaporeans seeking a connection to history and indigeneity walk among the overgrown graves of the nation's founders in the shadow of encroaching construction machines.

The Botanic Gardens are located amid Singapore's wealthiest districts, close to upscale shopping on Orchard Road and relics from colonial rule such as the Tanglin Club. These districts feature the private homes of many members of the Singaporean elite but also wealthy expatriates including significant American and British communities. The link between elite visions of Singapore and the promotion of the Botanic Gardens to UNESCO is not lost on some of the island's critical intellectuals, such as a local intellectual and writer, interviewed in December 2012: 'The only place that they [the government] will conserve – which is prime property – because it has value: Botanic Gardens. Botanic Gardens . . . And – I suspect because [Lee Kuan Yew] and family jog there frequently!'

The gardens were part of the British Colonial project from the very beginning, with Colony founder Joseph Stamford Raffles proposing a 'national garden' as early as 1822. In 1859 the gardens were laid out by botanists in the 'English Landscape Movement Style'. It is only since Singapore's independence in 1965, ostensibly, that the Gardens have been truly Singaporean. Still, little of the flora in the gardens is native to Singapore or even the Malay Archipelago: perhaps the most iconic tree, the 'rain tree', is native to South America. Colonial evidence is everywhere, from the 'black and white bungalows' scattered around the grounds to the orchid garden featuring, among its newest additions, a special orchid named for Kate, the Duchess of Cambridge. The Botanic Gardens are beautiful: their appeal resonates not only with locals who use the space but also with the international press: Wu (2015) listed the Botanic Gardens as the very first thing to do and see upon arrival in the City-State, noting (incorrectly) that the Gardens are Singapore's 'last remaining green lung'.

The promotion of the gardens to UNESCO for World Heritage Status fits within Singapore's broader state policy agenda: the gardens are part of the Prime Minister's vision for Singapore to be a 'City in a Garden', along with other similar spaces such as the Gardens by the Bay and the River Safari. All these spaces share the characteristics of being green spaces. They are also, however, largely devoid of the regional, Chinese-Malay character (culturally, botanically, aesthetically) and an *authentic* sense of history. These 'gardens' are also just that: tended, manicured and curated. Bukit Brown Cemetery henceforth emerges as an alternative green space: a 'guerrilla' place to transgress, stepping over branches and under fences. As such, Bukit Brown invites the tourist to 'step off these formal roadways, fashioning their own, uniquely personal pathways' (De Certeau 1984: 93).

Conceptualizing 'guerrilla tourism' as a form of transgressive tourism: *off the formal pathway*

Walking is a process of appropriation of the topographical system on the part of the pedestrian . . . a spatial acting-out of the place . . . [and] implies relations among differentiated positions.

(De Certeau 1984: 97)

Cool, old, abandoned buildings, you say? What's this about guerrilla tourism? First, a disclaimer: visiting old abandoned buildings – be it an empty insane asylum or the remnants of a hulking steel mill – is a potentially dangerous activity.

(Copeland 2015: n.p.)

In this chapter I define 'guerrilla tourism' as a particular form of tourist practices that takes place in an alternative space, i.e. a space which is not seen as a 'mainstream' tourist site. In other words, it is a form of tourism that transgresses, that crosses boundaries, that involves going, seeing and *doing* in places that are tucked away, hidden, swept aside or prohibited. Though the term 'guerrilla tourism' has not yet been clearly defined, 'guerrilla warfare' is often envisioned as non-traditional or underground warfare – rebels hiding in the jungle, etc. – with connotations of violence. In urban literature, the term 'guerrilla' has been extended to refer to non-violent but subversive practices of reclaiming urban spaces through unauthorized activities, e.g. 'guerrilla gardening' (see Adams and Hardman 2014; Reynolds 2014).

By extension, a similar conceptualization can be extended to 'guerrilla tourism' – a sort of rebel tourism, an underground tourism and a tourism that involves the performance of transgression (and within that, potentially, of micro-resistances). This may mean literally going into the jungle (in a place such as Singapore), but in urban contexts (like Pittsburgh or Detroit), this might mean stepping over a 'closed' sign to enter an abandoned building, dodging broken glass or venturing out in the dark, after 'official' operating hours. A cursory online search of the phrase 'guerrilla tourism' revealed the term to be used in unofficial, grassroots tourism advertising and media, normally referring to tourist activities *off the beaten track* or beyond the normative tourism script. Abandoned buildings, desolate urban stretches or even those spaces envisioned as 'haunted' or surreal frequently emerge as such 'guerrilla tourist' sites: one promotional article on Pittsburgh, USA (in *BootsnAll*, an online tourist e-zine) mentions 'guerrilla tourism' of Pittsburgh's 'haunted' abandoned industrial districts, remnants of the city's once-great steel industry (Copeland 2015). However, the term is used informally – not defined or with a reference to use elsewhere.

In academic literature, particularly tourism studies, 'guerrilla warfare' has been predominantly linked with the *risks* to tourism – with authors probing how 'terror' and 'tourism' impact one another and the ways in which tourists avoid places they associate with danger or risk (Ryan 1993; Brunt *et al.* 2000). However, other authors have explored how tourists might be actually drawn to such 'guerrilla places', how guerrilla war or a war-torn history can evolve into a tourism-generator and ways that tourism can help rebuild war-torn nations (see Chheang 2008 with regard to post-Khmer Rouge Cambodia). As of yet, though, there does not exist a cohesive literature on 'guerrilla tourism' as a transgressive or subversive form of tourism and the various contextualities of place, actors and methods through which such forms of tourism are performed across diverse and atypical contexts.

That said, 'guerrilla tourism' can be envisioned as an evolution of, and addition to, the literature on 'off the beaten track', 'alternative' or 'third place' tourism (that is more well-defined and has been a feature of tourism studies since the 1990s). Bhaba (1994) explored the hybridity of 'place' and 'culture', and the way that tourism can be a conduit for alternative narratives and understandings in the post-colonial world (to which Singapore belongs). Hollinshead (1998), however, notes that tourism research should go further to interrogate the spatial practice and performativity of the everyday tourism experience and urges researchers to probe how tourism can both reinforce and challenge 'people, places and pasts'. Amoamo and Thompson (2010) answer Hollinshead's call and build upon Bhaba's exploration of 'hybridity' to explore the ways that hybrid Maori identities and differing interpretations of indigenous history in New Zealand present challenges and alternatives to hegemonic narratives, essentialisms and 'othering'. No such literature exists about Singapore, however, which is (likewise) characterized by a multitude of different ethnic, religious and cultural histories and identities.

The search for 'authenticity' is another theme that can be linked to 'alternative tourism': Sharon Zukin (2011) highlighted how the search for 'urban authenticity' and authentic spaces increasingly drives decision-making (and processes of urban change like gentrification) in the contemporary city. She contrasts 'authentic' urban space (independent stores, small-scale architecture) against homogenized, 'Disneyfied', corporate urban space, such as New York's Times Square. Zukin stresses the importance of social media, blogs and sites like Twitter, Yelp and Tripadvisor in promoting and disseminating the ideas of what constitutes 'authenticity' and the relationship between cyberspace and urban space. Along these lines, Maitland and Newman (2014) have explored the capability of urban settings to stimulate 'off the beaten path' tourist practices and the transformation of urban tourism more generally. The concept of 'guerrilla tourism' fits within this 'authenticity turn', since 'guerrilla tourists' seek alternative experiences and hybrid understandings and definitions of what constitutes space, place and culture. They are tourists, but they are trying *not* to be too 'touristy' and would rather say 'I am not a tourist' (see Week 2012). Cresswell's (1996) definition of 'transgression' – exhibiting 'geographical deviancy' simply by showing up in a place and assembling (but not resulting in a legitimate threat to the state and therefore not resulting in large-scale societal/political change) – is another way to conceptualize 'guerrilla tourism'. Whether 'transgressive' 'guerrilla tourism' can also contain resistances – deliberate acts of contestation – is one question this chapter seeks to probe in Singapore's context, through the example of Bukit Brown Cemetery and the 'Save Bukit Brown' movement.

Doing 'guerrilla tourism' in Singapore: a walk in Bukit Brown Cemetery

Adjacent to the Singapore Botanical Gardens (separated by a highway) lies Bukit Brown Cemetery, also known as 'Kopi' (coffee) Hill. This is a 200-hectare site of forested hills containing as many as 100,000 graves (Figure 16.1); thus, Bukit Brown is the largest Chinese (ethnic) cemetery outside of China. For this reason, as well as its links to the history of Singapore and the wider Chinese diaspora, its natural beauty and its environmental diversity, it is a site of significant cultural importance, as well as one of the City-State's largest remaining green spaces.

Construction has begun on a new highway straight through the site, resulting in the exhumation of many thousands of historic graves. The planned destruction of Bukit Brown has made the site a place of activism and has helped to generate a strange and loose network of artists, activists and 'guerrilla tourists'. 'Save Bukit Brown' has emerged as one of the most cross-cutting, tenacious and visible activist movements in the City-State's recent history, triggering alliances that had not before had such a staging ground around which to coalesce. There have been other efforts to save historic buildings and historic sites: the old national library building, for example, generated outcry when it was demolished for a new road. Yet no historical preservation movements have been able to generate as much international publicity as 'Save Bukit Brown' has. This is partly because of the way that the 'Save Bukit Brown' grassroots movement has utilized social media to project its campaign way beyond the site itself.

Bukit Brown is one of Singapore's rare examples of what Foucault (1984) and Soja (1996) described as an 'other' (or 'third' space): until recently, left alone – untouched by the City-State's master planning and spared the redevelopment policies that have reshaped most of Singapore. As the space is now being slowly turned into a construction site to feed Singapore's need for economic and

Figure 16.1 Undisturbed graves at Bukit Brown, February 2014.

Source: Author.

physical urban development, graves are being exhumed and history is literally disappearing into thin air. Steve Pile considered what cemeteries mean to the modern city (2004: 217), pointing to Walter Benjamin's (1999 [1935]) ruminations of how the 'dead cling like chewing gum to the heels of the living' and thus the 'dialectic of history is brought to a shocking standstill'. Bukit Brown and what it represents haunts Singapore's modern cityscape. The ghosts of Singapore's past also haunt the authoritarian state's version of how Singapore should be represented and used as a tourist city: artists, naturalists, conservationists, historians and those curious to experience something different meet on mornings and evenings to walk among the ghosts, eschewing the shopping mall, the casino and the theme park. A strange network of people and practices has formed in a strange place.

The large size of the site and its 'other' status – a spiritual site, a site of the non-living – allow it to host spontaneous gatherings and activities that do not often occur in Singapore. One anecdotal example of the emancipatory (and spontaneous) potential of Bukit Brown (that I learned about on one of the walking tours I joined) was the occurrence of a raucous moonlit rave, held on the site of the largest and most ornate grave in the cemetery well into the early morning one hot night. This was spread wholly via word of mouth – text messages and

Facebook posts. By literally dancing on the grave of one of the nation's most eminent (and wealthy) pioneers, the moonlight grave-rave was a whimsical and subversive reimagining of space. The moonlight grave-rave was only one of many examples of the way that the cemetery has led to practices which have gathered various individuals and groups that may not otherwise have joined together.

The 'Save Bukit Brown' movement began as a collective response to the cemetery's impending destruction through the joined-up organizing of historic preservationists, environmentalists, Taoist groups and artists, as well as a few academics from the National University. The movement started a Facebook and Twitter page in 2011 and slowly gained followers; tours were organized (usually held once or twice a week); and community forums were held at venues around Singapore (including the Substation theatre). The movement continued to grow, culminating in a petition in 2012/13 that (unsuccessfully) aimed to stop development of the site.

Some members of this loose network of Bukit Brown supporters have a direct, personal link to this space, as they may have family members buried there (or who have had their graves exhumed), or in some more indirect way feel connected to these few hundred acres. Other members are connected in a more spiritual way (adherents to Chinese folk religion, Taoism, paranormal societies). The arts community features heavily and plays a large role in organizing events: these artists range from those interested in the cemetery's ceramics legacy to members of Singapore's critical arts/art-activist community who often coordinate outdoor gatherings and performances. In this loose network of supporters are also people just *taking part*, such as tourists – who may have found out about the site via blogs, social media or travel sites such as Tripadvisor and may only visit the site once. These accidental, temporary members of the network who may only join briefly – by 'liking' a Facebook page or post, writing a Tripadvisor review or recommending the site to another tourist – are nonetheless part of the crucial 'glue' holding the wider movement together because of their ability to spread awareness outside of the City-State.

'Save Bukit Brown' has gained attention from the national and international press, as well as from organizations such as UNESCO and the World's Monuments Fund which put Bukit Brown on its 'Watch List' (WMF 2014) and has closely been monitoring developments there. Tripadvisor, the travel site, listed Bukit Brown as a top attraction in Singapore (13 out of 318 reviewed attractions, as of August 2014) with all but two reviews as 'excellent' or 'very good'. The inclusion of the cemetery on the World Monument's Fund's 'Watch List' (as well as the hundreds of Tripadvisor reviews) has fuelled a counter-movement of 'guerrilla tourism'. While the state promotes the Botanic Gardens, the grassroots asserts its *right to heritage* and the historical commons.

A walk through Bukit Brown (instead of the Botanic Gardens) may thus be interpreted as *being a guerrilla tourist*, and simply by crawling under vines and over old gravestones, a visitor performs resistance and contestation (albeit perhaps unconsciously) by going 'off the pathway' and making the effort to find the tucked-away, hard-to-find cemetery entrance. I myself attempted to be a guerrilla tourist by walking in Bukit Brown. On one occasion, I walked around the paved pathway that encircles this site, with a colleague that I brought for company.

Place: Bukit Brown Cemetery (Singapore)
Date: February 2013
Time: 3 p.m.

We did not talk; we observed the birds in the trees and felt the humidity of the afternoon paste our T-shirts to our chests. When we saw a grave of interest, we walked up to it and tried to interpret the rich carvings on it, which are often Confucian fables of filial piety. We were observers and participants, and in some ways also activists. By being here, taking pictures and writing about it, we were helping to raise awareness of this site and helping to protest its destruction. We were not in an air-conditioned mall. We were not at the Singapore Botanical Gardens. Therefore we were not doing what we were supposed to be doing, according to the official narrative and expectations of tourism promotion authorities. We were transgressing. I noticed on the one hand how meticulously arranged the graves were, in *feng-shui* orientation, in neat rows. On the other hand I noticed now messy and jumbled this space was: vegetation had crept across the gravesites in a whirl of vines and giant banana trees.

A woman on a horse came by. She was a member of the Singapore Polo Club, which is located nearby, and often uses the cemetery to exercise the horses. She was part of the eclectic network of people who uses this place, allied to the resting dead, the angry activists and, for a moment, to me. Other members of this loose network, observed on this and other research walks (at different times of the day), include what I have termed *spiritualists* (who come to connect with their ancestors); *gamblers* (who come at night to ask for favours from their ancestors); *Chinese family members* (who perform *Qing Ming* and other graveside ceremonies and offer gifts to those deceased); *tourists* (the American couple walking ahead of me, holding a map and taking pictures, who may have heard about this place from Tripadvisor); *joggers* (who take advantage of the traffic-free pathways and rolling topography); *activists* (in 'official' groups, such as 'Save Bukit Brown'); *environmentalists* (who are concerned with the loss of habitat for endemic species, including birds and monkeys); *artists* (who help to run tours of the site and also represent Bukit Brown in their art, ranging from photography to abstract displays at the museums); *academics* (such as myself, and staff members at the National University of Singapore, who now use Bukit Brown as part of the core Geography curriculum); and *ghost hunters and paranormal investigators* (who come at night, in the dark, and try to connect with the non-living).

Conceptualizing Bukit Brown as an activist and *counter* space (and *guerrilla tourist* site), I point to Foucaultian notions of governmentality (see Foucault 1991), and thus present Bukit Brown as a non-governable space within a highly-governed island. In Rose's (1999) conception of 'governable space', power operates largely through the creation of spaces as 'a matter of defining boundaries, rendering that within them visible, assembling information about that which is included, and devising techniques to mobilize the forces and entities thus revealed' (p. 33). These spaces, in turn, 'make new kinds of experiences possible, producing new modes of perception . . . they are modalities in which a real and material governable world is composed, terraformed and populated' (p. 32). And thus, 'the creation of governable spaces is also the creation of governable subjects' (ibid.).

Envisioning Bukit Brown as a non-governable space, we can also propose that those taking part in 'Save Bukit Brown' are non-governed subjects, free to assemble in strange and novel ways that are not possible elsewhere in Singapore (and are certainly not possible in 'official' tourist spaces such as the Botanic Gardens). Bukit Brown then becomes more than a cemetery: it becomes the most open space of outdoor activism in the City-State and a site of possibility, a spatial rejection of the glossy promotions sent out via official tourist channels. Therefore it is also, by proxy, a rejection of the authoritarian power structure.

However, one may ask whether Bukit Brown is truly 'ungoverned': it is also a bounded space with many limitations and impossibilities. Despite the protest movement and small concessions and compromises from state planners (such as the construction of a 'wildlife bridge' over a stream), destruction of the site is continuing. Construction equipment invades more of the site each day and policy-makers have not changed course significantly, with plans to turn the entirety of the site, eventually, into an urban extension. On a return visit in 2014, I found the cemetery almost unrecognizable due to construction barriers and fencing.

An even bigger (and perhaps more controversial) question also emerges: is 'guerrilla tourism' itself an externality of privilege, the domain of those with time, resources and the intellectual and cultural capital to make a hobby of visiting 'out of the way' places? The social media and Tripadvisor conduits through which 'Save Bukit Brown' resonated are the domain of a particular subset of the populace – as Habermas (1989) described the (then emerging) digital realm as part of the 'bourgeois public sphere' which is 'privately owned and operated for profit', and in which 'subordinated social groups lack equal access to the material means of equal participation' (in Fraser 1990: 64–5). Migrant labourers, for example, are not part of the network to save Bukit Brown. They are, however, part of the construction teams involved in its destruction.

The campaign to save Bukit Brown also raises other important questions, e.g. what is more important – housing for Singaporeans (at a time when the cost of living is higher than ever) or a historical green space? What happens in *real-world* situations where the 'right to the city' clashes with the 'right to cultural heritage'? For many Singaporeans, Bukit Brown is simply too abstract and removed from daily life to become an issue, or place, capable of resonating with the majority of the population and mobilizing a critical mass to push for real change. One research participant interviewed in December 2012, a satirical local author, summed up how he thinks most Singaporeans feel about Bukit Brown, based on a number of conversations he had with friends on the topic: "What do I care! It's just a cemetery, they're all dead, right? I've got my rice bowl to think about! I've got my house to think about! I've got my car payments to think about! I don't give a shit about the dead people.'

The Bukit Brown campaign then cannot be considered a grassroots victory, but rather a focus of micro-victories: connections have been made between tourists and a wide group of normally unrelated activists (and non-activists) that may outlast Bukit Brown itself. The ability of Bukit Brown to galvanize attention internationally, and also across the 'planetary scale' of digital space (Merrifield 2013), tells a wider story about the potential for tourists and tourism to link with activist networks coming together around other issues (and other material places) in Singapore. Even though the movement has failed to save the cemetery, it was able to slow construction long enough for thousands to visit the site that would not have otherwise visited. The movement also induced an important conversation about how Singapore will deal with its remaining sites of cultural history, perhaps giving rise to a permanently more critical, more aware local community. Activism with regard to Bukit Brown cannot be evaluated therefore based on 'winning' or 'losing', but rather the possibility that momentum will continue: whether, as Solnit (2005) theorizes, one cannot stop the 'spring' of activism once it has begun. In the hopeful words of an interview participant, a blogger and

Figure 16.2 Construction under way as 'Save Bukit Brown' tour is conducted, February 2014.

Source: Author.

316 Jason D. Luger

activist, in January 2013: 'So even if they lose? The fight to save Bukit Brown – and it's not really a total win or loss situation, there can be some compromise – . . . it creates the material for the art and literature to come. And the audience for it.'

Therefore, as the cemetery disappears, the compelling question emerges of how, where and in what forms the activism momentum will continue, and how it could impact other sites and policy areas in Singapore. Whether the 'guerrilla tourism' of Bukit Brown Cemetery is indicative of the Singaporean grassroots' potential to truly induce transformative policy shifts is unclear, but it offers a hint of the tactics and strategies that can be used to open up space for a new debate.

Conclusion: the living versus the dead – 'guerrilla tourism' versus the authoritarian state

This chapter has conceptualized 'guerrilla tourism' as an extension of Michel de Certeau's ideas on spatial practice, the act of walking itself as a form of transgression/resistance by charting new pathways within (and against) the hegemonic urban landscape (as devised and formed by state elites, planners and market forces.) In Singapore, where top-down master planning has an especially strong precedent (and the use of urban space carries authoritarian restrictions), the concept of 'going off the pathway' is a challenge, as are the contextualities of what 'resistance' and 'transgression' mean in a setting where the state owns at least 80 per cent of all land in a geographically limited small island. It is this unique political and geographical context that frames the understanding of 'formal' versus 'guerrilla' tourism in the City-State.

The case of Bukit Brown demonstrates the possibilities of 'alternative' tourist spaces in Singapore to take on roles as important sites of (deliberate and non-deliberate) activism and transgression. Bukit Brown also demonstrates the ability for 'unofficial', 'guerrilla tourism' to reshape the City-State's self-identity and world image by forcing open a new narrative and inducing an alternative conversation. Capable of bringing together groups that may not usually encounter one another and allowing those groups to experience urban space and interact in an 'ungoverned' manner, Bukit Brown is part of a growing global momentum of alternative readings of urban spaces (and the reappropriation of the urban touristscape).

Tan (2008) has suggested that the 'elitism' associated with Singapore's 'global shift' has pitted 'cosmopolitans' against 'the heartland' and threatens the nation's social balance. I have proposed the Botanic Gardens as a material representation of the elite's notion of what it means to be a global tourist city, whereas Bukit Brown Cemetery is representative of an alternative, hybrid cultural identity and heritage, born out of grassroots networks and 'off the pathway' tourist flows. 'Guerrilla tourism' in authoritarian Singapore is not merely capable of constructing new meanings about urban space, but also provides 'prospects for a *new political opening*' (Scott 2011: 316; Long 2013) within the wider context of global capitalism through the cultivation of a shared aesthetics of protest. As a 'guerrilla' site, Bukit Brown has allowed a coming together of popular sentiment that represents not only a connection to history but also a rejection of Singapore's developmental, hyper-modern cityscape, as expressed by a blogger and activist interviewed in January 2013: 'It is both the green movement coming together . . . [and] the idea that uh, you know, you don't disturb my family's grave . . . – it represents precisely this anti-steel-and-glass ethos that has been gradually gaining ground.'

UNESCO World Heritage Status has now been awarded to the Botanic Gardens, but will never be awarded to Bukit Brown as the cemetery melts into thin air. Nevertheless, the resonance of Bukit Brown Cemetery as a counter-site of tourism (and activism) may change urban planning debates at the top level in Singapore, to allow more space for collective conversations on the historical, built and natural commons – or the 'Save Bukit Brown' campaign and network will reassert itself in a new place, in a new form. The destruction of the cemetery has instigated the blossoming of a grassroots response that may increasingly seek to question – and challenge – the *authoritarian tourist city*.

Notes

1 The field work was carried out in Singapore from September 2012 to March 2014 in two separate research visits and was part of a research study funded by King's College London in partnership with the National University of Singapore. Methods incorporated semi-structured interviews with activists, artists and policy-makers (N = 30) along with site and participant observation as well as policy document/media discourse analyses.
2 Severe Acute Respiratory Syndrome, which impacted East/Southeast Asia in 2003/4.
3 A historic vernacular architecture common in Singapore and the Malay Archipelago.
4 Housing Development Board (HDB) 'estates' are state-owned residential new towns where most Singaporeans live.

References

[Unless otherwise stated, all URLs were last accessed 31 March 2015.]

Adams, D. and Hardman, M. (2014) 'Observing guerrillas in the wild: reinterpreting practices of urban guerrilla gardening', *Urban Studies*, 51(6): 1103–19.

Amoamo, M. and Thompson, A. (2010) 'Reimagining Maori tourism: representation and cultural hybridity in postcolonial New Zealand', *Tourist Studies*, 10(1): 35–55.

Arnold, W. (2005) 'Singapore, courting tourists, allows casinos', *New York Times*, 19 April. Online. Available at http://www.nytimes.com/2005/04/19/business/worldbusiness/singapore-courting-tourists-allows-casinos.html.

Benjamin, W. (1999 [1935]) 'Paris, the capital of the nineteenth century', in W. Benjmain, *The Arcades Project*. Cambridge, MA: Harvard University Press.

Bhabha, H. (1994) *The Location of Culture*. London: Routledge.

Brunt, P., Mawby, R. and Hambly, Z. (2000) 'Tourist victimisation and the fear of crime on holiday', *Tourism Management*, 21(4): 417–24.

Chang, T. C. (2001) 'Configuring new tourism space: exploring Singapore's regional tourism forays', *Environment and Planning A*, 33(9): 1597–619.

Chang, T. C. (2004) 'Tourism in a borderless world: perspectives from Singapore', *Asia Pacific Issues*, 73: 1–8.

Chang, T. C. (2016) 'New uses need old buildings: gentrification aesthetics and the arts in Singapore', *Urban Studies*, 53(3): 524–39.

Chang, T. C. and Huang, S. (2009) 'Geographies of everywhere and nowhere: place-(unmaking in a world city', *International Development Planning Review*, 30(3): 227–47.

Chang, T. C. and Huang, S. (2014) 'Urban tourism and the experience economy', in A. A. Lew, C. M. Hall and A. M. Williams (eds) *The Wiley Blackwell Companion to Tourism*. Oxford: Wiley.

Chang, T. C. and Lim, S. Y. (2004) 'Geographical imaginations of "New Asia-Singapore"', *Geografiska Annaler*, 86(3): 164–84.

Chang, T. C., Savage, V. and Huang, S. (2004) 'The Singapore River thematic zone: sustainable tourism in an urban context', *Geographical Journal*, 170(3): 212–25.

Chheang, V. (2008) 'The political economy of tourism in Cambodia', *Asia Pacific Journal of Tourism Research*, 13(3): 281–97.

Cohane, O. (2011) '36 hours in Singapore', *New York Times*, 28 April. Online. Available at http://www.nytimes.com/2011/05/01/travel/01hours-singapore.html?_r=0.

Copeland, D. (2015) 'Guerrilla tourism in Pittsburgh, Pennsylvania', *BootsnAll*, 6 April. Online. Available at http://www.bootsnall.com/articles/05-04/guerilla-tourism-in-pittsburgh-pittsburgh-pennsylvania.html.

Cresswell, T. (1996) *In Place/Out of Place*. Minneapolis, MN: University of Minnesota Press.

De Certeau, M. (1984) *The Practice of Everyday Life*. Berkeley and Los Angeles: University of California Press.

Economist Intelligence Unit (2015) *Annual Cost of Living Index*. Online. Available at http://www.economist.com/blogs/graphicdetail/2015/03/daily-chart.

Florida, R. (2002) *The Rise of the Creative Class*. New York: Basic Books.

Florida, R. (2004) *Cities and the Creative Class*. New York and London: Routledge.

Foucault, M. (1984) 'Of other spaces, heterotopias', *Architecture, Mouvement, Continuité*, 5: 46–9.

Foucault, M. (1991) *Governmentality*, trans. Rosi Braidotti and revised by Colin Gordon, in g. Burchell, C. Gordon and P. Miller (eds), *The Foucault Effect: Studies in Governmentality*. Chicago: University of Chicago Press.

Fraser, N. (1990) 'Rethinking the public sphere: a contribution to actually existing democracy', *Social Text*, 25/26: 56–79.

Goh, D. (2014) 'Walking in the global city: the politics of rhythm and memory in Singapore', *Space and Culture*, 17(1): 16–28.

Habermas, J. (1989) *The Structural Transformation of the Public Sphere: An Inquiry into a Category*, trans. T. Burger with F. Lawrence. Cambridge, MA: MIT Press.

Hollinshead, K. (1998) 'Tourism, hybridity and ambiguity: the relevance of Bhabha's "third space" cultures', *Journal of Leisure Research*, 30(1): 121–56.

Humphreys, N. (2012) *Return to a Sexy Island*. Singapore: Marshall Cavendish International (Asia).

Long, J. (2013) 'Sense of place and place-based activism in the neoliberal city. The case of "weird" resistance', *City*, 17(1): 52–67.

Maitland, R. and Newman, P. (eds) (2014) *World Tourism Cities: Developing Tourism Off the Beaten Track*. London: Routledge.

Merrifield, A. (2013) *The Politics of the Encounter: Urban Theory and Protest Under Planetary Urbanization*. Athens, GA: University of Georgia Press.

O'Keeffe, K. (2014) 'Singapore's casinos face obstacles to growth', *Wall Street Journal*, 30 May. Online. Available at http://www.wsj.com/articles/singapores-casinos-face-obstacles-to-growth-1401388732.

Olds, K. and Yeung, H. (2004) 'Pathways to global city formation: a view from the developmental city-state of Singapore', *Review of International Political Economy*, 11(3): 489–52.

Pile, S. (2004) 'Ghosts and the city of hope', in Lees, L. (ed.), *The Emancipatory City: Paradoxes and Possibilities*. London: Sage.

Reynolds, R. (2014) *On Guerrilla Gardening: A Handbook for Gardening without Boundaries*. London: Bloomsbury.

Rose, N. (1999) *Powers of Freedom: Reframing Political Thought*. Cambridge: Cambridge University Press.

Ryan, C. (1993) 'Crime, violence, terrorism and tourism: an accidental or intrinsic relationship?', *Tourism Management*, 14(3): 173–83.

Scott, A. (2011) 'Emerging cities of the third wave', *City*, 15(3/4): 289–321.

Singapore Government (2013) *Population White Paper*. Online. Available at http://www.population.sg./whitepaper/downloads/population-white-paper.pdf.

SMTI (Singapore Ministry of Trade and Industry) (2011) 'Tourism 2015 goals', *MTI Insights*, 12 August. Online. Available at http://www.mti.gov.sg/MTIInsights/Pages/Investments.aspx.

Soja, E. (1996) *Thirdspace*. Malden, MA: Blackwell.

Solnit, R. (2005) *Hope in the Dark: The Never Surrender Guide to the Changing World*. San Francisco: Cannongate.

STB (Singapore Tourism Board) (2013) *Navigating the Next Phase of Tourism Growth*. Online. Available at https://www.stb.gov.sg/news-and-publications/publications/Documents/TIC_Discussion_Paper.pdf.

Tan, K. P. (2008) 'Meritocracy and elitism in a global city: ideological shifts in Singapore', *International Political Science Review*, 29(1): 7–27.

Trip Advisor (2014) *Bukit Brown Cemetery. Reviews*, August. Online. Available at http://www.tripadvisor.co.uk/Attraction_Review-g294265-d2547770-Reviews-Bukit_Brown_Cemetery-Singapore.html.

Week, L. (2012) 'I am not a tourist: aims and implications of "travelling"', *Tourist Studies*, 12(2): 186–203.

WMF (World Monument Fund) (2014) *Bukit Brown*. Online. Available at https://www.wmf.org/project/bukit-brown.

Wu, D. (2013) '10 things to do in Singapore', *Time Magazine*. Online. Available at http://content.time.com/time/travel/cityguide/article/0,31489,1845806_1845592_1845547,00.html.

Yew, L.K. (2000) *From Third World to First: The Singapore Story: 1965–2000 and the Asian Economic Boom*. London: HarperCollins.

Yue, A. (2007) 'Hawking in the creative city: "Rice Rhapsody", sexuality and the cultural politics of new Asia in Singapore', *Feminist Media Studies*, 7(4): 365–80.

Zukin, S. (2011) *Naked City: The Death and Life of Authentic Urban Places*. Oxford: Oxford University Press.

17 'Fantasies of antithesis'

Assessing Hamburg's Gängeviertel as a tourist attraction

Nina Fraeser

Introduction

Located in the touristic centre of Hamburg, just a few minutes walk from the opera and the Jungfernstieg with its upscale retail stores and beautiful views of the river Alster, the Gängeviertel stands out between the neighbouring glass and steel office towers. This is not only due to the visual appearance of this nine-teenth-century brick building complex, but also because the current uses, the 'look and feel' of the place, are in sharp contrast with the polished adjacent shopping and business districts. This last ensemble remaining from what was a historic working-class district had not seen major investments since the 1940s, and was left decaying and mostly vacant in expectance of redevelopment when it was squatted by a diverse group of artists, political activists, architects and planners in 2009. They organized exhibitions and art performances in the buildings and inner courtyards to make a loud and colourful statement against the selling out of not only the city's architectural heritage but also its subcultural milieu.

Despite not having started as a protest movement against tourism as such, the case of the Gängeviertel sheds light on tourism-related resistance in three inter-related ways. First, as outlined in the introduction to this volume, tourism-related policies are part of a broader neoliberal urban agenda deploying creativity for urban marketing purposes in the context of inter-city competition. Thus, subcultural producers of alternative spaces are often caught up in processes of co-optation and instrumentalization fuelling the aims of policy-makers to establish their city as a brand. Second, the Gängeviertel with its central location and rich cultural offer has been struggling with the dynamics of commercialization by also becoming a tourist attraction in itself. Third, the case of the Gängeviertel allows us to reassess the notions of the tourist and tourism as such, as this space has attracted very different kinds of visitors. Some passively consume the qualities of the place, while others get involved in the social, cultural and political practices of the activists and local residents. It is thus not tourists *per se*, but particular kinds of visitors who differ from the 'locals'. Yet the positive reporting potentially generated by those 'passive' visitors contributes to the public image and renown that has helped to prevent the demolition of the Gängeviertel. Those other visitors who engage with the practices of the Gängeviertel activists contribute to show that different ways of living collectively in the city are possible, becoming part of the Gängeviertel's 'commoning' process.

This chapter first introduces the politics of urban tourism in Hamburg as part of the city's neoliberal policy agenda and its focus on inter-urban competition, city branding and the notion of 'creativity'. This lays out what the 'anti' is referring to when describing the Gängeviertel's 'fantasies of antithesis'. The following section presents the case of the Gängeviertel occupation within the context of a broader range of social mobilizations that brought forward the 'Right to the City' network and challenged mainstream policies and urban development trends in Hamburg at the time of its emergence in 2009.[1] Subsequently, reflections are made on the transformation of the *Komm in die Gänge* initiative[2] and how it has shaped the liveliness of the Gängeviertel in the six years up to the time of writing in 2015. The narrative is divided into four stages: the occupation; the path to legalization; institutionalization, co-optation and commercialization; and the contestations over the renovation and the aim to ensure self-management. Particular attention is paid to the ways in which the openness to visitors and references to the city's official branding policy agenda influenced the development of the Gängeviertel initiative. Finally, the transformation of the Gängeviertel into a tourist attraction itself and the implications of that process are discussed.

The entanglement of the politics of urban development and tourism: the case of Hamburg

> The destructive logic of competition inherent in capitalist economies is borne out in the tourism political economy.
>
> (Bianchi 2009: 469)

Despite being located roughly 100 kilometres from both the North and the Baltic Seas, Hamburg is mostly known for its harbour and tradition of trade. As the second largest city in Germany, the city-state counts 1.75 million inhabitants and its population is growing. Due to Hamburg's three rivers and many canals, more than eight per cent of the city's surface is covered by water and its harbour is the second largest in Europe. Hamburg is one of Europe's most prosperous cities.[3] However – as with many cities with economies based on trade, finance and the tertiary sector – Hamburg displays high levels of intra-urban inequalities and social segregation (Friedrichs and Triemer 2009; Birke 2010). Not only the city's population, but also its tourism sector has been growing. In 2014 the city's tourism trade reached an all-time high and recorded 6.1 million visitors and 12 million overnight stays (Hamburg Tourismus 2015). Visitor numbers increased 103 per cent between 2004 and 2014 (ibid. 2015) and the gross turnover in tourism-related industries has, according to the Chamber of Commerce, quadrupled in the twenty years up to 2010 (Bohnenstengel *et al.* 2011). This illustrates how tourism contributes to local prosperity and thus has become high on the local political agenda.

The emergence of tourism promotion as 'being favoured for ailing urban economies' (Harvey 1989: 13) needs to be traced back, in Hamburg, to the crisis of harbour-related industries in the 1970s. The shift towards post-Fordism resulted in high unemployment rates, low economic growth and rising welfare expenditure. This led to a new urban strategy and political regime emphasizing the importance of science, technology and culture (Birke 2014). The inaugural speech by the city's mayor in 1983, Klaus von Dohnányi, under the title *Unternehmen Hamburg* (Corporation Hamburg) marked a turn towards an entrepreneurial approach to urban governance, in contrast to the Keynesian local political tradition of a 'solidary city'[4] (Berger and Schmalfeld 1999). Dohnányi stated that the city should be seen in an international competition for attracting creative people and capital (Dohnányi 1983), an approach which would shape the local political agenda for the subsequent decades.

When cities are transformed into destinations, culture becomes 'more and more the business of cities' (Zukin 1995: 1) and a tool to mask growing inequalities, segregation and distributional issues (Häussermann and Colomb 2003). Almost twenty years after the first reference to 'corporation Hamburg', the strategic development document for the city, titled *Metropolis Hamburg – Growing City* (HH 2002), set the increase in the city's international attractiveness as one of four political objectives. This urban strategy focused on the creation of an image of Hamburg as a unique brand for attracting international enterprise and capital as well as tourists and 'creative people' (Dettmann *et al.* 2006; Birke 2010). This led to the foundation of Hamburg Marketing GmbH in 2003, a holding merging the city marketing agency with three other agencies: Hamburg Tourism, the Hamburg Convention Bureau and Hamburg Business Development, exemplifying the interconnection between urban marketing, tourism, large-scale events and the local economic development strategy. The spatial development plan based on the *Metropolis Hamburg* document links lively and economically strong neighbourhoods to the presence of 'creative urban milieux' in these areas (Pedersen *et al.* 2007: 134). The focus on city marketing and tourism promotion was reaffirmed in a follow-up monitoring report to the Growing City strategy, which states that 'the tourism industry plays an outstanding role in relation to growth and employment and is essential for the service-centred metropolis Hamburg' (Enderlein and Jackisch 2007: 52).

By 2007 it had become unmistakably clear how 'creative city politics' (Peck 2005; Markusen 2006; Mayer 2012a) had begun to influence Hamburg's policy discourse and urban development. The city government integrated the concept 'Hamburg, city of talents' into the strategic development programme, directly referring to Richard Florida and his claims that cities need to be appealing to the 'creative class'. In 2009 a brand consultancy report indicated the importance of local subcultures as a factor in attracting people and enterprises to Hamburg (Marketing-Hamburg 2009). The follow-up strategic development document of 2010 entitled *Growth with Foresight* introduced a post-2008 austerity discourse while still holding onto the idea of growth, with a focus on public spending to support renewable energy, the health sector and – again – the 'creative economy'.

The city chamber argued that 'creativity is not only the key to economic success and innovation in society, but it is also facilitating lively cities and the wellbeing of its inhabitants' (Senat-Hamburg 2010: 2). Olaf Scholz, who was elected mayor in 2011, vowed to further enhance Hamburg's position as a 'cultural metropolis' (Briegleb 2011) and stated in 2013 that his way forward for Hamburg would involve ramping up efforts to compete internationally for capital and well-educated 'creative' future residents (Scholz 2013).

Irrespective of the missing proof of a correlation between the presence of a creative class and the economic well-being of cities (Peck 2005; Krätke 2012), the 'cult of urban creativity' has evolved into a central concept within Hamburg's city branding programme (Walz 2011). During the late 2000s, Hamburg's tourism and marketing agencies discovered the importance of local forms of cultural expression as a promotion tool, and consequently decided to use images of subcultural venues and music bands in their advertisements. This exemplifies how city marketing policies harness (sub)cultural milieux 'as location-specific assets in the intensifying interurban competition' (Mayer 2012c: 76). Thus city branding relies on people who actually live in a place, contributing through their everyday practices to the 'look and feel' and production of local (sub)cultures (Zenker and Beckmann 2012), while the cultural capital generated becomes appropriated by profit-maximizing private interests (Hoffman *et al.* 2003; Spirou 2011; Harvey 2012).

In the context of a neoliberal urban policy agenda upholding the international attractiveness and touristic image of the city, the thesis of the 'creative city', however, has also led to contestations – a 'class struggle within the "creative class"' (Krätke 2012: 147) and a critical demand for 'the Right to the Creative City' (Marcuse 2012). In Hamburg such struggles are embedded in a strong existing local squatters' movement which emerged in the 1980s, predominantly centred on the Hafenstraße and Rote Flora. Both locations are currently mentioned in many tourist guides and presented as a 'symbol of resistance' (Schellhammer and Vogler 2008: 234) or 'myth of the autonomous scene' (Freydag 2006: 105). The efforts of the Hamburg city marketing and tourism agency to capitalize on this 'subcultural creative class' led up to various social mobilizations and served as a hotbed for the occupation of the Gängeviertel.

'Fantasies of antithesis'[5] – the Gängeviertel

> Space is a doubt: I have constantly to mark it, to designate it. It's never mine, never given to me, I have to conquer it.
>
> (Perec 1997: 91)

In June 2009 a protest under the slogan 'The city belongs to everyone – against rising rents, privatization and displacement' mobilised more than one thousand people in Hamburg. It was followed by the formation of the local 'Right to the City'[6] network, which served as a linking platform for struggles related to the urban realm (personal interview, Twickel 2013). This brought together various local anti-gentrification groups such as No BNQ resisting urban renewal plans in the St Pauli neighbourhood, or the more artistic initiative *Es regnet Kaviar* ('It's raining caviar') with its creative repertoire of protest actions. The local community centre Centro Sociale opened its doors in 2008, offering space for counter-cultural and social projects in the heart of the highly gentrified and commercialized area of the so-called Schanzenviertel, a tourist hotspot with boutique stores, bars and restaurants. By 2015, the Right to the City network comprised around sixty initiatives, ranging from anarchist and autonomous groups to residents' associations, addressing a wide range of urban issues (Fritsche 2015). All the initiatives involved keep their individual agendas and approaches, but act in solidarity in calls for protest (personal interview, Ziehl 2013) – for instance in 2014 when the existence of the autonomous social centre Rote Flora was endangered – or develop common campaigns, most recently an anti-Olympic bid campaign in 2014 and 2015.

The occupation of the Gängeviertel, further described below, was closely related to the emergence of the Right to the City network which has been active in connecting struggles against urban development in Hamburg. Fuelled by the extensive public interest that accompanied the occupation, the Gängeviertel was seen as symbolic for the network's demands for 'free spaces' and the self-organization of cultural producers (Gabriel *et al.* 2011). Another amplifying effect for the increasing involvement of people with this broader issue was the publication of a popular manifesto by local artists entitled *Not in Our Name* (NION) in October 2009. The opening line of the manifesto states: 'A spectre has been haunting Europe since US economist Richard Florida predicted that the future belongs to cities in which the "creative class" feels at home'. The text then rejects the exploitation of cultural production and the festi-valization of the city for the needs of upper middle classes and tourists:

> We refuse to talk about this city in marketing categories. [. . .] We say: a city is not a brand. A city is not a corporation. A city is a community. We ask the social question which, in cities today, is also about a battle for territory. This is about taking over and defending places that make life worth living in this city, which don't belong to the target group of the 'growing city'. We claim our right to the city – together with all the residents of Hamburg who refuse to be a location factor.
>
> (NION 2010)

What is today known as the Gängeviertel is the last part of a historic working-class district that combined housing and small-scale manufacturing. Since 1945 it had barely seen any investment. Covering a total surface of 0.45 ha, the Gängeviertel consists of twelve buildings, four courtyards and narrow passage-ways, with a former belt factory built in 1903 in the centre (Figure 17.1). In 2008 the local government agreed on selling the (then publicly owned) site to the Dutch investor Hanzevast, which had development plans involving the demolition of large parts of the Gängeviertel (Donsbach 2012). In 2009 though, a small

Figure 17.1 The Gängeviertel captured from the neighbouring office block – the former Unilever tower – in June 2012.

Source: Franziska Holz.

group primarily made up of artists, whose presence had previously been tolerated in the vacant ground floor spaces of the building complex, started to call secret meetings in the cellar of one building to collectively imagine a different future for the Gängeviertel (Schuller *et al.* 2012). In the context of the tensions generated by the entrepreneurial urban political agenda of Hamburg's city leaders, it was soon decided that something needed to be done in this particular space. The small group was gradually joined by interested architects, planners, political activists and others, but remained discreet, an attitude which had stemmed from the experiences of previous squatting actions in Hamburg and the state violence that occurred in response to them (Birke 2010).

Weeks in advance of the beginning of the occupation of the Gängeviertel, the group had secretly filled the abandoned spaces inside the buildings with art. Additionally, a logo, a red circle, and the slogan *Komm in die Gänge* were agreed upon. In a strategy reminiscent of contemporary guerrilla marketing techniques, the logo appeared on different walls of the city. The group decided to fix a date for a two-day festival in the quarter in August 2009 and announced a courtyard party to the police. They ordered portable toilets, fixed up the buildings, organized food and drinks, and hoped for ample attendance. The occupation unfolded during the event: while more and more visitors arrived, the seemingly abandoned buildings were opened one after the other in a secret orchestration. The visitors discovered the interiors of the historic buildings and the exhibitions and performances that had been set up. Throughout the two days there were regular meetings between the core activists. Banners were prepared for a protest march in case of eviction, a refuge inside one of the buildings was ready to hold the squat, paramedics and lawyers were on call, and a media centre was even set up, with activists trying to reach out to local politicians inviting them to the Gängeviertel – most of this unnoticed by the hundreds of visitors who enjoyed a colourful and exciting party (Stillich 2012). Mayer (2012b) referred to the approach developed on this first weekend as a form of 'squatting with performance character' and a left-wing newspaper critically named it 'squatting with marketing competence' (Eckhorst 2010). The police did not come near the buildings to carry out any evictions and on the following Monday the activists sat down and realized that they were now officially squatting twelve buildings in a prime location within Hamburg's inner city.

In the years which have followed the occupation, the Gängeviertel initiative has embraced its ongoing 'processual state', meaning that its performative condition is always in the making, never finished (Gängeviertel e.V. 2012). Internally the organization of the quarter is based on principles of horizontality, consensus and decentralization through working groups and building collectives, while the main decision-making body is a weekly general assembly. The initial group of squatters consisted mainly of artists and cultural producers but grew rapidly due to an open policy of posters put up on the walls of the quarter for interested visitors to note down their names and qualifications and the activities they would be interested in helping with. The activists in the Gängeviertel became an increasingly heterogeneous group – political activists from the local autonomous scene joined the initiative as well as socially excluded people who did not have an artistic background.[7]

Countless cultural, artistic, social and political activities, events and initiatives have taken place since 2009. More than 200 people have joined the Gängeviertel association and about half of them consider the Gängeviertel as their everyday living space. The quarter today is as much a creative working and living space as it is a cultural venue, experimental zone, political centre and party location. It has also become a tourist attraction. Despite its very diverse visitors and the heterogeneous background of the activists, the common thread between their activities is to claim the Gängeviertel as a social cultural 'free space' and experimental zone.

In the following I will analyse in more depth the particular ways in which the dynamics in the Gängeviertel since 2009 have been entangled with urban marketing and tourism policies and practices, demonstrating how the activists have mobilized the official city marketing discourse and the ways in which the city government has integrated the Gängeviertel into its discourses on culture, creativity and urban development.

The arts of resistance: struggling with negotiations

> We are concerned with battles or games between the strong and the weak, and with the 'actions' which remain possible for the latter.
>
> (De Certeau 1984: 32)

We came to stay! The weekend of the occupation

From the very beginning the activists embraced a peculiar subversive tactic of taking the 'creative city' policy discourse of the city government, the city marketing agency and the urban development department seriously. The people engaged in the Gängeviertel occupation were fully aware of the importance of a city's (sub)cultural offer for international attractiveness. By carving out a creative and artistic image instead of one of radical political activity, they sought to gain the support of a broader public, resulting in overall positive initial media coverage. The absence of police eviction during the most critical first 48 hours of the occupation was due to the many visitors to the spectacular, family-friendly festival. In fact, they seemed to offer exactly what the policy-makers in Hamburg were so desperately looking for: hip and somewhat neat subcultural activities – precisely what attracts millions of tourists nowadays to the rival city of Berlin. Before the occupation, the group had already utilized marketing and branding strategies to generate a positive curiosity towards the activities in the quarter. They quickly improvised ways to communicate actively with the media and invited local authorities to visit the quarter, while strategically avoiding the highly charged term 'squat' (*Besetzung*). On the Monday after the occupation weekend, a press conference was carried out with a tactical mixture of improvisation, professionalism and humour. It announced: 'We had a great deal of tourists here in the past walking around the inner city looking for activity and they stood here [at the Gängeviertel] and asked themselves why is there no life?' and further, 'with this [occupation] we have lightened the workload of the city, considering their intention to better support "creatives" and the creative economy. We chose a location [. . .] and there is art and a concept which can now be discussed' (Gängeviertel 2009, min. 1:00–3:00).

Second phase: towards legalization

That weekend was followed by a period of direct action mixed with tactical negotiations between the rapidly growing group of activists and the public authorities, who in the first instance tolerated and then permitted the use of the space. The city government was soon pressured to act, since the legal owner Hanzevast did not tolerate the occupation. Under public pressure and thanks to the tactical campaigns led by the activists, only four months after the occupation, the city government invested 2.8 million euros in December 2009 to buy back the whole building complex from the developer and committed itself to invest another 20 million euros to renovate the run-down buildings for social housing, artist studios, workshops and subsidized cultural uses.

In the critical phase up to the repurchase, the activists put the focus on maintaining constant cultural work at the site, organizing events and exhibitions, as well as taking a rather cooperative stance towards the public authorities. The Gängeviertel communication tactics integrated an emphasis on the architectural heritage of the quarter resonating with broad support from local elites and the media. This put pressure on the city government to accept responsibility for the preservation of this unique piece of built heritage. By tapping into the city government's discourse on the importance of creativity (Figure 17.2), cultural programming and attractiveness for visitors, by offering guided tours and an archive of the quarter's history supplementary to the exhibitions, events and concerts in the quarter, the Gängeviertel activists consciously traded cultural capital to the local government in exchange for the legalization of their activities.

Third phase: institutionalization, negotiations, co-optation and commodification

After the repurchase by the city government, a sigh of relief went through the Gängeviertel activists, who shifted their energies towards longer-term plans. There was a need to broaden their claims and carefully balance their language again, in part because they had fallen into disgrace among some activists from the autonomous, radical left scene in Hamburg and beyond. A broad critique of neoliberal urban development including issues such as social exclusion, housing

Figure 17.2 Gängeviertel 'advertisement', a week after the occupation, August 2009. The banner reads: '10,000 square metres of unrenovated housing and working quarter – vacant for years! Starting from €0 per square meter. Already 80% creative use!'

Source: Christine Ebling.

shortage and rising living costs seemed to be more resistant to co-optation (Katz and Mayer 1985) than a narrowly focused protest around artistic workspace and heritage preservation.

In April 2010 the *Komm in die Gänge* initiative presented a concept for the future of the Gängeviertel – an alternative development plan for the quarter, which included reflections on its future management and endangered state of autonomy. With this document the activists laid the grounds for further negotiations with the city council's departments. While the text pointed out the enormous influx of visitors – 30,000 within the first half year (Komm in die Gänge 2010: 4) – and highlighted the architectural quality of the buildings, it did not reduce the initiative's demands for renovation and future self-management. It placed the Gängeviertel as a movement within the broader struggle for a 'right to the city' against the dominant form of 'luxury-regeneration' aimed at corporations and tourists and displacing lower-income inhabitants, public spaces and historic structures (ibid.: 5). In order to realize their aims, members of the initiative institutionalized its existence into a legally registered non-profit association (Gängeviertel e.V.), and later into a separate cooperative (Gängeviertel Genossenschaft 2010 eG). The latter's main purpose was to start fundraising and form the future legal administrative body for the self-management of the quarter.

Parallel to this, the city council prided itself in having an open and supportive attitude towards the Gängeviertel in the policy document *Growth with Foresight* (Senat-Hamburg 2010). In 2011 the Gängeviertel cooperative applied for the UNESCO heritage title 'site of cultural diversity', which it was awarded in 2012 as one of only two initiatives in Germany. At the time of writing (August 2015), the following description of the Gängeviertel could be found on the official website of the city government under the section promoting Hamburg's key public spaces and heritage sites:

> Since a private investor wanted to demolish the remaining parts of the old Gängeviertel for new commercial buildings, a citizens' group consisting of planners, artists, and creative people squatted the buildings in 2009. [. . .] Everyone can freely move around in the quarter. If you are lucky one of the residents will tour you through the Gängeviertel.
>
> (HH 2015a)

In addition, the city government integrated the Gängeviertel into its discourse on creativity as a means for urban development. A whole set of articles about the local development scheme of the Gängeviertel and its participatory process can be found in a special section of the city's website (HH 2015b). The idea of a 'lively inner city quarter combining low rents with artistic uses' (ibid.) is presented as if it was the city council's initial plan. The city's government has benefited from co-opting the social, cultural and political engagement that has been keeping the Gängeviertel alive and vibrant since 2009.

With reference to the case of the squatter's movement in Amsterdam, scholars have shown that creative and cultural capital is traded by the social movement for legalization, subsidies and generally a better position in negotiations with public authorities (Pruijt 2003, 2004; Uitermark 2004; Martínez 2014). Owens (2008: 44) furthermore suggests that in a political context of urban competitiveness and city policies aiming at tourist attractiveness, squatters can stabilize their situation by 'fashioning themselves as an alternative tourist attraction'. Despite the differences between Amsterdam and Hamburg, the processes of negotiation and institutionalization in the Gängeviertel seem to support such an argument. This also shows that co-optation of a social movement is not a passive process, something that happens 'to' the movement; neither is co-optation fully antithetical to the maintenance of radicalism and a continuous militancy (Uitermark 2004). If co-optation means at its core that oppositional social groups are turned into service providers (ibid.) and implies that 'the state officials accept the ultimate goal of the movement' (Pruijt 2003: 144), the case of the Gängeviertel has been an ambivalent one. While the activists are producing a cultural and social programme based on voluntary engagement, they still keep a close eye on their own goals of establishing a permanent self-managed space for counter-cultural production, with social housing and workshop uses, and a socio-cultural centre in the inner city. The activists have instrumentalized the marketing-oriented policy discourse in order to improve their situation and have then found themselves instrumentalized by the city authorities as the proof of their open and liberal attitude towards subcultures.

As Uitermark (2004) analysed with the case of the Amsterdam squatters' movement, those squats with an artistic appeal were particularly targeted by co-optation and found themselves – in their struggle for legalisation – increasingly put in the role of a cultural service provider and thus also caught up in processes of commercialization. In light of the culturalization of the urban economy, artists and other cultural producers within a social movement seem to be in an ambiguous position. On the one hand they have a better stance in negotiations for legalization and subsidies as well as a better public image. On the other, they find their cultural activities exploited and co-opted, potentially causing alienation among them when they realise the 'first-hand appropriation and exploitation of their creativity' (Harvey 2012: 110).

The cultural appeal and authenticity the activists create in the Gängeviertel – which is desperately needed for city branding activities to attract tourists as well as capital – face the risk of fading away through processes of commodification. Constantly trying to keep their cafe, tea house, bar, exhibitions and events visitor-friendly, the activists have to emphasize their openness and the importance of their contribution to a culturally diverse city. They also run a gift shop for those visitors who wish to acquire an artwork produced in the Gängeviertel as a souvenir. These activities were, however, at the time of writing, mainly driven by voluntary work and did not generate a substantial profit. The growth of the tourism economy amplifies processes of commodification in subcultural spaces, and potentially of loss of authenticity (Hoffman *et al.* 2003). Such processes can be seen as both a necessity and a danger for a creative autonomous space such as the Gängeviertel.

Fourth phase: renovation, public investment and the aim of self-management

From the summer of 2013 onwards the quarter underwent a process of refurbishment, carried out by the municipal housing development agency working closely with the Gängeviertel association, which constantly sought to shape the process and future space allocation according to its strategic concept plan. Thanks to constant negotiations, internally as well as with the authorities, it seems likely that all buildings will stay in the hands of the activists (Gängeviertel e.V. 2012). At the time of writing (August 2015), the activists were still running the Gängeviertel and shaping the development and refurbishment of the quarter. However, conflicts kept cropping up – whether they concerned technical and heritage-related matters in the renovation process or the public authorities' perceived upper hand over future uses of the Gängeviertel. Due to this, the Gängeviertel association left the renovation advisory board in February 2015 and by doing so temporarily put on hold the future planning and construction works (Gängeviertel 2015).

Instead of analysing urban social movements in terms of their 'successes', or giving another account of how a neoliberal urban regime co-opts, commodifies and exploits subcultural activities, I want to call for a different perspective. Describing the political context of Hamburg and the case of the Gängeviertel shows that, in some places, the contradictions inherent in current capitalism can be 'hacked' for the benefit of social movements and spaces of collective inventiveness, while at the same time commodification and co-optation take place to some extent. After the refurbishment of the Gängeviertel, the people who decide to stay will have to pay social-housing rents and provide financially viable commercial-cultural concepts for the shops, offices, exhibition spaces and other venues. Some will not be able to afford living in the Gängeviertel, particularly not if the provision of activities in the quarter continues to depend on mostly voluntary and unpaid work (Figure 17.3). So far the activists had viewed their work in the quarter as self-exploitation for the benefit of the collective, but they have been increasingly aware that the moment may arise when this voluntary labour could become exploited by others. The Gängeviertel remains an endangered space of possibility – a *Möglichkeitstraum* (Kahn 2012).

Due to the public ownership of the land and buildings of the Gängeviertel,[8] the allocation process for both housing units and other spaces has to follow a standardized procedure with individual rental contracts. The shops that opened in the first refurbished buildings were a bike workshop and a vegan cafe, both projects developed by activists from the Gängeviertel. Another consequence of the renovation is the changing visual image of the quarter, as the newly painted facades of the refurbished buildings are decorated with flowerpots, while on the last floor an 'antifa' (Anti Fascist Action) flag remains displayed on the balcony. When asked about what can be done to oppose the transformation into a beautified commercialized cultural quarter, some activists have stated in news interviews: 'Make holes in the facades as soon as they are refurbished' (Freitag 2014) and

Figure 17.3 Graffiti reading: 'It works 'cause we work', on the wall of the first building
handed over for refurbishment in the Gängeviertel, August 2013.

Source: Author.

'continue to resist' (Schipkowski 2014). At the time of writing, the stream of
visitors had not dried up while the activists in the Gängeviertel were preparing
their sixth birthday celebration, for which the flyer read: '6 year alarm!', depicting a protest whistle shaped like the number six.

The Gängeviertel as a tourist attraction: tensions and contradictions

> Tourist attractions do not spring fully formed into travel guides, ready for tour-
> ists' consumption, but are rather products of contestation and construction.
>
> (Owens 2008: 44)

The Gängeviertel has entered commercial tourist guides (e.g. Fründt 2015) and is
described as a squatted space for subcultural and alternative art production which

was heavily fought for, where 'the inhabitants are very helpful and willing to tell more about the story of the quarter' (Smit 2012: 19). The activists' aim to be open to visitors contains, however, the potential for conflict. The built structure of the Gängeviertel's passageways displays spatial porosity and it is also a conscious attempt by the activist group not to become enclosed but to stay open for all visitors and tourists. In fact, one of the main aims of the activists is to offer collective activities and events with no financial and commercial barriers, unlike the consumption-based public spaces of the surrounding area. An exemple of the contradiction that may arise from this openness was the decision to veto the request of a tourist agency that actually wanted to include the Gängeviertel as an attraction in one of their city tours. Although the courtyards of the quarter are public spaces, the residents considered that this went too far, some of them feeling that they already lived in a zoo with a constant influx of tourists photographing their everyday lives.

Not only has the Gängeviertel become a tourist attraction, but there are also different patterns of tourism taking place inside the quarter. As part of the cultural programme, many international artists and activists have been invited for concerts, exhibitions, workshops and debates hosted on the site, often temporarily integrating themselves into its social structure. The Gängeviertel contains a donation-based 'hostel' and an artist residency. It is therefore clear that certain kinds of tourists fit in better in spaces such as the Gängeviertel than others. The term 'counterculture travellers' – used by Owens (2008) to describe tourist squatters in Amsterdam – refers to visitors who are part of international networks of resistance and subcultural struggles and engage in local activism when travelling. In fact, 'tourism can be both target and outcome of activism. Activism can both attract and resist tourism' (ibid.: 44). Visitors who are used to alternative ways of living seem to have an easy time integrating into the functioning of the Gängeviertel and its social practices. This was illustrated by the example of a travelling social-political theatre group involved in a cooperative project between Germany and Latin America, who visited Hamburg in the summer of 2014. The group was hosted in the Gängeviertel's hostel and used the kitchen, courtyards and other facilities for the time of their stay. For an observer it was clear that those visitors were used to non-commercial and collectively run spaces. They showed a high familiarity with the cultural codes, behaviours and ways of organizing of the Gängeviertel. On their second day, the visiting group organized an open dinner in the common cooking facilities and mingled effortlessly with the local activists.

However, not everyone feels welcome in the Gängeviertel: those tourists who are primarily drawn by the consumption-based spaces of the rest of the city centre are often challenged by the different 'look and feel' of the place and its different socio-spatial practices. Many only stop at the passageway which connects the courtyards of the quarter to the street, but do not dare to go inside, as if they were crossing the threshold of a private space. But the public character of the Gängeviertel's courtyards just differs from the more sanitized and clean spaces of the adjacent shopping and business district. It offers spaces of encounter that overturn the dichotomy of public and private – towards a space of 'commoning' (Stavrides 2016). While the discomfort of many visitors still points to this present radical imaginary, its openness makes the exchange of experiences and knowledge of different lives possible.

Visiting spaces of creative autonomy – a different tourism narrative?

The presence of tourists and visitors in the quarter has become a topic of discussion within the activist group, and it is important to reflect on the internal dynamics between the people who are engaged in the Gängeviertel and the issue of tourism. The Gängeviertel can be seen as a space of what I have called 'creative autonomy' which is characterized by a twofold internal tension. On the one hand, the activists are caught up in constant internal negotiations between the desire to protect the self-management and autonomy of the space and the willingness to institutionalize and cooperate with the city authorities. On the other, there is a tension between artistic production and political activities in the Gängeviertel (Fraeser 2013). I want to argue, in line with Owens (2008), that the tourism issue intensifies the split within social movements of politics versus culture, arts and creativity.

The activists have been challenged by the constant influx of visitors. However, it appears irrelevant whether those visitors are actual tourists or residents of Hamburg. What matters is their approach to, and involvement with, the space: whether they passively consume the produced culture or become engaged in the processes of collective production of the space together with the activists, consequently becoming (temporary) activists themselves. For spaces such as the Gängeviertel this means that those socio-spatial practices actually taking place are not primarily defined by questions of ownership (Birke 2010) but by the degree of active engagement with the activities – in opposition to the passive consumption of a cultural programme. Such spaces are not completely pre-fixed, but are under constant negotiation in which activists create relatively open spaces of possibilities (Stavrides 2010). By challenging the dominant production of space and offering alternatives to neoliberal urban development, the Gängeviertel makes some tourists feel like 'locals' and other (often local) visitors feel alienated by the prevalent socio-spatial practices in the quarter, which they may not be familiar with. Due to its openness and central location, the quarter remains a point of entry into social movement activity and political engagement for those visitors not (yet) active in emancipatory urban struggles – may these be locals or tourists. Beyond this, the Gängeviertel as a collective project has constantly been shaped by the enthusiasm and engagement of newcomers.

Conclusion: resisting fantasies – within and beyond an antithesis

This chapter has explored some of the dynamics and tensions present in the Gängeviertel in relation to tourism policies and the influx of tourists. The analysis underlined the interlinkage of 'creativity politics' with city branding and showed that subcultural spaces have become selling points in the conventional tourism strategy of the city. I argued that – in addition to the central location and cultural programme on offer – the primacy given by the activists to openness to visitors (more than radical autonomy) has turned the Gängeviertel into something resembling a tourist attraction. In this context, it is necessary to call for a renegotiation of what is understood as 'antithetical', as spaces such as the Gängeviertel can take advantage of having become attractive for policy-makers and tourists alike, notwithstanding the co-optation and commercialization that this entails (Uitermark 2004; Novy and Colomb 2013). As this analysis has shown, it is not only inhabitants who shape an urban 'free space' and socio-cultural centre, but it is also those visitors who participate in the cultural projects and everyday life of the Gängeviertel who contribute to its diversity and quality.

It is within such 'spaces of creative autonomy', temporally taken out of the harshest effects of the logic of capitalist profitability, that it seems possible to focus on social reproduction as a battleground for creating spaces 'beyond contemporary forms of domination' (Stavrides 2016), and to collectively work towards a 'radical imagination' (Haiven and Khasnabish 2014). At the same time it is the 'fantasy of antithesis' to neoliberal political agendas that keeps alive such projects refusing to be business ventures, attractions refusing to commercialize their spectacle, and creativity refusing to be trapped in the demands of productivity and profitability. The crucial question is not whether the Gängeviertel has become a tourist attraction but how visitors act out in this socio-cultural space. This implies that resisting the pressure of commodification brought upon such spaces of creative autonomy in the context of a growing tourism economy will not be achieved by a general 'anti-tourism' attitude and by enclosure, but rather the opposite, as also argued by Arias-Sans and Russo in their account of the commoning process of Parc Güell in Barcelona (see Chapter 13). Ensuring openness to visitors needs to be a central concern to foster collective engagement in the making of a different city.

Notes

1 This chapter is based on a mixed-method research design including exploratory visits to Hamburg and expert interviews during the winter of 2012 and spring of 2013, intensive ethnographic fieldwork carried out during the months of July and August 2013 conducting participant observation in the Gängeviertel, and a follow-up visit during July 2014. Additionally, a review of policy documents, political speeches and media reports in relation to urban development, city marketing and tourism policies in Hamburg, as well as media- and indie-media reports on local protest movements focusing on the Gängeviertel was conducted in late 2014. Unless otherwise stated, all quotes from original German sources mentioned in this book chapter were translated by the author.
2 *Komm in die Gänge* is the name of the initiative that later developed into both the Gängeviertel e.V. (association) and the Gängeviertel cooperative (Genossenschaft). The title is a play on words inviting people to come into the alleyways (Gänge) of the Gängeviertel on the one hand, and on the other it is a German phrase meaning 'get things moving' (Novy and Colomb 2013).

3   Hamburg is the fourth most prosperous region in Europe after Inner London, Luxembourg and Brussels Capital Region (https://www.de.statistik/daten/studie/150072/umfrage/regionen-mit-dem-hoechsten-bip-je-einwohner-in-europa/ (accessed 23 October 2014)). Within Germany its GDP per capita is the highest of all federal states, at 61,700 euros in 2015, roughly 25,000 euros above the national average (http://de.statista.com/statistik/daten/studie/73061/umfrage/bundeslaender-im-vergleich-bruttoinlandsprodukt/ (accessed 22 April 2016)).

4   The political discourse around tourism, cultural policies and creativity displayed here had over time been accompanied by various social policies, although these were not able to stop rising living costs and housing prices as well as continuous social segregation and urban poverty (Alisch 1997; Berger and Schmalfeld 1999).

5   I want to thank a squatting activist in Vienna who, in a discussion around the contemporary interrelatedness of radical political action with processes of gentrification, labelled the persistent aim of living differently a 'fantasy of antithesis'. Beyond this, I am grateful to those activists who allowed me to enter their living and working spaces and, by telling me their stories, made me learn from their realities and their fantasies.

6   The 'Right to the City' is a notion based on Henri Lefebvre and his 1968 publication *Le droit à la ville*. It has ever since been interpreted and reused by critical scholars and activists. In the words of David Harvey (2012: 5): 'To claim the right to the city [. . .] is to claim some kind of shaping power over the processes of urbanization, over the ways in which our cities are made and remade, and to do so in a fundamental and radical way.' The concept became a slogan (Brenner *et al.* 2012) and 'is less a juridical right, but rather an oppositional demand' (Mayer 2012c: 71).

7   In the 2010 publication 'Concept for the Future of the Gängeviertel' it is stated:

> Who we are: painters, urban planners, graphic designers, illustrators, cooks, designers, social workers, gold- and silversmiths, unskilled labourers, photographers, architects, web designers, ivory sculptors, upholsterers, carpenters, gardeners, poets, social-welfare benefiters, project-developers, geriatric nurses, violinists, teachers, event managers, scientists, movie directors, restaurateurs, authors, psychologists, plumbing and heating installers, camera-men, performance- and conceptual- artists, hedonists, remedial teachers, DJs, street artists, scene designer, glassblower, musicians, programmers, lighting technicians, wood-, stone- and metal-sculptures, massage therapists, drama advisors, saddlers, educators, light-artists and non-artists, film-makers, media artists, students, stand builders, sinologists, bookbinders, scholarship-holders, retail dealers, fashion designers, singers, kindergarteners, and ecological vegetable sellers. (Komm in die Gänge 2010: 7)

8   The future scenario preferred by the Gängeviertel activists is that the cooperative would sell enough shares to be able to buy the buildings off the city government and self-organize the allocation and maintenance process autonomously.

References

[Unless otherwise stated, all URLs were last accessed 23 November 2015.]

Alisch, M. (1997) 'Soziale Stadtentwicklung – Leitlinien einer Politik für benachteiligte Quartiere. Das Beispiel Hamburg', in W. Hanesch (ed.), *Überlebt die soziale Stadt?* Opladen: Leske + Budrich.

Berger, O. and Schmalfeld, A. (1999) 'Stadtentwicklung in Hamburg zwischen "Unternehmen Hamburg" und "Sozialer Großstadtstrategie"', in J. Dangschat (ed.), *Modernisierte Stadt – gespaltene Gesellschaft*. Opladen: Leske + Budrich.

Bianchi, R. V. (2009) 'The "critical turn" in tourism studies: a radical critique', *Tourism Geographies*, 11(4): 51–77.

Birke, P. (2010) 'Herrscht hier Banko? Die aktuellen Proteste gegen das Unternehmen Hamburg', *Sozial.Geschichte Online*, 3: 148–91.

Birke, P. (2014) 'Sozialproteste im "unternehmerischen" Hamburg. Notizen zu ihrer Geschichte', in N. Gestring, R. Ruhne and J. Wehrheim (eds), *Stadt und Soziale Bewegungen*. Wiesbaden: Springer VS.

Bohnenstengel, K. *et al.* (2011) *Die Welt zu Gast in Hamburg*. Hamburg: Handelskammer Hamburg.

Brenner, N., Marcuse, P. and Mayer, M. (2012) 'Cities for people, not for profit: an introduction', in N. Brenner, P. Marcuse and M. Mayer (eds), *Cities for People, Not for Profit*. London: Routledge.

Briegleb, T. (2011) 'Ende der musischen Bewusstseinstrübung', *Süddeutsche Zeitung*, 21 February. Online. Available at http://www.sueddeutsche.de/kultur/hamburger-kultur-politik-ende-der-musischen-bewusstseinstruebung-1.1063027.

De Certeau, M. (1984) *The Practices of Everyday Life*. Berkeley, CA: University of California Press.

Dettmann, M.-A., Haas, O. J. and Reimer, R. (2006) 'Paradigmen der Hamburger Stadtentwicklung', in R. Volkmann (ed.), *Erfolgsmodell 'Metropole Hamburg Wachsende Stadt'? Ein neoliberales Leitbild und seine Folgen*. Hamburg: VSA Verlag.

Dohnányi, K. von (1983) *Unternehmen Hamburg*. Online. Available at http://www.ueber-seeclub.de/resources/Server/pdf-Dateien/1980-1984/vortrag-1983-11-29Dr.%20Klaus%20von%20Dohnanyi.pdf.

Donsbach, H. (2012) 'Von alten Steinen und neuen Wünschen. Auf den Spuren des historischen Gängeviertels', in Gängeviertel e.V. (ed.), *Mehr als ein Viertel*. Berlin and Hamburg: Assoziation A.

Eckhorst, K. (2010) 'Besetzer mit Marketingkompetenz', *Jungle World*, 15. Online. Available at http://jungle-world.com/artikel/2010/15/40731.html.

Enderlein, R. and Jackisch, A. (2007) *Monitor Wachsende Stadt. Bericht 2007*. Hamburg: Statistisches Amt für Hamburg und Schleswig-Holstein.

Fraeser, N. (2013) *Spaces of Creative Autonomy. Artistic Groups in Contemporary Urban Social Movements*. MA thesis 4CITIES programme, Vienna, University of Vienna.

Freitag, J. (2014) 'Gängeviertel will Off-Art bleiben', *Die Zeit*, 24 August. Online. Available at http://www.zeit.de/hamburg/kultur/2014-08/gaengeviertel-kuenstler-hamburg/komplettansicht.

Freydag, N. (2006) 'Hurra Hurra, die Schanze brennt!', *Geo Spezial*, 2: 102–8.

Friedrichs, J. and Triemer, S. (2009) *Gespaltene Städte? Soziale und ethnische Segregation in deutschen Großstädten*. Wiesbaden: VS Verlag für Sozialwissenschaften.

Fritsche, T. (2015) *Recht auf Stadt*. Online. Available at http://www.rechtaufstadt.net/ras.

Fründt, H.-J. (2015) *City Trip Hamburg*. Paderborn: Reise Know-How Verlag.

Gabriel, R., Sitte, U. and Walter, M. (2012) 'Scheibchen für Scheibchen. Verhandlungschronologie bis Status Quo', in Gängeviertel e.V. (ed.), *Mehr als ein Viertel*. Berlin and Hamburg: Assoziation A.

Gängeviertel (2009) *Press Conference Gängeviertel* [video]. Online. Available at https://www.youtube.com/watch?v=8GbvZANBM2Q.

Gängeviertel (2015) 'Planungsstopp im Gängeviertel', *das-gaengeviertel.info*, 24 February. Online. Available at http://das-gaengeviertel.info/neues/details/article/planungsstop-im-gaengeviertel.html.

Gängeviertel e.V. (ed.) (2012) *Mehr als ein Viertel. Ansichten und Absichten aus dem Hamburger Gängeviertel*. Berlin and Hamburg: Assoziation A.

Haiven, M. and Khasnabish, A. (2014) *The Radical Imagination: Social Movement Research in the Age of Austerity*. London: Zed Books.

Hamburg Tourismus (2015) *Beherbergungen in Hamburg*. Online. Available at www.hamburg-tourism.de/business-presse/zahlen-fakten/tourismusstatistiken/beherbergungen/.

Harvey, D. (1989) 'From managerialism to entrepreneurialism: the transformation in urban governance in late capitalism', *Geografiska Annaler* B, 71(1): 3–17.

Harvey, D. (2012) *Rebel Cities*. London: Verso.

Häussermann, H. and Colomb, C. (2003) 'The New Berlin: marketing the city of dreams', in L. Hoffman, S. Fainstein and D. Judd (eds), *Cities and Visitors*. Malden: Blackwell.

HH (Hansestadt Hamburg) (2002) *Leitbild: Metropole Hamburg – Wachsende Stadt, Staatliche Pressestelle 11.07.2002*. Hamburg: Freie und Hansestadt Hamburg.

HH (Hansestadt Hamburg) (2015a) *Gängeviertel Peterstraße*. Online. Available at http://www.hamburg.de/oeffentliche-plaetze/4257220/gaengeviertel-peterstrasse/.

HH (Hansestadt Hamburg) (2015b) *Gängeviertel Hamburg*. Online. Available at http://www.hamburg.de/gaengeviertel/.

Hoffman, L., Fainstein, S. and Judd, D. (2003) 'Making theoretical sense of tourism', in L. Hoffman, S. Fainstein and D. Judd (eds), *Cities and Visitors*. Malden: Blackwell.

Kahn, K. (2012) 'Die prekäre Einheit von Kunst und Leben', in Gängeviertel e.V. (ed.), *Mehr als ein Viertel*. Berlin and Hamburg: Assoziation A.

Katz, S. and Mayer, M. (1985) 'Gimme shelter: self-help housing struggles within and against the state in New York City and West Berlin', *International Journal of Urban and Regional Research*, 9(1): 15–46.

Komm in die Gänge (2010) *Konzept für das Gängeviertel*. Online. Available at http://das-gaengeviertel.info/uploads/media/Konzept_Gaengeviertel_01.pdf.

Krätke, S. (2012) 'The new urban growth ideology of "creative cities"', in N. Brenner, P. Marcuse and M. Mayer (eds) *Cities for People, Not for Profit*. London: Routledge.

Lefebvre, H. (1968) *Le Droit à la Ville*. Paris: Anthropos.

Marcuse, P. (2012) *The Right to the Creative City*. Lecture given on 29 July 2011, London. Online. Available at https://creativecitylimits.wordpress.com/4-the-right-to-the-creative-city/.

Marketing-Hamburg (2009) *Waraus besteht die Marke Hamburg*. Online. Available at http://marketing.hamburg.de/Markenanalyse.161.0.html.

Markusen, A. (2006) 'Urban development and the politics of a creative class: evidence from a study of artists', *Environment and Planning A*, 38(10): 1921–40.

Martínez, M. A. (2014) 'How do squatters deal with the state? Legalization and anomalous institutionalization in Madrid', *International Journal of Urban and Regional Research*, 38(2): 646–74.

Mayer, M. (2012a) 'Beyond austerity urbanism and creative city politics', *City*, 16(5): 558–9.

Mayer, M. (2012b) 'Hausbesetzungen als politische Aktionsform seit den 1970er-Jahren', in M. Nußbaumer and W. M. Schwarz (eds), *Besetzt! Kampf um Freiräume seit den 70ern*. Vienna: Czernin Verlag GmbH und Wien Museum.

Mayer, M. (2012c) 'The "right to the city" in urban social movements', in N. Brenner, P. Marcuse and M. Mayer (eds), *Cities for People, Not for Profit*, London: Routledge.

NION Not in our Name (2010) 'Not in our name! Jamming the gentrification machine: a manifesto', *City*, 14(3): 323–5.

Novy, J. and Colomb, C. (2013) 'Struggling for the right to the (creative) city in Berlin and Hamburg: new urban social movements, new "spaces of hope"?', *International Journal of Urban and Regional Research*, 37(5): 1816–38.

Owens, L. (2008) 'From tourists to anti-tourists to tourist attractions: the transformation of the Amsterdam squatters' movement', *Social Movement Studies*, 7(1): 43–59.

Peck, J. (2005) 'Struggling with the creative class', *International Journal of Urban and Regional Research*, 29(4): 740–70.

Pedersen, M. *et al.* (2007) *Räumliches Leitbild. Entwurf.* Hamburg: Behörde für Stadtentwicklung und Umwelt.

Perec, G. (1997) *Species of Spaces and Other Pieces.* London: Penguin Books.

Pruijt, H. (2003) 'Is the institutionalization of urban movements inevitable? A comparison of the opportunities for sustained squatting in New York City and Amsterdam', *International Journal of Urban and Regional Research*, 27(1): 133–57.

Pruijt, H. (2004) 'Squatters in the creative city: rejoinder to Justus Uitermark', *International Journal of Urban and Regional Research*, 28(4): 699–705.

Schellhammer, S. and Vogler, J. (2008) *Hamburg.* München: Travel House Media.

Schipkowski, K. (2014) '"Wir sind im Stress"', *taz*, 22 August. Online. Available at http://www.taz.de/Gaengeviertel-Sprecherin-Christine-Ebeling-ueber-Zusammenarbeit-mit-der-Stadt/!144678/.

Scholz, O. (2013) *Hamburg – eine dynamische Stadt wandelt sich.* Online. Available at http://www.ueberseeclub.de/resources/Server/pdf-Dateien/%20Scholz%20Internet.pdf.

Schuller, C., Tampe, F. and Walter, M. (2012) 'Die Kaschemme. In den Keller und zurück in die Welt', in Gängeviertel e.V. (ed.), *Mehr als ein Viertel*. Berlin and Hamburg: Assoziation A.

Senat-Hamburg (2010) *Leitbild Hamburg – Wachsen mit Weitsicht, Mitteilung des Senats an die Bürgerschaft, 23.02.2010.* Hamburg: Bürgerschaft der Freien und Hansestadt Hamburg.

Smit, S. (2012) *100% Hamburg.* Berlin: mo media.

Spirou, C. (2011) *Urban Tourism and Urban Change: Cities in a Global Economy.* New York: Routledge.

Stavrides, S. (2010) *Towards the City of Thresholds.* Professional Dreamers. Online. Available at http://www.professionaldreamers.net/?p=1980

Stavrides, S. (2016) *Common Space: The City as Commons.* London: Zed books.

Stillich, S. (2012) 'Handys aus, Akkus raus. Der Tag der Besetzung', in Gängeviertel e.V. (ed.), *Mehr als ein Viertel*. Berlin and Hamburg: Assoziation A.

Twickel, C. (2013) Personal interview: *Recht auf Stadt, Hamburg, NION, Gängeviertel.* Held in Hamburg, 1 August.

Uitermark, J. (2004) 'The co-optation of squatters in Amsterdam and the emergence of a movement meritocracy: a critical reply to Pruijt', *International Journal of Urban and Regional Research*, 28(3): 687–98.

Walz, M. (2011) *City Branding as Colonization of the Lifeworld? Analysing the Branding Process in Hamburg from a Critical Perspective.* Paper presented at the 21st NFF Conference, Stockholm, 20–24 August.

Zenker, S. and Beckmann, S. (2012) 'Place branding: the issue of a narrowed tourism perspective', in R. H. Tsiotsou and R. E. Goldsmith (eds), *Strategic Marketing in Tourism Services.* Bingley: Emerald Publishing.

Ziehl, M. (2013) Personal interview: *Leerstandsmelder, Recht auf Stadt, Gängeviertel, Hamburg.* Held in Hamburg, 26 June.

Zukin, S. (1995) *The Cultures of Cities.* New York: Wiley.

Index